BYZANTIUM AND THE RENAISSANCE

Greek Scholars in Venice

BYZANTIUM AND THE RENAISSANCE

Greek Scholars in Venice

Studies in the Dissemination of Greek Learning from Byzantium to Western Europe

DENO JOHN GEANAKOPLOS

ARCHON BOOKS
1973

Library of Congress Cataloging in Publication Data

Geanakoplos, Deno John.
    Byzantium and the Renaissance.

    First published under title: Greek scholars in Venice.
    Bibliography: p.
    1. Greek philology—History. 2. Greek in Italy.
3. Philologists. 4. Learning and scholarship—Italy. I.
Title. II. Title: Greek scholars in Venice.
[PA57.G4   1973]   089'.8   72-11550
ISBN 0-208-01311-3

*To my father
and my brother Christie*

PREFACE

The idea of doing research on the general subject of this work first occurred to me years ago while a student of Professor A. C. Krey at Minnesota University. The more I read of medieval and Renaissance history the more interested I became to find out all I could about these curious Byzantine or post-Byzantine Greek refugees in the West, who usually appear briefly in the pages of textbooks with a line or two about their significance for the revival of Greek studies and then as suddenly disappear. A thesis at Pisa University in Italy after the war and a seminar paper on Erasmus and the Aldine Academy of Venice, written in 1948 for Professor Myron Gilmore of Harvard University, further whetted my interest. It was this paper, in fact, that was the genesis of the present study. For as I examined in detail the careers of several Greek scholars I began to realize that these poor, often disdained Greeks from the wreckage of the Byzantine world were not quite the isolated figures usually portrayed. Their country was perishing, but, along with many refugees or voluntary exiles of various classes and professions, they poured into the West in increasing numbers. Soon they set up, in Italy especially, large and flourishing colonies, and in one case at least, in Siena, they even had ambitions to establish a sort of revived Greek nation. Whether the scholars actually lived in these Greek communities or whether necessity forced them to reside elsewhere, there is no doubt that most of them communicated frequently with one another, that they had a certain rapport, and that in greater or lesser degree they felt that they had, in Venice especially, a kind of substitute homeland. It is this broad setting of the Greek diaspora in the West, an awareness of the feeling of patriotism imbuing the scholars' thinking even when they worked on Greek texts for Western patrons, and, no less important, the little-known Byzantine or post-Byzantine Eastern background of their careers that I have tried to provide, for the first time I believe, for the various figures discussed in this book.

During the four or five years of preparation for this work I have had the assistance of many persons, scholars and others, who have generously given of their time and knowledge. Besides Professor Gilmore, who has encouraged the work in all its stages, I am most grateful to two persons: to my colleague Professor Alexander Turyn of Illinois University and to Professor P. O. Kristeller of Columbia University. Professor Turyn has at all times graciously permitted me to draw on his great fund of knowledge of Greek and Byzantine philology for help with the most recondite of manuscript or historical problems; and Professor Kristeller kindly read the entire book in manuscript and made a great number of very valuable suggestions for improvement.

Space does not permit reference to all who have been of assistance. I should like to mention Professor George Williams of the Harvard Divinity School, who has always encouraged my researches, especially during the past year when I was studying the problem of the Greek Uniates and the Orthodox church of San Giorgio dei Greci in Venice. I want also to acknowledge the help of the University of Illinois Research Board, the American Council of Learned Societies, and the Fulbright Commission, all of which gave me substantial grants to carry on research in the archives and libraries of Greece and Italy during the year 1960–61. In Greece Professors D. Zakythinos, N. Tomadakes, and G. Zoras of Athens University suggested bibliographical material and pertinent Greek manuscripts, while Dr. M. Manousakas, Director of the Medieval Archives of the Academy of Athens (and now Professor at Thessalonica University) discussed with me many perplexing problems and gave me a number of his valuable publications. At the Vatican Library I was at all times courteously permitted to use its printed and manuscript materials. I wish to thank Dr. G. Ferrari, Vice-Director of the Marciana Library in Venice, for showing me a manuscript containing new information pertinent to the Aldine circle. To the Director of the Hellenic Institute in Venice, Prof. Sophia Antoniadis, and her aide Mr. S. Messinis I am grateful for permission to explore the fascinating records, documents, and inventories of the Greek community of San Giorgio dei Greci, which is in some respects an untapped mine of information. (Dr. Antoniadis also kindly gave me the picture of the Greek church of

Venice, drawn by R. M. Zamichieli.) Mr. K. Mertzios, the scholarly former Greek consul in Venice, has kindly provided me with bibliographical items and permitted me to utilize several unpublished documents he found in the Venetian archives. And Professor A. Pertusi of the Catholic University in Milan graciously offered me new manuscript material from his forthcoming book on Pilatus and Boccaccio. Although she claims to have done nothing to promote this work, I want to express appreciation to my wife, who has constantly encouraged my research and who, despite the care of two children and a profession, has made the task of preparation much easier than it might have been. I am also very grateful to my close friend Solon Karalis of Greece, who helped me in numerous ways, including the discussion of various problems and the tracking down of documents. To my research assistants and students at the University of Illinois during the past years Mrs. Catherine Byerly, Christ Patrinelis (now of the Medieval Archives of the Academy of Athens), and Dr. Mark Naoumides (now on the staff of the Classics Department of the University of Illinois) I am grateful for their valuable and tireless help during the many stages of this work.

The Vatican Library kindly allowed me to reprint six pictures of Greek scholars, sixteenth century engravings by Tobias Stimmer, from its copy of Paolo Giovio's *Elogia virorum literis illustrium* (Basle, 1577), and the Houghton Library of Harvard the opening page of its copy of the Aldine edition of Erasmus' *Adages*. Zanichelli, publishers of Bologna, have granted their permission to reproduce the map of some of Venice's eastern colonies from Bruno Dudan, *Il dominio veneziano di Levante* (Bologna, 1938). *Greek, Roman and Byzantine Studies* has permitted me to draw upon my two articles "A Byzantine Looks at the Renaissance: The Attitude of Michael Apostolis toward the Rise of Italy to Cultural Eminence," I (1958) 157–162, and "Erasmus and the Aldine Academy of Venice: A Neglected Chapter in the Transmission of Graeco-Byzantine Learning to the West," III (1960) 107–134; the latter, with certain changes, appears as Chapter 9 of this work. Mrs. Stephen Fisher has made the index.

D. J. G.

Urbana, Illinois
November 1961

CONTENTS

xi

CONTENTS

ILLUSTRATIONS

On the title page is the printer's mark of Zacharias Calliergis: the Byzantine imperial double-headed eagle, with the printer's initials.

PORTRAITS

Engravings by Tobias Stimmer, from Paolo Giovio, *Elogia virorum literis illustrium* (Basle, 1577), courtesy of the Vatican Library.

BYZANTIUM AND THE RENAISSANCE

Greek Scholars in Venice

INTRODUCTION

> It is through your efforts, Musurus, in the celebrated and
> very renowned city of Padua [then the university city of
> Venice], where you teach publicly from that chair as
> from the height of a throne, that one sees depart each
> year from your school, as from the flanks of the Trojan
> horse, so many learned pupils that one could believe
> them born in the bosom of Greece or belonging to the
> race of the Athenians.
>
> —Demetrius Ducas, in volume I
> of the Aldine *Rhetores Graeci.*

THE MOVEMENT which more than any other served to widen
the intellectual horizon of western Europe during the later Middle
Ages and the Renaissance was the restoration of Greek letters. In
the history of this revival a significant role was played by the Greek
scholar-exiles from the Byzantine, or former Byzantine, areas of the
East. Beginning in the late fourteenth century and extending well
into the sixteenth, a more or less steadily increasing flow of refugees
or voluntary exiles from the Greek East — a veritable diaspora —
seeking to escape the Turkish domination of their homelands,
poured into the West. Many of these émigrés were well educated
in the Greek language and literature, and through their work of
teaching, manuscript copying, and preparing of texts for the press
contributed materially to the advancement of Greek studies in
western Europe.

Of these exiles the more prominent ones — Chrysoloras, Bessarion, Gaza, Trapezuntios, Argyropoulos, Callistos, Chalcondyles,
and Janus Lascaris — have already been the object of considerable
attention.[1] But there are scores of others whose careers, less spec-

---

[1] Constantine Lascaris should also be included in this group of important exiles,
a monograph having recently appeared on his life: A. de Rosalia, "La vita di
Costantino Lascaris," *Archivio storico siciliano,* III (1957–58) no. 9, pp. 21–70. The

tacular but perhaps more typical of the experience of the average refugee humanist, have not yet been closely investigated. This book is primarily concerned with the lives of several of these lesser-known figures whose careers are closely associated with the city of Venice in the period of the Renaissance when she attained the primacy in the study of Greek.

Venice in the closing years of the fifteenth century and the first decade of the sixteenth was indisputably the chief center of Greek scholarship not only in Italy but in the entire Western world. Because of her own schools and the great university of her nearby satellite Padua, her many scores of printing establishments [2] staffed by scholars preparing first editions of the Greek classics, and the Venetian colonial administrators' need to learn Greek, Venice had become a mecca for devotees of Greek coming from other parts of Italy as well as from the more distant areas of western Europe. In Venice these visitors could benefit from contact with some of the most brilliant Hellenists of the age, including many refugees or exiles from the wreck of the Byzantine world. And having profited from their association, the visitors on their return home or on their movement to other regions would themselves become agents in transmitting Greek letters. As a result of this combination of factors — the return of students from Venice to their homes, the movement elsewhere of professors of Greek, and, not least, the wide circulation of the numerous Greek editions produced by the Venetian press — Europe witnessed a remarkable diffusion of Greek learning from Venice to many important cultural areas of the West. It is this process of the dissemination of Greek learning from the asylum of the city of the lagoons to such centers as Rome, Alcalá in Spain, Paris, Cambridge, areas of Germany and Hungary, as revealed in the activities of the Greek exiles

famous Neoplatonist Gemistos Pletho was of course not an exile (though he appeared in Florence in 1439). Works written on these various scholars are cited below, *passim*.

[2] On the number of Venetian presses in the fifteenth century, L. Hain, *Repertorium Bibliographicum* (Stuttgart, 1838) IV, 540; M. Ferrigni, *Aldo Manuzio* (Milan, 1925) 95; and H. Brown, *The Venetian Printing Press* (London, 1891) 50, cite 207, 250, and 268 presses respectively. Cf. G. Fumagalli, *Lexicon Typographicum Italiae* (Florence, 1905) 451–52, who says the figure of more than 200 is exaggerated. Also see below, Chapter 5, note 32, for V. Scholderer's estimate of the number of Venetian editions and volumes published.

under discussion, that constitutes the underlying theme of this work.

Venice was of course not the only transmitter of Greek learning to the West, nor were the Greek refugees alone responsible for her part in this process. Despite the widespread ignorance of Greek in western Europe during the medieval period, a knowledge of that language had never disappeared from the Byzantine, or former Byzantine, areas of southern Italy and Sicily. At the Hohenstaufen and Angevin courts of Palermo and Naples, during the thirteenth and fourteenth centuries, Greek was still known, and it was not uncommon for Greek writings to be copied by scribes or translated into Latin.[3] And of course earlier, in the twelfth and thirteenth centuries, a considerable selection of the philosophic and scientific works of Aristotle and certain other ancient Greek authors, but principally in the form of Latin translations, had been made available for the use of the Western scholastics.[4] Moreover, the enthusiasm for the Greek language subsequently manifested by the early Renaissance humanists of Italy (whose emphasis was primarily on grammar, rhetoric, ethics, and politics in contrast to the prevailingly theological and scientific proclivities of the scholastics) may

[3] See R. Weiss, "The Translators from the Greek at the Angevin Court of Naples," *Rinascimento* (1950) 195–226, and bibliography cited there. Also see his "The Greek Culture of South Italy in the Later Middle Ages," *Proceedings of the British Academy*, XXXVII (1951) 23–50. Certainly not a few other cases of a Western knowledge of Greek can be cited for the medieval period, for example, the tradition of the Irish monks in the seventh and eighth centuries (although John Scotus Eriugena is the only sure case), the tradition of Greek in certain Greek monasteries in Rome virtually throughout the entire period, at the Ottonian court of Germany (tenth century), and with Robert Grosseteste and Roger Bacon in thirteenth century England and France. On this general problem (and especially the translations made from the Greek during the medieval period) see C. H. Haskins, *Studies in the History of Medieval Science*, 2nd ed. (Cambridge, Mass., 1927); *Aristoteles Latinus*, ed. G. Lacombe, et al., I (Rome, 1939); A. Siegmund, *Die Ueberlieferung der griechischen christlichen Literatur in der lateinischen Kirche bis zum zwoelften Jahrhundert* (Munich-Pasing, 1949); J. Muckle, "Greek Works Translated Directly into Latin before 1350," *Medieval Studies*, IV (1942) 33–42, V (1943) 102–14; L. Loomis, *Medieval Hellenism* (Lancaster, Pa., 1906).

[4] The role of the Arabs of Spain, Sicily, and North Africa from the eleventh to thirteenth centuries as transmitters to the West of Aristotle and other Greek scientific and philosophic authors (but largely in Arabic versions) is of course well known. It is striking evidence of anti-Byzantine feeling that for a long time some Western scholars preferred Latin translations made from the Arabic to those made from the Greek manuscripts preserved in Byzantium. See works cited above in previous note.

3

be dated from at least as early as the middle of the fourteenth century. Traditionally ascribed to the pioneer efforts of the Tuscan humanists Petrarch and Boccaccio, this revived Renaissance interest in Greek was therefore already over a century old when Venice came to the fore.

Of the various Italian centers of the Renaissance that achieved prominence in humanistic endeavors, several, by the end of the fifteenth century, had made considerable progress in the pursuit of Greek learning. Most notable were Florence, with its tradition of Greek teaching solidly established in 1397 by the Byzantine Manuel Chrysoloras, and its revival of Platonic philosophy during the next century under the patronage of the Medici;[5] Ferrara, with its school for young Hellenists and Latinists presided over by the Constantinople-trained Guarino of Verona (1436–1460); and Rome of the mid-fifteenth century, where under the aegis of the Greek Cardinal Bessarion and Pope Nicholas V various classical Greek authors were translated into Latin.[6]

Northern Europe lagged far behind Italy in developing an interest in Greek studies. No centers comparable to the Italian existed there before 1500. Nor did the few Byzantines or Italian teachers who journeyed across the Alps during this period meet with any permanent success. In France, for example, Gregorius Tifernas (from 1456 to 1458) and the rather incompetent Spartan refugee George Hermonymus (about 1476) taught Greek for a time in Paris. But no regular instruction in the language occurred until the coming of the learned Byzantine exile Janus Lascaris and especially the arrival in 1508 of the Italian Hellenist Girolamo Aleandro from Venice.[7]

---

[5] P. O. Kristeller, in *The Philosophy of Marsilio Ficino* (New York, 1943) 346–74, and in "Humanism and Scholasticism in the Italian Renaissance," *Byzantion*, XVII (1944–45), has shown that Ficino did not simply revive a Platonic and Neoplatonic philosophy that had lain dormant for centuries; there was also an influence of Aristotle and the scholastic tradition remaining.

[6] Other important centers that deserve mention are Mantua, where Greek (among other subjects) was taught by Vittorino da Feltre, and Bologna, for which see Umberto Dallari, *I rotuli dei lettori, legisti, e artisti dello studio bolognese dal 1384 al 1799*, 3 vols. (Bologna, 1889–1919). For references to all these Italian centers, see below.

[7] On the teaching of Greek in France, particularly in Paris before 1500, see especially A. Renaudet, *Préréforme et humanisme à Paris pendant les premières*

We know that in the first half of the fifteenth century several Englishmen went to Ferrara to study at the school of Guarino [8] and that in certain private households of Oxford and Canterbury there was fostered an interest in Greek. But the attention of these circles, as in other northern areas at the time, was focused on theology and philosophy and very little on secular learning. Even in the last decades of the fifteenth century such persons as the physician Thomas Linacre and the theologian-educator John Colet had to go to Medici Florence or other Italian centers to perfect their knowledge of Greek.[9]

In Germany too and the Low Countries a beginning in Greek instruction had been made by Rudolf Agricola at Heidelberg, who, like his more famous contemporary John Reuchlin, had been a student in Italy, and by John Wessel of Groningen who had also been indebted for his Greek to his Italian studies.[10] To the south, Spain manifested no great interest in Greek studies before the sixteenth century. Indeed, despite the sporadic attraction of the Castilian court to the Italian humanist movement and the comparatively early initiation of Greek instruction on a university level at Salamanca in 1498 by Ayres Barbosa, pupil of the Florentine

guerres d'Italie (Paris, 1916); and cf. Chapter 5, note 75, citing the French scholar François Tissard, who preceded Aleandro in teaching at Paris (1507). Robert Gaguin (d. 1501), whose Paris circle was the cradle of French humanism, had studied with Tifernas, though he made little progress. The work of Budé, the greatest French Hellenist (who studied mainly with Lascaris), falls after 1500. For references to all of these persons, see now also the summary of R. Weiss, "Learning and Education in Western Europe from 1470 to 1520," *New Cambridge Modern History*, I (Cambridge, 1957) 103-105.

[8] On Guarino see Chapter 1, text and notes 53-55.
[9] On England in general see R. Weiss, *Humanism in England during the Fifteenth Century* (Oxford, 1941), and "Learning and Education in Western Europe," 108-10. Weiss mentions several Greek refugees teaching Greek or copying manuscripts in England, for example, a certain Emmanuel of Constantinople and John Serbopoulos (*Humanism in England*, 144-45 and 147-48).
[10] Weiss, "Learning and Education in Western Europe," 112-13, 119. Germany's first contact with the Italian Renaissance was probably at the Council of Constance (1414-1418), where Chrysoloras, Bruni, and Poggio appeared. More important was the Council of Basle (1437-1450), which Aeneas Silvius, among others, attended. On the developments in Europe in general see the standard work of J. Sandys, *A History of Classical Scholarship*, 3 vols. (Cambridge, Eng., 1903-1908; new printing, 1958). Regarding Switzerland it might be noted that the Byzantine refugee Andronicus Contoblachas (with whom Reuchlin studied for a time) was teaching in Basle at the end of the fifteenth century. Wessel had taught Greek in Paris in 1473. His career has not yet been entirely clarified.

Angelo Poliziano, the militantly religious ethos of Spain was not conducive to promoting the study of Hellenic literature.[11]

Such in brief was the state of Greek studies in western Europe shortly before 1500, when Venice succeeded Medici Florence to the intellectual leadership of the Renaissance. Though it is evident that interest in Greek had grown, there was not so widespread a knowledge of the language as one might expect, not even in Italy with its now firmly established tradition of Greek instruction. Nor could every large Italian city offer facilities for study of the language.[12] A serious drawback, moreover, to mastery of Greek literature in the original was the lack of such indispensable scholarly tools as adequate Greco-Latin grammars and dictionaries and, above all, of correct editions of the classical Greek texts. With the multiplication of such instruments in the late fifteenth and early sixteenth centuries, especially after the establishment in Venice of the Aldine press with its learned Academy of Greek and Latin Hellenists, great strides were to be taken in filling these needs.

Much has been written about the Florentine phase of the Greek revival, and somewhat less on the work of the circle of Bessarion in Rome. But comparatively little attention has been paid to the intellectual contribution of Venice, which in certain respects is as notable as that of Florence. To be sure, the work of the Aldine press in producing first editions of the Greek classics is widely recognized; but all too often this activity is conceived of as an isolated phenomenon having little connection with previous Venetian history and divorced from other equally significant Venetian contributions to the development of western Hellenism. Only one

[11] On Spain, see Chapter 8, text and notes 25–30. The statements above apply more to Castile than to Aragon, where, owing to later 14th century Catalan relations with Greece and Byzantium, interest in translations from Greek was evidenced at the courts of Pedro IV and John I. See A. Rubio y Lluch in *Estudis Universitaris Catalans*, X (1917–18), and K. Setton's important "The Byzantine Background to the Italian Renaissance," *Proceedings of the American Philosophical Society*, C (1956) 64ff.

[12] V. Rossi, *Il Quattrocento*, 3rd ed. (Milan, 1933) 92, says that "a knowledge of Greek [after Chrysoloras] was diffused in Italy more slowly than one might think"; and Weiss, "Learning and Education in Western Europe," 99, notes that in 1492 the Venetian Pietro Bembo had to go to Messina to secure a good knowledge of Greek from the Greek exile Constantine Lascaris. (According to P. de Nolhac, *La bibliothèque de Fulvio Orsini* [Paris, 1887] 152, the Venetian Angelo Gabrielli accompanied Bembo.) Finally, see P. Kristeller, *The Classics and Renaissance Thought* (Cambridge, Mass., 1955) 16: "Knowledge of Greek was [with respect to Latin] comparatively rare even during the Renaissance."

work of synthesis, the old study of A. Firmin-Didot, has been written on the period of Venetian primacy in Hellenism; none focuses on the role of the Greek exiles in that development.[13]

As far back as the early medieval period Venice had enjoyed close relations with that repository of ancient Greek learning, the Byzantine East. Indeed, Venice's rise to world power was the direct result of her share in the Latin conquest of Constantinople in 1204. On the ruins of old Byzantium Venice had erected a great colonial empire, and even after the fall of Constantinople to the Turks in 1453 she continued to maintain substantial territories in the East, especially the great island of Crete. With the Turkish invasions of the Greek mainland and the Aegean islands large numbers of Greeks were persuaded to flee for refuge to Venice itself. There many remained to become members of a substantial Greek colony of merchants, mercenaries, intellectuals, and others which began to flourish within the city.

The exposure to Greek culture resulting from this long inter-action of East and West is a fundamental (though by no means the only) factor in the transfer of Greek letters westward. Therefore in the first chapter of this book we shall briefly summarize the history of Venetian relations with the Byzantine East. The next chapter will consider the unique role of the island of Crete, whose scholars contributed notably to the copying of manuscripts and to the development of the Venetian printing press. A third intro-ductory chapter will be devoted to the history of the Greek colony in Venice, which served as a kind of homeland in exile for many of the Greek refugees. Then, with this setting provided, we shall

---

[13] Firmin-Didot's book, which was a pioneer in its field and which is still of considerable help to researchers, is rather narrow in its approach, devoted as it is exclusively to Aldus and his circle. As will be noted below, it is now outdated (a number of important studies and articles having appeared since its publication), it contains numerous errors, and it garbles many of the French translations made from the Greek. See criticism in R. Proctor, *The Printing of Greek in the Fifteenth Century* (Oxford, 1900) 123ff., and esp. the rather severe view of P. de Nolhac, "Les Correspondants d'Alde Manuce," *Studi e documenti di storia e diritto*, VIII (1887) 246: "Le travail d'Ambroise Firmin-Didot, précieux à beaucoup d'égards, est tout-à-fait insuffisant. L'*Alde Manuce* . . . renferme, en effet, beaucoup d'iden-tifications inexactes et des erreurs de fait considerables; le livre est donc à refaire tout entier." Nor does the basic work of E. Legrand, *Bibliographie hellénique ou description raisonnée des ouvrages publiés en grec par des grecs au XV ͤ et XVI ͤ siècles*, 4 vols. (Paris, 1885-1906), focus on the Greek scholars and their environ-ment in Venice. On this important work see below, *passim*.

move to the principal section of the work, a detailed examination of the lives of certain representative Hellenists, each of whom exemplifies a particular aspect or phase of the dissemination of Greek letters.

Five are scholars of Greek origin, none of whom has yet been the subject of an adequate biography and most of whom have not yet been treated in monographic form.[14] First, the Constantinopolitan refugee Michael Apostolis, whose work provides us with a prime example of Greek scholarship in Crete, that halfway point between Venice and the East. Second, Marcus Musurus, a Cretan émigré resident in Venice and Padua, whose importance for us lies in the extraordinary number of Greek first editions he edited for the Aldine press and in the influence of his teaching on a large group of Western students. Then Arsenios, son of Michael Apostolis, whose career spans virtually the entire period under discussion and who figures not only in the intellectual life of Crete, Greece, and Venice, but in that of Florence and Rome. Fourth, Zacharias Calliergis, another Cretan, who went from Venice to Medici Rome, there to establish its first Greek press. And, lastly, Demetrius Ducas, still another Cretan, whose career, never heretofore treated, is notable because of his teaching at Alcalá University in Spain and his contribution to Cardinal Ximenes' Polyglot Bible.

As a climax to the process of transmission there is added a discussion of the sojourn of the celebrated Erasmus in Venice with the Aldine circle of Hellenists — an episode of capital importance not only for his own intellectual development but, in view of his far-reaching influence, for the development of Greek letters in Northern Europe as a whole. In the final chapter of the book an attempt is made to summarize and evaluate the contribution of the Greek exiles to the Venetian rise to primacy in Greek studies and to draw certain conclusions on the role played by the Queen City of the Adriatic in the dissemination of Hellenic learning in western Europe.

A word about the often lengthy translations from the Greek

[14] For references to whatever previous work has been done on the scholars whose biographies are treated here see the opening notes, and corresponding text, to each chapter.

8

which have been incorporated into the text. These have been included not only because very few of the selections have hitherto been translated but because through the words of the authors themselves — tortuous as their expressions often may be — we can best gain insight into the mentality and attitudes of these uprooted, unassimilated scholars from the East.

PART I

THE BACKGROUND

Chapter 1

BYZANTIUM AND VENICE

T HE GEOGRAPHICAL POSITION of Venice at the head of the Adriatic and between the eastern and western halves of the Mediterranean permitted her early to assume the function of intermediary between the Greek East and the Latin West. Indeed, from at least the eighth and ninth centuries the practical-minded merchants of the lagoons had been attracted by Byzantium, its splendor and its opportunities for commercial enterprise. So close in fact did Venetian ties with the East become that the Emperors accorded lofty honorary titles to the Doges (such as that of Protosevastos) and a place in the hierarchy of the Greek imperial court.[1]

As a virtual satellite of Byzantium, Venice rendered valuable military service by the dispatch of a fleet to aid the Empire against the Arabs at Bari in 1003, and again during the Greco-Norman wars in the last part of the eleventh century. In exchange the Venetians were granted a substantial quarter of their own in the capital city of Constantinople, in which merchants from the home city could reside and carry on trading activities unmolested by imperial regulation and the payment of imposts.[2]

The existence of a virtually independent Venetian colony along the Golden Horn in the heart of the Greek metropolis is of prime

[1] For the titles, see G. Tafel and G. Thomas, *Urkunden zur älteren Handels- und Staatsgeschichte der Republik Venedig*, pts. 1–3 (Vienna, 1856–1857). In some cases the Byzantine titles even precede the Venetian. Also see H. Brown, "The Venetians and the Venetian Quarter in Constantinople to the Close of the 12th Century," *Journal of Hellenic Studies*, XL (1920) 68–88, esp. 71.

[2] On the Venetian colony see especially W. Heyd, *Histoire du commerce du Levant au Moyen-Age* (Leipzig, 1885) I, 464–71, and Brown, esp. 70–72. On Bari see J. Gay, *L'Italie Méridionale et l'Empire byzantin* (Paris, 1904) 369.

importance in the development of Greco-Venetian relations. By the end of the twelfth century, we are informed by a contemporary chronicler, the Venetian community comprised some twenty thousand persons.[3] With Constantinople possessing from eight hundred thousand to possibly one million inhabitants, this figure may not seem unduly large. But when one considers that Venice in 1170, as has been estimated, had a population of some sixty-four thousand and Paris of perhaps less than a hundred thousand, it is remarkable indeed.[4]

Opportunities for social contact in Constantinople between Greeks and Venetians were considerable, and intermarriage was not uncommon, the issue of such unions being termed Gasmules.[5] Among the inhabitants of the Venetian quarter were not only merchants and their families but a number of Latin priests and monks who had been summoned to officiate in the churches provided for Latin use.[6]

Extensive as were her economic privileges in Constantinople, Venice nevertheless desired to control the entire lucrative trade of Byzantium. And it was especially her hope of displacing all other Western merchants from a share in the rich Greek markets that motivated her participation in the Fourth Crusade of 1204. In the ruthless sack of Constantinople and the carving up of Byzantine territories which followed that Crusade, Venice, from the economic

[3] Eustathius of Thessalonica, De Thessalonica a Latinis capta (Bonn, 1842, with Leo Grammaticus) 394, says there were then 60,000 Latins in Constantinople; of these by far the largest group was certainly Venetian: see A. Paspates, Βυζαντιναὶ Μελέται (Constantinople, 1877) 147, and esp. Brown, 82, who cites the Historia ducum Veneticorum, MGH SS, XIV, 78, quoting 20,000 Venetians. But cf. C. Diehl, Byzantium: Greatness and Decline (New Brunswick, 1957) 192, who says there were over 10,000 Venetians (no source cited).

[4] On the population of Paris see T. Chandler, Cities of the World (New York, 1940) 10, which, for ca. 1100, gives Paris less than 100,000 people (and for ca. 1250 assigns her 155,000); also L. Bréhier, La civilization byzantine (Paris, 1950) 83. For Constantinople, see Bréhier, 82–83, and C. Diehl, "Byzantine Civilization," Cambridge Medieval History, IV (New York, 1927) 750. On Venice see W. Hazlitt, The Venetian Republic, I (London, 1900) 71, n. 2.

[5] On the Gasmules, see D. Geanakoplos, Emperor Michael Palaeologus and the West, 1258–1282: A Study in Byzantine-Latin Relations (Cambridge, Mass., 1959) 127, 132 and bibliography cited. On the frequent intermarriage of Greeks and Venetians (in Venice as well as Constantinople) before 1204, see A. Frothingham, Jr., "Byzantine Art and Culture in Rome and Italy," American Journal of Archaeology, X (1895) 162–63.

[6] On the specific provisions of various Greco-Venetian treaties that reveal such contacts, see Heyd, Histoire, I, 464–71; also Geanakoplos, esp. 301.

point of view, secured the choicest of the Greek areas. Together with three-eighths of the capital city (including the cathedral of Hagia Sophia), Venice acquired most of the isles of the Aegean and Ionian Seas, the great island of Crete (actually secured shortly after 1204), and several important points in the Morea (Peloponnese), including the fortresses of Modon and Coron. A virtual monopoly of the Eastern trade accordingly fell into Venetian hands, and, equally important, there came under her sway large segments of the Greek population. These eastern possessions of Venice soon assumed such importance in Venetian eyes that in

EASTERN COLONIES OF VENICE

1214 the Doge Pietro Zeno actually contemplated transferring the seat of government to Constantinople.[7]

The attitude of the Greeks toward their conquerors is worthy of note. While some, especially among the nobility, collaborated with their new masters in the aim of retaining their privileges,[8] the large majority of the Greeks bitterly resented the Westerners, looking upon them as oppressors and interlopers. This resentment was intensified on the religious side by the fact that the Greeks were now compelled to accept Roman Catholicism. Pope Innocent III himself informs us that after the performance of a Latin rite in the Byzantine churches, the Greeks were accustomed to scrub their altars, in their eyes polluted by the Latin ceremony, and also to rebaptize their children in the Greek rite.[9] Though all the Western peoples were generally distrusted, the Greek animus seems to have been directed primarily against the Venetians, who were held chiefly responsible for the destruction of the Greek Empire.[10]

With the Greek recovery of Constantinople in 1261 by the Emperor Michael VIII Palaeologus, most of the Venetian commercial privileges in the capital were awarded to their arch-rivals, the Genoese. This fact notwithstanding, Venice did not lose control of her Greek island possessions in the Aegean and Adriatic Seas.[11] Even after the fall of Constantinople to the Turks in 1453, Venice managed to retain a firm foothold in the east. And it was these island possessions which, as late as the latter part of the fifteenth and early sixteenth centuries, kept her attention directed to that area.

During the medieval period we find far greater evidence of social and economic interaction between Venetians and Greeks in Constantinople than of intellectual exchange. This is, of course, largely because virtually all the Venetians in the capital, with the notable exception of the ecclesiastics, were merchants, characterized by the narrow interests of their class. Quite rapidly, to be sure, in

[7] See S. Romanin, *Storia documentata di Venezia* (Venice, 1925) II, 208. On the Venetian acquisitions in 1204, see Tafel and Thomas, *Urkunden*, I, 452ff.

[8] W. Miller, *Latins in the Levant* (London, 1908) 57ff.

[9] See a canon of the Fourth Lateran Council (1215), in C. J. Hefele and H. dom Leclercq, *Histoire des conciles* (Paris, 1914) V, pt. 2, 1333.

[10] Geanakoplos, 132, 153.

[11] Geanakoplos, *passim*. For a convenient list of the many Venetian possessions see Diehl, *Byzantium*, 194. Also below, Chapter 3, text for note 3.

16

order to be able to carry on their trading activities with the Byzantines, the merchants learned to speak a certain amount of Greek.
But this was undoubtedly the popular form of the language, which
was somewhat different from the ancient Greek of the classical
works as well as from the artificial, highly stylized Greek employed
in the Byzantine literary productions of the medieval period. Thus
the colloquial Greek of which the Venetian merchants had knowledge probably did not lead to any really fruitful exchange of ideas.
Moreover, the Western view of the Greeks as schismatics and
especially the Greek antipathy for the Latins — feelings which
were always lurking in the background — might well have served
as barriers even in the case of a Venetian who managed to learn
more of the language.[12]

Despite these drawbacks some significant examples do exist of
cultural interchange on a more intellectual level. Aside from the
well-known influence of Byzantium on Venice in the sphere of
art, we have evidence that during the twelfth century Latins rep-
resenting the highest learning of the period were sent to Constantinople to participate in ecclesiastical disputations held before the
imperial court. Present at one such *pourparler* was a certain James
of Venice, who is said to have translated from Greek into Latin
and written commentaries on Aristotle's *Topics*, *Prior* and *Posterior
Analytics*, and the *Elenchi*. James has been singled out by Haskins
as "the first scholar of the Twelfth Century who brought the New
Logic of Aristotle afresh to the attention of Latin Europe." [13]

It seems probable that there were many more instances of Vene-
tian-Greek intellectual exchange than our sources have yet di-
vulged. But on the basis of the present state of research [14] it can-

[12] For a brief but good discussion of Greco-Latin attitudes, see Diehl, 221–24.

[13] Haskins, *History of Medieval Science*, 144–45, 227–32; cf. L. Minio-Paluello,
"Jacobus Veneticus Grecus," *Traditio*, VIII (1952) 265–304, who believes James
was of Greek extraction, and Setton, "Byzantine Background," 24–25. On the
various libraries of Constantinople at this time that Venetians like James might
well have visited, see Diehl, 230, who cites in particular the 30,000 volumes in the
great library of the Basilica. Also Bréhier, *La civilization byzantine*, 484, 492, and
the article of S. Padover in J. W. Thompson, *The Medieval Library* (New York,
1957) 310–29.

[14] Our information is drawn principally from imperial decrees on trade and
from enactments of the Venetian *baillis* (governors) of the Venetian colonies in
the East. See, for example, C. Diehl, "La colonie vénitienne à Constantinople,"
Etudes byzantines (Paris, 1905) 245ff., which deals exclusively with the institu-
tional and economic factors relating to that colony during the fourteenth century.

not safely be said that the intellectual intercourse occurring in the East between Venetians and Greeks in the two centuries before 1453 was very far-reaching in scope. For any exchange to have occurred, more penetrating and on a broader scale, a shift in attitude would have had to take place. And indeed, the Venetians, as a result of centuries of residence in the East, were gradually becoming conditioned to toleration of the Greek religion and social practices. (The lure of economic profit was here of course no unimportant consideration.) As for the Greeks, diminution of their deep-seated hatred for Venice was a more difficult matter. What helped to produce a change in the attitude of some Greeks during the later fourteenth and fifteenth centuries was the increasingly grave threat of the Ottoman Turks to the very existence of the Byzantine state. To be sure, most Greeks remained fanatically anti-Latin. But others, *politiques* and intellectuals in particular, began to look to the West for military aid and even to favor ecclesiastical union with Rome as a means of salvation for the state.[15] Thus by the time of the final fall of Constantinople to the Turks in 1453, a relatively small but influential segment of the Greek population was able to look upon the Venetians, with their eastern possessions, no longer as the hated oppressors of the crusading period but rather as the people best able to render effective military assistance, and, especially after 1453, as the ones most likely to offer refuge for displaced Greeks fleeing the Turk.[16] This partial but significant mitigation of the ancient ill-feeling between Greeks and Venetians in the fourteenth and fifteenth centuries also served to help open the way to greater receptivity in the intellectual sphere. But the interest in Greek learning which began to manifest itself in Venice, and indeed in Italy in general, during this period cannot of course be attributed simply to an improved rapport between East and West. The problem is tied up with the broader, more complex question of the origins of Italian humanism.

We need not enter here into the various meanings of this much-

---

[15] See the important example of Demetrios Cydones, whose treatise on this matter of aid from the West is discussed in D. Zakythinos, *La Grèce et les Balkans* (Athens, 1947) 52–56. Also see D. Geanakoplos, "The Council of Florence (1438–39) and the Problem of Union between the Greek and Latin Churches," *Church History*, XXIV (1955) 333 and n. 78.

[16] On the Greek fugitives see especially Chapter 3.

debated term — whether it should primarily be conceived of as a passion for the recovery and study of the classical Greek and Latin texts, or (what seems to have been a later development) as a wider, more liberal interest in "human values" as the basis for the formulation of a new philosophy of life.[17] For our purposes we shall understand humanism to embrace the broad range of classical studies as originally conceived of by the Italian scholars of the fourteenth century — the study of the writings, especially literary, of the ancient authors, the recovery of manuscripts of lost or rare texts, and the desire to learn Greek and to write Latin, utilizing the refined style of the ancients as a model.[18] This emphasis on the imitation of the antique style constituted an important difference between the attitude of the Italian Renaissance humanists and the medieval scholars, who, though having at their disposal a not inconsiderable selection of the classical writings, were primarily interested in them (especially the philosophic and scientific works of Aristotle) as a means of bolstering Christian theology.[19]

Recent investigation has indicated that the beginnings of Italian humanism probably grew out of the fusion of two different currents: first, the tradition of the medieval Italian rhetoricians (*dictatores*) and the students of the Roman law, with their emphasis on rhetoric and analysis of legal texts, and second, and less important, the study of the classics which was introduced from France, where it had flourished during the twelfth century. It was in the latter

[17] Cf. Kristeller, *Classics*, 8 and 10.
[18] On the meaning of humanism, there is of course a large literature. I cite here only a few important recent works dealing with the problem: Kristeller, *Classics*, esp. 9–10; Kristeller, "Humanism and Scholasticism in the Italian Renaissance," *Byzantion*, XVII (1944–45) 346ff. (reprinted in his *Studies*), which stresses the role of the rhetoricians in the origins of Italian humanism; W. Ferguson, *The Renaissance in Historical Thought* (Boston, 1948); and R. Weiss, *The Dawn of Humanism in Italy* (London, 1947). See especially P. Kristeller, *Studies*, 23–26: "The core and center of Renaissance humanism [was] the emphasis on the Greek and Latin classics as the chief subjects of study and as unrivaled models of imitation . . ." On the classics see especially the old works of J. Burckhardt, *The Civilization of the Renaissance in Italy*, new ed. (Oxford-London, 1945), G. Voigt, *Die Wiederbelebung des klassischen Altertums*, 3rd ed. (Berlin, 1893), and, on the rediscovery of manuscripts, R. Sabbadini, *Le scoperte dei Codici latini e greci nei secoli XIV e XV*, 2 vols. (Florence, 1905–1914). Other works are cited below.
[19] C. H. Haskins, *Renaissance of the Twelfth Century* (Cambridge, Mass., 1927) ch. 4, discusses the classical Latin works available to twelfth century western Europe and in chs. 4 and 9 the translations from Aristotle. See also Kristeller, *Classics*, esp. 28–36.

part of the thirteenth century, and in the context of the growing Italian urban centers with their increasing awareness of secular values, that the French influence seems to have been grafted upon the earlier native tradition of medieval Italian rhetoric. The result was a revived appreciation in Italy of the literature of classical antiquity.[20]

Of the several Italian towns in which this incipient humanism seems almost simultaneously to appear,[21] some scholars believe that Padua, with its circle of jurists around Lovato dei Lovati (in the late thirteenth century) and the group surrounding the rhetorician and poet Albertino Mussato (in the early fourteenth century), is one of the very first in point of time.[22] However that may be, those in whom the traits of humanism, as we have defined them above, first appear in really clear form are the fourteenth century Florentines Petrarch and his pupil Boccaccio. And they are commonly considered to be the founders of humanism as a definite movement.

Until the time of Petrarch and Boccaccio the humanistic interests of Italy appear to have been focused on Latin learning, as was only natural in a country where the Roman tradition was dominant. As a result of their activities, the scope of humanism was broadened to include the study of Greek.[23] The desire of Petrarch and Boccaccio to learn Greek was primarily inspired by

[20] On the Italian rhetoricians see especially Kristeller, *Classics*, 11–13, and Weiss, *Dawn of Humanism*, esp. 5. Also Kristeller, "Humanism and Scholasticism," *Studies*, 565, n. 32, for bibliography. On the French influence see Kristeller, *Studies*, 570, and bibliography cited; for the thirteenth century in particular, see G. Bertoni, *Il Duecento*, 3rd ed. (Milan, 1939) and for the fourteenth century, B. Ullman, "Some Aspects of the Origin of Italian Humanism," *Philological Quarterly*, XX (1941) 20–31.

[21] Weiss, 5, cites Padua, Verona, Vicenza, Venice, Milan, Bologna, Florence, and Naples. He also notes (23) that as of 1947 no work had been done on the earliest humanism of Florence or of Bologna.

[22] Weiss, 6ff., and esp. bibliography on 22. Also the work of L. Lazzarini, *Paolo de Bernardo e i primordi dell'umanesimo in Venezia* (Geneva, 1930) 4–40. Cf. Kristeller, *Classics*, 13, who emphasizes the addition to the practice of the medieval rhetoricians of the humanistic view that imitation of the ancient style was important.

[23] See Sandys, *History of Classical Scholarship*, II, 15: "Boccaccio, the first of modern men to study Greek in Italy and Europe." Also see P. de Nolhac, *Pétrarque et l'humanisme* (Paris, 1907) *passim*. On Petrarch's predecessors see G. Toffanin, *Storia dell'umanesimo* (Naples, 1933), and Sabbadini, *Scoperte dei codici latini e greci*. There is a large literature on Petrarch. We cite here only F. Lo Parco, *Petrarca e Barlaam* (Reggio, 1905) and de Nolhac.

their contact with Greek culture, as represented by Byzantine envoys to the papal court at Avignon, where Petrarch lived for a time,[24] and especially by the formerly Byzantine areas of southern Italy and Sicily. There Greek was still a living language, and in the libraries of Greek monasteries such as Casole and San Salvatore in Messina many ecclesiastical and some classical Greek codices (including even the profane ones of Aristophanes) were preserved, if not always read.[25] Moreover, in Petrarch's time at the Angevin court of Naples, translations were still not infrequently being made from ancient Greek texts.[26] Eager to read the few Greek manuscripts in their possession (Petrarch's precious Homer and Plato, for instance), they turned for instruction to two south Italian Greeks, Barlaam and his pupil Leontius Pilatus. Petrarch failed to learn Greek, but Boccaccio was somewhat more successful.[27] And in 1361 he was able to induce his home city of Florence to establish a position for the teaching of the Greek language at its *studium*.[28] The original occupant of this first Western chair for

[24] It was at Avignon (or possibly Verona) that Petrarch met the Byzantine envoy Nicholas Sigeros, who later presented him with a manuscript of Homer: see Petrarch, *Le familiari*, xviii, 2; III (Florence, 1937) 275ff. Also see the forthcoming book of A. Pertusi, *Leonzio Pilato, Petrarca e Boccaccio: Omero e la cultura greca nel primo umanesimo*, which discusses Sigeros.

[25] See Chapter 1, note 76. Also for classical works at Casole, see E. Aar, "Gli studi storici in Terra d'Otranto," *Archivio Storico Italiano*, VI (1880) 104-05; S. Borsari, "Sulla cultura letteraria nei monasteri bizantini del Mezzogiorno d'Italia," *Archivio storico per Calabria e la Lucania*, XVIII (1949) 143ff.

[26] See especially Weiss, "Translators," 195ff. And on Byzantine Italy see especially Weiss, *Greek Culture of South Italy*. On the Angevin library at Naples, however, cf. C. Coulter, "The Library of the Angevin Court of Naples," *Transactions of the American Philological Association*, LXXV (1944) 141-55, who shows that no Greek books were acquired for the library in the Angevin period.

[27] On Barlaam see especially M. Jugie's article in *Dict. hist. et géog. ecclésiastique*, VI, cols. 817-34, and Lo Parco, *Petrarca et Barlaam*. Petrarch remained only an elementary Hellenist, a fact for which Barlaam has sometimes been blamed. At Constantinople Barlaam was able to engage in debate with some of the most learned Byzantines of the age (for example, Nicephoros Gregoras). He therefore possessed a mastery of Greek as Petrarch himself admitted; see Barlaam's works in Migne, *Patrologia Graeca*, Vol. 151, cols. 1243ff. Pilatus, however, was evidently considerably less learned. Petrarch's failure to learn his Greek satisfactorily was probably due to the briefness of his study with Barlaam, his lack of grammars and dictionaries, and, to some degree, his own failings. Boccaccio acquired from Barlaam (via Paolo da Perugia, librarian at the Angevin court in Naples) much information on ancient mythology, which resulted in his *Genologia deorum*, the first treatment of the ancient myths in their original context and disconnected from medieval Christianity.

[28] Greek seems to have been taught even earlier, in 1325, at the University of Paris, according to J. Nordström, *Moyen Age et Renaissance* (Paris, 1933) 81, but

instruction in Greek was his teacher Pilatus, who is known for translating Homer into Latin verse, thus making that author available to the West for the first time since antiquity.[29]

Despite the interest in Greek generated by Petrarch and Boccaccio, enthusiasm for the language remained limited to the circle connected with the Florentine monastery of Santo Spirito and a few individuals such as Palla Strozzi and Niccolò Niccoli,[30] who made up for their lack of knowledge of Greek by their zeal in seeking to learn the language. It was clear that for any real progress to be made someone who was expert in the language and at the same time an effective teacher must be found. Such a person was the Byzantine nobleman Manuel Chrysoloras, and it is with his coming that we may speak of the true beginning of Greek studies in Italy.

In Byzantium, where Greek was of course the common tongue and where the Greek classics were a staple of education, the scholarly study of the Greek language and literature had undergone a series of revivals and declines since the time of the great patriarch and scholar Photius in the ninth century.[31] The last and one of the most notable of these literary revivals is often considered to have begun after the Byzantine recapture of Constantinople from the Latins in 1261. But this so-called Palaeologan Renaissance (so called because the study of the classics had never died in Byzantium) was rather, it appears, a continuation of that revival which

---

in connection with scholasticism, not humanism, and no chair was then created nor was a stipend assigned (Sandys, II, 168–69).

[29] A. Pertusi, "La scoperta di Euripide nel primo Umanesimo," *Italia medioevale e umanistica*, III (1960) 101–152. See also his (and E. Franceschini's) "Un' ignota Odissea latina dell' ultimo del Trecento," *Aevum* (1959) 323–55, and his forthcoming book(see above, note 24). Professor Pertusi kindly informs me that Pilatus translated Homer not from the codex possessed by Petrarch but from a Paduan codex owned by a jurist of Padua, who was, interestingly enough, probably a Cretan or Cypriote Greek who had become a Paduan citizen. Cf. below, note 40.

[30] See G. Voigt, *Pétrarque, Boccace et les débuts de l'humanisme en Italie*, trans. P. Le Monnier (Paris, 1894) 185.

[31] Photius was an encyclopedic scholar, the center of a group of literati, who wrote the famous *Bibliotheca*, which preserves the names and, in summary-form, parts of the contents of many ancient Greek works, including some now lost. See F. Fuchs, *Die höheren Schulen von Konstantinopel im Mittelalter* (Leipzig-Berlin, 1926) 21; also V. Vasiliev, *History of the Byzantine Empire* (Madison, 1952) 297; and R. Bolgar, *The Classical Heritage and its Beneficiaries* (Cambridge, Eng., 1958) 68. Also now see R. Henry's edition of Photius' *Bibliothèque*, 2 vols. (Paris, 1959–60).

had already begun at Nicaea, in western Asia Minor, a few decades before, perhaps as a kind of reaffirmation of the Hellenic spirit in the face of the Latin domination of Constantinople.[32] At Nicaea Nicephorus Blemmydes, George Acropolites, Manuel Holobolos, the Emperor Theodore II Lascaris, Nicephoros Choumnos, and Maximos Planudes had inaugurated a new emphasis on the study of the Greek classics, including works of a scientific nature. And it was this movement that was intensified and expanded by the late thirteenth and fourteenth century scholars of the Palaeologan period such as Maximos Planudes, Manuel Moschopoulos, Theodore Metochites, Demetrius Triklinios, and Thomas Magister.[33] These Byzantines compiled or edited lexica and treatises on grammar and syntax, wrote scholia on poetry, prose, and scientific literature, and developed certain philological techniques for editing the classical texts. Though their endeavors have often been subjected to severe criticism by nineteenth century scholars on the ground that in their work of editing they often corrupted the genuine texts, there is little doubt that through the interest they aroused in the ancient literature they were instrumental in preserving for the modern world valuable manuscripts of classical texts.[34]

While these rhetorical and literary activities were being carried on at Constantinople and Thessalonica, there was also developing at Mistra during the first half of the fifteenth century an increasing preoccupation with the philosophic works of Plato.[35] (Aris-

---

[32] On this theory, see especially A. Tuilier, "Recherches sur les origines de la Renaissance byzantine au XIIIe siècle," *Bulletin de l'association G. Budé*, III (1955) 71–76. He shows that "the aristocratic civilization of the Palaeologan Renaissance lived on the intellectual heritage of Nicaea."

[33] On these men in general, see Fuchs, 54–62; Sandys, I, 427–432. Tuilier, 76, also shows that new sources were sometimes utilized after 1261, as for example in Planudes' text of the *Greek Anthology*. Planudes also possessed a good knowledge of arithmetic and science. On him see below, text and note 48. Also see H. Beck, *Theodoros Metochites* (Munich, 1952); J. Verpeaux, *Nicéphore Choumnos Homme d'état et humaniste byzantin* (Paris, 1959); and R. Guilland, *Essai sur Nicéphore Grégoras* (Paris, 1926). The historian Pachymeres (13th century) also is notable for his knowledge of science.

[34] See, for example, F. Hall, *A Companion to Classical Texts* (Oxford, 1913) 44, and Sandys, I, 427. As Hall says, they were not just scribes but scholars; however, they had inadequate theories of meter and language and laid a heavy hand on the texts they edited. It may be said that they had less in common with Photius than with the Italian Renaissance humanists.

[35] On the philosophy of Plato in this period, especially that of Pletho, see F. Masai, *Pléthon et le Platonisme de Mistra* (Paris, 1956).

totle of course, because of the early synthesis made of his philosophy with Greek Christian thought, had generally held a position of honor in the Byzantine world.) By virtue of the passion of these various scholars for classical learning, their attempts to edit the ancient texts, however imperfect their methods, and their efforts to imitate the style of the ancient authors and thus to recapture something of the spirit of antiquity, many of these Byzantine intellectuals of the Palaeologan period may rightly be termed humanists.[36] It was through Manuel Chrysoloras, himself a later representative of this Palaeologan revival, that the Italian humanists, with their not dissimilar interests, were now able to draw directly upon the rich classical tradition of Byzantium.

Sent to the West by the Byzantine Emperor Manuel II Palaeologus to implore aid against the Turks, Chrysoloras in 1396 accepted an appointment as professor of Greek at the University of Florence.[37] The response to his teaching was highly enthusiastic, and leading Florentine statesmen and humanists, including Leonardo Bruni, Palla Strozzi, and perhaps Coluccio Salutati, flocked to hear him. The Florentine chancellor Bruni is quoted as saying that Chrysoloras inspired him to learn a language no Italian had understood for the last seven hundred years.[38] Though this often repeated statement cannot now be considered completely accurate (since the Italo-Greeks Barlaam and Pilatus knew Greek, and at least one erudite Byzantine, Simon Atumano, seems earlier to have taught Greek in Italy, in 1380–81),[39] there can be no doubt of the tremendous impetus given by Chrysoloras to the development of Greek studies in the West. His reputation, however, seems to have owed less to the profundity of his learning, inspiring as was his instruction, than to the widespread influence of his many pupils.

[36] See Fuchs, *Die höheren Schulen,* 65: "Durch Männer wie Planoudes war in Byzanz eine letzte Phase des Humanismus. . . ." Bolgar, *Classical Heritage,* 85, and Sandys, I, 427: "These Byzantines [of the Palaeologan era] have less in common with Photius, Arethas, and Eustathius than with the earliest representatives of the revival of learning in the West." Also Verpeaux, 199ff.

[37] On the dates of Chrysoloras' appointment and initial lecture (probably early 1397), which are disputed, see the summary of Setton, "Byzantine Background," 57, and G. Cammelli, *Manuele Crisolora* (Florence, 1941) 34, 39.

[38] Cited, for example, in Sandys, II, 19–20.

[39] See Setton, esp. 49–50, on whether Simon taught Greek (in Rome in 1380–81) privately or publicly; also see G. Mercati, *Se la versione dall' Ebraico del Codice veneto-greco VII sia di Simone Atumano* (Vatican, 1916) 40–41.

The origins of Greek studies in Venice are neither so spectacular nor so easily determinable. As we have seen, long before the thirteenth and fourteenth centuries there were Venetian merchants of long residence in the East fluent in the speaking of the Greek vernacular. Moreover, the chancery of the Republic had a continual need for persons with a knowledge of the language to participate in the administration of Venice's eastern colonies. From the practical point of view, therefore, there had long been an interest in the Greek language in Venice.

During the late fourteenth and fifteenth centuries, however, this Venetian interest in Greek was gradually transformed into an appreciation of the language on a more literary plane, rather than exclusively for practical considerations. What stimulated the Venetians to approach the study of Greek in this new manner seems to have been the influences of the rising humanism of Italy, especially of nearby Padua. Padua was situated only some twenty miles from Venice, and it was perhaps inevitable that any Paduan intellectual ferment would sooner or later penetrate in some measure to Venice. Although relations between the two cities were often far from cordial — in 1405, in fact, the Venetians conquered their rival — Padua was able to exert a strong attraction on the more intellectual-minded citizens of her neighbor city.[40]

From as early as the year 1222 Padua had been the site of a university, and it was one of the first Italian university centers to look with favor on the new humanistic studies.[41] Venice, lacking a university of its own, adopted the habit of sending potential lawyers, doctors, and grammarians there for training.[42] And these

[40] See Lazzarini, *Paolo de Bernardo*, 5–6: "Strette erano le relazioni tra i poeti di Venezia [esp. Mussato] e quelli di Padova" (in the early fourteenth century). Professor A. Pertusi informs me that in his forthcoming book he will show that he has found the first evidence of a knowledge of Greek at Padua (before 1358) in two notes in the hand of Pilatus, in his copy of Homer's *Iliad* (Ven. Marc. gr. IX, 2; no. 1447–48 de l'inv.). Here Pilatus mentions that when in Padua he had heard a jurist (elsewhere Pilatus terms him a legist) defending a law case by reciting verses from the codex of Homer's *Iliad* which he was holding in his hand.

[41] On Padua University, see J. Facciolatus, *Fasti gymnasii patavini* (Padua, 1757) I. Also on early humanism at Padua University, see Weiss, *Dawn of Humanism*, 6ff.

[42] See, for example, G. Fabris, "Professori e scolari greci all'università di Padova," *Archivio veneto*, XXX (1942) 130, who emphasizes the number of Greeks from Venice or her colonies attending Padua university in the schools of arts and

men, after exposure to the Paduan faculties of law and arts, brought back with them the widened outlook of humanism, with its focus on the culture of antiquity. In the later fourteenth century, the Venetians were brought into even closer contact with the humanism of Padua by way of the frequent visits made by Petrarch to their city during his periods of residence with the Paduan rulers, the Carrara. As is well known, he finally fixed on Arquà, near Padua, as his residence, and he died there in 1374. Petrarch's influence on the origins of Venetian humanism left its mark in particular on a number of the notaries connected with the Chancery of the Republic.[43]

The wave of excitement produced by the presence of Chrysoloras at Florence spread to other areas of Italy, and soon reached Padua. In 1397 Piero Vergerio, a teacher of arts, left that university to study with Chrysoloras in Florence. And Guarino of Verona, a student at Padua under Gasparino Barzizza, became so imbued with a desire to learn Greek that he returned to Constantinople either with Chrysoloras or shortly after, in order to master the language in its own milieu.[44] These two men, Vergerio and Guarino, are the links between the University of Padua and Chrysoloras.[45]

Despite the early appearance of a humanistic tradition at Padua and the various contacts with Chrysoloras, there seems to have been no attempt to inaugurate formal instruction in Greek at the University. Indeed, there were even those who considered its study unimportant — such as the Latin professor (and former pupil of Petrarch) Giovanni da Ravenna, who we are told advised someone

---

law. He in particular discusses the Corfiote Thomaso Diplovataccio (at Padua 1486–1489), who was an important name in the sphere of juridical studies in the period.

[43] On Petrarch at Padua and his Venetian connections, see especially Lazzarini, 24–54, and bibliography cited there.

[44] Cammelli, *Manuele Crisolora*, 133, disputes the traditional view that Guarino actually *accompanied* Chrysoloras to Constantinople. A whole series of Westerners (probably more than we have record of) went to the East to learn Greek: we might add to the names of those well known that of Rinucius Aretinus (d. 1456), who studied in Crete and Constantinople, where he dedicated his translation of Plato's *Crito* to the Emperor. He returned to Italy about 1423. See D. Lockwood, "De Rinucio Aretino Graecarum Litterarum Interprete," *Harvard Studies in Classical Philology*, XXIV (Cambridge, Mass., 1913) 51–109. For the names of others see below, Conclusion, note 3.

[45] A good account of Padua in this period is provided by W. Woodward, *Vittorino da Feltre and Other Humanist Educators* (Cambridge, Eng., 1905) 12ff. On Vergerio, see Cammelli, 52–57. Guarino could speak as well as write Greek, an ability in which no Italian could equal him except Filelfo and Aurispa.

not to address him in Greek or he would consider him a barbarian! (Giovanni did however recognize the possible value of translations from the Greek for the enrichment of Latin learning.) [46] Even Barzizza, the greatest Latin scholar of the age, who in 1407 assumed the new chair of rhetoric at Padua, probably knew very little Greek, though he had been with Chrysoloras at Pavia.[47]

Of no little importance in stimulating Venetian interest in Greek on a more humanistic basis were the visits of learned Byzantine dignitaries to Venice. As early as 1296 the Byzantine scholar Maximos Planudes had appeared in Venice as the ambassador of the Greek Emperor. What influence he could have exerted on Venetian cultural life during his brief and not altogether happy stay is hard to say, though we know that his sentiments were pro-Western and that he had translated into Greek various Latin writings of Ovid, Macrobius, Augustine, and Boethius.[48] Another visitor was the Byzantine scholar and Archbishop of Latin-held Thebes, Simon Atumano, who in 1373 was granted the honor of Venetian citizenship, at a time when he seems to have been at work on his remarkable trilingual Bible.[49] Even more important is the case of Simon's friend, the famous Byzantine scholar and prime minister Demetrius Cydones, who in 1391, after a year's residence in Venice, was also awarded the coveted honor of Venetian citizenship — a mark of high esteem for a foreigner in view of the jealousy with which the Serenissima guarded its municipal privileges. In Byzantium Cydones too had turned a number of Latin theological treatises into Greek, including Thomas Aquinas' *Summa Contra Gentiles* and *Summa Theologiae* (which had resulted in the formation of a virtual circle of Thomists in the Byzantine court).[50] Though it is probable that the honor granted to Cy-

[46] See R. Sabbadini, *Giovanni da Ravenna, Insigne figura d'umanista* (Como, 1924) 103 and 220: "athice autem si peroraveris, barbarus michi eris . . . Quod si . . . codices habes grecos, interpretare."

[47] See Woodward, 16, n. 1.

[48] We know that Planudes was sent to Venice because he knew Latin. His mission was to mollify the Venetian anger over the murder of Venetians in Constantinople. On Planudes, see especially C. Wendel, entry under Planudes in Pauly-Wissowa, *Real-Encyclopädie*, XX (1950) cols. 2202–53, with bibliography. It is often stated (e.g., in Sandys, 427) that Planudes also translated Caesar, but this is incorrect.

[49] See Setton, "Byzantine Background," 51.

[50] See M. Jugie, "Démétrius Cydonès et la théologie latine à Byzance au XIVe

dones was primarily the result of some political service rendered by
him, or of a Venetian desire to curry favor with the Greek government, it is certain that Venetian respect for his scholarly attain-
ments must have played some part in the award.[51] Later, in 1397,
Cydones once more returned to Venice, this time as a companion
to Chrysoloras on the occasion of the latter's memorable journey
to Italy. Chrysoloras himself stayed twice in Venice, and after
teaching in Florence for over three years (1397–1400) returned to
that city, where he may well have continued to instruct, though
not formally.[52]

The first humanist school to be established in Venice was that of
Chrysoloras' student, Guarino of Verona.[53] The study of Greek
literature was an integral part of the curriculum, valued for its
ability to educate the intelligence and train the mind in principles
of sound morality. So successful was Guarino in his instruction
(1414–1418), we are told, that to his school came the leaders of
the Venetian patriciate.[54] Among these were several Venetians
who appear later in England: Fantino Zorzi, Tito Livio Frulovisi
(who was not actually a Venetian but was brought up in Venice),
and Piero Del Monte, the collector of the papal revenues, who,
when he looked for Greek books in England in order to resume

et XVᵉ siècles," *Echos d'Orient*, XXXI (1928) 385–402, and especially G. Mercati, *Notizie di Procoro e Demetrio Cidone* (Vatican, 1931), which prints sections of Cydones' translations of Aquinas. Also Setton, 52–54, for bibliography.
Cydones is often said also to have translated Augustine's *De Trinitate*, but this is
probably wrong and should be attributed to Planudes: see M. Rackl, *Miscellanea
F. Ehrle*, I (= *Studi e testi*, XXXVII [Rome, 1924]) 9–17. For Cydones' correspondence see now R. J. Loenertz, *Démétrius Cydonès: Correspondance* (Vatican, 1956–1960), and on Cydones' movements at this time see esp. vol. 2, no. 442,
p. 406, Cydones' letter written on his return from Venice.
    [51] Cf. R. Loenertz, "Démétrius Cydonès, citôyen de Venise," *Echos d'Orient*,
XXXVII (1938) 125–26. Simon Atumano's awards of citizenship in 1373 had been
for his literary activities. See note above, bibliography listed.
    [52] Cf. Cammelli, *Manuele Crisolora*, 144, 164–65.
    [53] Among Chrysoloras' many pupils, according to some authorities, was per-
haps the Camaldulensian Ambrogio Traversari, later bishop of the Venetian colony
of Coron (in the Morea). Also two young Florentines, Roberto Rossi and Iacopo
Angeli da Scarperia, who, it is known, on the arrival of Chrysoloras and Cydones
in Venice, rushed there to receive instruction from them (Cammelli, 66ff., and
Setton, 56–71).
    [54] Woodward, *Vittorino da Feltre*, 18, and R. Sabbadini, *La scuola e gli studi di
Guarino Veronese* (Catania, 1896) 26; also Sandys, II, 49. Guarino of course later
established a school at Ferrara which taught a very large number of subsequently
famous Hellenists and Latinists.

his studies, could find no suitable texts.[55] One of Guarino's associates in Venice was the noted educator Vittorino da Feltre. Though not a regular student, Vittorino took advantage of his stay to learn some Greek from Guarino. And subsequently for one year (1432) Vittorino himself conducted a school for the sons of Venetian nobles.[56]

Of Guarino's students in Venice the best was probably the statesman-humanist Francesco Barbaro. As a boy Francesco had learned some Greek from the noble Zaccaria Trevisan, a Venetian who had returned in 1403 from his post of Captain in Crete. Barbaro, whom his biographer Percy Gothein believes to have done more than anyone else to bring about a greater Venetian receptivity to the new principles of humanism,[57] was deeply inspired by Guarino's instruction, and while still a youth undertook to translate certain of the lives of Plutarch (which he regarded as a model of conduct for Venetian political life) [58] and to collect a library of Greek manuscripts. Barbaro's interest in Greek was undoubtedly intensified by his own term of administrative service in Crete, where he was afforded an opportunity to enlarge his library by patronizing the growing activity of the scribes of the island. Barbaro profited also from friendship with enthusiasts of Greek in Florence: Ambrogio Traversari, Niccolò Niccoli, and even Cosimo de'Medici, with all three of whom he considered a journey to the Holy Land for the purpose of searching for Greek manuscripts.[59] In the formation of Barbaro's intellectual interests the East played a significant part. But the one who probably exerted the most

[55] See Weiss, *Humanism in England*, 26.
[56] Woodward, esp. 18. Also see E. Ferrai, *L'ellenismo nello studio di Padova* (Padua, 1876) 26. Vittorino's reputation was mainly built, however, on his teaching in Mantua.
[57] P. Gothein, *Francesco Barbaro: Frühhumanismus und Staatskunst in Venedig* (Berlin, 1932) 10, stresses throughout that Barbaro's humanistic interests were of use to him, a man of action, in affairs of state. For other works concerning Barbaro, see R. Sabbadini, *Centotrenta lettere inedite di Francesco Barbaro* (Salerno, 1884) and Kristeller, *Studies*, 347. On Trevisan see G. degli Agostini, *Notizie istorico-critiche intorno la vita, e le opere degli scrittori viniziani* (Venice, 1752–1754) I, 310–25.
[58] Gothein, 54–55, who says the Plutarchan influence was important during both the youth and manhood of Barbaro and was the main force behind the composition of Barbaro's most important work, *De re uxoria*, written in the first year of his Greek studies. Barbaro, says Gothein, became almost the personification of Plutarch's vision.
[59] Gothein, 105.

direct influence upon him was Guarino, himself a product of Eastern training. It was Barbaro, together with his young patrician friend, Leonardo Giustiniani, another student of Guarino, who in 1423 formally greeted for the Republic in faultless Greek the Byzantine Emperor Manuel II Palaeologus, who had come to Italy in the hope of securing military aid against the Turks.[60] Throughout his life Barbaro maintained an active interest in Greek studies, which was shared by other members of his family, notably his nephew Ermolao and his grandson, both of whom had the same name. At the end of the fifteenth century, the younger Ermolao would help prepare the way for instituting at the University of Padua the teaching of Aristotle in the original Greek.[61]

In 1417 Barbaro brought from Crete to Venice the young George of Trebizond, soon to become one of the most famous of the Greek exiles. Born in Crete (his parents were from Trebizond), he spent his early days in Italy learning Latin and copying manuscripts for Barbaro. Of a perpetually contentious disposition, George soon entered into conflict with his teacher of Latin, Guarino (whom he charged with knowing less Latin than he!), and also with his patron, Bessarion (who accused George of gross negligence in his translation of Plato's *Laws*).[62] In 1460 or the beginning of 1461 George, by dedicating his translation of the *Laws* to the Doge (the Senate was persuaded that the work could serve as a practical guide for the management of Venetian public life), obtained an instructorial position in the School of the Ducal Chancery,[63] which had recently been established for the Venetian youth destined to enter the administrative offices of the Republic. It must be noted, however, contrary to what is often believed, that in this post

[60] See Gothein, 178, also 50; and G. Mazzuchelli, *Gli scrittori d'Italia* (Brescia, 1753-1763) II, pt. 1, 265. Also on Giustiniani see degli Agostini, I, 135-76.

[61] See Kristeller, *Studies*, 343, who shows that Ermolao still used the medieval Latin translations, though referring to the Greek text in his lectures. The first course on the Greek text of Aristotle seems to have been a bit later, by Nicolaus Leonicos Thomaeus, who was an Epirot Greek (or perhaps Albanian) born in Venice. See below, Chapter 8, note 18.

[62] See Chapter 4, text and note 55.

[63] On George's life in general see Gothein, 147ff. and esp. 150-51 for this incident. Also see the authoritative article of G. Castellani, "Giorgio da Trebisonda, maestro di eloquenza a Vicenza e a Venezia," *Nuovo Archivio Veneto*, XI (1896) 123ff. I follow his date for George's arrival in Italy (1417), explained on page 129. Further on Trapezuntius see the notes of R. Sabbadini in *Giornale Storico della letteratura italiana* (1891-1904).

Georgius Trapezuntius.

GEORGE OF TREBIZOND
(1395–1486)

George taught only Latin, though it is very likely that he was at the same time giving Greek lessons privately.[64]

Barbaro was not the only Venetian patrician to be attracted to Greek studies. We may cite the case of Carlo Zeno who had been Venetian ambassador in the Greek East and who, at the ripe age of eighty, decided to learn Greek. Earlier he had offered hospitality at his house in Venice to Chrysoloras, Vergerio, and Guarino.[65] There were also the nobles Zaccaria Trevisan, Captain of Candia, who, as we have seen, had originally taught Barbaro Greek,[66] and Marco Lipomanno, the jurist and Duke of Candia, who seems similarly to have acquired much of his knowledge of the Greek language in the East.[67] Among the group of diplomats and administrators who utilized the opportunity of service in the East to enrich their knowledge of Greek learning, the best known is Francesco Filelfo. An attaché of the Venetian embassy in Constantinople from 1420 to 1427, he served at the same time as secretary to the Greek Emperor. His growing reputation in Greek scholarship persuaded the noble Venetian family of the Giustiniani to have him recalled to Venice. There he taught for a time but soon moved on to Florence, still the principal center of Greek studies, where he succeeded the Sicilian Giovanni Aurispa in the Greek chair formerly occupied so illustriously by Chrysoloras.[68]

Although not a few members of the Venetian nobility were thus beginning to share in the growing humanistic interest — no negligible factor was the conviction that such studies might provide the youthful nobility idling on the piazzas with something more use-

[64] Castellani, 135-36, dispels the theory that George's appointment marked the institution of Greek teaching in Venice on a public basis. Cf. E. Bertanza, I maestri scuole e scolari in Venezia fino al 1500 (Venice, 1907) p. xvii. Also P. Molmenti, Venice; Its Individual Growth from the Earliest Beginnings, trans. H. F. Brown (Chicago, 1907) pt. 2, I, 255.

[65] Lazzarini, Paolo de Bernardo, 131. Zeno died in 1418.

[66] On Trevisan, see Lazzarini, 131-32 and Gothein, 7. See also note 57, above.

[67] F. Cornelius, Creta Sacra (Venice, 1755) II, 377f., and S. Mercati, "Di Giovanni Simeonachis Protopapa di Candia," Misc. G. Mercati, III (Vatican, 1946) 3.

[68] On Filelfo (who married a relative of Chrysoloras), see C. De' Rosmini, Vita di Francesco Filelfo, 3 vols. (Milan, 1808), esp. I, 11, 19-20; Gothein, 147; also bibliography in Rossi, Il Quattrocento 69, n. 44. Florentine women, we are told, stepped aside with reverence when meeting Filelfo on the street! Giovanni Aurispa had returned from the East to Florence in 1424 with a cache of no less than 232 Greek manuscripts, and Filelfo in 1427 with a goodly number. H. Noiret, Lettres inédites de Michel Apostolis (Paris, 1889) 49, thinks Filelfo may have studied Greek in Constantinople with Michael Apostolis (on whom see below, Chapter 4).

ful to do! [69] — not all of the aristocracy by any means looked with favor on the study of Greek letters. Nor can it be said that Venice before the last half of the fifteenth century was of any real importance as a center of humanistic culture.[70] A secretary to the Venetian Senate, Lorenzo de Monaci, who was a friend to the Florentine humanist Leonardo Bruni and also to Francesco Barbaro, expressed a profound hostility to everything Greek and in fact declared that the study of Greek and translations from that language were useless.[71] Even Filelfo's hopes were deceived (though probably partly on account of the faults of his own personality), and, as we have seen, he left Venice for the more congenial environment of Florence. More significant with regard to the development of Greek studies in Venice is the fact that no public chair of Greek had yet been established in that city or even at the nearby University of Padua, which since 1405 had been under Venetian control. This seeming paradox, the lack of interest in Greek instruction on a public basis despite the long history of close relations with Byzantium, is attributable not only to the traditional absorption of the Venetian aristocracy in economic affairs but also, it would seem, to the very ease of communication with her Greek colonies in the East, which rendered such instruction as yet unnecessary.

A powerful new impetus was given to the Western cultivation of Greek scholarship by the arrival in 1439 of a Greek delegation to attend the famous Council of Florence, the aim of which was to unite the Greek and Roman churches.[72] The delegation remained in Florence for a year and a half, and it was, as is well known, the presence in Florence of this huge group of seven hundred Greeks, many accomplished in Greek literature and philosophy, that led to the revival in western Europe of an interest in the Platonism and Neoplatonism of antiquity.[73]

[69] Gothein, *Francesco Barbaro*, 140; Woodward, *Vittorino da Feltre*, 9.

[70] See Weiss, "Learning and Education in Western Europe," 95. Also Burckhardt, *Civilization of the Renaissance*, 94.

[71] See degli Agostini, *Scrittori viniziani*, II, 364ff., and Lazzarini, *Paolo de Bernardo*, 110, who also notes that in 1416 Francesco Barbaro actively opposed Monaci's views on Greek (cf. Rossi, *Il Quattrocento*, 92). Also see F. Thiriet, *La Romanie vénitienne au Moyen Age* (Paris, 1959) 288, n. 3, who refers to Lorenzo as Chancellor of Crete.

[72] For the problem of ecclesiastical union see Geanakoplos, "The Council of Florence," 324-46.

[73] On this revival see A. della Torre, *Storia dell' Accademia Platonica di Firenze*

On their way to and from the Council the Greek delegates spent some time in Venice. The impression made by their stay, brief though it was, has been vividly preserved for us by several contemporary sources. To quote from one, the illuminating if not highly literary account (called *Acta Graeca*) of the' Greek ecclesiastic Dorotheos of Mitylene:

[Venice is] truly marvelous and most marvelous — rich, varied, golden, and adorned in various ways. Worthy [indeed] of many encomia is the most sage Venice. Whoever would call it a second promised land is not mistaken . . . What could one ask for there and not find? . . . The entire city bestirred itself and went to welcome the Emperor and made a great amount of noise and applause . . . The marvelous church of St. Mark, the magnificent palace of the Doge, and the great houses of the nobles, red and decorated with much gold, beautiful and more than beautiful. Those who have not observed these can perhaps not believe. But we who have seen the city cannot describe its beauty: its site, its order, the intelligence of its men and women, the multitude of people all standing and looking, rejoicing in and enjoying the arrival of the Emperor . . . When then we reached the great bridge, called the Rialto, it was raised and our boat passed underneath. A great crowd of people was there, with gilded banners and trumpets, and there were cries and applause. In brief, I am unable to write of or to describe the spectacles of that day.[74]

It is true that Dorotheos was a pro-unionist and hence favorable to the Latins. But even the strongly anti-unionist account of the Greek cleric Sylvester Syropoulos, despite the bitterness he expresses over the Venetian looting of Constantinople in 1204, reveals a grudging admiration for the splendor of Venice.[75]

From sources such as the above we may derive some indication of the mutual attitudes of Venetians and Greeks in this critical period. Significantly, the Greeks of the delegation were impressed

---

(Florence, 1902). For important qualifying remarks regarding this revival see Kristeller, *Marsilio Ficino*. Also see above, Introduction, note 5.

[74] My translation, from J. Gill, *Quae supersunt Actorum Graecorum Concilii Florentini* (Rome, 1953) pt. 1, 4–5. Father V. Laurent is preparing a much-needed critical edition of Syropoulos.

[75] See M. Creyghton's edition of S. Syropoulos, *Historia vera unionis non verae . . . Concilii Florentini* (The Hague, 1660), esp. sect. 4, chap. 16, on the richness of the Venetian churches and the plunder taken from Constantinople. Cf. S. G. Mercati, "Venezia nella poesia neo-greca," *Italia e Grecia* (Florence, 1939) 312. For still another contemporary account of the reception in Venice see the Greek historian Ducas (Bonn ed.) 212.

by the toleration of the Venetians and their growing appreciation for the Byzantine ways and habits. In fact, the memory of the warm reception accorded them was to play no small part in inducing many of these same Greek prelates and scholars to return later to Venice in order to settle there permanently.

The most prominent of the Greek intellectuals who returned to Italy subsequent to the Florentine Council was Bessarion, Archbishop of Nicaea and, after the Council (where he was the leading Greek proponent of union), a Cardinal of the Roman church.[76] Pupil of the Greek Neoplatonist Gemistos Pletho (whose exposition of Platonic philosophy had created such a sensation in the Medici circle of Florence), Bessarion lost no opportunity in the Curia of Pope Nicholas V for preaching the necessity of launching a crusade to save Constantinople from the advancing Turks. Besides his unceasing efforts in behalf of his homeland (about which there will be more to say later), Bessarion opened his home in Rome to a large number of learned Greek refugees whose patron he became and who, in exchange, sought out for him Greek manuscripts, many of which at his request they translated into Latin. This circle, under his guiding spirit and that of Pope Nicholas V, was the first manifestation of a Greek Renaissance in Rome, and was the precursor of the more famous sixteenth century revival of Greek letters under Pope Leo X.[77]

Though Bessarion spent most of his time in Rome, on several occasions he made extended visits to Venice. Indeed, such was his regard for that city that, after some hesitation, he chose it rather than Rome or Florence as the permanent repository for his remarkable collection of manuscripts, which included some five hundred written in Greek. A letter he wrote in 1468 to the Doge informs us of the reasons for his bequest:

As all peoples of almost the entire world gather in your city, so especially do the Greeks. Arriving by sea from their homelands they debark first at Venice, being forced by necessity to come to your city and live among you, and there they seem to enter another Byzantium (*quasi alterum Byzantium*). In view of this, how could I more appro-

[76] On Bessarion, see Chapter 4.
[77] See Chapter 4, text and note 72. According to Weiss, "Learning and Education in Western Europe," I, 95, there was little interest in Greek in Rome before the days of Leo X.

Beſſarion.

CARDINAL BESSARION
(c. 1403–1472)

priately confer this bequest than upon the Venetians to whom I myself am indebted and committed by obligation because of their well
known favors to me, and upon their city, which I chose for my country after the subjugation of Greece and in which I have been very
honorably received and recognized.[78]

By the late fifteenth century, intellectual pursuits were becoming a more and more essential part of the education of the Venetian
aristocracy. Indeed the nobles' very manner of life was now under-
going an important change. No longer did wealthy Venetians invariably send their sons on state galleys to learn trade and navigation. Commerce was of course still the basic source of wealth, but
more time was being devoted to humanistic activities.[79] It was felt
increasingly that an awareness of the ideals of Greek and Roman
antiquity would be useful in molding the character of the Venetian youth, the education of which had always been of vital concern to the government of this rather regimented society. However,
in spite of the gradually changing attitude, there were still no
facilities for the advanced study of Greek, and those desirous of
such training had to go elsewhere — to the East, to Bologna, or
frequently to Florence, which until the last years of the fifteenth
century continued to maintain its position as the leading center of
Greek studies.

Already in 1434 the Venetians had been brought into more
direct contact with the literary ideals of Tuscany by the arrival
in their midst of the wealthy Florentine statesman Palla Strozzi.
Strozzi, a man of deep humanistic interests, had originally been
responsible for bringing Chrysoloras to Florence (a fact sometimes overlooked in the widespread admiration for the accomplishments of Medici patronage). But having run afoul of Cosimo de'
Medici in the tangled politics of the Tuscan metropolis, he was
exiled to Venice, to the benefit of the latter. Once ensconced in
that city — or rather in Padua, where he maintained his residence

[78] See H. Omont, "Inventaire de manuscrits grecs et latins donnés à Saint-Marc
de Venise (1468)," *Revue des bibliothèques*, IV (1894) 129-87. For Latin text
which I have here translated, see Omont, 139. Cf. also on Bessarion's manuscript
collection Setton, "Byzantine Background," 74. Bessarion secured a large number
of manuscripts from the south Italian Greek monastery of Casole, on which see
C. Diehl, "Le monastère de S. Nicolas di Casole près d'Otrante d'après un manuscrit inédit," *Mélanges d'archéologie et d'histoire*, VI (1886) 173-88.

[79] See Molmenti, *Venice*, 227-31. Also W. Elwert, "Venedigs literarische Bedeutung," *Archiv für Kulturgeschichte*, XXXVI (1954) 261ff.

— he began to instill in his Venetian friends something of his own avid interest in Greek culture. Thus he sent to Constantinople and other Eastern areas for Greek manuscripts, and was able to attract to Venetia teachers noted for their mastery of Greek letters. Two young Byzantines John Argyropoulos and Andronikos Callistos lived in Strozzi's own house and gave him lessons in Greek.[80]

It was partly because of the preparation of the terrain by Strozzi, partly because of the suggestions of Filelfo and the Greek émigré Theodore Gaza,[81] and possibly also from a desire on the part of the Venetians to emulate the examples of Florence and Bologna that the Venetian Signoria in 1463 took the important step of establishing a chair of Greek letters, providing for a fixed stipend, at the University of Padua. The first occupant was the celebrated Athenian Demetrius Chalcondyles. By virtue of the excellence of his instruction, Chalcondyles became the center of a group of enthusiasts of Greek studies, among his better-known pupils being the Venetian humanist Giovanni Lorenzi and the Greek (or at least Hellenized Albanian) Leonicos Thomaeus, the young Greek protegé of Bessarion Janus Lascaris, and perhaps the Western Hellenist Varinus Favorinus of Camerino.[82]

After teaching for about a decade at Padua, Chalcondyles left to go to Florence, where in 1475 he assumed the Greek chair vacated by Argyropoulos.[83] After Chalcondyles' departure, successors to his Paduan post seem to have been the (Uniate) Greek priest Alexander Zeno and the Venetian Lorenzo Camerti, com-

[80] See G. Cammelli, *Demetrio Calcondila* (Florence, 1954) 30, and Sandys, *History of Classical Scholarship*, II, 63, 76, who say that Strozzi studied in 1441 with Argyropoulos and in 1461 with Callistos.

[81] Cammelli, 29. Gaza, Chalcondyles' teacher, may well have recommended him to Filelfo, who was interested in the appointment to the Paduan chair.

[82] On the foundation of the chair see Facciolatus, *Fasti gymnasii patavini*, I, pp. liv–lv. Florence's chair dated from 1361 and that of the University of Bologna from 1455. On the Florentine *studium* and university to 1472, see A. Gherardi, *Statuti della Università e Studio Fiorentino* (Florence, 1881), and on Bologna see below, Chapter 9, note 11. On Chalcondyles' pupils see Cammelli, *Demetrio Calcondila*, 31–36; also Ferrai, *L'ellenismo di Padova*, 29 and 63, n. 16. On Favorinus as Chalcondyles' student, Cammelli, 36 n. 1, cites E. Mestica, *Varino Favorino Camerte* (Ancona, 1888), who bases his statement on the often untrustworthy N. Papadopoli, *Historia gymnasii patavini* (Venice, 1726).

[83] See Cammelli, 50–55, who says that Chalcondyles was teaching in Padua as late as 1472 and was definitely at Florence teaching in 1475. Argyropoulos left Florence in 1471, and up to 1475 Callistos taught privately in Florence, at which time he left to go to Milan, and Chalcondyles was called.

monly called "the Cretan" because of his years of study in the east.[84] Following these came the Cretan-born Marcus Musurus,[85] during whose tenure, as we shall see, the Greek chair of Padua was to achieve a prestige unequaled in all Europe.

It may be concluded from the above discussion that the origins of the Western interest in Greek owed far less to the native traditions of rhetorical practice or medieval precedents than to direct or indirect contact with the Byzantine East.[86] But in the case of Venice, as we have observed, close relations between the Republic and the East had already existed for centuries, and the development of a more humanistic attitude toward the study of Greek must therefore originally have been due to some other factor. This was, in considerable part, the rising humanism of Padua and, to a lesser extent, that of more distant Florence. Without the creation of a more receptive Venetian outlook, the influence of Chrysoloras, Bessarion, and the many other Greek visitors, and conversely of the Venetian administrators serving in the East, would have had little more effect on the development of Venetian Greek studies than did the earlier centuries-long Greco-Venetian exchanges. To be sure, the primarily economically oriented mentality of the Venetian citizenry for a long time permitted only slow progress to be made in humanistic endeavors. But once the aristocracy came to realize, under the guidance of such persons as Francesco Barbaro, Giustiniani, and perhaps to some extent George of Trebizond, that Greek humanism not only was intellectually rewarding but could be utilized to serve the highest interests of the state, Venice, more than any other Italian center, could take full advantage of her unique relationship to the old Byzantine East and begin to make rapid advances in the cultivation of Greek letters.[87]

[84] It should be noted that in this period (1490) the Hellenist Urbano Bolzanio of Belluno, who had learned his Greek in the Greek East and was an intimate of the Doge (we shall later see him as a member of Aldus' Academy), opened a private Greek school in Venice (Molmenti, *Venice*, I, pt. 2, 254).

[85] The succession at Padua is often confused, partly because professors of "rhetoric" are sometimes taken for professors of Greek. I follow here the order of Facciolatus, *Fasti gymnasii patavini*, I, p. lv.

[86] See Kristeller, *Classics*, 84. Also Kristeller, *Studies*, 24: "The study of Greek language and literature . . . [was] now introduced from the Byzantine East where it had been kept alive throughout the medieval centuries."

[87] This is not, of course, to deny that a *practical* knowledge of the Greek lan-

These, then, were the beginnings of Greek studies in Venice that prepared the way for the remarkable flowering of Venetian Hellenism at the close of the fifteenth and early sixteenth centuries. But before we examine this later period, in which the Greek exiles from the East were to play a central role, let us investigate the situation on the Venetian-held island of Crete. For with the destruction of the Byzantine state after the capture of Constantinople in 1453, Crete became a veritable center of refuge for the entire Greek world. And it is the conditions on the island which constitute the background for the careers of most of the figures to be discussed in this book.

---

guage had earlier been useful to the state, as, for example, in the case of her administrators in the East. But in the later fifteenth century the state could benefit from the developing *humanistic* interest in Greek by way of the prestige accruing from the hospitality it accorded to Greek scholars (as we shall see, for instance, in connection with the Aldine press), from the classical precepts of education, which could serve to mold the character of the youth, and from the practical examples to be drawn from the ancient works on politics and government (for instance, George of Trebizond's translation of Plato's *Laws* and Barbaro's of Plutarch's *Lives*, both mentioned above). On this question of the Venetian use of humanism to serve the state, see Weiss, *Dawn of Humanism*, 6, 11, and cf. esp. Lazzarini, *Paolo de Bernardo*, 20ff., who emphasizes the early role of the notaries in the Ducal Chancery for the origins of Venetian humanism. Lazzarini does not, however, consider the problem of why the relations between Venice and the East for a long time produced no "humanistic" results. See also Gothein, *Francesco Barbaro*.

Chapter 2

CRETE AND VENICE

IN THE REVIVAL of classical scholarship in the West, Cretan men of letters occupy a noteworthy position. Beginning in the early fifteenth century with the Cretan Pope Alexander V (born Peter Philarges) and extending to the end of the sixteenth with Nicholas Tourriano (Della Torre), librarian of King Philip II, a surprisingly large number of Cretan intellectuals spread over the Mediterranean area, from Syria in the East to as far as Spain in the West. As émigrés to Western Europe, Cretans filled teaching positions in leading universities, copied manuscripts for patrons of virtually every Latin country, and were closely associated with the early development of the Greek press in Venice and elsewhere. Nevertheless, despite a certain recognition of the importance of the Cretan contribution, insufficient attention has been directed to the social and intellectual conditions on the island which constituted the early environment for these expatriates. Without a delineation of this background no real understanding is possible of the sudden emergence of Crete to intellectual prominence or of the reasons for the movement of the Cretan scholars westward.

By the end of the fifteenth century Crete had become the most important colonial possession of Venice in the east. To maintain Venetian domination over the island, however, was no easy matter. In the first place the island was situated a considerable distance from Venice. Moreover, the people were of a different culture and religion and they had a tradition of being the most rebellious of all Greeks. Revolutions, lasting sometimes for decades, repeatedly broke out which the Venetians were often hard put to suppress.

In these uprisings prominent Cretan families (*archontes*) such as the Callierges and Vlastos families acted as leaders, and their names recur constantly in the sources.[1]

In the face of these difficulties the Venetian government sought to strengthen its position by encouraging Venetian colonists to settle on the island. Consisting primarily of colonial officers and merchants, the newcomers tended at first to remain aloof from the Cretans and to reside exclusively in the two or three principal towns, in Candia (the modern Herakleion), Rethymnon, and Canea. A few Venetian peasants were also transferred to Crete, but by the fifteenth century they seem to have been completely absorbed by the Greeks.[2] For the Venetian nobles on the island, never very numerous, Cretan customs and culture came to exert a strong attraction. Indeed, according to evidence adduced by historians, intermarriage and even adoption of the Greek religion were not uncommon. One scholar, for example, emphasizing the degree of assimilation of many noble Venetians, notes that they spoke Greek "alla Greca." [3] Xanthoudides, a leading recent historian of the Venetian period of domination, affirms that many of the Venetians sent to colonize Crete soon adopted the Greek language and customs — far more than the Greeks did the Italian. And Kyrou shows that sometimes members of the best Venetian families in Crete would even join the Cretan revolutionaries against their own government.[4]

[1] The chief modern work on Crete under Venetian rule has been that of S. Xanthoudides, Ἡ Ἐνετοκρατία ἐν Κρήτῃ καὶ οἱ κατὰ τῶν Ἐνετῶν ἀγῶνες τῶν Κρητῶν (Athens, 1939) esp. 99–110, 113ff. (cited hereafter as *Venetian Crete*). Also see W. Miller, "Crete under the Venetians (1204–1669)," in *Essays on the Latin Orient* (Cambridge, 1921) 177–98. More recent is the work of Thiriet, *La Romanie vénitienne*, and especially that of M. Manousakas, Ἡ ἐν Κρήτῃ συνωμοσία τοῦ Σήφη Βλαστοῦ (*1453–54*) καὶ ἡ νέα συνωμοτικὴ κίνησις τοῦ *1460–62* (Athens, 1960), and his articles cited below. See also the articles of N. Tomadakes, below. Finally, the work of N. Zoudianos, Ἱστορία τῆς Κρήτης ἐπὶ Ἐνετοκρατίας, I (Athens, 1960), provides little information of importance for us.

[2] Xanthoudides, *Venetian Crete*, 159, and documents in Cornelius, *Creta Sacra*, II, 373, and in Gerola, *Monumenti Veneti*, II, 7–8, 252, 258.

[3] Gerola, II, 7, 8, 252, 258. Miller, "Crete," 179: "The Venetian colonists . . . became Hellenized and embraced Orthodoxy."

[4] Xanthoudides, 159, and A. Kyrou, " Ἡ πνευματικὴ ἀκμὴ τῆς Κρήτης κατὰ τὸν 15 ον καὶ 16 ον αἰῶνα," Ἐπετηρὶς Ἑταιρείας Κρητικῶν Σπουδῶν (1938) 313–15. Also B. Dudan, *Il dominio Veneziano di Levante* (Bologna, 1938) 134. On the Gasmules or *migades*, children of such mixed marriages, see Kyrou, 313, and above, Chapter I, note 5.

In view of the difficulty of establishing firm political control, the Venetian government felt it necessary to be more or less tolerant in its policy toward the Orthodox Church of Crete. There are in fact indications that not infrequently the Venetians would support their Orthodox subjects against papal pressures and Latin ecclesiastical propaganda.[5] This dominance of the political factor over the religious was typical of Venetian diplomatic practice, as is well attested by the famous Venetian saying, "Semo Veneziani e poi Cristiani" ("We are Venetians first, then Christians").[6]

Nonetheless, while the over-all policy of Venice toward the Greek church of Crete was one of nonviolence, the Venetian authorities sought to nullify the influence of the Greek episcopate. For the clergy with its fanatical adhesion to the Greek ritual was the nucleus around which men of independent spirit could best unite. Thus the Venetians astutely displaced the Greek metropolitans and bishops in favor of ten Latin episcopal appointees, to whom the ecclesiastical estates of the former were then assigned. Left untouched, however, were the lower clerical Greek ranks and the numerous monasteries with their landed possessions.

This reorganization of their church administration and especially deprivation of an ecclesiastical hierarchy (a situation which with rare exceptions would obtain until the Turkish conquest of Crete in 1669)[7] was bitterly resented by the Greeks. They were particularly indignant at the fact that a candidate for ordination to the Orthodox priesthood was forced to resort to the hierarchy of the Venetian-held territory on the Greek mainland — to Modon, Coron, or more often Monemvasia. Occasionally, it is true, Greek bishops might come secretly from Constantinople in order to

[5] G. Scaffini, *Notizie intorno ai primi cento anni della dominazione Veneta in Creta* (Alexandria, 1907) 17-18; also Xanthoudides, 156. E. Gerland, "Histoire de la noblesse crétoise au Moyen Age," *Revue de l'Orient Latin*, X (1903-04) 223, mentions the case of Alexios Kalliergis, whom the government defended against the pretensions of two Latin bishops.

[6] Xanthoudides, *Venetian Crete*, 156.

[7] An exception to the appointment of Cretans as bishops is the case of the scholar Gerasimos Palaiokapas (ca. 1580), who had studied and taught at Padua and for whom the Venetians had a great liking. His will left scholarships to Greek students attending Padua University. See Xanthoudides, 155. Also Kyrou, "Ἡ πνευματικὴ ἀκμή," 308. For other exceptions see the recent work of N. Tomadakes, Ὁ Ἰωσὴφ Βρυέννιος καὶ ἡ Κρήτη κατὰ τὸ 1400 (Athens, 1947) 83-85 (cited hereafter as *Iosef Bryennios*), and also below, Chapter 5, text and note 166, for Musurus' appointment to the bishopric of Hierapetra in Crete.

ordain the Cretan clergy, but the government meted out severe punishment if the persons involved were apprehended.[8] The Venetian officials, however, recognizing the need for some kind of authority among the Greek clergy of the island, appointed in the towns certain "first priests" (*protopapades*) who were to act as low-ranking heads of the clergy; but these in no sense were to constitute a genuine hierarchy.[9]

Despite the difficulty of ordination, the Orthodox clergy of Crete continued to increase, to become, by the end of the fifteenth century, very numerous indeed. (Xanthoudides cites the example of one area which had not long before supported four priests and now had forty.) Responsible in part for this remarkable growth after 1453 was the large number of ecclesiastical exiles, especially monks, entering Crete from Constantinople and other Greek areas.[10] Another factor of importance which attracted candidates for the priesthood was the special privileges enjoyed by clerics. Unlike other Venetian subjects, Greek ecclesiastics were exempt not only from military service but from the *angaria* (a particularly oppressive Byzantine form of *corvée*) and service as *paroichoi* (serfs on the great estates). Settling primarily in the cities, the Orthodox clergy posed a serious problem to the government, as many of them, especially the recent immigrants, did not hesitate to participate actively, though secretly, in the various revolutionary movements.[11]

The union of the Greek and Roman churches proclaimed at the Council of Florence in 1439, far from simplifying the relation of the Venetians to their Orthodox Cretan subjects, actually made for

[8] On the entire problem of the Cretan hierarchy under Venetian rule, see Xanthoudides, 152–55.

[9] Xanthoudides, 154; also 159, where he notes that, aside from the towns, where Latin churches were more numerous, it was rare to see the Latin mass celebrated. See also F. Hofmann, "Wie stand es mit der Frage der Kircheneinheit auf Kreta?", *Orientalia Christiana Periodica*, X (1944) 91–115, and now N. Tomadakes, "Οἱ Ὀρθόδοξοι παπάδες ἐπὶ Ἐνετοκρατίας. . . ," Κρητικὰ Χρονικά, XIII (1959) 39–72.

[10] Xanthoudides, 169; N. Tomadakes, "Μιχαὴλ Καλοφρενᾶς Κρής, Μητροφάνης Β' καὶ ἡ πρὸς τὴν ἕνωσιν τῆς Φλωρεντίας ἀντίθεσις τῶν Κρητῶν," Ἐπετηρὶς Ἑταιρείας Βυζαντινῶν Σπουδῶν, XXI (1951) 134; Manousakas (above, note 1) 35–37.

[11] See V. Lamansky, *Secrets d'état de Venise* (St. Petersburg, 1884) 1045–50, who relates that in the great revolt of 1458, curiously, the revolutionaries were betrayed by a Greek priest and a Jew, with the result that all the leaders were hanged by the Venetian authorities. Also Gerland, "La noblessee crétoise," 202. On the *angaria* in Crete see Thiriet, *La Romanie Vénitienne*, 231.

greater complexity. For as a result the Serenissima now had to deal
with three religious groups on the island: the Orthodox, the Greek
supporters of union termed Uniates (who were relatively few in
number), and the Venetian Roman Catholics. As might be expected, the Venetian government extended special protection to
the Uniates, toward whom the average Cretan felt a violent antagonism.[12] Rejecting the decree of union as unholy, uncanonical,
and the result of papal pressures, the fanatical Orthodox branded
the Greek supporters of union as traitors. In consequence, therefore, of their virtual ostracism from Orthodox society, the Uniate
Greeks tended to become even more pro-Latin. In their prosely-
tizing activities these Uniates were occasionally supported by
Greeks of high position in the West such as Bessarion, now a
powerful Roman Catholic cardinal who paid annual subsidies in
support of selected Uniate priests of Crete.[13] More typical examples of the outspoken Greek Uniates despised by most of their
fellow Cretans were Michael Apostolis and his son, the scholarly
Archbishop of Monemvasia Arsenios Apostolis, whose careers will
be examined later.

In view of the political and social unrest in Crete during the two
and one-half centuries of Venetian domination before 1453, it is
not surprising that, aside from certain important exceptions such
as the scholar-prelates John Simeonachis and John Plusiadenos,
there is little evidence of any substantial, sustained intellectual activity on the island for that period.[14] Admittedly, of course, our
source material is still meager. Thus while it is doubtful that there

[12] Tomadakes, "Μιχαὴλ Καλοφρενᾶς Κρής," 124ff., shows that the vast majority
of Cretans flatly rejected the union.
[13] See Chapter 4, text and note 45. In the early sixteenth century, the thirty
Greek pensioners of Pope Leo X's Greek (Uniate) College in Rome returned to
the Venetian-held Greek areas, where they created disturbances in support of
the Union of Florence. See J. Kalitsounakes, "Ματθαῖος Δεβαρῆς καὶ τὸ ἐν Ῥώμῃ
Ἑλληνικὸν Γυμνάσιον," Ἀθηνᾶ, XXVI (1914) 81ff. (cited hereafter as "Matthaios
Debares").
[14] According to M. Wittek, "Pour une étude du *scriptorium* de M. Apostolès
et consorts," *Scriptorium*, VII (1953) 289, we may discern some activity in manuscript copying there before 1453. And Tomadakes (above, note 9) 49–50, affirms
that in the period between 1350 and 1410 there were considerable educated Cretan
clergy in the towns (though not in the rural areas). Hence he tends less than
other scholars to minimize the educational level of the clergy. Yet this manifestation of learning in that period does not appear to have been sustained; cf. below,
note 19.

were schools in the rural areas, the future might well provide more than the scanty indications now available regarding the existence of Greek schools even in the towns. (In the case of the Cretan scholars of urban birth whose careers are discussed below, it is rare that the sources inform us where they obtained their early training.) And it goes without saying that there was no university, Greek or Latin, on the island. The only education of which we have solid record, in fact, seems to have been provided by the numerous monasteries, the chief aim of which was the preparation of monks and priests for ecclesiastical duties. The level of this learning was generally low, being limited to a knowledge of the Bible and various religious books which were copied and recopied. The result of such an educational system — combined with the lack of ecclesiastical leadership — was a clergy for the most part ignorant and not infrequently lacking in spiritual character.[15]

In contrast to this large group of more or less unlettered clergy we must not neglect to mention a small number of educated ecclesiastics, of whom the more important had evidently been instructed at the monastery school of St. Catherine in Candia (Herakleion). The school of St. Catherine, an offshoot of the famous parent monastery of the same name on the Sinai peninsula, was the leading Greek educational center in Crete.[16] Its curriculum consisted of ancient Greek, theology, religious music, and philosophy and rhetoric: only the rudiments of these subjects were taught, but these were sufficient to permit the pursuance of more advanced studies elsewhere.[17]

For the Venetians there were, it is true, some schools in the towns where the Latins were more numerous. But again these were in the main monastic schools which provided a meager instruction in Latin and Italian primarily for the training of monks and priests. The possession of a higher education among the Venetians was therefore rare, except among the administrative officials of high

[15] See Xanthoudides, *Venetian Crete*, 161–62, who quotes documents from Gerola, *Monumenti Veneti*, II, 156. Contemporary records indicate that the Greek patriarch of Constantinople often inveighed against the scandalous behavior of the Cretan clergy. See Xanthoudides, 162. Xanthoudides' work, however, unfortunately does not distinguish sufficiently with regard to the Cretan educational level during the various centuries.

[16] Xanthoudides, 163.

[17] Xanthoudides, 171.

position sent from Venice to govern the island — dukes, rectors, generals, and secretaries [18] — and in the rather infrequent cases of educated Italians such as Rinuccio of Arezzo, who in the early fifteenth century studied Greek in Crete with the learned Cretan *Protopapas* John Simeonachis.[19]

If the education of most of the Greek clergy was of generally low caliber, one can imagine the educational level of Cretan lay society.[20] And yet we know that by the late fifteenth century Crete was sending talented students to the west to complete their education, to assume positions in the rising printing industry, or even to occupy university chairs as professors of Greek. In Crete itself the copying of manuscripts was intensified. This was a type of work for which the Cretans were soon to become famous. And indeed, with the dispersion of Cretan intellectuals as far west as Spain, not a single major manuscript collection of western Europe was to be without at least one specimen of Cretan calligraphy. If one accepts these phenomena as manifestations of a genuine efflorescence of learning in Crete in the half century or so after 1453, one would expect to find concrete evidence of the existence of institutions of higher learning on the island. But there are few indications that the common level of education and learning among the Cretans had become markedly superior to what it had been during the earlier period of Venetian domination. Since the internal situation had not essentially changed, what accounts in the period after 1453 for the appearance in Crete of so many learned men?

[18] Xanthoudides, 169.

[19] See text and note 32. A. Pertusi is about to publish a paper showing that certain Italian scholars visited Crete as early as 1350, esp. Pilatus. N. Tomadakes, it is true, points out in *Iosef Bryennios*, 85–102, and in his "Μιχαὴλ Καλοφρενᾶς Κρής," 124–25, that because Crete around 1400 and later was the scene of a sharp struggle between unionists and antiunionists, a number of important Greek theologians then appear there (for example, Joseph Bryennios from Constantinople and the Cretans Joseph Philagres and Nilus Damilas, as well as the pro-unionist Constantinopolitan Maximos Chrysoberges). But these men, coming in the main from the outside, seem to have affected the general cultural level of the Cretan populace relatively little.

[20] The generally low level of education is reflected in the few Greek documents preserved, for example, notarial records, which are written in a bad mixture of the Byzantine written language and the *koine* ("vulgar" tongue). Cf. Legrand, *Bibliographie hellénique* II, letter 26, l. 6, of Michael Apostolis, who says the Cretans "who once were scholars now hate learning."

During the years when the Turkish threat to Constantinople was becoming more perilous, ever greater numbers of refugees began to flee to Crete and Greece proper. The capture of the capital in 1453 sent an especially great wave of displaced persons to the island, seeking not only Venetian protection and religious tolerance but to be able to carry on their customs in an essentially Greek environment. This movement of Greeks to Crete was not without precedent, for already in the 1380's, when panic gripped Constantinople because of the Turkish approach, many citizens left the city as well as the tiny nearby island of Tenedos to go to Crete.[21] After the great influx resulting from the fall of Constantinople (when some persons must merely have passed through Crete on their way to Italy), there was, in 1460, still another exodus of Greeks to Crete from the Morea, now prostrate before the Ottoman advance. These came principally from the areas of Nauplion, Monemvasia, and Mani.[22] As a result of these various emigrations, Crete, in the years after 1453, may be said to have become the main center of Hellenism in the old Byzantine world.

While the fact of a large number of refugees fleeing to Crete just before and especially after 1453 has permitted the noted Italian scholar S. G. Mercati to speak (perhaps exaggeratedly) of an "inundation" of Crete by Constantinopolitan exiles,[23] it is difficult to estimate how many of the refugees were scholars. But at any rate those émigrés (and children of émigrés) about whom specific information remains seem in many cases to have been of the intellectual class.[24] Among the more famous names are those of George of Trebizond, already mentioned, who was born in Crete of parents who had fled to the island at the end of the fourteenth

[21] Cornelius, Creta Sacra, II, 355, and Gerland, "La noblesse crétoise," 204. C. Mertzios, "Περὶ Παλαιολόγων καὶ ἄλλων εὐγενῶν Κωνσταντινουπολιτῶν," Γέρας Α. Κεραμοπούλλου (Athens, 1953) 355–72, discusses the flight, on the day of the Turkish sack of Constantinople in 1453, of many noble Byzantines to Crete.

[22] Xanthoudides, Venetian Crete, 189. At the end of the sixteenth century a less numerous group moved to Crete from the Peloponnese and Cyprus. Gerland, 172, also notes that yet another migration — this time of Cretans to the Ionian islands — occurred in 1669 after the Turks finally took Crete.

[23] Mercati, "Di Giovanni Simeonachis," III, 13.

[24] See Geanakoplos, "The Council of Florence," 333 and n. 78, and E. Udalcova, "The Struggle of Parties in 15th Century Byzantium and the Role of Bessarion of Nicaea" (in Russian), Vizantiysky Vremennik, II (1949) 294–307 and III (1950) 106–32. Also Zakythinos, La Grèce et les Balkans, 52–56, who shows that the Byzantine intellectuals were very often pro-unionist.

century; the Constantinopolitan exile Michael Apostolis, who came to Crete almost immediately after 1453 and became a copyist, teacher, and seeker of manuscripts for Bessarion; his son Arsenios, born in Crete; and the celebrated Janus Lascaris, who, according to Papadopoli, in 1453, while still a youth, fled from Constantinople to Crete with his father Theodore, to be well received by the Venetian prefect Thomas Celso. Janus evidently later went with Celso to Venice, lured by the gifts being distributed by Bessarion to promising young Greeks.[25]

The majority of the Constantinopolitan refugees came to Crete virtually stripped of worldly possessions. Without means of support, the learned among them turned naturally to teaching or to the trade of a copyist. As a result of the increasing Italian demand for manuscripts in the period, Crete with its swelling group of educated exiles now became a center for copying. The scribes of the island occupied themselves with transcribing old texts for a considerable number of Venetian patrons, not only those at home but those administrators stationed in Crete who, imbued with the developing humanist spirit of Italy, were eager to secure reproductions of whatever literary treasures Crete might contain.

The number of manuscripts in Crete at the time is difficult to estimate with any accuracy. But we know that there were codices possessed by the numerous monasteries, and that not a few of the refugees, anticipating a life of hardship, arrived on the island literally clutching a precious old manuscript or two in their arms. With the market for beautifully copied manuscripts rapidly increasing in the latter half of the fifteenth century,[26] the reputation of the Cretan copyists, natives as well as Byzantine refugees, now

---

[25] On Janus see Papadopoli, *Historia Gymnasii Patavini*, II, 187. Though Papadopoli offers no documentation, he has not been refuted on this point. On other Greeks fleeing to Crete, see Martinus Crusius, *Turcograeciae libri octo* (Basle, 1584), and B. Montfaucon, *Palaeographia Graeca* (Paris, 1708) 111, and the next two notes.

[26] The market for manuscripts subsequently declined under the impact of the flood of printed works, but again during the sixteenth century the demand for Cretan manuscripts revived because of the low quality of the printed books. For the names of more Cretan scribes and patrons, see H. Omont, *Fac-similés de manuscrits grecs des XV*e *et XVI*e *siècles* (Paris, 1887) 9-15; M. Vogel and V. Gardthausen, *Die griechischen Schreiber des Mittelalters und der Renaissance* (Leipzig, 1909); H. Pernot, "Les Crétois hors de Crète," in *Etudes de littérature grecque moderne* (Paris, 1916) 129-94, and the works cited below in notes 28-30.

spread throughout Europe.[27] It must be pointed out, however, that the astonishing productivity of the Cretan scribes, though invaluable for the preservation of the ancient writings, did not aim primarily at the most accurate reproduction of a text. Since their work was essentially for commercial purposes, it often lacked system and method; the transcribing was frequently done indiscriminately, either from the one available manuscript or from several, but without reference to the textual tradition so important for modern philology.[28]

Although as yet we know the identity of only some of the noble Venetian patrons of the Cretan scribes, the list available includes such names as that of the Barozzi family established in Crete (to the later members of which we owe the Barocci collection now in the Bodleian Library of Oxford University);[29] also a certain Sir George "the Frank," who, to quote a subscription of a Cretan scribe named George Tzangaropoulos, paid for the copying of manuscripts of Thucydides.[30] Further, there was the famous humanist and statesman Francesco Barbaro (who in one manuscript dated 1420 is termed a "Candiote lord"), and Marco Lipomano, the noted jurist and Duke of Candia (1435 to 1437)[31] for whom the Cretan *protopapas* John Simeonachis copied a Lucian, Aristotle's *Mechanics*, and Michael Psellus' *De operatione daemonum*. Other manuscripts reproduced by the diligent Simeonachis (whose work was first carefully discussed by Professor S. G. Mercati) were those of Aristotle's *De anima* and *Metaphysics*, the homilies of Gregory of Nazianzus, and, strikingly enough, translations of the Western

[27] For a list of the authors copied by the Cretan scribes, see Wittek, "Etude du scriptorium de Michel Apostolès," 294-95.

[28] See J. Irigoin, *Histoire du texte de Pindare* (Paris, 1952) 365-66, and A. Dain, "Le Moyen-Age Occidental et la tradition manuscrite de la littérature grecque," *Association G. Budé, Congrès de Nice* (Paris, 1935) 358-78.

[29] On the Barozzi (or Baroeci) family see Mazzuchelli, *Gli scrittori d'Italia*, II, pt. 1, 410ff., and J. Tomasini, *Bibliothecae Venetae* (Udine, 1650) 64. On the Barocci collection see C. Frati, *Dizionario Bio-bibliografico dei bibliotecari e bibliofili italiani dal sec. XIV al XIX* (Florence, 1933) 52.

[30] See J. E. Powell, "Cretan Manuscripts of Thucydides," *Classical Quarterly*, XXXII (1938) 107, who cites names of other Cretan scribes who copied for Venetians. Also E. Lobel, *The Greek Manuscripts of Aristotle's 'Poetics'* (Oxford, 1933) 3-15, and Omont, *Fac-similés de manuscrits grecs des 15ᵉ et 16ᵉ siècles*, 9-15.

[31] On Barbaro see preceding chapter. On Lipomano see Cornelius, *Creta Sacra*, II, 377f.; Tomadakes, "Μιχαὴλ Καλοφρενᾶς Κρής," 128, esp. note 3; and S. Lampros, Παλαιολόγεια καὶ Πελοποννησιακά, II (Athens, 1923) 23-24 (preface).

philosophers Thomas Aquinas, Anselm, and Boethius, and of the Latin liturgy. Associated with the name of Simeonachis is that of John Sirigos, who transcribed manuscripts of Herodotus.[32] Other Venetian patrons were Thomas Celso, prefect of Crete, who, as pointed out, had befriended Janus Lascaris following his flight from Constantinople; Lauro Quirini, a Venetian humanist of the fifteenth century; and the scholar of Greek Girolamo Donato, Duke of Crete from 1506 to 1508, whose arrival on the island, we are told, was greeted by the learned Cretan Arsenios Apostolis with verses written for the occasion.[33]

To summarize the principal reasons for the apparently sudden efflorescence of Cretan letters in the later fifteenth century: most obvious, though care should be taken not to exaggerate their numbers, is the influx of refugees from Constantinople and other Byzantine areas; second, the literary patronage of various noble Venetian administrators on the island; third, as will be emphasized later, the growing interest of Venice herself in Greek scholarship, which was in turn being accelerated by the presence there of the Greek refugees; and, finally, of course, a certain as yet undetermined degree of interest in scholarship on the part of a number of native Cretans. All four factors interact, and it is therefore not easy to evaluate the precise importance of each. But given the paucity of information available on the over-all cultural and social situation of Crete in the period, these factors would seem perhaps to offer the most adequate explanation that can be adduced — at least until such time as additional information is gleaned from the huge mass

[32] On all these manuscripts see Mercati, "Di Giovanni Simeonachis," 2–3, and 13, where he says a close analysis of Simeonachis' works might throw further light on Cretan conditions before 1453. Also see Lockwood, "De Rinucio Aretino," 51ff., and M. Manousakas, "Βενετικὰ ἔγγραφα ἀναφερόμενα εἰς τὴν ἐκκλησιαστικὴν ἱστορίαν τῆς Κρήτης," Δελτίον Ἱστ. Ἐθν. Ἑταιρ., XV (1961) 173–76, 181–90, and, on Plusiadenos, 212ff. And see below, Chapter 4, note 90.

[33] M. Manousakas, "'Αρχιερεῖς Μεθώνης Κορώνης, καὶ Μονεμβασίας γύρω στὰ 1500," Πελοποννησιακά, III (1959) 114 (cited hereafter as "Prelates of Monemvasia"), for the Greek verses composed for Donato by Arsenios, here termed Archbishop. On Quirini see A. Segarizzi, "Lauro Quirini Umanista Veneziano del secolo XV," Memo. R. Acc. Scienze di Torino, LIV (1904) 1–28. For names of still other Venetian manuscript collectors, see Molmenti, Venice, pt. I, vol. II, 167; also letter no. 17 of Manousakas, "Gregoropoulos Correspondence" (see Chapter 3, note 5, below), mention of the Venetian John De Monacis (?), who ca. 1499 sought to buy a Lucian.

of yet unsorted Cretan documents deposited in Venice's *Archivio di Stato*.

Crete afforded a tranquil enough refuge for the Eastern exiles. But for the more restless and ambitious it presented virtually no chance for advancement.[34] Opportunities were limited even for the native-born Cretans. Because of overpopulation certain areas had become economically depressed. (In one area, for example, we are told that fifteen to twenty priests, including recently arrived refugees, carried on the duties of two.) [35] Moreover, arrogation by the Venetian government to its own colonists of most of the island's commercial rights — a traditional Venetian practice — tended to diminish the Greek merchants' chances for genuine profit. The ecclesiastics, as we have indicated above, resented the Venetian refusal to permit them to rise to higher position in the church. Most intolerable, however, was the lot of the scholars. For with the lack of schools of higher education, the more able and ambitious were blocked from securing professorial positions. Hence they had to content themselves either with the private teaching of a few pupils or with the deadening monotony and meager recompense derived from long hours of manuscript copying.

In the light of this situation of frustration and stagnation many Cretan men of letters and merchants chose to emigrate to the west — to France,[36] Spain, or to the closer Italian centers of Milan, Florence, Rome, and, above all, Venice.[37] There they soon constituted a vital element in the largest concentration of Greeks in any single area of the Western world.

[34] See the example of Michael Apostolis, discussed below.

[35] Xanthoudides, *Venetian Crete*, 162. Also P. Pisani, "Les chrétiens de rite oriental à Venise et dans les possessions vénitiennes (1439–1791)," *Revue d'histoire et de littérature religieuses*, I (1896) 201ff.

[36] France, in the late fifteenth and early sixteenth centuries (during the reigns of Francis I and Henry II), received many Cretans who brought Greek manuscripts with them. Between 1518 and 1544 Blois had forty Greek manuscripts (which became the nucleus for the royal collection); in 1550, only six years later, Blois possessed 546. (In connection with France we might note that Andronikos Callistos had been in Paris in the later fifteenth century.) See H. Omont, *Inventaire sommaire des manuscrits grecs dans les bibliothèques autre que la Bibliothèque Nationale*, I (Paris, 1886) pp. vi–vii.

[37] On the Cretan emigration to the West in general, see the brief article of Kyrou (above, note 4), 302–15. Little has been written on this subject.

Chapter 3

THE GREEK COLONY IN VENICE

Owing to the development of a long-range trade, the city of Venice seems early to have contained a considerable foreign element. Among the first to settle there were Greek merchants. But Greeks in more substantial number do not seem to have appeared in Venice until after the Franco-Venetian capture of Constantinople in 1204, when there came, or were, in some cases, called, to Venice a group of Byzantines — among them skilled artists and artisans seeking employment — who in no small measure influenced the life and customs of the Venetian populace.[1] A much greater influx of Greeks occurred later, about the time of and during the half century following the Turkish capture of Constantinople in 1453, when there began a large-scale movement of Greek refugees to western Europe. Then, along with merchants and their families, crowds of Greek émigrés, often well-educated, in some cases indigent, occasionally even wealthy, entered Venice, there to become members of the growing Greek community. By the end of the fifteenth century this Greek colony had so burgeoned as to become

---

[1] Very little has been written on the Greek colony in Venice prior to 1453. See, however, the remarks in Frothingham, "Byzantine Art and Culture in Rome and Italy," 162–70; and, restricted to the centuries before 1204, M. Armingaud, *Venise et le Bas-Empire* (Paris, 1868) 432; Romanin, *Storia documentata di Venezia*, II, 279; and F. Zanotto, "Pittura, Architettura, Scultura, e Calcografia," *Venezia e le sue lagune* (Venice, 1847) I, pt. 2, 290ff., all of which stress the important influence of Byzantium on Venetian art in this period. Armingaud, 432–40, also points out (for the period before 1204) the Venetian adoption of Byzantine dress, titles, ceremonial, luxury goods, and useful arts such as glassmaking, as well as the Byzantine influence on the Venetian dialect and on the practice of employing family names.

one of the largest contingents of foreigners and certainly the most significant one, in the city.[2]

The Greeks resident in Venice in the years following 1453 seem to have come principally from Crete, the economy and social structure of which could not, as we have observed, contain the more energetic individuals. A lesser number came from such areas of Greece as the Venetian-held islands of Corfu, Zakynthos, Patmos, the Archipelago, Cyprus, and the mainland city of Monemvasia.[3] The inhabitants of these Venetian colonies found it only natural to gravitate to the capital, which always maintained close contact with its eastern possessions. Particularly close relations existed between Crete and Venice, with ships plying the well-established route between them by way of Modon, perhaps also putting in at Monemvasia. The journey from Crete to Venice usually took somewhat less than a month, a relatively short time for this period,[4] and we know from letters of Cretan intellectuals working in Venice that such voyages were very frequent. Young men would go to seek their fortune in Venice secure in the knowledge that provisions could easily be sent them if necessary, and that return home would not be difficult. Thus George Gregoropoulos wrote from Crete to his learned young son John, a member of the famous Aldine circle: "If you do not get along well in Venice, come home."[5] And another letter of George to his son reveals the ease and frequency of communications:

[2] On the Greek colony just before and after 1453 (up to the end of the nineteenth century), see the unique little work of G. Veludo, Ἑλλήνων Ὀρθοδόξων ἀποικία ἐν Βενετίᾳ, 2nd ed. (Venice, 1893) (cited hereafter as *Greek Colony*). An Italian version was published earlier, entitled "Cenni sulla colonia greca orientale," in *Venezia e le sue lagune*, I, pt. 2, 78–100. A very brief discussion of the Greek colony is included in Dudan, *Il dominio Veneziano*, 258–260, and in N. Kontosopoulos, "Τὰ ἐν Βενετίᾳ τυπογραφεῖα Ἑλληνικῶν βιβλίων," Ἀθηνᾶ, LVIII (1954) 288 (cited hereafter as "The Greek Press in Venice").

[3] Dudan, 259; he also mentions Greeks from Athens, Epirus, Corinth, and still other areas, but many of these came after the seventeenth century.

[4] See, for example, the voyage of a pilgrim from Venice to the Holy Land at the end of the fifteenth century, as described in H. Prescott, *Friar Felix at Large* (New Haven, 1950) 79, 93. Venice was still a main port of debarkation for pilgrimages to the Holy Land. Also see F. Thiriet, *La Romanie Vénitienne au Moyen Âge* (Paris, 1959).

[5] Legrand, *Bibliographie hellénique*, II, 271, dated April 10, but lacking the year. Now see M. Manousakas, " Ἡ ἀλληλογραφία τῶν Γρηγοροπούλων Χρονολογουμένη," Ἐπετηρὶς Μεσαιωνικοῦ Ἀρχείου (1957), 182 (cited hereafter as "Gregoropoulos Correspondence"). It is interesting to note that in the same letter the noted

We have received everything you have sent in the past as well as now, except for the boxes . . . Know that here there will soon be a real shortage of wine and wheat so that we are living very sparingly. Your brother is still in Carpathos [in the Dodecanese] and I expect him any day. I write you very often but I cannot understand why they don't give you my letters. I thank God that I always hear from you, which pleases me, and I hope that God will grant you more [success]. Don't worry about us because, thank God, our illness is better. The sausages (*konduloi*) and wine are being sent to you by another ship. I wonder why you ask that your nephew be sent to you since you realize how lonely I am. If God permits, George [nephew of John] will come there next spring . . . Your teacher, the pious deacon, is well and greets you. I have not yet received the ducats and that is why I have sent you nothing.[6]

What opportunities were open to Greek émigrés in Venice? In the first place, those possessing some capital were able to engage in commerce, perhaps becoming ship captains.[7] The more impoverished might labor in various factories or the Arsenal, perhaps become tailors, or work for established merchants until they could amass sufficient funds to venture on their own.[8] Not surprisingly, in the period immediately after 1453 there were very few examples of the type of wealthy Greek merchant who was to become so prominent in the Venetian economic life of the later sixteenth and seventeenth centuries.

An opportunity for military service, a chance to get back at the Turks, was afforded by the famous Venetian corps of the *estradioti* (from the Greek *stratiotes*, soldier).[9] This body, constituting

Greek calligrapher John Rhosos is mentioned as still living. He died in Venice ca. Feb. 1498 (see letter in Manousakas, 184, 177) and thus was not an Aldine Academy member, though he had earlier associated with Aldus' circle. Cf. page 130.

[6] Legrand, II, 273–74, dated simply September 18; cf. Manousakas, "Gregoropoulos Correspondence," 201, who assigns it to 1501.

[7] The archives of the Greek colony of Venice (termed *Mariegola*) reveal that, especially in the later sixteenth and seventeenth centuries, many of the Greeks of the community were captains of vessels. No Greeks of the colony, however, seem ever to have been slaves. Nor is there evidence, Mme. Antoniadis, Director of the Hellenic Institute of Byzantine and Post-Byzantine Studies in Venice, informs me, that Greeks were fishermen or that Greek artisans worked in Venetian glass factories, though this might be expected.

[8] See S. Antoniadis, "Πορίσματα ἀπὸ τὴν μελέτην προχείρων διαχειριστικῶν βιβλίων τῶν ἐτῶν 1544–47 καὶ 1549–54 τῆς παλαιᾶς κοινότητος Βενετίας," Πρακτικὰ τῆς 'Ακαδημίας 'Αθηνῶν, XXXIII (1958) 477ff.

[9] A recent work referring to the *estradioti* is that of K. Mertzios, "Περὶ Παλαιολόγων καὶ ἄλλων εὐγενῶν Κωνσταντινουπολιτῶν," Γέρας 'Α. Κεραμοπούλλου (Athens,

the republic's light cavalry, consisted of youths from the Greek and to a perhaps lesser extent Albanian colonies, and was one of the most important military arms of Venice in its wars of the late fifteenth and sixteenth centuries.[10] The officer's cadre of the corps was generally appointed from among the Greeks,[11] though supreme command was exercised by Venetian nobles. Possessing excellent *esprit de corps*, the *estradioti* were noted for their daring, and a certain pride in their Byzantine heritage doubtless inspired their actions. The corps is described as a colorful unit in the Venetian military forces by the Venetian scholar Pietro Bembo, who relates that in 1491, when a reception was tendered the ex-Queen Catherine Cornaro of Cyprus, dashing *estradiot* troops from Crete held a joust on the frozen Grand Canal.[12] Well known in Europe were their exploits against not only Turkish but Western enemies of Venice, as, for instance, against the Germans in 1510. In the words of one historian, the *estradioti* were "the flower of the Venetian land forces." [13]

The Republic also recruited sailors from its eastern island possessions, but the exploits of the Greek mariners have attracted less attention than those of the *estradioti*. The modern historian Pisani would have us believe that certain less savory professions — spying,

---

1953) 355–72. Cf. C. Sathas, *Documents inédits relatifs à l'histoire de la Grèce au Moyen Age* (Paris, 1882) IV, pp. liv–lvi, who says the term *estradiot* derives from *strada* (route). Most recently see K. Bires, Ἀρβανίτες, οἱ Δωριεῖς τοῦ Νεωτέρου Ἑλληνισμοῦ (Athens, 1960) 183ff. Also C. Sathas, " Ἕλληνες στρατιῶται ἐν τῇ Δύσει καὶ ἀναγέννησις τῆς Ἑλληνικῆς τακτικῆς," Ἑστία, XXIX (1885) 371–76, and later issues.

[10] Veludo, *Greek Colony*, 15–16, mentions Greeks, Albanians, and Spalatines, though emphasizing that with the passage of time the Greek character of the troops became strong. Dudan, *Il dominio Veneziano*, 259, includes Albanians and Dalmatians, but these, too, seem largely to have been Greek-speaking. Pisani, "Les chrétiens," I (1896) 202, says part of the militia was Greek (though elsewhere on p. 202, he refers to the Greeks in Dalmatia), while Molmenti, *Venice*, I, pt. 2, 74, affirms that the troops were Cretan. See also E. Barbarich, "Gli stradioti nell' arte militare italiana," *Rivista di cavalleria*, XIII (1904) 52–72; and Bires, esp. 188ff., who seems to exaggerate the significance of the Albanian element among the *estradioti*, while noting that they always appear as "Greeks" in the sources. Bires states flatly (p. 185) that the *estradioti* saved the Republic from the dissolution with which it was threatened by the Franco-German alliance.

[11] Veludo, *Greek Colony*, 16.

[12] Pietro Bembo, *Della istoria viniziana* (Venice, 1790) I, 37. Cf. Molmenti, I, pt. 2, 74.

[13] Veludo, 17. Cf. F. Guicciardini's praise of the corps, *Storia italiana*, ed. G. Rosini (Pisa, 1819–1820) bk. II: "Their dexterity is incredible . . ."

counter-spying, or in other ways acting as go-between for question-
able purposes — also lured some of the Greeks of Venice,[14] a not
unlikely possibility in view of the hardships of exile and resettle-
ment.

Another opportunity affording employment to the émigré Greek
was provided in the late fifteenth century by the newly developing Greek press. The art of printing had been introduced to
Venice in 1469 by the German John of Speyer [15] — a date, in the
view of certain scholars, marking the true beginning of intellectual
activity in the commercial metropolis of Venice. Soon thereafter
brief Greek passages were included in the publications of the
printer Nicholas Jenson. But what may perhaps be the first Greek
book printed in the city of St. Mark (it consisted of a Greek text
together with Latin translation) was Manuel Chrysoloras' *Erotemata* (grammar), published in 1484 by the Italian Peregrino da
Bologna.[16]

The possibilities of Greek printing served increasingly to attract
intellectuals from Crete and to a lesser extent other Greek areas,
and from the very start these exiles played a prominent role in the
evolution of the Greek press. The first dated entirely Greek book
to be printed in Europe, the *Erotemata* of Constantine Lascaris,
had been published in Milan in 1476 by Demetrius Damilas, of
Latin descent but born in Crete. In 1488 the Athenian Demetrios
Chalcondyles summoned Damilas from Milan to Florence and together they produced a Homer, which, though not, as is sometimes

[14] Pisani, "Les chrétiens," 202. A. Fortescue, *The Uniate Eastern Churches*
(London, 1923) 136, n. 1, also refers to Greek fishermen at Venice.

[15] John of Speyer printed Cicero's *Epistolae ad familiares.* On this see the authoritative V. Scholderer, *Catalogue of Books Printed in the XV Century Now in
the British Museum* (London, 1924) pt. V, p. ix; also Fumagalli, *Lexicon Typographicum Italiae*, 455, and more recently, F. Norton, *Italian Printers 1501–1520*
(London, 1958) p. xxiv. Brown, *Venetian Printing Press*, 24, wrongly cites an
earlier date (1461), and correctly makes much of the fact that Venice had available in neighboring Padua a great paper industry. The first editions of any kind
printed in Italy were done by Sweynheim and Pannartz in Subiaco and Rome in
1467.

[16] On Chrysoloras' *Erotemata* see especially Scholderer, pt. V, pp. xxxiii–xxxiv;
also A. Firmin-Didot, *Alde Manuce et l'hellénisme à Venise* (Paris, 1875) 44 and
21, and Brown, 20. Cf. Legrand, *Bibliographie hellénique*, I, 5, who believes that the
work issued from Florence. In the view of Fumagalli, 139, Legrand may be right.
V. Scholderer's important *Greek Printing Types 1465–1927* (London, 1927) 5,
however, affirms the priority of a work of the Cretan Laonikos. See page 58, below.

affirmed, the first Greek book to appear in the West, can lay claim to being one of the first published classical works.[17]

In 1486, even before the printing of the Homer, two Cretans had established a Greek press in Venice and produced two works, one the *Batrachomyomachia* of the so-called "Homeric" school, the other a Psalter. The two men, Laonikos (who edited the *Batrachomyomachia*), the chief priest of Canea in Crete, and Alexander (editor of the Psalter), called the son of George the Priest, are of significance because they seem to stand at the head of the long tradition of Greek printing in Venice; Scholderer, in fact, says Laonikos produced Venice's very first Greek book. Only a few details are known of the background of the pair, notably the interesting fact that Laonikos was a pupil of and corresponded with Michael Apostolis [18] (whose career is discussed below), and that the father of Alexander, George of Crete, was close to Pope Alexander VI, and as a mark of special favor was granted the right to read the Bible in Greek while the Pope was celebrating mass.[19]

The outstanding example of the Cretan contribution to the development of the Greek press of Venice is provided by the printing establishment of Zacharias Calliergis, whose entire staff consisted of Cretan compatriots. But the most decisive strides in the development of Greek printing and scholarship were made by the celebrated press of the Italian Aldus Manutius. Founded in Venice in 1494 or 1495, the Aldine press gave employment to a host of

[17] Cf. Sandys, *History of Classical Scholarship*, II, 104. It must be noted that two Greek works, but undated and unsigned, may well have appeared in Italy very shortly before the Lascaris. See Scholderer, *Greek Printing Types*, 3–4.
[18] See Legrand, I, 6–7. J. Darkó, "Michael Apostolios levelei Laonikoshoz," *Csengers Emlékkönyv* (Szeged, 1926) 108–12, says that this Laonikos is the same as the historian Chalcondyles. But this seems incorrect, since the printer Laonikos was chief priest of Canea. Legrand, I, 6 (cf. I, p. lxx) quotes from the *Batrachomyomachia* the title of some verses written by Laonikos' teacher, Michael Apostolis. (Cf. Noiret, *Lettres*, 22–23, and Legrand, II, 245, letter 22, where Michael terms Laonikos φοιτητής τε ὤν.) See also on these verses Patrinelis, "Νόθα," 211. Laonikos was charged by Apostolis with collecting some of his correspondence (Noiret, 22; Legrand, II, letter 16). On Scholderer see note 16, above.
[19] See Legrand, I, 8. Recently an attempt has been made (I would disagree) to identify George with George Trivizius, a Cretan priest of the Greek colony in Venice, who copied manuscripts for Bessarion. See K. De Meyier, "Two Scribes Identified as One," *Scriptorium*, XI (1957) 99ff., and K. De Meyier, "More Mss. copied by George Trivizius," *Scriptorium*, XIII (1959) 86–88. On George the Priest see also Manousakas, "Βενετικὰ ἔγγραφα," 197–98. Finally, on this early Venetian printing see Proctor, *Printing of Greek*, 75, who suggests Laonikos and Alexander were brothers.

σκότος καὶ ὀλίσθημα· καὶ ἄ[νε]μος

· · ·

· Λ · Γ ·

ΟΜΗΡΟΥ ΒΑΤΡΑΧΟΜΥΟΜΗ
ΑΧΙ ΛΛΕΝ ΔΕ ΤΙΣ ΙΤΙ ΓΡΗ
ΤΟΣ ΤΟΥ ΚΑΡΟΣ

GREEK TYPE USED BY LAONIKOS THE CRETAN IN THE
Batrachomyomachia, VENICE, 1486

Greek compositors and scholars. Since nearly every figure to be discussed in the central section of this book is in some way associated with Aldus and his circle, we shall leave to a later chapter a discussion of his work and significance.

As the press in Venice developed, more and more opportunities were offered for those skilled in Greek. For the exile from the east, employment as editor or corrector at a press was more challenging than the work of a scribe and usually brought greater recognition. Furthermore, the growing popularity, convenience, and relative cheapness of printed works now greatly lessened the demand for manuscripts. Thus more and more Greeks, Cretans in particular, emigrated to Venice to seek employment.[20] Writing to a friend then in Venice, Marcus Musurus asks typically, "Have any more of our countrymen come from Crete?" [21]

It is true, of course, that not all the Greeks who came to Venice remained there. A few, unable to find satisfactory employment, had to return home. Others proceeded to areas farther west (like the Cretan scholar-printer Demetrius Ducas, who was summoned to Spain). But so many remained permanently in Venice that we are justified in saying that the Greek colony, which in 1478 totaled more than four thousand persons, continued to prosper, to form, at the end of the fifteenth century, a very substantial community — and this in a period when Venice herself contained little more than 110,000 people.[22] By 1580, one source says, perhaps exagger-

[20] On this point note the example of John Gregoropoulos and his father (who, like his son, was a copyist of manuscripts), both of whom planned to come west because of the diminishing profits of the copyists' trade in Crete. Actually the father was never able to come. See Firmin-Didot, 579. Also see above, Chapter 2, note 23, noting that later the copyists' trade revived for a time.

[21] Firmin-Didot, 518. Cf. below, Chapter 5, text and note 51.

[22] Our chief authority Veludo, *Greek Colony*, 6, cites 5,000 Greeks for 1478. Cf. B. Knös, *Un Ambassadeur de l'hellénisme: Janus Lascaris* (Uppsala-Paris, 1945) 21, who cites 4,000 Greeks. Pisani, "Les chrétiens," 205, quotes the figure of 600 in 1479 — certainly incorrect for the total Greek population. S. Antoniadou, in a brochure entitled "Museo di Dipinti Sacri" (Venice, 1959) (with Greek version attached) 7, 23, cites 4,000 Greeks for the later sixteenth century. On population figures for the entire city of Venice, see Molmenti, *Venice*, I, pt. 2, 2, n. 1. The figure I have used (110,000) refers to the year 1509. Cf. G. Beloch, "La popolazione d'Italia nei secoli XVI–XVIII," in *Bulletin de l'Institut international de statistique*, III (1888) and "La popolazione di Venezia nei secoli XVI e XVII," *Nuovo archivio veneto*, n.s., III, p. 1. More recently, Chandler, *Cities of the World*, 12, gives Venice for the year 1450, as the West's largest city, 150,000 inhabitants, and for 1550, 158,000.

atedly, there were fifteen thousand Greeks living in Venice, a figure that swelled greatly with the return to the city of the many Greek ships from Alexandria, Constantinople, Crete, and the islands.[22a]

We know little about the religious situation of the Greeks in Venice before the Council of Florence (1439). Certainly the Venetians, though perhaps less so than other peoples of the West, looked upon these Greeks as schismatics. As such the latter were not permitted by the authorities to celebrate the liturgy publicly, nor were they allowed to have their own church, being instructed to attend those of the Latins. Nevertheless, whatever the theory (and for the Venetians "religion of the state" was always important in principle), Venetian practice had to be flexible. Greek subjects of the Empire were very numerous in the areas where the Turkish power was still increasing. Moreover, vital Venetian military arms on both land and sea were composed in part of Greeks, while certain not unimportant activities in Venice itself were in Greek hands. Thus in this early period the Greeks appear to have enjoyed a certain degree of religious toleration,[23] though on occasion we do hear of measures taken against certain Greek *papas* who celebrated the liturgy *secundum morem Graecorum*.[24]

A decisive step in the amelioration of the religious situation of the Greeks in Venice was the signing of the decree of union at Florence. For the Venetian government was now induced to look with special favor upon the Uniates — upon those Greeks, that is, who accepted the union, with its provision for papal supremacy over the entire church. We may be sure, however, that the hardheaded citizens of the Serenissima viewed with some skepticism the numerous Greeks of the colony, especially of the intellectual class, who now claimed to be their coreligionists.

The Greeks, for their part, were still not satisfied with their position. Thus in 1456, soon after the fall of Constantinople, with

---

[22a] Statement of Andreas Darmarios, a contemporary Greek copyist of Monemvasia, in E. Legrand, *Notice biographique sur Jean et Théodose Zygomalas* (Paris, 1889) 254-55. On Darmarios see also C. Graux, *Essai sur les origines du fonds grec de l'Escurial* (Paris, 1880).

[23] Fabris, "Professori e scolari greci," 123, lists several Venetian churches in which he says the Greeks, before 1453, could celebrate their own rite. Cf. Pisani, "Les chrétiens," 203-204.

[24] Pisani, 203.

the reinforcement of their community through the arrival of more colonists from the East, they petitioned the Venetian government for the right to establish a church "for their own use." The spokesman for the community was the influential Uniate Isidore, former Byzantine Archbishop of Kiev and now Cardinal of the Roman church, who had come to Venice in order to recover certain ecclesiastical properties. The Venetian Senate replied to the request on June 18, 1456, issuing a decree granting the Greek colonists not a church, but the right to buy land on which to construct one. Subsequently, in 1470, at a time when the Venetians had urgent need of the *estradiot* arms against the advancing Turk, the Greeks of Venice were granted by the Serenissima the use of a side chapel in the Latin church of San Biagio in the *sestiere* of Castello, with the proviso that no Greek priest could celebrate the liturgy elsewhere under penalty of a fine of 100 lire.[25] (San Biagio still stands on the Riva dei Sette Martiri.) An exception to this ruling was made for the famous and wealthy Anna Notaras, daughter of the last Byzantine Grand Logothete (prime minister) Lucas Notaras, who was permitted to have religious services performed in her own home. As is little known, Anna had earlier made elaborate plans for the establishment of an independent Greek enclave in Tuscany within the territory of Siena. But this remarkable project — looking toward the formation of a kind of national Greek community in the West — was never realized, and she had remained in the more congenial environment of Venice.[26]

Nine years later, in 1479, the Greeks, still without a church of their own, requested permission to begin the construction of one, but were again told to "frequent the Latin churches." Evidently the Venetian government, observing the rapid growth of the Greek

[25] Pisani, 204–205. Veludo, *Greek Colony*, 7–8. Isidore had been named titular patriarch of Constantinople by the Pope and had come to Venice to secure the revenues from the patriarchal properties in Venetian-held Negropont. Also see Antoniadou, "Museo di Dipinti Sacri," § 1, pp. 4, 20. The *Practica* (*Mariegola*, in Venetian), the records of the community which I have examined in Venice, were maintained from the year 1470.

[26] Veludo, 8; Legrand, *Bibliographie hellénique*, I, p. cxxvii; and especially G. Cecchini, "Anna Notara Paleologa: Una principessa greca in Italia e la politica senese di ripopolamento della Maremma," *Bullettino Senese di Storia Patria*, XVI (1938) 1–41. Also see M. Manousakas, "Recherches sur la vie de Jean Plousiadénos (Joseph de Méthone) (1429?–1500)," *Revue des études byzantines*, XVII (1959) 41–43, esp. n. 78.

colony, feared that the Greeks, once in possession of a building of their own, would cast off any pretense of subordination to the patriarch of Venice, the city's highest-ranking ecclesiastic, and revert again to schism.

Despite their rebuff, the Greek exiles were able to achieve recognition in another sphere. On November 28, 1494, the Greeks, following the example, they affirmed, of the communities of Slavs, Albanians, and Armenians of Venice, asked permission to establish what they termed a "Brotherhood (*Scuola*) of Greeks," under the protection of the famous St. Nicholas of Myra (in Asia Minor). Approval was granted on condition that the initial membership would not exceed 250, exclusive of women and children. This marked the first formal organization of the Greek colony as a corporate body before the law, and may well have been due in large part to increasing Venetian recognition of the valuable services of the *estradioti*. A constitution was drawn up in imitation of the Venetian, with provisions for voting procedures, representation, and formation of councils.[27]

On October 4, 1511, after fifty-five years of religious services in San Biagio, the Brotherhood once again petitioned the Council of Ten for permission to buy land for the building of a church, to be dedicated, interestingly enough, to the patron saint of the soldier, St. George. The reasons cited in the request reveal something of the relations existing between the Greek émigrés and the Venetians at the time. The Greeks pointed to the troubles arising between the two religious groups and the fact that many Greeks could not understand what was said in the Latin churches. Moreover, the colonists wanted to provide proper burial for their dead, thereby putting an end to what they termed the awful scandal of mixing the bones of criminals with their own, or of having the remains of their deceased exhumed and thrown into the sea. (Evidently hitherto the Greeks had not had a cemetery of their own — no doubt the lack of available land in Venice had something to do with this — being forced to bury their dead in the Latin cemeteries, with the danger that their bones would be violated.) They

[27] Veludo, 9. Cf. Pisani, 205. Also see Antoniadis, "Museo di Dipinti Sacri," 5 and 21. Fortescue, *Uniate Eastern Churches*, 136, adds that no one could join the Brotherhood unless he was in union with the Holy See. The Venetian term *Scuola* refers to a religious-philanthropic society.

declared, finally, that the chapel then in use could not accommodate all the worshipers, now increasing greatly in number especially with the many *estradioti* and their families recently brought in by the Venetian government.[28]

It was not until three years later, after further appeals, that the Venetian Council of Ten (on April 30, 1514) at last approved the Greek request for a church with the right to possession of a cemetery on the same site. Two important stipulations were made, however — that the Greeks remain *veri e catolici cristiani*, and that approval for erection of a church also be secured from Rome.[29] Responding at once to the Greek appeal, the Medici Pope Leo X, on May 18, 1514, and again on May 10, 1521, granted consent for the building of a church with a bell tower and cemetery. The Greeks were authorized to name a priest, to be chosen by the community, who would officiate according to the Eastern (that is, Uniate) rite ("juxta ritum et morem vestrum"). More important, the colonists were granted freedom from local clerical interference.[30] As evidence of direct dependence on Rome, however, the community each year was to pay to the Holy See a token amount of white wax.[31]

Understandably, the Venetian Patriarch, Antonio Contareno, protested against this papal decision on the grounds that, once in possession of their own church, the Greeks would return to schism and might even lead Latins astray. Insisting that the Greeks should return to the provisions of the edict of 1479 (directing them to attend Latin churches), the Patriarch sought revocation of the papal directive. Pope Leo, however, always sympathetic, as we shall see, to representatives of Greek culture, and probably influenced by the growing circle of Greek scholars around him, proceeded even to enlarge on the scope of his concessions, enjoining (by a bull of 1521) the Venetian patriarch and bishops from interfering

---

[28] Veludo, 14. The petition is printed in F. Cornelius, *Ecclesiae venetae antiquis monumentis* (Venice, 1749) decade XV, pt. I, 372–73; see partial Greek translation in Bires, 'Αρβανίτες, 186–87.

[29] Veludo, 19; Pisani, 205.

[30] Pisani, 205–207, and Veludo, 19–20, both of whom cite the date June 3, 1514, for papal permission. Veludo, 20, who was of Greek descent, emphasizes more strongly than the Roman Catholic Pisani the freedom of the new church from Western clerical interference.

[31] Veludo, 20, affirms that this was never paid or even demanded.

in the affairs of "Catholics of the Greek rite." Furthermore, he directed the Greeks, in the absence of a bishop of their own, to appoint a vicar, whom the Latin episcopate was instructed to recognize.[32]

Circumstances, of which the most important was probably the accession of the austere Pope Adrian VI, intervened to prevent immediate implementation of Leo's pronouncements. But on March 26, 1526, the new Medici pope, Clement VII, confirmed Leo's authorization to build, and finally, on September 27, 1526, representatives of the colony (among them, we are told, the gallant old *estradiot* Theodore Palaeologus), decided on the purchase of a plot for the church in the section of San Antonin. After a voluntary payment to the Venetian government of five hundred ducats, construction of the church and adjoining cemetery began. The first service was held on March 4, 1527, with a priest from the Venetian-held Greek island of Cephalonia officiating.[33]

This was not the Greek church well known to Venetian history but a provisional one, constructed quickly to enable the congregation to remove itself from San Biagio.[34] It was not until November 1, 1539, that the cornerstone for the famous church of San Giorgio dei Greci, centrally located in the same spot, only a few hundred meters from San Marco and facing the canal called Rio dei Greci, was ceremoniously laid. Construction took thirty-four years, being completely finished (except for the addition of icons, paintings, and other decorations) only on July 11, 1573, at a cost of fifteen thousand ducats. Much of this sum was raised by a tax which the officials of the Greek community were in 1546 permitted by the Venetian government to levy on all Greek ships entering the port of Venice [35] — this despite the fact that most of the Greek areas were now subject to the Turk. Several architects, among whom were the noted Sante Lombardo and Zanantonio

[32] Veludo, 20; Pisani, 207.
[33] Veludo, 19–21, who also mentions construction of narrow cells for habitation of the priests. On Cephalonia see W. Miller, *Essays on the Latin Orient* (Cambridge, Eng., 1921) 203.
[34] Cf. Pisani, 207, who says the Greeks transferred their place of worship in 1527 to the chapel of Sant' Ursula. Veludo, 21, cites the neighborhood of San Antonin as the place where the Greeks constructed a provisional church.
[35] On the tax on Greek ships, see Greek translation of the document in Antoniadis, "Πορίσματα," 468–70.

Giova (Chiona), labored on the church.[36] Built of fine stone and adorned with paintings by famous artists, especially Greek, and precious icons, several of which had been brought from Constantinople by Anna Notaras,[37] this beautiful edifice, which still stands, was a remarkable monument to the efforts of the Greeks of the diaspora to preserve unbroken the traditions of their lost homeland.

CHURCH OF SAN GIORGIO DEI GRECI

From the foundation of the first Greek church and the selection of a priest in 1527 to the year 1550, the colony underwent a period of religious persecution at the hands of the Venetian episcopate. For it was still the fear of the latter that as the community grew stronger it would become increasingly independent of the

[36] It is an error to believe (with Veludo, 37–59) that the celebrated Venetian Jacopo Sansovino was one of the architects of the church, although the building is in the style of Sansovino.

[37] See Veludo, 37–39, who also refers to a *kibotion* (chest) once in the possession of the Byzantine Emperor Michael VIII Palaeologus (d. 1282), which was brought from Constantinople to this church later in 1577 by the Greek bishop Gabriel Severos.

Roman church. And so, under pressure from the Venetian Patriarch Girolamo Quirino, Pope Clement VII in 1528 even revoked
Leo's privileges. Quirino insisted on strict implementation of the
provisions of the Union of Florence — recognition of the pope as
head of the church, insertion of the *filioque* into the creed, and
especially his own authority over the Greek church and its clergy.
What specific provocation the Greeks may have given him we do
not know, but he took steps to excommunicate the entire congregation and anyone associating with the Greeks. According to the
nineteenth century Greco-Italian historian Veludo, he even locked
the worshipers in their church during the days of Holy Week.
For Quirino, we are told, a schismatic Greek was "worse than a
Jew" ("pezo che se fussino zudei").[38]

Disturbances seemed gradually to diminish until there appeared
on the scene a fanatic Uniate, the Cretan-born scholar and Archbishop of Monemvasia, Arsenios Apostolis, whose career will be
examined in Chapter 6. By an edict of the Council of Ten, dated
March 30, 1534, Arsenios was appointed preacher at the Church
of San Giorgio dei Greci, in which capacity he had ample opportunity for conducting propaganda among the congregation.
A second edict of the Venetian government, dated May 29, 1534,
ordered the appointment of two (Uniate) priests as assistants to
Arsenios. Greater disturbances now broke out and, according to
one report, many Greeks narrowly escaped death as a result of the
violence of their reaction to Arsenios' measures.[39] The death of
Arsenios in 1535 did not, however, do much to mitigate the turmoil, and troubles between clergy and community continued for
several more years. On May 11, 1542, the Senate went so far as to
decree that the Venetian patriarch had to approve every Greek
priest before admitting him to celebrate the liturgy. But the per-
sistence of the Greeks at last prevailed, and in 1549, during the
Council of Trent, Pope Paul III restored their old immunity from
local episcopal jurisdiction.[40]

It is not our aim here to trace the history of the colony beyond

[38] Veludo, 52–55. Cf. Pisani, "Les chrétiens," 207. For the protest of Quirino,
see B. Cecchetti, *Venezia e la corte di Roma* (Venice, 1874) II, 349–50.

[39] See Chapter 6, text and notes 98–101. Also Crusius, *Turcograeciae*, 151.

[40] Pisani, 207–208. Cf. Veludo, *Greek Colony*, 61ff., who is not clear on this
point.

the mid-sixteenth century, although in commerce and in artistic achievement the community was to experience its most flourishing period in the last part of the sixteenth and the early seventeenth century.[41] Nor should we devote more space to the religious issue, however important it is for providing a background to the careers of the various scholars to be discussed later. We may note briefly, however, that so complete was the victory of the Greeks of Venice in the religious sphere that from 1577 onward they were even permitted to place their church directly under the jurisdiction of the Greek Orthodox patriarch of Constantinople.[42] The latter, in the meantime, had consecrated their priest Gabriel Severo as Archbishop of Philadelphia (near Smyrna, in Asia Minor), a title henceforth to be held by Severo's successors in Venice. Pisani would have us believe that the triumph of the Greek colony over the Venetian patriarch was in great part due to the larger political events of the period — the advance of Lutheranism in western Europe and the fear that the Greeks might ally themselves with the new movement.[43] But this view seems much exaggerated. At least equally important must have been the traditional Venetian attitude of expediency, the benefits derived by the Venetians from the services of the Greek *estradioti*, mariners, and intellectuals,[44] and

[41] The area of the Greek community was termed Campo ($\pi\lambda\alpha\tau\epsilon\hat{\iota}\alpha$) dei Greci and was dominated by the church of San Giorgio and the school, Collegio Flanghinis (begun in 1626). It was the desire of the community that the generations born in Venice continue to speak Greek, and thus various schools were founded. For example, when the Brotherhood established a monastery in 1501, Greek was taught there to girls.

[42] See Pisani, "Les chrétiens," 208. Cf. Veludo, *Greek Colony*, 66–67; also Fortescue, *Uniate Eastern Churches*, 136–39, who affirms that, though nominally Uniate, the Greeks increasingly looked to Constantinople and considered themselves Orthodox. Interestingly enough, Veludo considers the Greek colony of Venice as the nucleus from which emerged the "generating seed" of modern Greek civilization.

[43] Pisani, 208–209, who even believes that the Protestant peril brought the fear the Greeks would enroll in the Lutheran army! Cf. Veludo, 64, whose reasoning seems more logical.

[44] It must be pointed out that, though many of the émigré intellectuals in the period covered by this book (up to ca. 1535) certainly must have had more or less close connections with the members of the Greek colony, it is rare that names of such intellectuals are to be found actually enrolled in the archives (*Mariegola*) of the community. But this is not surprising, since before 1558 (the date when decisions began to be taken by the forty representatives chosen to run the community) only very brief notices were kept, while even in the later period, where the information is far more detailed, names were merely listed without identifying material. The scholars, moreover, often had no children (hence no baptismal records, etc.), and we know that their interests usually lay elsewhere than in the

the increasingly thriving commerce of the Greek merchants. It was in the Republic's own interest to put an end to the turmoil so disquieting to an important and still rapidly growing segment of her population.

Before moving on to consider the careers of various individuals important in transmitting Greek learning to the West, it would be useful, as a backdrop, to present a picture of the city of Venice in the last years of the fifteenth and the early sixteenth century, when she was still near the zenith of her power politically and economically. Venice was then the richest, most populous metropolis of western Europe. The city was a meeting place for every race, and a veritable babel of tongues was spoken on the piazzas, in the market places, and in the shops. Prominent among these was the Greek language, with Greek songs and ballads heard in virtually all sections of the city. Thus, in a dialect half Venetian and half Greek, the popular poet Antonio da Molino (called the Venetian Burchiella) wrote the "Barzellete dei quatro compagni Strathioti: I fatti e le prodezze di Manoli blessi strathioto," verses recounting the brave deeds of Manoli and his companion *estradiot*.[45]

Visitors were deeply impressed by the city's appearance — the great ducal palace with its adjoining basilica of San Marco, so Byzantine in style and especially in decoration, the immense central piazza, witness to the lavish pageantry of state and religious processions, the Grand Canal lined with the magnificent houses of the nobles, the intense merchant activity on the Rialto and the wharves, the industry of the arsenal where ships were being turned out one after another, the numerous printing establishments, and the large

---

colony — with wealthy patrons, for example, able to support their work. The important point to be made, however, is that even if they were not formally inscribed as members of the colony, the community was able to provide them with a kind of homeland in exile — to give them a sense of security, as it were — where they could associate at will with people of their own race and customs.

It should be noted that the library of the Greek community of St. George has been lost; it may well have contained works of the Greek scholar-exiles.

[45] See B. Gamba, *Serie degli scritti impressi in dialetto veneziano* (Venice, 1832) 82. (Also Molmenti, *Venice*, pt. 2, I, 247, and Bires, 'Αρβανίτες, 184, who reproduces the title page of this work, about the *estradiot* who later became famous throughout all Europe for his military prowess.) This poem, actually written in 1561, is the most notable example of a genre typical of this and the earlier period, and is called "stradiotescha. See Gamba, esp. 82, for another such work of Molino, entitled "Manoli Blessi sopra la presa de Margaritin. Con un dialogo piacevole di un Greco et di un Fachino." Cf. Sathas, *Documents inédits*, VII, 236ff.

CIVITAS VENECIARU

VENICE IN 1483

colonies of Greeks, Armenians, and Jews with their colorful cos-
tumes. All this combined to produce an atmosphere of splendor
and cosmopolitanism unequaled in western Europe, which could
not but remind one of that great predecessor of Venice in the East.
Thus an anonymous Greek poet, writing at the end of the fifteenth
century, could exclaim: "There is no land that can rival Venice.
Its piazza has completely enthralled me." [46] Little wonder that the
Greek exile Cardinal Bessarion could refer to Venice as "almost
another Byzantium."

[46] Quoted in Molmenti, pt. 2, vol. I, 63.

PART II

THE DISSEMINATORS

Chapter 4

MICHAEL APOSTOLIS

Byzantine Copyist and Manuscript Collector in Crete

Of the six persons chosen for discussion, we begin, chronologically, with Michael Apostolis. He is not a major figure among the group of Greek emigré-scholars, but his career is perhaps more typical than those of such better-known individuals as Bessarion, John Argyropoulos, or Janus Lascaris. For in his perpetual lament for the lost Byzantium, in his constant penury (which reduced him even to begging for financial assistance), and in his futile attempts to obtain a professorial post in the West, Apostolis is representative of the large number of lesser-known and less fortunate learned Greek refugees during the difficult years immediately following Constantinople's fall in 1453. Moreover, he is the most notable of the group of Greek men of letters who spent their lives copying and searching for manuscripts in Crete, that Venetian-controlled island which served as a kind of mid-point between the old Byzantine world and the rising Italian centers of classical scholarship. For these reasons, and because no monograph has been written on his life, the career of Michael Apostolis is worth treating in detail.

Though the period in which Michael lived was one of turmoil and instability, his voluminous correspondence [1] enables us to re-

---

[1] Except for the brief sketches of Noiret, *Lettres*, introduction, 17–27; Legrand, *Bibliographie hellénique*, I (Paris, 1885) pp. lxvi–lxx; and S. Salaville, entry in *Dict. d'hist. géog. eccl.*, III, cols. 1030–35, no monograph exists on Michael. (See also the entry of Crusius in Pauly-Wissowa, II, cols. 1823–24.) As for his correspondence, 48 of Michael's letters (evidently he collected his own letters: cf. Chapter 3, note 18) are published in Legrand, II, 234–59; others appear in Noiret,

construct the principal events, if not all the details, of his career. Authorities differ over the spelling of his name, most preferring the form "Apostolios" to "Apostolis." But the latter seems more authentic, if we are to judge from the frequency with which it appears in his own writings.[2] From his works we learn also that he preferred the Hellenized form of his given name, "Michaelos" to "Michael."[3]

No definite information is available regarding the time and place of Michael's birth. The proud surname "Byzantios" adopted by him would surely indicate that he was born in Constantinople, though his family was evidently of Peloponnesian origin. The date is generally fixed as approximately 1422, on the slim and rather inadequate testimony of an obscure passage in a letter of Bessarion, dated 1462, in which Apostolis is termed "young."[4] The family of Michael, though not rich, was of sufficient means to

---

who also reprints a few from Legrand's collection. For a *list* of Michael's writings, see Legrand, I, pp. lxvi–lxx, which, however, contains errors. F. Mohler, "Aus Bessarions Gelehrtenkreis," *Quellen und Forschungen aus dem Gebiete der Geschichte*, XXIV (Paderborn, 1942) 478–84, prints six (unpublished) letters of Bessarion to Michael. See also notes below for individual letters and essays printed by B. Laourdas, almost all of which are listed in his "Κρητικὰ Παλαιογραφικά," Κρητικὰ Χρονικά, XI (1958) 381, n. 1. (For complete list see Laourdas, in Bibliography.) Laourdas there (381–82) remarks that though the publication of Michael's writings is now virtually complete, a monograph on his career is still lacking. On Michael's importance see P. Koukoules, Κρητικὰ Χρονικά, II (1948) 376. Finally, see now also the important article of C. Patrinelis, "Νόθα, ἀνύπαρκτα καὶ συγχεόμενα πρὸς ἄλληλα ἔργα τοῦ Μιχαὴλ 'Αποστόλη," 'Επετηρὶς 'Εταιρείας Βυζαντινῶν Σπουδῶν, XXX (1960) 202–13, where errors are pointed out regarding works written by or hitherto falsely attributed to Apostolis. See especially page 203 and notes for previous attempts by Fabricus, Boerner, Sathas, and G. Zavira, Νέα 'Ελλὰς ἢ 'Ελληνικὸν Θέατρον (Athens, 1872) 56–58, to list Michael's complete works. For additional articles see below.

[2] See, for example, Noiret, letter no. 94, ll. 17–18; also no. 5, ll. 7–8, and nos. 94 and 95, where the form "Apostolis" is used. But cf. no. 125, Michael's epistle addressed to the Venetian government, in which he writes "Apostolios." The spelling "Apostolis" has been accepted by Noiret, 18, though Legrand prefers "Apostolios" (I, p. lviii).

[3] On this point (i.e., his different uses of his name), which has not hitherto been examined, see Noiret, no. 94, ll. 16–17. Note that in this period it was the vogue in the West to Hellenize Latin and Italian names: for example, Forteguerri = the Greek Carteromachus.

[4] Bessarion's letter, addressed to Apostolis, is printed in Migne, *P.G.*, CLXI, cols. 688–92, esp. 688, where Bessarion upbraids Michael for attacking Theodore Gaza's views on Aristotle, telling him that as a "young man" (νέος) he should have respect for Gaza's old age (Gaza then was evidently 90). See also Noiret, 17–18; Legrand, I, p. lix; and Salaville's article on Michael in *Dict. d'hist. géog. eccl.*, III, col. 1031 (Salaville's account seems to be based on Noiret and Legrand).

provide him with a good education.[5] Scholarship, in fact, appears early to have attracted him, in part because of his association with the celebrated philosopher Gemistos Pletho either in Constantinople or, possibly, in the Peloponnesian city of Mistra,[6] where Pletho had established a school of philosophy.[7] That Apostolis actually pursued a formal course of study under Pletho is uncertain, but we know that he espoused the latter's philosophic ideal, Platonism [8] — more correctly Neoplatonism — and adhered to it throughout his entire life.

In 1448 we find Michael definitely established in Constantinople as a pupil of the famous teacher John Argyropoulos. Argyropoulos had fairly recently returned from several years of residence and study in Italy in order to become professor of Greek literature at the higher school of Byzantium, the Mouseion of the Xenon.[9] In Italy he had been in close contact with Western humanists, and at the University of Padua had directed Palla Strozzi in his study of Greek.[10] Michael's studies under Argyropoulos were evidently on

[5] On his education see below, text and notes 112-13, for certain remarks included in his discourse to the Italians. But one cannot always judge accurately from his statements, which are often highly rhetorical.

[6] The basic evidence for Michael's connection with Pletho is a letter of Michael to the latter (Legrand, II, letter no. 1, 233). This letter must have been written sometime before Pletho's death (which probably took place in 1452, though some argue he died in 1449 or 1450: see C. Alexandre, *Traité des lois* [Paris, 1858] p. xliii). C. Sathas, Νεοελληνικὴ Φιλολογία (Athens, 1868) 70, 72 (cited hereafter as *Neohellenic Philology*), believes that Michael had adopted Pletho's ideas already when he was in Constantinople (i.e., *before* Michael might have gone to Mistra) and even that Michael, like Pletho, had become a pagan — a view considered exaggerated today.

[7] On Pletho's school and the Platonism of Mistra, see especially Masai, *Pléthon et le Platonisme de Mistra*, esp. 368 and 208ff. Also M. Anastos, "Pletho's Calendar and Liturgy," *Dumbarton Oaks Papers, no. 4* (Cambridge, Mass., 1948) 270-303. Anastos objects to the thesis of the inclusion of Muslim ideas in the new religion that Pletho tried to establish in the aim of revitalizing Byzantine society.

[8] See again Michael's letter to Pletho in Legrand, II, no. 1, 233, where Michael writes he is ready, if necessary, to die for Pletho and declares his love for Plato. He says further that he has stolen and sent to Pletho two orations written by George Scholarios against Platonism. See also below, text and note 113, for Michael's statement in his oration to the Italians: "Plato . . . [I studied] in good measure before Constantinople's fall . . ."

[9] On Argyropoulos and the Xenon and the subsequent events of his career, especially in Florence where he lectured on Aristotle, see G. Cammelli, *Giovanni Argiropulo* (Florence, 1941) 30-33ff. Also Noiret, *Lettres*, nos. 4, 15, and 32 (all probably addressed by Michael to Argyropoulos). For Michael's encomium on Argyropoulos when the latter assumed the Xenon chair, see G. Hyperides, Μιχαήλου Ἀποστόλη πονήματα τρία (Smyrna, 1876) 38-41.

[10] Cammelli, *Giovanni Argiropulo*, 14ff.

Argyropylus.

JOHN ARGYROPOULOS
(c. 1415–1487)

an advanced level, and Michael himself in 1452 succeeded his teacher,[11] who may again have departed for Italy.

The military and political situation of Constantinople at this time was exceedingly critical. Since 1422 the city had been under virtually constant siege by the Ottoman Turks, whose territory now surrounded the capital. Even provisioning of the city was difficult. That the schools of Constantinople could function at all in view of this precarious situation seems remarkable. But the citizenry had grown accustomed to living from day to day. Moreover, intellectual activity might offer a temporary escape from the hard realities of life and perhaps spur the flagging courage of the people through contemplation of the glories of ancient Greece.

The attitude of the Greek populace in the face of looming destruction is not clear-cut or easily definable. There were, of course, the two extremes — the party favoring ecclesiastical union with Rome in order to save the state, and the anti-unionists, who saw in submission to the Western church the prelude to Latinization and Western political domination of Byzantium. Of the latter group, which included the common people and most of the clergy, a minority (stronger than is usually believed) accepted what it considered to be the inevitability of Turkish political domination.[12] Even among the unionists, the so-called *Latinophrones* (pro-Latins), there is reason to suspect that many, motivated entirely by political expediency, believed that once the pope had dispatched military aid and the Turks had been repulsed, it would then be clear who the "true *azymites*" (unionists) were.[13]

The Greek church itself was sharply anti-unionist and in general

[11] Information derived from the poem "Constantinopolis," vv. 662–667, of Ubertino Puscolo, an Italian from Brescia then living in Pera, a suburb of Constantinople: "Hunc [Argyropoulos] sequitur tanto dignus doctore Michael Byzantinus, erat cognomen Apostolus illi" (quoted in Legrand, I, pp. lviii–lix); see the entire poem in A. Ellissen, *Analekten der mittel- und neugriechischen Literatur* (Leipzig, 1857) III, Appendix. Michael's speech to the Italians (Noiret, 148) also contains a passage of possible pertinence here: "I have been . . . a teacher in the realm of letters to some of you . . . in Byzantium or in Crete." On Argyropoulos' journeys see Cammelli, 35.

[12] For documentation see the works cited in my article, "The Council of Florence," esp. 343–44, nn. 78–80. Cf. now J. Gill, *The Council of Florence* (Oxford, 1959).

[13] See M. Ducas, *Historia byzantina* (Bonn, 1834) 255, who notes that the papal ambassador to Constantinople, the Greek Isidore, ex-metropolitan of Kiev and now a Roman cardinal, was not taken in by these various attitudes.

its clergy sought to preserve its independence even at the risk of complete destruction of the state.[14] After all, the Turks had already shown themselves tolerant toward the conquered Christians of Anatolia, and the Greek church and hierarchy of Constantinople might therefore remain intact. This view is reflected in the attitude of Gennadius, the first patriarch to be appointed after the Turkish conquest of Constantinople, who perhaps even had aspirations for the conversion of Mohammed II to Christianity and the transformation of the Ottoman Empire into a Greco-Turkish state on the ruins of the old Byzantine Empire.[15]

Apostolis could not, of course, escape this conflict of ideas. It was probably in 1449 that he addressed a speech to the Emperor Constantine XI in which he attempted to refute the accusation that he was a worshiper of the old pagan Greek gods.[16] It has commonly been believed that in the same year he directed a speech to this same Constantine on the occasion of the latter's assumption of the imperial throne, but it has recently been shown that this particular speech was rather the work of Michael's teacher and friend John Argyropoulos.[17]

In November of 1452, when the Greek prelate Isidore, now a cardinal of the Roman church, appeared in Constantinople publicly to proclaim the unionist decree of the Council of Florence to the capital's populace, Apostolis and Argyropoulos in the ensuing turmoil took the side of Isidore.[17a] Michael continued to maintain unionist proclivities even after the fall. But whether his attitude stemmed

---

[14] See my article "The Council of Florence," 332-35.
[15] See G. Zoras, *George of Trebizond and his Efforts toward a Greco-Turkish Compromise* (in Greek) (Athens, 1954); N. Tomadakes, *George Scholarios and his Political Ideas* (in Greek) (Athens, 1954) 23; and Tomadakes, "Mohammed's Discourses in Critoboulos' History" (in Greek) (Athens, 1952) lvi, 61ff.
[16] Published in Lampros, Παλαιολόγεια καὶ Πελοποννησιακά, IV, 83-87, esp. 85. Masai, *Pléthon et le Platonisme de Mistra*, discusses the speech.
[17] Lampros, IV, 67-82. Cf. Patrinelis, "Νόθα," 204-205. On 203-204, he also shows that the μονῳδία written on the death of Emperor John Palaeologus and sometimes ascribed to Michael is that of Argyropoulos. Finally, F. Masai, "Un περὶ οὐσίας faussement attribué à M. Apostolis," *Scriptorium*, I (1946-47) 162, shows that another work, "On Substance," was not written by Michael, but is a chapter (Λ) from Aristotle's *Metaphysics*.
[17a] See Ubertino Puscolo's poem "Constantinopolis," bk. III, vv. 662-66 (above, note 11). On these events see also the historians Chalcondyles (Bonn, 1843) bk. VI, 155, and Ducas, 119. Cf. L. Mohler, *Kardinal Bessarion als Theologe, Humanist und Staatsmann* (Paderborn, 1923) 270-72.

from deep personal conviction or was rather the result of the influence first of Argyropoulos and later of Bessarion, is impossible to determine. However, in view of Michael's character — "a big child of good heart but without judgment," as the editor of his correspondence, H. Noiret, puts it,[18] perhaps somewhat too forcefully — it seems likely that in each case he was following the example of his stronger-willed associates.[19] There is no further evidence of Michael's role in the exciting events immediately prior to the Turkish capture of the capital, despite Legrand's statement that, with Argyropoulos, he was "à la tête" of the unionist party.[20]

It is unnecessary here to repeat the events of the seven-week siege of the capital: the populace's avoidance of its beloved cathedral of Hagia Sophia after its "pollution" by Isidore's ceremony of union; the stand of the seven to eight thousand defenders able to bear arms [21] against the Ottoman army of 150,000 Janissaries and mercenaries; the battering of the walls by a huge cannon; and the final Orthodox service in the cathedral the night before the last Turkish assault — a virtual litany of death preceding the Empire's final agony.

In the sack of the capital, which began on the 29th of May, 1453, and lasted for three days and nights, Michael, along with many other Greek scholars, was taken prisoner.[22] He was transported to the nearby Asiatic coast of the Black Sea, where he remained in captivity for a period of something less than a year.[23] How he secured his freedom we are not informed, though in the manner of Cardinal Isidore he may have managed to escape,[24] or,

---

[18] Noiret, *Lettres*, 24, and esp. 26.

[19] On Pletho's antiunionism see Geanakoplos, "Council of Florence," n. 108, which tells of his warnings to the emperor not to go to the West for a unionist Council. On Michael's vacillation, Sathas, *Neohellenic Philology*, 73, says perhaps too strongly: "In Italy he posed as a Westerner, while in Greece as Orthodox."

[20] Legrand, I, p. lviii; cf. Noiret, 19, who believes that during the siege Michael's role was not important.

[21] Only about 5,000 were Greeks, the rest mainly Genoese. See E. Pears, *The Destruction of the Greek Empire and the Story of the Capture of Constantinople by the Turks* (London, 1903) 247, and Vasiliev, *History of the Byzantine Empire*, 647ff. Gill, *The Council of Florence*, 87, quotes authorities to the effect that in 1453 the population of Constantinople had shrunk to 40,000–50,000 people.

[22] Noiret, no. 78.

[23] Legrand, II, nos. 4, 26, and 46. Noiret, 19.

[24] Sathas, *Neohellenic Philology*, 37 and n. 1, on the authority of Aeneas Silvius, says that Isidore escaped by disguising himself in another man's clothing. Cam-

as one authority suggests, he may have been ransomed by Bessarion.[25] Were the latter true, however, one would expect Michael
to have emphasized this in the many effusive letters he later addressed to his patron.

After his liberation Michael seems to have gone first to Italy
and subsequently to the island of Crete, though another view holds
that before proceeding to Crete he visited Thessalonica.[26] At any
rate, in early 1454 we find Michael definitely established on the
island, where he soon took in marriage the daughter of an Orthodox
priest.[27] Michael's reasons for settling in Crete are set forth in one
of his later writings:

Ever since the ruler of the Turks and of many other peoples captured
Byzantium and has ruled over us and our possessions, we [Greeks]
have been scattered to the four corners of the earth. I thought it wise
then to establish myself in Crete, after I had first visited Italy and other
countries of the world (*oikumene*) [28] — in Crete which is very ancient
and glorious on account of the virtue of its forebears and the antiquity
of its culture, and also because of its Greek race and speech and the
fact that it lies in wait to destroy the Turks — a hope that I cherish
and that has been cherished by many others better than I.[29]

If our chronology is correct, as early as autumn of the same year
Michael left his bride in Crete in order to go to Italy, where he

---

melli, *Giovanni Argiropulo*, 44, says nothing about Isidore's capture. On the capture and ransom of the noted Byzantine scholar Constantine Lascaris, see Legrand,
I, p. lxxi.

[25] Mohler, *Kardinal Bessarion*, 306, states flatly that Bessarion purchased
Michael's freedom, citing as evidence, however, only the general statement of B.
Platina, *Panegyricus in laudem Bessarionis*, P.G., CLXI, col. 115ff., that Bessarion
spent money to free many Greek prisoners. See also D. Thereianos, *Adamantios
Koraes* (in Greek), II (Athens, 1889) 94.

[26] See Michael's letter in Noiret, 149, l. 1, reading: "I thought it wise, after
visiting Italy and other countries of the world, to establish myself in Crete"
(see below, text for note 28). Also cf. Noiret, no. 125, p. 136, and p. 19. Laourdas,
in "Κρητικὰ Παλαιογραφικά," VI, 58, believes Michael went first to Thessalonica,
then Crete, and lastly to Italy.

[27] Shown in Laourdas, VI, 58. Cf. Salaville, *Dict. d'hist. géog. eccl.*, col. 1031,
who says he was already married before 1453 (i.e., in Constantinople).

[28] Possibly Michael here refers in part to a visit to Dalmatia, where an uncle of
his was bishop.

[29] Noiret, 148–49; for a translation of the work as a whole see below, text and
notes 109–114. Actually Crete was supposed to play an important role in projected
papal plans for a crusade. See a document in Noiret, 82, where the Pope instructs
Venice to prepare a Cretan army and, evidently, to use Crete as a base for such
an expedition.

hoped to meet Bessarion at Bologna.[30] From the year 1450 Bessarion had been governor and papal legate in the great but turbulent Romagnole city. And in that capacity he had rendered valuable service, maintaining order, reconstructing the municipal university, and gathering there as teachers many leading professors of the time, whom he paid himself and encouraged in the study of the classics.[31]

This is Apostolis' first recorded meeting with Bessarion,[32] and it was to mark the beginning of a relationship in which, from Michael's viewpoint at least, the Cardinal-humanist would act as Michael's guide and patron. Michael's aim was evidently to secure the support of Bessarion, then the most influential Greek in the West, for the establishment of a school in Crete or preferably in Italy under his own direction. Though he failed in this attempt, Michael did succeed in obtaining a commission to seek out ancient manuscripts, which were to be purchased or copied at Bessarion's expense and then sent to him. Bessarion's letter of instruction to Michael emphasizes his own fears for the loss of the ancient works as a result of Constantinople's fall, and, what is more revealing, his feeling about his duty as a Greek to preserve the ancient heritage for the benefit of future generations of his countrymen:

I lack quite a few works of our teachers [the Christian] and of the others [the pagan]. As long as the common and single hearth of the Greeks [Constantinople] remained standing, I did not concern myself [with gathering manuscripts] because I knew they were to be found there. But when, alas! it fell, I conceived a great desire to acquire all these works, not so much for myself, who possess enough for my own use, but for the sake of the Greeks who are left now as well as those

[30] Because of the difficulty of winter travel Michael probably went to Italy in the fall. See Noiret, no. 7 (bis), no. 11, and p. 19. Also Salaville, cols. 1030-31, who dates this meeting with Bessarion before March, 1455; Legrand. I, p. lix, says 1454.

[31] On Bessarion's activities in Bologna, see Mohler, *Kardinal Bessarion*, 258-269, and L. Pastor, *History of the Popes* (St. Louis, 1894) I, 322ff.

[32] If we are to accept the view that Michael had made trips to Italy before settling in Crete, it would seem strange that he had not already met Bessarion there. In any case possible evidence for two previous trips to Italy may be the following passage of Apostolis, in Noiret, no. 7 (bis) (dated 1455): κατήχθημεν ἐς . . . Ῥώμην . . . ἣν τρὶς ἰδών. Cf. the previously quoted passage in Noiret, pp. 148-49: "I established myself in Crete, after I had first visited Italy . . ." Also Noiret, no. 27 (Legrand, II, 248) dated 1462-63, where Michael says he has made the voyage to Italy twice.

who may have a better fortune in the future (for many things may happen in the course of the years). Thus the Greeks may be able to find intact and preserved in a safe place all the records of their language which remain up to now, and, finding these, may be able to multiply them, without being left completely mute. Otherwise, they would lose even these few vestiges of these excellent and divine men — which have been saved from what we have lost in the past — and they [future Greeks] would differ in no way from barbarians and slaves.[33]

By the fall of 1455 Michael had returned to Crete, settling in the capital city of Candia (Herakleion) in the north central part of the island, which was to be his home for almost all his remaining years.[34] It was probably in the latter part of the same year that his wife died, leaving him a widower with two small children.[35] In this period his father, who was living in the Peloponnese,[36] also died bequeathing to him a small patrimony. Apostolis, however, soon lost the inheritance and with it any hope he may have had of ameliorating his economic condition.[37]

We have little information on Michael's family life during the next few years except that, against the advice of Bessarion, he remarried, espousing the daughter of one Count Theodosios Corin-

[33] The letter (dated Bologna, 1455) is printed in S. Lampros, "'Ανέκδοτος Ἐπιστολὴ τοῦ Βησσαρίωνος," Νέος Ἑλληνομνήμων, VI (Athens, 1909) 393ff., esp. 394 and later in Mohler, Aus Bessarions Gelehrtenkreis, 478–79. The letter indicates that Michael was not the first person to be commissioned to seek out manuscripts for Bessarion.

[34] Michael's epistles for the period before 1461 are sparse and we cannot always be certain of his movements before that date. B. Laourdas, "Ἡ Γόρτυνα καὶ ὁ Μιχαὴλ Ἀποστόλης," Κρητικὰ Χρονικά, IV (1950) 240ff., depicts Gortyna (situated thirty miles from Candia) as a center of scribal activity and as the home of Michael. But S. Alexiou, "Ὁ Χαρακτὴρ τοῦ Ἐρωτοκρίτου," Κρητικὰ Χρονικά, VI (1952) 395, shows that Michael's references to Gortyna apply rather to Candia. Michael's archaizing tendency caused him to prefer the ancient name Gortyna to the medieval Candia. Gortyna, it should be noted, is in the district of Candia (Herakleion).

[35] On the death of his wife see Noiret, no. 83. On his daughter Penelope and a son, see also Noiret, nos. 28, 31, 125, 57, 58. (Legrand, I, p. lx, speaks of "several children.") Questions relating to the number of his children and the dates of their birth have not yet been adequately explained.

[36] Exact place unknown; the Peloponnese did not fall to the Turks until 1461, though a few small areas remained in Latin hands. (Monemvasia remained Greek for about a decade after 1461.)

[37] See Noiret, Lettres, 18, and no. 86. We may assume that the property did Michael little good because his first complaints about his poverty date from the same period (Noiret, nos. 2, 5, 8).

thios, a Greek of Monemvasia.[38] This second matrimonial venture provoked the ire of the father of Michael's first wife, to whom Michael, in order to justify his action, addressed a lengthy discourse appealing to Platonic ideas, which he entitled "Address to his father-in-law on his being incensed at his second marriage." [39]

Michael did not find the Cretan environment a congenial one. Because of his unionist attitude he felt himself cut off from the Orthodox society of the island; [40] nor does he seem to have had warm relations with the Venetians. Adding to his sense of insecurity was the general Cretan fear of an imminent Turkish invasion.[41] Michael, moreover, could not put out of his mind the idea of founding a school on the island or preferably somewhere in Italy for the teaching of ancient Greek literature and philosophy. But Crete offered little opportunity for the implementation of such designs. He lacked funds of his own, and the Venetian authorities took no interest in his schemes. His sole hope was Bessarion, and throughout his life Michael never ceased to beseech his patron to help him leave Crete and establish a school or secure a teaching position elsewhere. Michael himself relates that though he preferred to emigrate to Italy [42] he would also look with favor on England, Germany,[43] "Frankish" Cyprus, or even Turkish-dominated Constantinople.[44]

Bessarion evidently never approved Michael's plan for the foun-

---

[38] See Noiret, no. 11, and p. 17; and Legrand, *Bibliographie hellénique*, II, no. 26, p. 248, and I, p. lx.

[39] Published by A. Demetracopoulos in Ἐθνικὸν ἡμερολόγιον of M. Vretos (Athens, 1870) 359ff. (Cf. Noiret, no. lxxxiii.) There is little of value in this discourse. The appeal to Platonic ideas only repeats thoughts on the divisions of the functions of the body and soul and provides no facts on Michael's life. Michael's second wife seems to have produced four children. See Noiret, no. 96 (ll. 15). Also Legrand, II, no. 26. Patrinelis, "Νόθα," no. 3, 205–206, shows that sometimes confused with this letter of Michael to his father-in-law is another he wrote to George Amiroutzes, the Greek scholar (Noiret, no. 64).

[40] See Noiret, no. 70: "From the time that I expressed my opinion of the Latins and supported the adherents of the Roman church with words and especially with deeds, rejecting the first church [the Greek] — whenever I appear in the city they [the Greeks] call out to me, 'Look the devil got him too. Look at the accursed one; see the wretch!'"

[41] Noiret, nos. 73, 90, 91, 105.

[42] Noiret, nos. 27, 93, 105.

[43] Noiret, no. 92.

[44] Legrand, *Bibliographie hellénique*, no. 5, and Noiret, no. 27 (bis). The word "Frankish" here refers to Latin domination.

dation of a school in the West. (Did he consider Michael incapable or of greater usefulness simply as a purveyor of manuscripts?) Instead he granted to Michael an annual pension to be used for the support of Michael's family and to finance Michael's search for old codices. Michael was only one of many Greek Uniates assisted by Bessarion, for out of the revenues provided by his ecclesiastical estates in Crete, Bessarion had established a fund to be apportioned annually among some twelve to sixteen persons, most of them Greek priests of Crete who had accepted the unionist decree of the Council of Florence.[45]

As a pensioner of Bessarion, Michael each year (or at least after 1463, when Bessarion was named Latin Patriarch of Constantinople) [46] received from Bessarion's agent in Crete, a Latin named Lorenzo Daphnis Quirino, the sum of twenty ducats.[47] This amount, as Michael's numerous outspoken complaints indicate, was too meager for the proper support of his family. Michael's correspondence is replete with complaints about his penury, and he likes to dramatize his condition by terming himself "the king of the destitute." [48] His complaints are of course directed mainly to Bessarion, his chief charge being Quirino's delay in paying his pension. To Quirino he says: "Because your purse is full of gold coins do you think mine is also? Those whose stomachs are full cannot comprehend the need of the hungry." [49] In one of the most

[45] See Cornelius, *Creta Sacra*, II, 35–36, who mentions the names of sixteen Uniate Cretan priests supported by Bessarion (also quoted in Tomadakes, "Μιχαὴλ Καλοφρενᾶς Κρής," 131'). Cf. Noiret, no. 125, p. 136, for Michael's letter to the Venetian government after the death of Bessarion, saying that eighteen Cretans were on a yearly pension. In 1462 Pope Pius II requested part of the revenues of the Sinai monastery of St. Catherine to be given for the support of the Uniate clergy of Crete. See G. Hoffman, "Sinai und Rom," *Oriens Christianus*, IX (1927) 267–70. But now see, on the Cretan pensioners of Bessarion, Manousakas, "Βενετικὰ ἔγγραφα," 215–19.

[46] From the fact that Michael's numerous outspoken complaints about the inadequacy of the funds all date after 1463, we may assume that the pension was regularized at this time.

[47] Bessarion's orders were transmitted either directly to Michael or to Quirino, Bessarion's properties providing a revenue of 800 ducats per year. Quirino, whom Apostolis calls Daphnis (Greek for Lorenzo), also provided aid to the unfortunate Catholics of Crete and to certain individuals such as the son of Pletho. See Noiret, 40.

[48] Actually a subscription on certain of his manuscripts, for example, the *Icones* of Philostratus, now at Bologna. See Salaville, *Dict. d'hist. géog. eccl.*, col. 1033.

[49] Noiret, no. 54.

outspoken of a long series of querulous letters to Bessarion, Michael
writes that he lacks money even for the necessities of life, that he
owes the rent for his house, that his wife "revolts" and makes this
and that demand upon him. Bessarion's replies are always couched
in consoling terms: "Don't worry and everything will come out all
right." But Apostolis was never fully reassured, and a typical response of his was, "Hope is sweet but vain." [50]

It seems, however, that Apostolis was not entirely dependent on
Bessarion's subsidy. For manuscripts in Apostolis' hand preserved
in various European libraries indicate that he was employed as a
copyist by persons other than Bessarion.[51] Moreover, even if he
never did open the type of school he wanted in Crete, he was able
to take in for instruction a number of private pupils, notably
Laonikos, later the editor of the first book to be published entirely
in Greek in Venice, and Emmanuel Adramyttenos, a talented
young man who subsequently taught Greek in Italy to Aldus
Manutius.[52] But these additional sources of income were evidently
sporadic and uncertain, and did little to alter the picture that has
been drawn of Michael's poverty-stricken existence.

It was in the hope of currying further favor with Bessarion that
Michael became involved in the famous controversy between the
Platonists and Aristotelians. The philosophic conflict — which was
to have important ramifications for Western as well as Eastern in-
tellectual history — had begun among the Greek delegates to the
Council of Florence during their one and one-half year stay in
Italy (1438–1439). At the home of Cosimo de' Medici, the aged
Greek Neoplatonist Gemistos Pletho had pronounced a discourse

[50] For all these expressions see Noiret, no. 57 (for Apostolis' complaints to Bessarion and Quirino) and nos. 54, 57, 58, 69 (for Apostolis-Quirino correspondence).
For the letter of Apostolis to Bessarion mentioning his wife and the rent see
Noiret, no. 92, and Legrand, *Bibliographie hellénique*, no. 26. Also Noiret, no. 27.
[51] Michael's work as a scribe was typical of the production of the other Cretan
scribes — often indiscriminate as to the texts copied, with frequently arbitrary
correction of supposed errors, and lacking in system. See Chapter 2, text and
note 28, and, e.g., Irigouin, *Pindare*, 376.
[52] See text following note 109, where Michael speaks of being a "benefactor"
(teacher) to pupils in Crete and Byzantium. Also text and note 110. More manuscripts copied by Michael survive in the Bibliothèque Nationale and the Vatican
than were included in Bessarion's collection. See Vogel and Gardthausen, *Die
griechischen Schreiber* 305–10. On Adramyttenos see below, Chapter 5, note 24,
and for another pupil, Michael Lygizos, and others see Wittek, "*Scriptorium* de
Michel Apostolès," 293, and Laourdas, "Κρητικὰ Παλαιογραφικά," 242–45.

(in Latin known as "De Platonicae et Aristotelicae philosophiae differentia"), on the question of the philosophic and religious differences between Plato and Aristotle, an address which eulogized Plato and which he later set down on paper.[53] And in 1441 Bessarion received from his old teacher Pletho answers to certain questions irenically posed by the former as to the respective merits of the two philosophic systems.

The discussion over the two philosophies was not to become acrid until the return to the East of the Greek delegation. In 1448 there was made public in Constantinople an attack on Pletho by the learned Aristotelian George Scholarios (later as patriarch of Constantinople called Gennadios), who, like the earlier Western scholastics, had sought to reconcile Aristotelianism and Christianity.[54]

Meanwhile in the West the seeds of controversy had taken firm root, and the dispute was carried on by the Greek exiles in Italy. The most violent in his attitude was George of Trebizond, who in the year 1455, against the supporters of Platonism, wrote a libelous, pro-Aristotelian treatise comparing the views of Plato and Aristotle. The main defense of Plato's views was provided by Bessarion, who sometime between 1455 and 1459 made public his carefully reasoned and subsequently famous work entitled *In calumniatorem Platonis*. Shortly before this, it might be noted, George of Trebizond had become incensed at Bessarion because the latter had exposed to Pope Nicholas V, one of whose secretaries George had been the inadequacies of George's translation of the *Laws* of Plato.[55]

At the same time that this dispute was transpiring, minor personal quarrels, branching off from the main issue, were being carried on. The starting point for one such quarrel was a second,

[53] Περὶ ὧν 'Αριστοτέλης πρὸς Πλάτωνα διαφέρεται. See J. W. Taylor, *Georgius Gemistus Pletho's Criticism of Plato and Aristotle* (Menasha, 1921) 38ff. Text printed in Migne, *P.G.*, CLX, cols. 889–934. See on this conflict the more correct and more recent work of Mohler, *Kardinal Bessarion*, 46ff. and 339ff.

[54] On this dispute see Mohler, 47, and cf. W. Gass, *Gennadius und Pletho: Aristotelismus und Platonismus in der griechischen Kirche* (Breslau, 1844).

[55] For George's activities and his relations with Bessarion, see Mohler, 358–60, and H. Vast, *Le Cardinal Bessarion* (Paris, 1878) 338–39. Also on the philosophic questions involved (for example, the immortality of the soul), see B. Nardi, *Saggi sull' Aristotelismo padovano dal secolo XIV al XVI* (Florence, 1958) 407–408, 446–47.

briefer essay of Bessarion's, Πρὸς 'Αριστοτέλη περὶ οὐσίας, in which he again supported the views of Plato. To certain philosophic questions raised by Bessarion in this work, the mild Aristotelian Theodore of Gaza responded with a small treatise entitled "In behalf of Aristotle against Pletho." [56] It was at this point that Apostolis entered the fray.

Coming to the defense of his patron, Michael (who himself, as we have seen, may well have studied with Pletho) composed a violent attack on Gaza and his Aristotelianism.[57] The work he sent to a Cypriot friend of his living in Rome, the learned Uniate monk Isaias, who seems to have been on friendly terms with protagonists on both sides of the conflict.[58] Isaias proceeded, at Apostolis' request, to circulate the polemic among several persons. When the treatise came into the hands of the Constantinople-born Andronikos Callistos, a pupil of Gaza then teaching in Italy, he composed an answer to Apostolis and sent both treatises on to Bessarion.

Thereupon Bessarion, who strongly disapproved of the scurrilous tone of Michael's work, dispatched a letter to his protégé (dated May 19, 1462), taking him severely to task for his diatribe against Aristotle, "our guide and master in all manner of learning." In the same communication Bessarion affirmed his deep respect for *both* Aristotle and Plato ("Know that I like Aristotle as well as Plato and I respect both as the wisest of men").[59] Thus in the end Michael,

---

[56] See Mohler, 393–94. Sandys, *History of Classical Scholarship*, II, 74–75, is confused here. On Theodore and his role, see especially A. Gercke, *Theodoros Gazes. Festschrift der Universität Greifswald* (Greifswald, 1903) (and, as a corrective, Mohler). Theodore belonged to Bessarion's circle despite his mild anti-Platonic attitude.

[57] Printed in Hyperides, Μιχαήλου 'Αποστόλη. Dated 1461 by Mohler, 395. Cf. above, note 8. Patrinelis, "Νόθα," no. 11, 212–13, shows that incorrectly attributed to Michael is a letter (Cod. Vallicell. gr. 190) in which the writer supports Bessarion's defense of Plato against the attacks of George of Trebizond.

[58] Mohler, 392–95; also Cammelli, *Demetrio Calcondila*, 22–23. For Isaias' works see Migne, P.G., CLVIII, cols. 971–76. Puscolo in his poem "Constantinopolis," bk. III, vv. 705–707, says of Isaias: "Nec monachorum decus, Esaia Cyprie, versu transierim indictum. Pulchra virtute decorus, quamvis nulla tibi collata potentia, vultus . . ." (quoted in Legrand, *Bibliographie hellénique*, I, p. lxi).

[59] See Mohler, *Kardinal Bessarion*, 396; also Taylor, *Pletho*, 14. Bessarion's letter is printed in Migne, CLXI, cols. 687–92, esp. 689, and more recently by J. Powell, "Michael Apostolios gegen Theodoros Gaza," *Byzantinische Zeitschrift*, XXXVIII (1938) 71–86; and finally by Mohler, *Aus Bessarions Gelehrtenkreis*, 511–13, who evidently did not know it was already published by Powell.

instead of securing the approbation of his patron — not to mention drawing further on his liberality — evoked only a sharp rebuke.[60]

But relations between the two were not broken off, and Michael continued to seek out ancient writings for Bessarion. In his search for manuscripts Michael at this time made two journeys to Constantinople, the first in 1460–61 and another in 1463–64.[61] It was probably on his first trip that Apostolis was able to transcribe in Constantinople a valuable manuscript of Thucydides, a copy of which he brought back with him to Crete.[62] Michael no doubt took advantage of his stay in Constantinople to investigate the possibility of establishing a school there. Higher schools for the Greeks had been forbidden by the Sultan Mohammed II, it is true, but the Greek patriarch Gennadius was permitted to open a school, the primary aim of which was the training of Orthodox clergy.[63]

With the stabilization of conditions in Constantinople after the Turkish conquest, the situation became somewhat more favorable for the recovery of old manuscripts. The average Turk, still largely illiterate, had no interest in Greek codices and was as yet generally unaware of their commercial value. As the Byzantine historian Michael Ducas reports, at the time of the conquest the Turks had gathered together a large number of ancient manuscripts with which to build a fire for roasting meat. Among these codices were copies of certain plays of Euripides, several of which are no longer extant. Ducas also relates that during the pillage an enormous number of books were loaded upon carts and scattered throughout various countries with the works of Aristotle and Plato, and treatises on theology and other subjects, being sold for "one gold coin." [64] But the barbaric, indiscriminate destruction of codices that had occurred in 1453 was now a thing of the past. Of the number of manuscripts that Constantinople still possessed, the

[60] See Noiret, *Lettres*, no. 31 (Legrand, II, 251), to Bessarion (in 1463), in which Michael accepts the reproaches of Bessarion for his attack on Gaza and asks Bessarion's aid and advice.
[61] Noiret, no. 32, and p. 22.
[62] See Powell, "Cretan Manuscripts of Thucydides," 103.
[63] On the situation of the schools in Constantinople immediately after the fall, see Diehl, *Byzantium*, 292. More important is F. Babinger, *Maometto il Conquistatore e il suo tempo* (translated from German) (Turin, 1957) 183–184.
[64] Ducas, *Historia byzantina*, 312. See Pears, *Destruction of the Greek Empire*, 411–12; cf. Vasiliev, *History of the Byzantine Empire*, 653.

majority were probably to be found in the monastic libraries. And
it was therefore the monasteries of the capital that Apostolis now
must have visited.[65]

The many difficulties faced by Michael in locating manuscripts
and the methods he used in procuring or copying them can be seen
in a letter he sent to the "admirable" Bessarion in 1467, probably
soon after his return to Crete after a stay in Rome: [66]

In the belief that you would prefer to hear some *good* news regarding the books you want — books desirable both because of the ancient
beauty and usefulness of their content as well as because most present-
day Greek and Western scholars are perhaps not even aware of their
titles [67] — I have until now kept silent. I have taken advantage of every
opportunity, every moment, and any other factor involved in order
that I might procure and offer to you the books you want — all or at
least most of them. Since, however, my hopes are not very high because of what has happened, and since the adversities of fortune and
time, and the death of the first of the vice-governors here — who was
very kind to me for the sake of your excellency — did not work out in
my favor, I shall tell you how fortune has treated me. And this I do
rather unwillingly. The wretched evil owners of books, whom demons
and all the wicked spirits in the world have made guardians and despots
of them in order to cause us distress, have quarreled with one another.
Though the son of the priest Genesius, Genesius Manuel by name, has
sailed from Crete to Chios and has used every means of persuasion and
appealed to every possible reason, he is ready to die from chagrin at
not being able to serve you. I too suffered the same thing — oh, by
Greek letters and your great-souled spirit! However, despite all these
obstacles, there is some little hope of success, but this depends on me,
the "detective" of rare books (*bibliophanes*), and on Quirino, son of
Daphnis, who is more interested in copying ancient manuscripts than
in eating or obtaining honors or money. I agreed with the valiant
Quirino that we should try to convince our good rulers [of Crete] by
any means of persuasion, stratagem, or trick, to compel those ac-

[65] Knös, *Janus Lascaris*, 48, says that when manuscripts were sold, Constantinopolitan monks were among the first to buy them. See also a letter of Bessarion
to Apostolis, ed. Lampros, in "'Ανέκδοτος 'Επιστολὴ τοῦ Βησσαρίωνος," 394, where
he suggests the existence of Greek manuscripts in Adrianople, Gallipoli, Athens,
Thessalonica, and elsewhere. It is not unlikely that Michael may have visited some
of these areas. Janus Lascaris, we know, was later to procure many manuscripts
from the Athonite monasteries (see enumeration of the manuscripts found by
Lascaris in Constantinople, Crete, and elsewhere, in Knös, 46–48).

[66] Noiret, *Lettres*, no. 70.

[67] Noiret, no. 70, p. 88: 'Ελλήνων καὶ 'Ρωμαίων σοφῶν οἱ πλείους γε ἴσως οὐδὲ τὰς
ὀνομασίας τούτων ἐγνώκεσαν — an interesting but exaggerated remark!

cursed owners of books needed by you to hand them over to us. This will come about soon even though famine and plague and the failure of the wine crop be upon us. . . . I would already have left here if my tender care for the books you desire had not restrained me. Were it not for my hope of finding such books, I would prefer to die or to leave everything and find a city better and more attractive than that of the Cretans. But for all this God will provide as also will you, who are easily able to correct this state of affairs. I am now copying a work of Galen, "Concerning Simple Drugs," another which is entitled "The Physician," works of his on the (suffering) parts of the body [De locis affectis], and, in addition, a work of Artemidoros.[68]

After his return from a second trip to Constantinople, Michael again journeyed to Italy (1465–66), possibly to carry to Bessarion the manuscripts he had discovered in the East. Whatever his motive, there can be little doubt that he took advantage of the visit to explore the possibility of establishing himself there permanently.[69]

The journey from Crete to Venice generally took about a month or less, the route extending from Crete to Modon in the southwest Peloponnese and thence northward along the Dalmatian Coast. Such a voyage must always have been fraught with a certain danger, given the conditions of navigation in the period. In one epistle (written at the end of 1466 or beginning of 1467) Michael vividly sets forth the perils of his voyage to Venice via Modon, Ithaca, and Corfu. With frequent allusions to Poseidon, Odysseus, and other classical figures, Michael affirms that he would prefer "to have been born inland away from the sea and thus to have remained ever ignorant of it" — so much did he suffer from a terrible storm in which "Poseidon pursued me." [70] On one of his trips to Rome, in 1466, Michael stopped briefly at Scutari, on the Dalmatian coast, in order to see his uncle Manuel, the Uniate bishop of that see. On arrival, however, he heard of his uncle's recent death. We can imagine his reaction when, as the uncle's heir, he requested

[68] On Galen's work "Physician," see Noiret, 89, n. 4; in n. 5, Noiret says that in another letter, no. 7, Michael refers to Artemidoros of Ephesus, who wrote On the Meaning of Dreams.

[69] Michael seems to have taken at least two trips to Italy after 1455. One is referred to in a letter dated 1466–67 (Noiret, no. 61), and another in a letter written in 1468–69 (no. 84). The latter may well have been his last trip to Italy because in his letters dated 1468 to 1472 he entreated Bessarion for permission to return to Italy (no. 93), a desire, as we know, that was not to be realized.

[70] Noiret, no. 60.

information as to the latter's estate only to learn that whatever property his uncle had possessed had been eaten up in liaisons with prostitutes! [71]

Surprisingly enough, none of Michael's letters provides information of value on his activities in Rome, though, in Bessarion's palace on the Quirinal, he must have mingled with many important Greek refugees and Western humanists. In this brilliant circle of Bessarion, which took the form of an "academy" (as Bessarion's secretary Niccolò Perotti terms it) and the prime aim of which was the translation of Greek works into Latin, the philosophy of Plato and other branches of learning were discussed in familiar conversation. Among the members of the group at one time or another were the Greeks Theodore Gaza, John Argyropoulos, George of Trebizond, Janus Lascaris, Demetrios Chalcondyles, and Andronicos Callistos, and the Latins Poggio Bracciolini, Lorenzo Valla, Perotti, Flavio Biondo, and Bartolomeo Platina.[72] Despite the lack of any substantial evidence from Michael or other sources regarding his Roman sojourns (a fact which of course may indicate visits of only short duration)[73] we may assume that he was well informed about current gossip, in particular the latest developments in the Aristotelian-Platonic controversy, which was still far from over.

In 1464 the irascible Cretan, George of Trebizond, took up the cudgels with a bitter invective against his old opponent Bessarion, to which the latter replied in the same year or the year following.[74] Subsequently Michael, who had returned to Crete, in 1467 once

[71] Noiret, no. 61.

[72] See Mohler, *Kardinal Bessarion*, I, 252, 325-31, and his *Aus Bessarions Gelehrtenkreis, passim*. Also Pastor, *History of the Popes*, I, 319ff. On Chalcondyles' membership in the group, see Cammelli, *Demetrio Calcondila*, 20.

[73] See Legrand, *Bibliographie hellénique*, I, p. lix, and Bessarion's brief mention of Michael's reception in the Roman Curia in Bessarion's letter printed in Mohler, *Aus Bessarions Gelehrtenkreis*, 481. Noteworthily, Bessarion writes Michael in another letter printed by Mohler (483) that he desires the latter to send him the *Syntaxis* of Ptolemy as well as the *Problems* (*Problemata*) of Aristotle. And in still other letters (483-84) Bessarion seeks Theophrastus, Dionysius of Halicarnassus, the "Pyrrhoneia" (probably the *Pyrrhoneioi Hypotyposeis* of Sextus Empiricus), Quintus (doubtless Smyrnaeus), Galen, commentaries on the *Rhetoric* and *Poetics* of Aristotle (Bessarion says he had the *texts*), and the *Rhetoric* of Apsines.

[74] Mohler, *Kardinal Bessarion*, I, 392. Bessarion's treatise was entitled *De Natura et Arte*. It will be recalled that Bessarion had been instrumental in having George expelled from the circle of Pope Nicholas V because of his faulty translations.

more viciously attacked a champion of Aristotle in the person of Demetrius Chalcondyles, then professor of Greek at Padua, in a work bearing the lengthy title, "Response to Chalcondyles' defense of Theodore Gaza against Gregory's views on substance." But to Apostolis' attack Chalcondyles did not, evidently, deign to respond.[75] This battle of words, initiated in the West by the Greek scholars at the Council of Florence and then carried back to the East, had now begun to involve some of the leaders among the Italian humanists. Perotti wrote an invective against George of Trebizond, and Ficino, Filelfo, and others addressed letters to Bessarion complimenting him on his learned defense of Plato. Thus the conflict, which had as its principal result the popularization of a knowledge of the Platonic and Aristotelian philosophies (based, it should be noted, on the original text and ancient interpolations rather than on medieval translations and commentaries), entered the mainstream of Italian Renaissance thought.[76] As a defender of Platonism Michael too played a certain part. But, like George of Trebizond, he does not stand up well in comparison to the serene Bessarion and the more moderate Gaza and Callistos.

Except for his second intrusion into this conflict, Michael on his return to Crete continued to spend his time in seeking out and copying manuscripts. The area of his activities was not limited to Crete, but extended to Constantinople, Cyprus, and other regions of the East, as may be observed from the following letter he addressed to Bessarion in 1467: [77]

. . . Badios [evidently a Latin of Cyprus] has many books very useful to us, the titles of which I have copied exactly and sent to you, together with his letters. I do not know why you did not ask me to copy them

[75] For Michael's work see Hyperides, Μιχαήλου Ἀποστόλη. Here Michael, according to D. Kampouroglou, Οἱ Χαλκοκονδύλαι (Athens, 1926) 195–96, descends to gross insults. He terms Chalcondyles' mother a woman of easy virtue and, punning on Chalcondyles' name, remarks that his *kandulen* (vessel with oil placed before an icon) is not of copper (*halkos*) but of glass, which itself is of bad quality!

[76] See Kristeller, *Marsilio Ficino*, 12. For the historiographical literature on this entire philosophic controversy, see Sandys, *History of Classical Scholarship*, II, 75, n. 8. Also Vast, *Cardinal Bessarion*, 265ff., and recently G. Cammelli, "Andronico Callisto," *Rinascita*, XXIII–XXIV (1942) 17ff. On Perotti's role and the letters of Ficino and Filelfo to Bessarion, see Mohler, *Aus Bessarions Gelehrtenkreis*, 343–44, 544–45, 598–600, and his *Kardinal Bessarion*, 384–89. There are also a number of unpublished treatises on the controversy, mostly by western scholars.

[77] Printed in Noiret, *Lettres*, no. 76.

but only to indicate what they were, along with their subject matter and contents. I cannot promise to do this immediately, since the books are not here but in Cyprus, which is 700 miles distant. Consequently, the information you want will take a long time to secure, not because the books are so far away but because Cretan ships rarely go to Cyprus and more rarely do Cypriote ships come to Crete. Meanwhile, so much time I fear will elapse that the books will escape us. Nonetheless, I will do what I can, but not so much as I could if I had enough money to go to Cyprus myself. Proclus' *On Geometry* was to be found here when there resided here the owner of the book, a student of mine named Lord Thomas Phykarnos the Sicilian (*Sikeliotes*).[78] He is now living in Modon. [I might mention] also a man of Epidauros [Monemvasia],[79] an uncle on my wife's side named Theodore, an old servant in religion of your excellency as was his father (who was Count of Corinth and Grand Ecclesiarch of Epidauros). This Theodore wrote me that he found a manuscript of Hippocrates containing the complete works of that blessed author. I am sending you in addition the letter containing the titles which Theodore sent me from Epidauros. All these things and more, most pious Lord, cannot be copied without money, hard work, and the risking of many dangers. But if Quirino the son of Daphnis would pay me the gold lire on time, I would by now have sent you these works and perhaps others too. I have explained to you and described the situation. The decision about these books and also about my affairs remains at the discretion of your holiness.

Lack of funds was not Michael's only complaint, for he continued to meet with difficulty in gaining access to manuscripts. In another section of the same letter he wrote that

concerning the many other books recently requested by you I have not yet ascertained for your lordship the details on the titles of Plutarch, Proclus, and Galen. But this was not voluntary (for I am not distinguished for my laxity) but rather because of that very bad Nicholas,[80] the gold-lover and book-burier (*bibliotaphos*),[81] a man small of body and resembling a monkey, very shrewd in mind and chameleon-like. Many times he has informed me that he has numerous books (and he

[78] An unknown person, according to Noiret, 97, though of interest because he may possibly be an example of a Latin pupil of Apostolis.
[79] Cf. Noiret, no. 77, p. 97, n. 2, who wrongly says that this also could refer to Ragusa. Noiret has confused Epidauros with the ancient name of Ragusa, Epidamnos.
[80] The identity of Nicholas is unknown. Doubtless he went back and forth to Constantinople and Michael asked him to search for books. See Noiret, 88.
[81] Letter printed in Noiret, 76. On *bibliotaphos* see Firmin-Didot, *Alde Manuce*, 221, who has not noted that this apt term was employed by Apostolis before its use by Aldus Manutius and Musurus.

spoke the truth), but he showed me what was least useful to us and not at all valuable. These I looked at and read — some quickly, others with a little more attention (for he did not leave me alone but kept pestering me) and those of which I noticed the titles I wrote you. But I could not examine them, as he did not permit it. Since he had heard of the 200 gold pieces his only aim was to obtain them, and he demanded them just for copying the books. He permitted me to copy a few only; he knew what you wanted, and these manuscripts he hid.

There is little doubt that Michael's perseverance brought its reward. For in this age when the collection of manuscripts had become a virtual mania, the library of his employer, Bessarion, grew to be the largest and best collection of Greek books in all of Europe. As we have noted, before his death Bessarion left to the Venetians 746 manuscripts, of which 482 were in Greek.[82] According to the contemporary papal historian Bartolomeo Platina, Bessarion — aside from his Latin library — expended some 30,000 florins on his Greek collection, with Greek manuscripts being copied at his expense in the monasteries of Constantinople, in the Morea, and in southern Italy, as well as in Crete.[83] Of these codices a considerable number are from the hand of Apostolis,[84] to whom, as to other scribes of Crete, we are therefore indebted for our knowledge of a substantial number of ancient Greek texts.

Michael was no more content in Cretan society on his return from Rome in the years after 1467 than he had been previously. Indeed his stay in the papal capital had, if anything, made him more Latinophile. He now became more vocal against the Orthodox

[82] See Omont, "Manuscrits grecs et latins donnés à Saint-Marc," 129–87. Also Setton, "Byzantine Background," 74, n. 24.
[83] Passage cited in Vast, Cardinal Bessarion, 304. Bessarion procured many manuscripts from the library of the south Italian Greek monastery of St. Nicholas of Casole. See above, Chapter 1, note 25 (cf. Mohler, Kardinal Bessarion, 258).
[84] For a list of the manuscripts copied for Bessarion by Michael and listed in the latter's correspondence, see Noiret, Lettres, 43. Vogel and Gardthausen, Die griechischen Schreiber, 305–10, list a total of about 115 manuscripts copied in whole or in part by Michael, not all, of course, for Bessarion. See also Montfaucon, Palaeographia Graeca, 82, 103, 111; Bolgar, Classical Heritage, 462. The Greek manuscripts owned by Bessarion and now contained in the Marciana library are listed in A. Zanetti, Graeca D. Marci Bibliotheca Codicum Manu Scriptorum (Venice, 1740). Finally, see Noiret, Lettres, 27–28, for a list of MSS copied by Michael and now to be found in the Bibliothèque Nationale, Vatican, Palatine library, Venice, Florence, London, Oxford, Munich, Escurial, Brussels, Vienna, Berlin, and Naples. On an Iliad copied by Michael, now in Warsaw, see L. Politis, Ἑλληνικά, XVI (1958–59) 408.

population of Crete, viewing them as schismatics — "wretched and ignorant who [think] they do something meritorious in criticizing the Latins." [85] And the head of the Orthodox church, the Constantinopolitan patriarch, Mark Xylokaraves, he described as a "lover of gold, an evil-thinking man, a monkey with a tail, who disturbed and agitated all of Crete." [86] So partisan did Michael now become in support of the Latins that in 1467 he denounced two Orthodox monks to the Venetian government, which resulted in their exile.

After this incident Michael's position in the eyes of his fellow-Cretans deteriorated even further. In a letter to Bessarion he tells of the increasing animosity toward him:

The new order and directive which you established I gladly accepted [regarding the Uniates pensioned by Bessarion?], recalling the words of the epic [Hesiod]: "He is a fool who tries to withstand the stronger, for he does not get the mastery and suffers pain besides the shame." And all this even though I am a stranger [to Crete] and destitute and homeless, for not only am I cast aside by the Greeks but looked upon as a hated, irreconcilable, and ostracized enemy. From the time I expressed my opinion of the Latins and supported the adherents of the Roman church with words — and rejected the other [Greek] church — from that time, whenever I am in the city [Candia] they [the Greeks] call out to me: "Look, the devil got him, too. Look at the accursed one, behold the wretch!" [87] And these men, who would have killed me long ago had they not feared the authorities, drew my students away from me.[88] So now I live miserably by my pen wondering where on earth to go and thinking especially of the place where you are, my lord and master . . .[89]

Michael's words describing the intensity of anti-Catholic feeling were not without justification. Thus a letter written soon after 1467 by a Greek Uniate bishop, Joseph of Modon (John Plousiadenos), to the Cretan Orthodox clergy reports that so recalcitrant was the Greek populace that, despite the proclamation of union at

[85] Noiret, no. 93.
[86] Noiret, p. 95. Cf. Tomadakes, "Μιχαὴλ Καλοφρενᾶς Κρής," 134.
[87] Noiret, no. 70 (in 1467) ll. 28–37.
[88] Cf. Noiret, no. 81 (dated 1467–68) to Bessarion, esp. p. 102, ll. 3–6, where the sentiment is expressed that Michael's pupils rejected him because they feared they would become Latinized. Cf. Tomadakes, "Μιχαὴλ Καλοφρενᾶς Κρής," 110ff., esp. 130–33.
[89] Noiret, no. 70.

Florence, it refused to accept the sacraments from the hands of the Greek unionist clergy.[90]

Despite Michael's ostensible antagonism to the adherents of the Orthodox church, he felt very strongly the fate of the Greek East, and it was his hope that Latin power would not only dispel the fear of an imminent Turkish invasion of Crete but even liberate Constantinople from the Turkish yoke. To be sure, the fervor of the Crusading period had long since disappeared in the West, but there were still those who saw in a concerted effort on the part of Christendom the sole means of repelling the Turk. The most vocal proponents of a renewed crusade were the refugee Greeks, especially those like Bessarion, who through their presence in the papal court were in a position of influence. The hope for Byzantine liberation is expressed with particular intensity in some of Michael's writings. One of his works, in fact, is devoted exclusively to this theme — an oration addressed to no less a personage than the Holy Roman Emperor Frederick III.[91] Although an early editor of the speech says it was composed in 1457, it seems more likely to have been written — and perhaps sent to the Emperor in the custom of the time — in 1468, on the occasion of Michael's last trip to Italy. For certain expressions employed in the text presuppose the Turkish conquest of the Morea, which was not completed until after 1460.[92]

In 1468 Michael had again journeyed to Italy to see Bessarion.

[90] Joseph Plusiadenos' letter to Cretan clergy in Tomadakes, 124–39, esp. 139. And more recently, M. Manousakas, "Recherches sur la vie de Jean Plousiadénos (Joseph de Méthone)," *Revue des études byzantines*, XVII (1959) 41. Patrinelis "Νόθα," no. 10, 211–12, shows that a work against the decision of the Council of Florence is falsely attributed to Michael.

[91] We have two different versions of this speech, the earlier edited by B. Struve in *Rerum Germanicorum Scriptores*, I (Strasburg, 1717) cols. 47ff., entitled "Ejusdem oratio in laudem Friderici III imperatore" (previously published by M. Freher in *Rerum Germanicorum scriptores*, II [Frankfurt, 1602] 33ff.). The later, more complete edition, which is translated here, is edited by B. Laourdas, " Ἡ πρὸς τὸν αὐτοκράτορα Φρειδερίκον τὸν Τρίτον ἔκκλησις τοῦ Μιχαὴλ Ἀποστόλη," Γέρας Α. Κεραμοπούλλου (Athens, 1953) 516–27. The speech is listed (not quoted or analyzed) in Legrand, *Bibliographie hellénique*, I, p. lxvi, but no mention is made of it by Noiret or Salaville.

[92] See Laourdas, 521, ll. 1–5, mentioning the Turkish "destroyer" of Achaia and the Peloponnese. For a similar type of oration (anonymous) addressed later to the Emperor Charles V see George Zoras, "Κάρολος ὁ Ε΄ τῆς Γερμανίας καὶ αἱ πρὸς ἀπελευθέρωσιν προσπάθειαι," Περὶ τὴν ἅλωσιν τῆς Κωνσταντινουπόλεως (Athens, 1959) 193–211.

The Emperor Frederick was then in Rome in order to secure the crown of Bohemia and to discuss with the recently enthroned Pope Paul II military measures to be taken against the Turks. We know that at this time Bessarion had an audience with Frederick and that they discussed the project of a crusade. To Bessarion's earnest exhortations,[93] however, Frederick's response was merely a proposal that a congress be convened in Constance to consider the problem.[94] It is entirely possible that on this occasion Michael met a member of Frederick's court in Rome — perhaps the Greek Staurakios whom he mentions in his address — and that through him he sought to add his own appeal to the proposals of Bessarion.[95]

Address of Michael Apostolis of Byzantium to the most holy, pious,
serene, and great Emperor of the Romans and all Christians,
Lord Frederick

I have been encouraged to address you by a servant of yours well known to your majesty (by a Byzantine, son of a wealthy and wise father), who is my best friend and familiar to the magistrates and leading men and who is also a herald of your virtues — though you have no need of such, your virtues themselves being your herald . . .[96] Now since you are such [an ideal emperor], as I have said, a fact confirmed by my friend [John] and attested to by your reputation, you, I firmly believe, will prevail over all, even over the ruler of the Turks [Teucri], the destroyer of all Greece, and of Thrace, the Chersonese, Macedonia, Epirus, Lower Moesia [Bulgaria], Achaia, Attica, Thessaly, Boeotia, Plataea, and the Peloponnese, the latter of which is such a renowned and divine land that if I called it "the eye of the world" I would not be far wrong . . .[97] [After enumerating all the former Byzantine territories of Asia now under Turkish domination, Michael proceeds to inquire of the Emperor:] But you might ask how I know that this [your triumph over the Turks] will come about. From necessity itself, which the philosophers termed *Adrasteia*, and from [the cycle of] revolution and change of things which are always uncertain and constantly in flux, and, above all, from the oracles, of which none, or

---

[93] See also in this connection Bessarion's famous "Oration against the Turks" addressed to the Venetian Doge in 1453, in Migne, *P.G.*, CLXI, cols. 641–76. English translation in *Viking Portable Renaissance Reader*, ed. J. Ross and M. McLaughlin (New York, 1953) 70–74.

[94] Mohler, *Kardinal Bessarion*, 416.

[95] See next note.

[96] Laourdas, 519, ll. 19–26. Also 520, l. 4, referring to John Staurakios, a Greek member of the German imperial court, who has not been identified. Struve's earlier version mentioned one Aristomenus, a Greek friend of Michael.

[97] Possibly further evidence that Michael's family was Peloponnesian.

very few, turn out to be false. In this I call you as a witness, great Emperor, you who are very wise and versed in astronomy, you whose fame in this respect has reached Greece, you who understand the movement of the heavenly bodies and the forces of the ether, of the spheres and the two poles North and South, the eclipses of the sun and phases of the moon — which of the stars move and which are fixed, which are the planets (*pursa*) and which fall through the air — the meaning of each formation of stars, when we shall have rain and drought, epidemic or health. Who does not marvel at your heavenly mind (*nous*) which communes with the first mind and the spheres, whence our intellect derives and dwells within us, which comes to us according to the law of Adrasteia. So Plato believes and with him all the Platonists following him . . . You, most wise mind, you illuminate the earth each night and day. How can I speak of the great worth of your virtues, the natural, ethical, and the political, which, they say, follow only upon reason and prudence. You, model of Emperors and statue molded by God, you can see clearly into the future. All these things reveal that this is no time for words but only for war and battle. It is time to gaze at the stars which help us to understand the problems of the world . . . O very wise Emperor, I am certain it will soon be the year about which all speak and the soothsayers foresee, and the oracles which those inspired by God have prophecied. You, I believe, are the sleeping dragon who will shortly arise and strike the upstart and will liberate the Greeks and reduce the Turks to slavery. You will be the author of our happiness, you the sole anchor and basis of our hopes.

Arise, then, O Emperor, seize the golden imperial spear, wield the weapon and the shield against the barbarians. Appoint as our emperor your son Maximilian, the most fortunate, who will succeed you on the throne in your advanced age. Restore our people — which is scattered everywhere on earth — to our country, our people which was ever very proud and wise but has now crumbled to nothingness and is very humble. Think that you hear the Byzantines clamoring to invite you, the very great Emperor, to free them and that Constantine, the Emperor, summons you to avenge those who died in battle with the Turks.[98] Hear me also, O Emperor, who am left without country or city, who am poor and destitute, and who may perish because of my misfortunes.

But for this, God and our most sacred Emperor will provide. As for the faithful servant of your majesty, John Staurakios, Count Palatine and knight, he requests through me that your most holy majesty grant him, in addition to what he has already received, another gift which he, with proper deference and on his knees, will come to, ask of you. May you, O Emperor, add this kindness to your former ones, imitating

[98] Refers to Constantine XI, last Byzantine Emperor.

yourself and your benevolence. If you also remember my name — I who am unfortunate and destitute on account of my country's misfortunes but rich and hopeful in my dependence on you, most serene Emperor — you will have in me a herald who will proclaim your deeds with the voice of Stentor, and you will find me the last and most faithful of all your servants. What more can I say? Nothing, but to pray and say no more. May you live, O most glorious and great Emperor Frederick, who are endowed by God with so many virtues. May you see Maximilian live long and may you have many and good sons and daughters. Would that we may see both of you rulers of Byzantium and the entire East!

This speech, which is modeled after the ancient declamatory oration,[99] is typical of Michael's style, prolix in the extreme and overly servile, but at the same time containing some interesting thoughts and curious allusions — to Neoplatonic ideas, to astronomical lore (an interest common to the later Byzantines and evidently also shared by Frederick), and, above all, to the woes of the Greek people. The discourse concludes with an appeal to the "Emperor of the Romans" to extend his hegemony over the entire *oikumene* (including the former Byzantine territories now occupied by the Turkish Sultan) and to assign to his son Maximilian the crown of the East — a remarkable suggestion recalling the administrative organization of the later Roman Empire at the time of Diocletian.[100]

If Frederick deigned to respond to Apostolis (and the speech, of course, may not even have been brought to his attention), his general reaction was probably much the same as it had been to the proposals of Bessarion. Suffice to say that Frederick, not unmindful of the lamentable fate of Pius II's recent crusade at Ancona,[101] never launched an expedition to the East. But had he been so inclined he certainly would have been persuaded more by the forceful yet subtle exhortations of Bessarion than by this curious, though nonetheless earnest, conflation of flattery, rhetoric, and unrealism.[102]

[99] Note the Homeric quotations employed.

[100] Cf. Laourdas' remarks in his edition of the speech, "Ἡ πρὸς τὸν αὐτοκράτορα . . . ," 526–27.

[101] On Pius II's crusading activities see A. Atiya, *The Crusade in the Later Middle Ages* (London, 1938) 230.

[102] Unrealistic because Michael based his opinion that Frederick would crush the Turk on the "law" of change, and on oracles (already supposedly prophesy-

On one of his trips to Rome, Michael had promised a former secretary of Bessarion, Gaspar Zacchi by name, Bishop of Osimo near Ancona in Italy,[103] that he would compile for him a collection of proverbs and wise sayings extracted from the classical Greek authors.[104] The task, according to the authority of Noiret, was completed sometime during 1471–72, at which time Michael sent to the Bishop the finished work, which he had entitled *Ionia*. He apologized for his delay in fulfilling the Bishop's request, and noted that the proverbs included reference to the provenience of most of them. Typically, he attributed the delay not to his own fault but to "circumstances of fortune on account of which everything comes to its end even when we do not expect it." And he added, "In any case, it is better that what you wanted be late and correctly done than executed earlier and badly." [105] This subsequently famous collection of proverbs is Michael's best known work. At his death the *Ionia* passed into the hands of his son, Arsenios, who enlarged and published part of the collection, as will be discussed in Chapter 6.

The trip to Rome in 1468 marked Michael's last visit with Bessarion, for only a few years later the great cardinal died, in November of 1472. His demise was a severe blow to Michael, who mourned the passing of his patron in an eloquent funeral oration written in Crete.[106] With the death of Bessarion, Michael's main hope of establishing himself in Italy disappeared. And now even his pension was curtailed. In a letter addressed to the Venetian Signoria of Crete Michael complained bitterly of this reduction. Invoking the name of Isidore, the first titular patriarch of Constantinople, as well as that of Bessarion, Michael pleaded the cause of the eighteen Greek Uniates (most, except for himself, clerics) who had been

---

ing the fall of the Turkish Empire), while saying absolutely nothing of Frederick's military and economic strength.

[103] C. Walz, ed., *Arsenii Violetum* (Stuttgart, 1832) p. ii, wrongly places this reference to Osimo, in Spain.

[104] See Michael's (undated) letter to Gaspar in Noiret, *Lettres*, 126.

[105] Noiret, 126–27. The question of the manuscript tradition of this collection of proverbs is a bit complex because Gaspar and Lauro Quirino both possessed exemplars of the work, along with Arsenios. See E. Leutsch, *Paroemiographi Graeci* (Göttingen, 1851) II, p. xff.

[106] Published in Migne, *P.G.*, vol. CLVI, cols. 127ff. See also his two epitaphs on Bessarion in Legrand, *Bibliographie hellénique*, I, p. lxv.

supported by Bessarion. Then he inveighed against the successor of Bessarion, the new archbishop of Crete, Jerome Landi, whom by implication he charged with the responsibility for reducing his pension. He ended dramatically by portraying himself, a person with no racial or linguistic connections with Venice, as willing to remain in Crete to die for the Venetians and the Cretans.[107] Unsuccessful in his bid to Landi for continuation of the subsidy, Michael was reduced to virtual destitution.

Michael made one last attempt to establish himself in the West. In the period after the death of Bessarion, Michael wrote a long, rather tedious but at the same time informative, discourse on the most effective way of teaching Greek, which is entitled "Exhortation from Gortyna [Crete] to Rome in Italy."[108] Doubtless he hoped thereby to be invited to a professorship at one of the Italian universities or even to a newly established school for the teaching of Greek to children. In view of the value attached to the study of Greek in the educational systems of the period, for example, in the schools of the Italian humanists Guarino da Verona and Vittorino da Feltre, a consideration of Michael's views on the subject is appropriate. For that reason and because no translation of it has yet been made into English, the discourse, despite its great length, is quoted in extenso: [109]

O Men of Italy and the West, you who have inherited the virtues of both the Greeks and the Romans: necessity has again brought me among you from Greece, I who am worthy of charity and sympathy because of the conquest of my country and the hardships I subsequently suffered. I have been as much a benefactor in the realm of letters to some of you as I could (when I was residing in Byzantium or in Crete). And now perhaps I will appear as a greater benefactor if I succeed in this, namely that the proposals I shall now set forth might appear to you as fruitful and efficacious . . . You Westerners who are eminent in everything as well as in letters — letters are a divine gift to man and, one may perhaps say, even a god. But whatever we may call them, if they be acquirable they should be preferred to everything else and transmitted to all who seek this end, as in fact is the case with the more

---

[107] Noiret, 137.

[108] Cf. a letter of Apostolis in Noiret, no. 110, p. 127, where Michael informs his friend Troilus (on whom see Noiret, 32) of his sending a discourse to the Italians, which he has translated into Latin.

[109] Printed in Noiret as an appendix, 148–53. Also cf. Legrand, I, p. lxix.

eminent men of letters . . . If you decide to teach your children our [the Greek] tongue in the same way that you instruct and educate them in your own tongue [Latin] — that is, beginning with the letters, then the syllables, the words, syntax and the deeper meaning of the ideas involved, step by step by means of a systematic method and not for the sake of exhibition and merely to make sounds — then your children will become as skillful in Greek as they are in your tongue. What then is this which I am alluding to? I shall describe it for you as clearly as I can.

For a long time now, O men of Europe, Greeks [the refugees or exiles] distinguished in family, wisdom, and letters, have been increasingly coming among you. These men, who attend your institutions and associate with your professors because of their love for Western literature, you appoint as professors for yourselves as well as your sons in the other [Greek] of the two best literatures. In this you do well and deserve praise. But their manner of teaching is, in my opinion, wrong. How can it be otherwise? Because you permit them to teach both literatures in the Latin language and not in accord with what is natural and peculiar to each particular tongue. The natural method of teaching Latin is in Latin, but the other literature [Greek] should be taught in Greek. According to your method it is the teachers who always benefit with respect to both languages, while the students, as may be expected, make progress in neither one tongue nor the other. Whether I am telling the truth will soon be clear. See how much time has elapsed since you began to cultivate Greek, and yet there is nobody among you nor will there be — if you persist in your method of learning the language of the Athenians — who knows the rules of grammar and etymology, or who can compose a discourse without error, or, at the very least, set forth and teach others what he has learned. And yet there are Greeks in Italy at this time who can express themselves quickly and well in Greek and are able to teach and write in it not only letters and sentences but books in such number that theirs outnumber, I think, all other books. Whence did this situation take its beginning [i.e., the Italian inability to learn Greek]? How did this condition spread so easily? Where did it start and what facilitated its progress if not that which I indicated before so accurately? — namely the fact that the Greeks do not teach the Westerners Greek in Greek. What do you gain returning home [from such a lesson in Greek] except a few words and the general idea, one might say, as I perceived in some places in Italy — things which students can themselves acquire without a teacher if they know how to read sufficiently and recite the rules of grammar. Don't you realize that the spirit of letters and all subjects is grammar, which assists those endowed with eloquence because of its strength and impressiveness? Grammar, as defined by the grammarian, is a thorough knowledge of what the poets and the other writers speak of in general terms. Who can be a rhetor, fluent, skillful, and concise, who does not have a good knowledge of grammar, which is the flavor of the arts, the leaven, the soul of wisdom, the eye of all the sciences? What philosopher, what mathematician or theologian is perfect without it? Who can be called a learned man without experience of this first of the arts, and how can one write on any subject without being trained in this queen of the sciences . . . This being so and as you agree, as I believe, you ought therefore to be educated in grammar and to call on experts in it without regard to the labor involved, to objections, to considerations of the body or of money or anything else so that you may acquire what is superior to all else . . . I can inform you, willingly, whether you need a pedagogue or simply a conductor (*porthmeus*), even if the latter be the best of his kind among the Greeks. If you want merely a conductor, it is useless to affirm anywhere that you are learning, since the real beauty of the arts would be lacking in you — that is, etymology, language, analogy, history — which are the organs and purpose of grammar. But if you want a real pedagogue with strength and virtue, then why do you neglect the fruits for the leaves? . . . And so I think it futile and without profit to study the Greek language via the Italian [i.e., Latin] — this is what prevents you from surpassing the Greeks. Sometimes I marvel, in the name of education, when I hear some Italians translating Homer and Thucydides into the language of the Romans [Latin], destroying the choice of words, and above all even the grace and expression of the words, which Athena gave birth to and for which the choir of Muses acted as midwife — which Apollo nourished and Hermes prescribed for the Greeks. And without these qualities, it seems to me that those who teach Greek thus [via Latin] hear a lyre playing which is false and discordant. What does one benefit from a song lacking in harmony? What is it worth to the flutist or trumpeter if the music has no harmony? . . .

If one should say that the Roman [Western] teachers translate the Greek language into their own tongue and manner very well and intelligently, what connection does this have with the Greeks and their wisdom? Rather it is a great injustice meriting strong penalties on the part of those who try gradually in this manner to obliterate the Greek language and to do against the Greeks what even the Romans did not. Indeed it will be possible for them [Western teachers] thus to appropriate works of the Greek writers by changing [to their own language] the titles and names of the authors. Those who do this should be punished by a fine of 10,000 talents, in particular because after we remnants of the Greeks (*ta ton Hellenon elleimmata*) are gone, not only letters but the whole Greek language, alas, will end up this way.

But if you love those wise and valiant men [the ancients], show your love through your efforts and become as skillful and proficient in the Greek language as you are in yours.

Only with effort can great things be accomplished and when accomplished bring much glory to those exerting the effort . . . Whenever an Italian reads Homer, Demosthenes, or Thucydides in Latin or the two philosophers [Plato and Aristotle], what fruit does he gain of Greek culture? All he acquires is the bare meaning that even barbarians can understand . . . To all men intelligence and thought are common, but not the words employed and the expression, which is something alloted only by divine gift.

But someone may say: how can the students understand the teacher of grammar if the teacher is unable to translate the words and thoughts when he instructs them . . . ? A good question, my friends. I do not say that the teacher should never communicate with you in Latin. But this should be rare and less frequent and only when the rudiments — the words and rules of grammar — are being explained, but it should not be done this way always, from the beginning to the end. You should try to learn from him [the teacher] and not he from you. You, however, deceiving yourselves, practice the opposite; you train the teacher in your way and not yourself in his. If I should wish to be taught by you, would I not force myself to understand your language and teachings and also the words and whatever is necessary? Otherwise, it would be like asking a wolf to give me wings or a chicken to produce milk. Or like trying to take liquid from a jar with holes in it.

It is in this manner that I insist you learn Greek. It was this way before and after Caesar; thus did Dion [Dio Cassius], and Albinus, Artemidorus, Hegesippus, Julian, Anatolius, thus did every Roman or Greek who wanted to learn the other's language. Or do you think I speak inaccurately? If you think me right, I thank you now and guarantee my gratitude in the future. If not, I shall show that you are wrong through my actions by opening a school (*mouseion*) in Italy. And if within ten years I do not have more students than other teachers have had in double the time, you may condemn me.

What can I say in conclusion? If any Italian city is fond of Greek letters — and I am sure there is more than one . . . give me for two years a salary to be agreed upon. And if I do not accomplish what I promise — even before the term is finished — impose any fine or penalty upon me that I deserve, and if you think it just, beat me and belabor me . . . if I am wrong in all I pledge. But if the opposite results [and I am successful], you should bestow the credit on me and my descendants.

The children to be taught should be between five and ten years of age, perhaps a bit less, and should know as much Latin as they are able. They should have available the books I will suggest and should spend the entire day with me except for lunch at noon, as is the custom. After lunch they will return to school; and I will not sit on a high chair and raise my voice but will sit on a stool or chair on the same level with them — as I have been accustomed to do until now in Byzantium and Crete.[110] For this reason I have had more students from among the Latins and Greeks (even if I was young and knew less) than those who knew much and were older than I, and that I think was a gift of God, so that I might not remain alone without virtue.

I assure you in addition that I will teach you better than I myself have been taught and more quickly than I have learned — oh, in the name of literature! — regarding those things into which I have been initiated so many times and instructed. First grammar, the eye of language, and the art of poetry, which is many-sided and broad.[111] These indeed I learned better than any of my contemporaries. And of course rhetoric, which breathes forth fire, in accord with my natural strength and the teachers I heard. I also studied the [Greek] authors and orators who made use of rhetoric, [and this I did] as well as anyone of our age. And I have learned everything that has been written in Greek on these disciplines — namely, logic and physics and other aspects of Apollo's arts that I was taught in my homeland. Nothing was I taught abroad [112] because of fate or the evils of the times and because of all that has befallen me until now. [I also studied] Plato the valiant, the genius, in good measure before Constantinople's fall, and after its capture my love for Plato spurred me on to study further either by myself or with other teachers whom I had the good fortune to meet.[113] I have told you sufficiently and briefly what I could about the method of learning Greek. It is now up to you to show that my exhortation will not remain mere words but will be translated into ac-

[110] Evidently in contrast to the practice of Byzantium and Crete, the teacher in Italy sat on a high chair, as had been the case in the medieval period. See another possible reference to the high professional chair of Italy in Demetrius Ducas' dedication to Marcus Musurus of the *Rhetores Graeci*, which reads: "You teach publicly from the chair as from the height of a throne" (cf. Chapter 5, text for note 107).

[111] Michael in fact wrote a rhetorical work, typical of the Byzantine period, entitled *De figuris poeticis* ('Επιδιόρθωσις ποιητικῶν τρόπων) (see Legrand, I, p. lxx). But he was *not* the author of two works supposedly called *De figuris rhetoricis* and *Expositio in artem rhetoricam* (see Patrinelis, "Νόθα," nos. 6–7, 208–10).

[112] This phrase, "Nothing was I taught abroad" (l. 19), is important because unless simply rhetorical, it may contradict the belief of Noiret and Legrand that before 1453 Michael had studied in Italy. Of course, Michael may simply be disparaging what he may have learned in Italy.

[113] We do not know whom Apostolis studied with after 1453. Argyropoulos was noted rather as an Aristotelian than a Platonist and Pletho had already died before that date. Professor E. Garin, however, informs me that he is publishing a study relating to Argyropoulos' Platonic interests.

tion. "Who knows but that heaven helping thou mightest rouse his spirit with thy persuading? A good thing is the persuasion of a friend." [114]

Michael was no doubt sincere in his program for a more effective manner of teaching Greek, but his proposed change in educational method must be viewed in the general context of his aim of advancing his career and ameliorating his economic condition. In this framework, then, one should perhaps not attach too much importance to such of his phrases as refer to numerous pupils in Crete, more students than other, more experienced teachers had, or to implied references to a regularly established school under his direction on the island. One may smile, moreover, at Michael's naiveté in "threatening" the Italians that he would open a school in Italy through his own efforts in the event they should refuse him the position he requested.

Despite the more practical considerations actuating Michael's composition of the discourse, we must admit that some of his ideas are not without importance, even a certain originality — especially the notion of teaching Greek "in Greek" and not via the Latin language, as was then evidently the prevailing practice in the West. It would be interesting to speculate what impact his theories might have had on contemporary methods of pedagogy had his ideas been seriously considered by the contemporary Italian humanists.[115] A leading modern scholar believes that there is much truth, acuteness, and modernity to be found in Michael's program, and today in the mid-twentieth century we have increasing evidence that foreign languages can successfully be taught to students in the original language at a very early age. In his proposed method of teaching Greek Michael was evidently ahead of his time, if we are to judge from the well-known treatise of the learned son of the great Guarino of Verona, Battista Guarino, "Upon the method of teaching and of reading the classical authors," in which the implication is clear that the teaching of Greek in Greek is impossible. Over a quarter of a century later one of the greatest Greek scholar-

[114] From Homer, *Iliad*, XI, 792–93.

[115] Aldus, who understood the difficulties of teaching Greek, later (1515) made a similar type of suggestion for the instruction of that language in the original, saying that in order to learn Greek well students should practice memorizing and copying out long passages in Greek. See Firmin-Didot, *Alde Manuce*, 366.

exiles, Marcus Musurus, would still be teaching Greek to his students at Padua via Latin translations.[116]

Michael's letters shed little light on the last part of his life. With almost no information available, we may therefore leave him vegetating a few years longer in Crete, perhaps amusing himself with occasional trips through the island to visit friends or to participate in religious festivals. A pathetic picture is drawn by the pen of his son Arsenios, who relates that Michael's last years were saddened by his long suffering from an incurable disease which did not permit him to work — a harsh fate for one financially dependent on his talents as a copyist.[117] The final notice we have of Michael is provided by a manuscript dated 1474, which is in his own hand.[118]

The date of his death is unknown. Noiret, Salaville, and others, with evidently no supporting evidence, have fixed on approximately 1480, overlooking, it seems, the possibility of his still living in 1486, in view of the appearance of his verses in the *Batrachomyomachia*, printed in that year in Venice by his pupil Laonikos the Cretan.[119] A dreamer to the end, Michael composed for himself the following epitaph, a kind of rationalization for the frustrations of his career, which seems to sum up what he would have liked his life and death actually to have been:

Issue of an indigenous stock of ancestors, Michael, who has lived independently without bowing his head before anyone, has fled to the

---

[116] For brief comments on Michael's discourse, see Rossi, *Il Quattrocento*, 91–92. For an English translation of Guarino's treatise, see Woodward, *Vittorino da Feltre*, 161–78. Guarino believed, contrary to the advice of the Roman Quintilian, that it was virtually impossible to teach Greek beginning with Greek instead of Latin because, as he put it, Greek is a learned, not a colloquial, language. For additional information on the humanist method of teaching Greek, see R. Sabbadini, *Il Metodo degli umanisti* (Florence, 1920) 17–29. On Musurus' method see Chapter 5, text and notes 105–106. The modern, so-called "conversational" method of teaching languages resembles what Apostolis suggests.

[117] See Arsenios' letter to Pope Leo X in C. Walz, ed., *Arsenii Violetum* ('Αρσενίου 'Ιωνιά) (Stuttgart, 1832) 1: καὶ νόσῳ ἀνηκέστῳ περιπεσών. Regarding religious festivals, Michael wrote verses (see B. Laourdas, "Μιχαὴλ 'Αποστόλη ἀνέκδοτα ἐπιγράμματα," 'Επετηρὶς 'Εταιρείας Βυζαντινῶν Σπουδῶν, XX [1950] 177–200, entitled "Στίχοι ἡρωϊκοὶ καὶ ἰαμβικοὶ καὶ ἐλεγειακοὶ εἰς διαφόρους ἑορτάς."

[118] Noiret, *Lettres*, 27.

[119] Theory of Legrand, *Bibliographie hellénique*, I, 7. The validity of this view of course depends on whether it was customary to print in this manner only the verses of living authors. See also Noiret, 24.

isles of the blest, to enjoy happiness forever with his many friends —
as is just.[120]

What may be said in evaluation of the career of Michael
Apostolis? He was not an outstanding figure, always overshadowed
by the more successful Greek expatriates. He never realized his
ambition to settle in the West. Nor was he in a position to put his
educational views into practice. His appeal for a crusade bore no
fruit. Were it not for his correspondence, most of the details of
his life would hardly be remembered. We would know him only
as the copyist of numerous manuscripts contained in Bessarion's
collection and other European libraries.[121] And yet because of the
valuable codices he collected or copied, his influential collection
of proverbs, and the fact that at Candia, which under his influence
was becoming an important center of calligraphic activity, he
taught at least two Cretans intimately connected with the development of Greek learning in Venice, the pioneer Greek editor
Laonikos and Aldus' instructor Emmanuel Adramyttenos, Michael
serves as an important connecting link between the Hellenism of
Crete and the rising interest in Greek studies in Venice. Michael
therefore stands forth as representative of an era of transition. Indeed, as we may gather from his writings, he himself realized that
he was living at a turning point in history. Cultural leadership, he
believed, was passing from the dying Byzantine world to the rising
humanistic centers of Italy. But to his way of thinking, the Italians,
though heralding the dawn of a new age, were merely the heirs of
the Greeks, whose superior culture had never been surpassed.

These views of Michael's are most clearly expressed in a speech
he wrote not long after Constantinople's fall, entitled "Michael
Apostolis to those who claim that the Westerners are superior to

[120] For the Greek text see Legrand, I, p. lxvi. On the date of his death also see
Legrand, and Salaville, *Dict. d'hist. géog. eccl.*, 1030; also cf. Lobel, *The Greek
Manuscripts of Aristotle's 'Poetics'*, 13.

[121] For the location of his manuscripts see Vogel and Gardthausen, *Die griechischen Schreiber*, 305–10. Besides Venice, Paris, and the Vatican contain a considerable number; for example, a magnificent Eusebius (*De praeparatione evan-
gelica*), copied in Michael's hand, is now in the Vatican (see Nolhac, *La Bibliothèque de Fulvio Orsini*, 148). Interestingly enough, the *Batrachomyomachia*
(1486), probably the first Greek book published by Greeks (Laonikos the Cretan)
in Venice, includes verses of Apostolis. See Legrand, I, p. lxx and cf. Chapter 3,
text and note 18.

the Easterners with respect to the whole of philosophy and that
they [the Westerners] explain perfectly the first birth of Christ
and the procession of the Holy Spirit." [122] Responding to the claim
of the superiority of the Western view on this particular point of
theology, Michael seizes the opportunity emphatically to affirm the
primacy of the Greek intellect:

Did you understand therefore how great a difference there is in theology and in the other branches of philosophy between the Greek and
the European [Western] fathers? Would you not make obeisance before the Easterners who have discovered the beauty of letters and of
philosophy itself? Who among the Europeans is wiser than Socrates,
Timaeus, and Pythagoras? Who among the Westerners is equal to
Plato and Aristotle and Zeno; who equal to Herodotus, Thucydides,
and Xenophon? Who can rival Antiphon, Hyperides, and Demosthenes? Who can be compared with Orpheus, Homer, and Stesichorus
in poetry; who with Plotinus, Proclus, and Porphyry; with Arius,
Origen, and Eusebius, men [i.e., heretics] who have split the seam of
Christ's garment? Who can be compared with Cyril, Gregory, and
Basil; who, in the field of grammar, can equal or approach Herodian,
Apollonius, and Trypho?
I think you might say Cicero, the savant, and the poet Vergil. But
as the saying goes, "Not even Hercules can vanquish two men!" Much
less the [Westerners] in comparison with two thousand men [of the
East]. "But we [Westerners]," you may say, "have more than two
thousand." I agree completely, and I have even anticipated such an
answer. But do you not understand that Athens alone of all Greece
was able to give birth to more philosophers than all Italy had or has?
Now, however, I admit, we are the remnants of the Greeks, a view
with which you of course agree willingly.
You Italians of the present age are the foremost (ta prota) of the
Italians. I say that you are the foremost and that we are the remnants
(ta leipsana) because, in the cycle of civilization, which has a beginning, a middle, and an end, we are in the closing stage of our culture,

[122] Discourse published by B. Laourdas under title "Μιχαὴλ 'Αποστόλη Λόγος περὶ
'Ελλάδος καὶ Εὐρώπης," 'Επ. 'Ετ. Βυζ. Σπ., XIX (Athens, 1949) 235-244. This discourse was written in answer to the views of one who was probably a Greek
Uniate. (Note that Michael here defends Greek theology, though he himself was
a Uniate). See D. Geanakoplos, "A Byzantine Looks at the Renaissance: The Attitude of Michael Apostolis toward the Rise of Italy to Cultural Eminence," Greek
and Byzantine Studies, I (1958) 157-162. Patrinelis, "Νόθα," no. 5, 207-208, shows
that this speech is sometimes referred to as "Περὶ ἐκπορεύσεως τοῦ 'Αγίου πνεύματος."
According to Patrinelis, Apostolis probably wrote no discourse on the procession
of the Holy Spirit; in any case, none upholding the Latin viewpoint (though of
course he was a fervent Uniate).

while you are in the first phase. And we are enslaved whereas you are free. Yet though we are in such a condition, one can observe, now as well as in the past, that throughout all Italy many Greeks are teaching Latin to Westerners. No one, however, has ever seen or heard a Westerner teaching Greek in Greece. And even if anyone can or should desire to do so it would be impossible, as the ruler of the Turks [Huns] has devoured all Greece and is now already seeking to enslave Europe.

May he be destroyed by God who has permitted him to become so strong and sated with our blood. O Christ-Emperor, stop him, stay his violence and deflect his knife and spear. Have pity on us, be merciful, reconcile yourself with us and watch over us who are again like the lost drachma.[123] Recall our scattered race, so downtrodden and humble. Grant to your servants of the West concord, strength, and force of will, zeal and mercy. Remove from us the bitter executioner and enemy; grant harmony to all who bear the name of Christ even if this hitherto has been impossible. But now let them [the Christians] enjoy concord because of the Turks, who commit evil acts without ceasing and tread upon your holy vessels, insulting the pure faith and the church itself, to which you have promised, "Nor can the gates of Hell prevail over the Church." [124] Yours is the will when you will, yours the strength when the time is worthy, yours the honor, glory, and strength throughout the centuries.[125]

The excerpts taken from this speech — especially the moving last section, which is so different in tone from many of Michael's other writings — epitomize for us the paradox of his life, that of an impoverished Byzantine rhetorician of rather exaggerated but not ignoble sentiments, caught between the old world and the new. Unable to adapt himself to the realities of changing conditions, Michael nevertheless from his asylum in Crete contributed no little to make possible the emergence of a cultural synthesis combining the new and youthful spirit of the Italian Renaissance with the older disciplined learning of Byzantium.

[123] Luke 15:8.
[124] Matthew 16:18-19.
[125] Doubtless these are phrases taken from the Greek ecclesiastical tradition. The concluding paragraph is a kind of appeal — and a moving one — to a higher unity of all Christendom, Western as well as Eastern, without regard to political or religious differences.

Chapter 5

MARCUS MUSURUS

*Cretan Editor with the Aldine Press and
Professor at Padua University*

O F THE MANY CRETANS who went to the West and achieved
recognition in intellectual circles, the most influential, certainly
the most productive in terms of the works he edited, was Marcus
Musurus.[1] From Crete, his relatively short but many-faceted career
as student, editor, and teacher of a host of Western Hellenists was
to take him to Florence, then Venice, and ultimately to Rome —
three centers whose leadership in humanistic endeavors coincided
with the period of his residence there.

Practically nothing is known of Musurus' earliest years. Even
his place of birth is uncertain, though it would seem to be Candia,
capital of Crete rather than the western Cretan town of Rethymnon,
as some have believed.[2] The date of his birth is generally cited by

---

[1] Musurus' life has been treated by Legrand, *Bibliographie hellénique*, I, pp.
cviii–cxxiv and especially by R. Menge, "Vita Marci Musuri" (in Latin), in M.
Schmidt, *Hesychii Alexandrini Lexicon* (Jena, 1868) V, 1–57. But Legrand's
treatment is brief, while Menge's, though very useful and fuller in many respects,
has certain deficiencies: virtually exclusive focus on the problem of Musurus'
printed editions and relationship with Aldus (for example, little discussion of his
teaching career and nothing on the early Florentine phase of his life); inability to
benefit from the work of subsequent researchers; and lack of integration with the
larger intellectual developments of the period. Firmin-Didot, *Alde Manuce* has
made no attempt to write a connected biography of Musurus, though the remarks he makes and his publication of Musurus' letters are very helpful (see esp.
460–65). His French translations, however, are much too free and often interpolate
meanings not to be found in the original texts. Articles on specific aspects of
Musurus' career are cited below.

[2] See undocumented reference to Rethymnon in the often unreliable work of
Papadopoli, *Historia gymnasii patavini*, I, 294, followed by Legrand, I, p. cviii;

scholars as approximately 1470, an assumption based on a later statement of his friend Erasmus that he was "scarcely older than Musurus." [3] Marcus came of an old Cretan family presumably engaged
in the pursuit of commerce.[4] He always felt a sense of pride in his
Cretan ancestry, and to the members of his immediate family we
know that he was deeply devoted.[5]

A master of both Greek and Latin, Marcus must have begun his
formal education early. Unfortunately, little information is available on the Cretan phase of his training. Possibly Musurus pursued
studies in the monastery school of St. Catherine of Sinai at Candia;[6]
very probably he studied privately with Arsenios, son of Michael
Apostolis. We know definitely that John Gregoropoulos was a
fellow student,[7] and the intimate correspondence between the two
provides an important source for the career of Marcus.[8]

Menge, 8; Firmin-Didot, 460, 545. Cf. Manousakas, "Gregoropoulos Correspondence," 193, n. 3, citing a letter (Legrand, II, 394) showing that in boyhood Musurus
was a fellow student of John Gregoropoulos at Candia under Arsenios Apostolis.
When I was in Rethymnon I was shown a street called that of Marcus Musurus,
and a house which, tradition has it, belonged to Marcus' father. But these afford
no proof that Marcus was actually born in Rethymnon.

[3] See P. S. and H. M. Allen, Opus epistolarum Des. Erasmi Roterodami (Oxford, 1906–1958) V, 245 (cited hereafter as Epistolae Erasmi), and F. Nichols, Epistles of Erasmus (London, 1904) I, 450. Even Erasmus' year of birth is uncertain,
but it is generally fixed at 1467.

[4] For reference to their commercial activity see Papadopoli, 294. Following him
are Menge, 8; Sathas, Neohellenic Philology, 80; Firmin-Didot, 460.

[5] On his family and the name "Musurus," see Gerland, "La noblesse Crétoise,"
232. Also see Chapter 6, on Arsenios, note 41. Modern authorities have made
various errors with respect to Musurus' family: e.g., Firmin-Didot, 499, refers to
John and Manuel Gregoropoulos as beau frères of Marcus, and Sathas, 84, alludes
to John as brother of Musurus and member of the Aldine Academy. Actually
no relationship existed between Musurus and the Gregoropoulos family (Legrand,
Bibliographie hellénique, II, 264, n. 1). Marcus evidently had a sister, according
to Sathas, 81, who quotes a document mentioning the appointment, near the end
of Musurus' life, of his nephew Manoussos Sacellarios, to act as administrator of
his ecclesiastical estates in Crete and Cyprus. See below, text and note 166.

[6] Cf. Chapter 2, text and note 16.

[7] See Legrand, I, p. civ, and M. Wittek, "Manuscrits et Codicologie," Scriptorium, VII (1953) 292. Also see Marcus' letter (of October 1502) to Gregoropoulos (in Legrand, II, 394, and cf. Manousakas, "Gregoropoulos Correspondence,"
201, and Menge, 73), in which Musurus speaks of "the deacon, the instructor of
our youth" (probably Arsenios). But cf. Firmin-Didot, 456, who says, probably
mistakenly, that their teacher in Crete was rather Justin Decadyos. Firmin-Didot,
532, also prints a letter from Arsenios to Gregoropoulos in which Arsenios signs
himself "Your zealous deacon Aristoboulos [Arsenios]" (cf. Manousakas, "Gregoropoulos Correspondence," 201). See also Chapter 6, note 8.

[8] Gregoropoulos evidently saved his own correspondence. Unlike many others
of the Cretan scholars he did not later go to Rome, where so many letters were

Early in life, probably still in boyhood, Marcus Musurus went
to Italy. That he remained there for some time alone — though his
father may originally have accompanied him — would seem evident from one of his letters to Gregoropoulos, in which he speaks
of his mother and father as residing in Crete.[9] Unlike so many of
the scholars of Greek extraction in the West, Musurus is not to be
thought of as a refugee fleeing the Turkish yoke, but as a voluntary
exile from his homeland. In this period of Venetian hegemony over
Crete, the senate of Venice was in the habit of drawing promising
Cretan youths to the city to further their education [10] and probably at the same time to inculcate in them a feeling of allegiance to
Venice. Musurus may well have been one of these young men.

Toward 1486, at perhaps the early age of sixteen,[11] Musurus
went to Florence, then experiencing her Golden Age under the
aegis of the Medici prince Lorenzo the Magnificent. The city
swarmed with noted Byzantine and Western scholars, among them
the Constantinople-born poet and intimate of Lorenzo, Michael
Marullus Tarchaneiotes,[12] the famous Neoplatonist Marsilio Ficino,
then in his fifties, and the aged Athenian exile Demetrios Chalcondyles, who held the chair of Greek in Florence until 1491. Another attraction for the young Musurus may well have been the

---

lost in the sack of 1527. At Gregoropoulos' death his letters went to the humanist
John Conon, who willed them to Beatus Rhenanus. See A. Oleroff, "L'humaniste
Dominicain Jean Conon et le Crétois Jean Grégoropoulos," *Scriptorium*, IV (1950)
104-7. On the correspondence of the Gregoropouloi see Manousakas, 156-206.
   [9] Letter in Legrand, II, 316-19; for a French translation see Firmin-Didot, 30-35,
esp. 32. This letter is undated but written from Carpi, probably between 1499
and 1503 (on the residence of Musurus' parents in Candia, Crete, cf. Manousakas,
193, n. 2). The article on Musurus in *Biographie Universelle*, new ed. (Paris, 1843-
1865) XXIX, 655, says that his father originally accompanied him to Italy, but
cites no source. See Chapter 7, text and note 5, for an episode occurring years later
in Padua at which Erasmus, Musurus, and the latter's father were all present.
Erasmus playfully referred to himself and Musurus' father as "old men."
   [10] Menge, 9-10.
   [11] See text for note 15, especially the phrase regarding Janus Lascaris' guidance of "my infant steps." See also Legrand, *Bibliographie hellénique*, II, 312 (cf.
I, p. cix and French translation in Firmin-Didot, 517), for a letter of Marcus to
Calliergis referring to a manuscript of Galen which he (Musurus) copied in
Florence, "being still young." Lascaris was considerably older than Musurus, having been called to Italy by Bessarion before 1472.
   [12] See B. Croce, *Michele Marullo Tarcaniota* (Bari, 1938) and D. Zakythinos,
"Μιχαὴλ Μάρουλλος Ταρχανιώτης," Ἐπετηρὶς Ἑταιρείας Βυζαντινῶν Σπουδῶν, V (1928)
200-42. For his Latin poems see the edition of A. Perosa, *Michaelis Marulli Carmina* (Zurich, 1951).

presence of Chalcondyles' protégé, the Constantinopolitan Janus Lascaris,[13] a consummate master of both Greek and Latin, who at this time or a few years later was giving public lectures in Greek in the Tuscan metropolis.[14]

Marcus has left us, as testimonial of his devotion to, and study with, Lascaris, several verses which constitute part of his famous poem to Plato (written some years later):

> The first from Graecia, of distinguished fame,
> To whom, derived from Lascar's noble race,
> The triple-fronted God concedes his name.
> 'Twas he my infant steps, with ceaseless care,
> Guarded, and loved me with a parent's love;
> He bade me to the Muse's hill repair,
> And pointed out the glorious meed above.[15]

Whether Lascaris taught Marcus Greek, Latin, or both, or, as a recent biographer of Lascaris affirms, was chiefly responsible for starting Marcus on the difficult road to mastery of Greek poetry,[16] is not definitely determinable. But we may derive some idea of the content of Lascaris' instruction from the record of a lecture of his that is still extant. According to this lecture, Janus in the previous

---

[13] See Knös, *Janus Lascaris*, 25. It is unlikely that Musurus had already studied with Lascaris in Crete, though it seems true that Lascaris had several times resided briefly on the island. See Chapter 6, text and note 11, regarding a contract in Crete in which both Lascaris and Arsenios are listed. Papadopoli, *Historia gymnasii patavini*, II, 187 (again without citing his source) says that after fleeing Constantinople Janus Lascaris stopped for a time in Crete; but this would be long before Musurus' birth. Knös, 20–21, believes that some of Papadopoli's sources may have been lost.

[14] A fellow student of Musurus' during his study with Lascaris was the Greek Michael Trivolis, who was later to have a remarkable career in Italy and subsequently in Muscovite Russia. See E. Denissoff, *Maxime le grec et l'Occident* (Paris-Louvain, 1943), esp. 150. It is not clear if Lascaris and Chalcondyles were giving public lectures at the same time in Florence. Also see G. Papamichael, Μάξιμος ὁ Γραικός (Athens, 1951) 31ff.

[15] English translation from W. Roscoe, *The Life and Pontificate of Leo X* (Liverpool, 1805) II, 243. Greek original in Aldine ed. of Plato, dated 1513; see below. "Triple-fronted" is in the original.

[16] Knös, *Janus Lascaris*, 27; see also Wittek, "Manuscrits et Codicologie," 292. Firmin-Didot, *Alde Manuce*, 460, says Musurus studied Latin under Lascaris; G. Tiraboschi, *Storia della letteratura italiana* (Modena, 1792) VII, pt. III, 1094, believes Musurus learned *both* Greek and Latin from Lascaris (cf. Menge, "Vita Marci Musuri," 9). Papadopoli, *Historia gymnasii patavini*, I, 294, says Marcus learned Greek in Crete and Latin in Venice. The truth probably lies in a combination of all these opinions.

year had undertaken to comment on Sophocles and Thucydides and now intended to "interpret" Demonsthenes and the famous collection of Greek epigrams called the *Greek Anthology*.[17]

Marcus' study with Lascaris continued at least until 1490 or 1491, when, by commission of Lorenzo, Janus departed for the Greek East to search for and bring back Greek manuscripts.[18] This Florentine period extending from about 1486 to 1493 [19] must have been very formative in the educational and social development of the young Musurus, since he was exposed to the leading cultural movements of the time and moved in a select intellectual circle.[20]

Sometime before his final departure from Florence, Musurus seems to have returned to Crete to visit his family.[21] The journey to Crete, perhaps made at the same time as Lascaris' voyage to the East, was soon followed by Musurus' decision to leave Florence permanently. The reasons for his departure can best be understood in the context of the gradual political decline of Florence after the death in 1492 of the great humanist patron Lorenzo, along

[17] Cited in Legrand, *Bibliographie hellénique*, I, p. cxxxii (from the old work of H. Vast, *De vita et operibus Jani Lascaris* [Paris, 1878]). Cf. J. Hutton, *The Greek Anthology in Italy to the Year 1800* (Ithaca, 1935) 36–37, who places Lascaris' lecture in 1493. The *Anthology* was a collection of Greek epigrams evidently gathered by the late thirteenth century Byzantine Maximos Planudes, who had abridged and rearranged, with a few additions, the anthology of the tenth century Byzantine Cephalas (Sandys, *History of Classical Scholarship*, I, 427).

[18] Legrand, I, p. cxxiv, gives April or May 1491 as the date of this second voyage of Lascaris to the east, the first being in 1489 or 1490. See now Knös, *Janus Lascaris*, 34, and especially the old but valuable work of K. Müller, *Neue Mittheilungen über Janos Laskaris und die Mediceische Bibliothek, Centralblatt für Bibliothekswesen*, I (1884) 346ff.

[19] See Nolhac, *La bibliothèque de Fulvio Orsini*, 150, who adduces evidence that Marcus was still in Florence in 1493 on the basis of a fly leaf of an autograph manuscript of Musurus bearing the words (in Greek): "This book belongs to Musurus and all who use it." Cf. Wittek, *"Scriptorium* de M. Apostolès," 292.

[20] Weiss, *Biographie universelle*, XXIX, 656, n. 2, affirms that in 1491 Musurus corrected Ficino's translation of Plato, but few scholars have accepted or even noted this theory. (Legrand, for example, makes no mention of it). For the complicated history of this translation of Ficino see P. Kristeller, *Supplementum Ficinianum* (Florence, 1937–45), I, p. cxlviiiff.

[21] Journey deduced by Legrand, I, p. cix, from a letter (undated as to year but probably referring to September 14) of George Gregoropoulos to his son John. But cf. Manousakas, "Gregoropoulos Correspondence," 180, n. 3, who does not accept this. However, Foffano, "Marco Musuro Professore di Greco a Padova e a Venezia," *Nuovo archivio veneto*, III (1892) 455, includes a letter announcing Marcus' return. Foffano's view is that Marcus visited Crete while Lascaris was in the east.

with the complete dislocation of the Medici regime and the rise to power of the austere Dominican monk Savonarola.[22]

While Florence was producing its literary and philosophic masterpieces of the late Quattrocento, the ground was being prepared in Venice for a great flowering of Greek learning. Closely associated with this movement is the name of the printer Aldus Manutius. Because of the importance of his press for the development of Venetian intellectual life and, in particular, as a setting for much of Musurus' work, the early phase of Aldus' career will be summarized here.

Aldus Manutius, born in 1449 at Bassiano in the province of Rome, revealed early in his career a strong bent toward classical studies.[23] He learned Latin in Rome probably under Gaspar Veronensis. Greek he studied at Ferrara under Battista Guarino (son of that noted educator Guarino of Verona, who had gone to Constantinople to master Greek) and then at Mirandola under the young Cretan scholar and pupil of Michael Apostolis, Emmanuel Adramyttenos.[24] It was through the recommendation of the famous humanist Pico della Mirandola that Aldus moved to Carpi, in Lombardy, in order to become tutor to Pico's nephews, the young princes of the principality, Alberto and Lionello Pio.[25] Aldus became an intimate friend of the brothers, and it was during his stay

[22] Note the case of Janus Lascaris himself, who left Florence after the French invasion in 1494 to accompany the French king to Paris, where he taught Greek and later became envoy of the French ruler to Venice. See Knös, *Janus Lascaris*, 80.

[23] For the fullest account of Aldus' career see Firmin-Didot, *Alde Manuce*. This work, however, focusing almost entirely on his publications, is very spotty and frequently inaccurate. Cf. also Ferrigni, *Aldo Manuzio*. A. Renouard, *Annales de l'imprimerie des Aldes*, 3 vols. (Paris, 1825; 3rd ed., 1834), is the best account of the publications of the Aldine Press. For a full bibliography see L. Donati, "Bibliografia Aldina," *La Bibliofilia*, LII (1950) 188–204, and E. Pastorello, *L'epistolario Manuziano* (Florence, 1957). Works pertinent to our subject, especially on the Aldine Academy, are cited below, *passim*.

[24] On Adramyttenos, whose influence on Western humanists such as Aldus and Pico della Mirandola is insufficiently appreciated, see H. Semper, *Carpi: Ein Fürstensitz der Renaissance* (Dresden, 1882) 19, n. 107; Firmin-Didot, 7; and especially Noiret, *Lettres*, 155ff., for a rather abusive discourse of Michael Apostolis against Adramyttenos, formerly his favorite pupil. We learn also (156–57) that Adramyttenos studied as a boy seven years with Michael, including reading the Greek poets and orators. Also see Laourdas, "Μιχαὴλ ᾿Αποστόλη, ᾿Ανέκδοτα ᾿Επιγράμματα," 172–208, esp. 173–174.

[25] On Carpi and the two brothers see Semper, *Carpi*.

at Carpi that he conceived his remarkable plan to establish a press with the principal aim of printing, systematically and for the first time, correct editions of all the more important Greek authors.[26]

This was certainly a praiseworthy, if ambitious, design, for in this period of avid interest in classical antiquity no press yet established had been primarily devoted to such a purpose.[27] Indeed, before the opening of the Aldine press in 1494–95,[28] only a dozen Greek books had been printed in all of Italy,[29] despite the rapid development of the art of printing. Moreover, the now firmly established Turkish occupation of the Greek East was threatening the loss or destruction of many priceless codices.

Only one city could fulfill all the demands of a Greek press in this period — Venice — and it is to Aldus' credit that he was able to resist the urgings of his friends to set up his press in their palace at Carpi [30] and proceeded instead to Venice. Of all the Italian cities, Venice possessed the greatest fund of experience in printing. As we have seen, the city's first press had been established in 1469,[31] and of the numerous books printed in Italy before 1500, over one half

[26] It was about the same time that the Cretan Zacharias Calliergis also founded his press (unlike that of Aldus, it was *exclusively* devoted to Greek publication), but Aldus was able to issue works before him. See Chapter 7, on Calliergis, text and notes 12–14.

[27] See also, note 65.

[28] Renouard, *Annales*, I, 2–3, cites the year 1494, though Scholderer, *Catalogue of Books Printed in the XV Century*, V, p. li, says 1495. Aldus' first definitely dated work is the Lascaris of 1495; his publications of the *Galeomyomachia* and Musaeus' *De Herone et Leandro*, were, however, probably trial efforts and may well have appeared in 1494. The question of date also involves the problem of calculation according to the Venetian calendar. See Renouard, I, 2–3, and Proctor, *Printing of Greek*, 94.

[29] Sandys, *History of Classical Scholarship*, II, 97, lists these publications: the Greek grammars of Constantine Lascaris (Milan, 1476; Vicenza, 1488 [1489, says Proctor, 156]), and Manuel Chrysoloras (Venice, 1484 [Florence, according to Legrand]; Vicenza, 1490); two Psalters (Milan, 1481–86); Aesop (Milan, ca. 1479); Theocritus (Milan, ca. 1493); the "Battle of the Frogs and Mice" [*Batrachomyomachia*] (Venice, 1486); Homer (Florence, 1488); Isocrates (Milan, 1493); and the *Greek Anthology* (Florence 1494). (Sandys omits specific mention of the Venice psalter, 1486, done by the Cretan Alexander; see Chapter 3, text and note 19.) Thus prior to Aldus' first publication in 1494–95, very few Greek texts had been published. Cf. C. Castellani, *La Stampa in Venezia* (Venice, 1889) 37.

[30] They offered him financial support; moreover Carpi, though small, was then a rather remarkable humanist center. See esp. Semper, *Carpi*; also Castellani, 39; and Ferrigni, *Aldo Manuzio*, 82.

[31] On the date, see Chapter 3, note 13.

were produced in Venice.[32] It was thus reasonable to assume that skilled printers would be available.

Of further importance to Aldus must have been Venice's possession of several great libraries, especially that of St. Mark (Marciana), the nucleus of which was the great collection of manuscripts bequeathed to Venice by Bessarion.[33] Significant too, as we have seen, was the tradition of Greek studies established earlier in the fifteenth century (for example, in connection with Francesco and Ermolao Barbaro) and the instruction in Greek offered by Giorgio Valla and others. The presence nearby of the University of Padua, from certain points of view now one of the foremost universities of western Europe, was also important.[34] No small consideration in the thinking of the practical-minded Aldus, of course, must have been the economic prosperity of Venice as the center of a large and still flourishing empire, a fact able to guarantee a class sufficiently wealthy and with enough leisure to buy and read the printed classics.[35]

With Aldus' primary emphasis on the publication of Greek works, of considerable importance was the presence in Venice of a large, thriving Greek community, the history of which has been

[32] See V. Scholderer, *Printers and Readers in Italy in the Fifteenth Century*, in *Proceedings of the British Academy*, XXXV (1949) 6–7, n. 1, who believes that the figures of 5,000 books published in Italy and 2,835 in Venice before 1500, as cited by Sandys, II, 97, are far too low and that Venice instead put out 4,500 editions before 1500 (one-seventh of all Europe.)

[33] On Bessarion and his library see especially Omont, "Manuscrits Grecs et Latins donnés à Saint-Marc de Venise," 130, who says about 500, but the catalog he cites numbers 482 (pp. 149–69). Also see Chapter 4, esp. text and note 82. Other Venetian libraries, the manuscripts of which were used by Aldus, were those of the nobles Antonio Morosini, Daniel Ranieri, and Alvise Mocenigo (Firmin-Didot, *Alde Manuce*, 421). See also Conclusion, text and notes 20–23, for still other private collections in Venice. On today's Marciana building see note 131 below.

[34] On Padua, which served as the state university of Venice and the center for her empire, see Ferrai, *L'ellenismo di Padova*, 9ff.; Knös, *Janus Lascaris*, 38 (for its libraries of Greek manuscripts); Molmenti, *Venice*, I, 258–67; Papadopoli, *Historia gymnasii patavini* (for its professors and students — though Papadopoli is often unreliable); and most important as a documentary source, J. Facciolati, *Fasti gymnasii patavini*. H. Rashdall, *The Universities of Europe in the Middle Ages* (Oxford, 1936) II, 9–21, is not useful here, as his emphasis is on the earlier period of the University's life.

[35] As late as 1533 Erasmus could refer to Venice as "theatrum totius Italiae splendidissimum" (*Opera Omnia* [Leyden, 1703] I, 1483C). On Venetian luxury and literary interest in the late fifteenth and early sixteenth centuries, see Molmenti, *Venice*, I, esp. 227–30, who lists the many Venetian nobles interested in letters. Cf. Firmin-Didot, *Alde Manuce*, 16–36.

traced in an earlier chapter. Venice's position as the center of empire and traditional port of entry to the West made her the funnel through which passed most of the Greek refugees coming to Italy, a large number of whom, owing to the opportunities presented for employment, chose to remain in the busy metropolis. Thus, as a result of the influence of the more learned of the Greek element, as well as the activities of such Venetian Hellenists as Francesco and Ermolao Barbaro, the more intellectual of the Venetian citizenry were becoming increasingly imbued with an appreciation of the ideals of Hellenic learning. By the first decade of the sixteenth century, in fact, Greek appears to have been more widely known in Venice than anywhere else in the Western world.[36] In view of these considerations, Venice seems to have been the best location for the establishment of a Greek press — and it attests to Aldus' judgment and breadth of vision that he decided to establish himself in the city of the lagoons.

Publication of Greek texts entailed difficulties compared to which the printing of Latin works was relatively easy, and Aldus therefore still had to cope with numerous problems. To begin with, not only had the most authentic manuscripts of a particular author to be sought out from among those in the possession of libraries, perhaps recalcitrant monks, or cantankerous private owners of Italy, the Greek East, or even more distant lands such as Poland,[37] but after the finding of such a work permission had to be obtained to copy, borrow, or, as a last resort, buy it from its owner. Only after these often painful preliminaries could the laborious task of preparing the manuscript for the press begin.

Establishment of the original text was the basic problem. In an era when the science of paleography was in its infancy, this was indeed a slow, difficult process. After the "decipherment" and transcription of the manuscript — frequently from faulty, mutilated, or otherwise unsatisfactory documents — as well as attempts to solve the numerous philological questions that remained, the text would be set in type. Following these steps, the proofs had to

[36] Cf. Knös, 21. Also note the statement of Aldus that Venice could be called "a second Athens" (see below, text and note 124).
[37] In his adage "Festina Lente," in the Froben *Adagia* of 1526 (Chil. II, cent. I, prov. I, 405), Erasmus records that manuscripts were sent to Aldus from Hungary and Poland. Cf. Nichols, *The Epistles of Erasmus*, I, 437.

be read by a person not only skilled in the technical aspects of typography but also familiar with the style of the author in question.

It was while Marcus was still in Florence that Aldus was taking steps to establish his press. We are ignorant of the precise reasons for Musurus' decision to settle in Venice, though the decline of Florence and the attraction exerted by Venice upon its Cretan dependents must have had something to do with it. We have no definite information, moreover, about the circumstances of Musurus' first meeting with Aldus. Of possible bearing on these questions is a letter of Musurus to Gregoropoulos in which he implies that in Venice he hoped to deepen his philological knowledge and acquire some measure of wealth and fame.[38] In any case, Marcus was one of the first and most intimate associates of Aldus. Indeed, it should be noted that it was Musurus who provided the model (perhaps not his own hand) for the cursive Greek type Aldus had cast for his press.[39] Musurus also composed two Greek epigrams that appear in what may well have been Aldus' very first publication, the *editio princeps* of Musaeus' poem "Hero and Leander," ascribed by some scholars to 1494.[40] The Latin translation accompanying the Greek text of Musaeus' verses is usually attributed to Musurus.[41]

[38] Letter published in Legrand, *Bibliographie hellénique*, II, no. 6, 316ff. (undated). Also see F. Foffano, "Marco Musuro professore di greco a Padova," *Nuovo Archivio Veneto*, III (1892) 460, 461, where he says Marcus may have heard Sabellico and Giorgio Valla lecturing in Latin in Venice. G. Putnam, *Books and Their Makers during the Middle Ages* (New York, 1896) I, 421, thinks the link between Aldus and Musurus may have been Pico della Mirandola, who was an early friend of Musurus. Cf. Firmin-Didot, 460, saying that Musurus perhaps met Aldus at Carpi in the palace of Alberto Pio. Cf. below, text for note 61.

[39] In 1496 Aldus applied to the Venetian Senate for a patent for this cursive type (Brown, *Venetian Printing Press*, 42). C. Bühler, "Aldus Manutius, The First Five Hundred Years," *Papers of the Bibliographical Society of America*, XLIV (1950) 207–8, criticizes the Aldine imitation of the current "hurried hand" because it did not facilitate reading. And Proctor, *Printing of Greek*, 15, goes so far as to say that adoption by Manutius of the current written hand rather than continuation of the old, more uncial type of letters was "disastrous" for the development of Greek printing. Cf. Brown, 46, on Marcus' hand as model.

[40] On the problem of Aldus' initial publications see note 28 above.

[41] See Scholderer, *Catalogue of Books Printed in the XV Century*, 552; and Legrand, *Bibliographie hellénique* I, p. cxi, both of whom support Musurus' authorship of the Latin translation. For an opposing opinion see Menge, "Vita Marci Musuri," 13, who believes that had Musurus done the Latin version of Musaeus, his name would have appeared either in the 1494 or in the later 1517 edition.

There has been some controversy over the exact nature of Musurus' work at the Aldine press. Whereas a few authorities have regarded him exclusively as a corrector of manuscripts already set in type, the more accepted view is that his work consisted of comparing manuscripts and preparing them for publication — in other words. what today would be termed establishing the text.[42] Musurus was therefore an editor — indeed Aldus' chief editor — and as such he was responsible for or collaborated in the preparation of a remarkable number of first editions of basic Greek works.

Musurus' activities in the two or three year period following the Musaeus are not mentioned in the sources. But in December of 1497 he probably finished, for the Aldine press, the preparation of a Greek dictionary, which had originally been compiled by the learned monk Giovanni Crastoni. Crastoni's lexicon, with Latin explanations for the Greek terms, was the first of its kind to appear in western Europe, and, consequently, despite its many defects, it marked a noteworthy attempt to provide a basic tool for the advancement of Greek studies. Musurus reworked the very incomplete material of Crastoni, and the last section of the Aldine version was completed by Aldus himself, in whose honor two quatrains were included.[43]

The first attempt of Musurus at textual editing for which we have positive evidence [44] was the great *editio princeps* of Aristophanes,

[42] See Menge, 13, Legrand, I, p. cxi (who says that though Musurus corrected his own work he is not to be considered a mere proofreader), and Proctor, *Printing of Greek*, 8.

[43] On this lexicon see Menge, 14, and Firmin-Didot, *Alde Manuce*, 92. Crastoni (Crastone or Crestoni), a Carmelite monk of Piacenza, had previously published a Greek psalter in Milan (1481). Roscoe, *Leo X*, II, 268, is probably correct in terming the dictionary of Crastoni so defective that the one of Varinus Favorinus of Camerino (published in 1523; see Chapter 7, text for note 77) should be considered the first really useful Greco-Latin lexicon. (On Byzantine materials from which the Greek lexica printed in the West were frequently drawn, see R. Reitzenstein, *Zur Geschichte der griechischen Etymologika* [Leipzig, 1897].) Aldus himself in his preface to the dictionary decries the incompleteness of the work — he says he hoped to remedy this by his future publication of Suidas, Stephanus Byzantinus, and others. Use of the work was in fact very inconvenient, since it was necessary to look at the end of the volume for the Latin equivalents of the words of the Greek text. Moreover, the pages were unnumbered. See Firmin-Didot, 92–94, and Catalogue of Bibliothèque Nationale, no. 122, p. 259; also Irigoin, *Pindare*, 401.

[44] Musurus himself speaks in his preface of the difficulty and tedium of correcting.

printed in July of 1498. For the readers of this book Musurus composed a lengthy preface addressed to the "Philhellenes," in which, interestingly enough, he commends the nobles of Venice for their growing interest in Greek learning.[45] The precise extent of Musurus' contribution to the publication of this important work is still a matter of dispute. While it has been generally agreed that he was responsible for establishing the text of both comedies and scholia, recent opinion holds that part of the scholia were even composed by him as well. Musurus' prefatory statement says nothing to contradict this view: "Not only did I tire myself collecting the scholia and putting them into order . . . but we were also enabled to correct the proofs." [46] Musurus' next editorial work to appear under the Aldine imprint, in March 1499, was the *Epistolae diversorum philosophorum oratorum rhetorum sex et viginti*, a particularly rich collection of letters attributed to twenty-six classical and early Christian figures, including St. Basil, Libanius the Sophist, Chion the Platonist, Aeschines and Isocrates the orators, Phalaris the tyrant, Brutus the Roman, Apollonius, Julian the Apostate, and others.[47]

With the publication of this collection of epistles, Musurus' association with the Aldine press seems for a time to have ended. In July of 1499 we know that he went to Ferrara, whence he wrote to his fellow Cretan in Venice, Zacharias Calliergis, who had some years before opened his own press in Venice devoted entirely to

[45] Greek text published in B. Botfield, *Praefationes et Epistolae Editionibus Principibus Auctorum Veterum Praepositae* (Canterbury, 1861) 219. Faulty French translation in Firmin-Didot, 107–110.

[46] See Botfield, 220, ll. 28–33, esp. l. 32, which Firmin-Didot completely mistranslates (109, l. 8). Menge, "Vita Marci Musuri," 14; and Legrand, I, p. cix, n. 2, says that the scholia are *not* by Musurus, but that he gathered and put them in order. The edition included nine plays (seven under Musurus' subscription). Aldus had announced in the Greek dictionary of Crastoni that he was publishing ten. The reason a smaller number appeared is probably that Aldus, like other printers of his time, was overly ambitious in his prospectuses and also that not all the necessary Greek manuscripts were available in Venice. For the most recent authoritative view of Musurus' work on Aristophanes, see R. Cantarella, *Aristofane, Le Commedie* (Milan, 1953) II, 72–73, whose view is cited above. On the *Lysistrata* see especially Firmin-Didot, 93, n. 2, and cf. Legrand, I, 50.

[47] Again there is a difference of opinion as to Musurus' precise role: see Menge, 15, Firmin-Didot, 120, and Legrand, I, 53. But in a letter included in the third from the last folio of part 2, Musurus himself indicates that he had arranged the epistles in the order in which he had collected them, edited the text (restoring it in parts) and revised the proofs. He notes that the letters of Alciphron were in particularly bad shape.

Greek publication. From the contents of the letter we gather that Musurus had been sent to Ferrara to obtain manuscripts for Calliergis. From the moment of his arrival, Musurus wrote, he became acquainted with a Ferrarese doctor Nicolò da Lonigo (also called Leoniceno), who showed him certain manuscripts of Galen in his possession. Enclosing a list of these works with their prices, Musurus inquired of Calliergis whether he would care to buy them for publication.[48] Musurus' letter also provides us with the address of Calliergis' press at the time, "at the shop of Luca Antonio the bookseller, next to the *Crucechieri*." [48a]

Musurus remained some three months in Ferrara, as seems indicated by a letter (dated September 7, 1499) which he wrote to his close friend John Gregoropoulos,[49] then a corrector with the press of Calliergis.[50] The importance of this letter lies in its mention of a number of personalities famous in Venetian life and in its revelation of Marcus' feelings toward his homeland. Referring to a recent illness of his, Musurus is saddened, he says, not at the thought of death but at the possibility of dying on foreign soil, far from friends and parents. He inquires "if anyone of our countrymen has arrived [in Venice] recently among you," and also "concerning the fleet of our lords," a probable reference to Venetian arrangements for an expedition against the Turks.[51] He asks if the preparation of the Galen text has yet been undertaken or if Gregoropoulos is still concentrating on the "commentaries" (commen-

[48] Letter in Firmin-Didot, 516, trans., 517. Also see Legrand, II, 312; and on da Lonigo, see especially A. Visconti, *La storia dell' università di Ferrara* (Bologna, 1950) 45, and D. Vitaliani, *Della vita e delle opere di Nicolò Leoniceno* (Verona, 1892).

[48a] Legrand, 312. According to G. Tassini, *Curiosità veneziana*, 6th ed. (Venice, 1933) 31, the "Crucechieri" are the Crociferi; these fathers are nonexistent today in Venice. But the location would be in the Campo de' Gesuiti at the Fundamenta Nuova.

[49] For the letter see Legrand, II, 313, and for a French translation see Firmin-Didot, 519–20; cf. 461.

[50] Firmin-Didot, 30, Legrand, II, 264. Gregoropoulos acted as overseer for the press of Calliergis until it closed temporarily (ca. 1500), at which time Aldus hired him. See below Chapter 7 on Calliergis. Cf. Manousakas, "Gregoropoulos Correspondence," 203 n. 1, on whether John was overseer. The letter to Gregoropoulos was also addressed to the shop "dove si stampa in graeco . . . acante ai Crucechieri" (Legrand, II, 313).

[51] Firmin-Didot, 518: περὶ τῶν ἡμετέρων δεσποτῶν στόλου. Cf. in Denissoff, *Maxime le Grec*, 400–402, a letter of Michael Trivolis to John Gregoropoulos, dated 1499, mentioning war against the Turks and referring to the Greek, George Moschus (see below, note 53).

taries to the ten *Categories* of Aristotle?) "now that Simplicius has been printed." [52] Inquiring about George Moschus he then asks (perhaps ironically) if there is an "overabundance" of correctors at the press of Calliergis. He closes requesting a return letter via Pietro Bembo and sends regards to Calliergis and his associate Nicholas Vlastos.[53]

In the same month, or possibly in August, the press of Calliergis completed its first work, the magnificent *Etymologicum Magnum*. The text, a kind of combination dictionary and encyclopedia [54] compiled by a tenth century Byzantine, itself based on earlier works, was printed in red and black with the elaborate paginal ornamentation typical of Byzantine manuscripts. Calliergis further revealed his national sentiment by choosing as his printer's mark the Byzantine imperial double-headed eagle.[55]

Some have believed that Musurus was the editor of the *Etymologicum Magnum*,[56] but the view has been effectively opposed, and we may believe that Musurus' contribution lay mainly in the advice he gave to the actual editor, Calliergis.[57] Musurus, however, is

---

[52] Galen was first published in 1500 (21 October) by Calliergis, and Simplicius was completed in November 1499, also by Calliergis (see Chapter 7, text and notes 27–30).

[53] Firmin-Didot, 518. For identification of George Moschus, see Legrand, I, p. lxxxix–xc, and II, 313, n. 1. George was the son of John Moschus of Lacedaemon (Sparta) and brother of the learned Demetrius (with whom he is frequently confused). George taught Greek, rhetoric, and medicine in Corfu, and Demetrius instructed in Greek at Ferrara, Mirandola, Venice, as well as at Corfu. Demetrius may have taught Pico Greek. On Vlastos see Chapter 7 on Calliergis.

[54] See edition of T. Gaisford, *Etymologicon Magnum seu verius lexicon saepissime vocabulorum origines indagans ex pluribus lexicis scholiastis et grammaticis anonymi cuiusdam opera concinnatum* (Oxford, 1848), which also contains Musurus' preface and poem on the Cretan role in printing. Also see Reitzenstein, *Griechischen Etymologika*, 212–53.

[55] For reproductions of the marks of Calliergis and his associate Vlastos, see Legrand, *Bibliographie hellénique*, I, 56–58. Also Firmin-Didot, *Alde Manuce*, 546, who emphasizes Calliergis' attempt to reproduce the typical Byzantine manuscript page.

[56] Opinions summarized by Menge, "Vita Marci Musuri," 16–18, especially those of Schöt and Montfaucon.

[57] Menge, 17, is probably right in believing Calliergis to be the editor, on the basis of Musurus' preface, where Musurus refers to the one who prepared the text as "he." (In works that we *know* Musurus edited, he referred to himself in the first person). Legrand, I, p. cxi, however, believes that had the able Calliergis prepared the work, there is no reason for Musurus to have written the preface. Cf. also colophon of work (reproduced in Sathas, *Neohellenic Philology*, 120, and Firmin-Didot, 547) where Calliergis and Vlastos (and also Anna Notaras)

certainly the author of the preface to that work, addressed to the "Friends of letters at Padua," [58] and also of a very interesting poem, which we reproduce here, praising the role of the Cretan technicians, scholars, and patrons in the establishment and early development of the Greek press:

But why should one be amazed at the talents of the Cretans, since it is Athena herself who by order of her father taught them many arts? It is a Cretan who has fashioned the type. It is a Cretan who has joined together the copper letters, a Cretan who inserted the accents one by one. The man who poured the lead was also a Cretan. It is a Cretan [Nicholas Vlastos] who bears the name of Victory (*Nike*) who paid the expenses, and the one who closes this book with these [verses] is also a Cretan [Musurus]. May the Cretan Zeus be favorable to the Cretans. Let us now address another prayer to him: may the name [Nicholas], which the father of the man who provided for the expense of this edition (*choregos*) gave to his son, be prophetic. And may he defeat his rivals [a reference to Aldus, among others?]. Zeus has decreed it; for the sons of sacred Greece may lay claim to Greek printing.[59]

In late 1499 or early 1500 Musurus moved to the small town of Carpi,[60] near Ferrara, in order to become the teacher and companion of studies to Alberto Pio, prince of Carpi and an intimate friend of Aldus. Aldus had preceded Musurus in this position (for which, as noted, he had been selected by the uncle to the Pio brothers Pico della Mirandola), and it was probably Aldus who now recommended his friend to Alberto.[61] At Carpi Musurus' life was, in the early stage, very pleasant, as the letters he wrote at this time

are mentioned but *not* Musurus. On Anna see Chapter 7, note 20, and Chapter 3, text and note 26.

[58] See Chapter 7 on Calliergis, text and note 13. Evidently at this time Musurus already had contacts with Paduan men of letters.

[59] Greek text in Firmin-Didot, 549, with an extremely free, faulty French translation on 550–51. The Greek is also quoted in Gaisford, *Etymologicon Magnum*, cols. I–II. A quatrain by John Gregoropoulos mentioning the work's indebtedness to Vlastos follows Musurus' poem.

[60] Foffano, "Marco Musuro," 460, says in 1500. See letter of John Gregoropoulos to Arsenios Apostolis (Legrand, II, 267 and Manousakas, "Gregoropoulos Correspondence," 193, who dates it 1499 [Dec. 5]), saying Musurus is living in Ferrara (probably meaning Carpi, nearby) "with a lord distinguished in Greek and Latin" (presumably Alberto Pio).

[61] Legrand, I, p. cix, Firmin-Didot, 8. There is disagreement as to precisely where Musurus first met Alberto. Firmin-Didot, 469, says at Carpi (cf. Semper, *Carpi*, 21A). Menge, "Vita Marci Musuri," 21, believes they first met at Aldus' home.

to Gregoropoulos indicate. Once a day Musurus would read with Pio in various types of Greek literature.[62] Otherwise Musurus' time was his own, and he spent many hours perusing the 146 or 147 Greek codices of the extensive Pio library, of which he was curator, as is indicated by the ownership entries in Greek he lovingly inscribed on the books of the collection.[63] He also devoted time to preparing texts and to enjoyable conversation with other educated courtiers of the Pio circle, such as the Spanish scholar Giovanni Montesdocca.[64] For Alberto, at his court in the little feudal principality of Carpi, had taken care to surround himself with a number of learned men, one of whom was his relative Pico della Mirandola.[65]

Musurus was evidently not bound by formal agreement to Pio. As he himself informs us in a letter to Gregoropoulos, he was at liberty to leave at will and go to Padua "to pursue philosophic studies more diligently" or even to return to Crete, which it was still his intention to do in order to take care of his aging parents. In the same letter [66] Musurus indicates that he is becoming a bit

[62] See letter in Legrand, II, 316–19 (cf. French translation in Firmin-Didot, 30–36). Also in Legrand, II, 396 (Firmin-Didot, 214, trans.), Aldus' dedication to Musurus of Statius (August, 1502), in which he says "you diligently taught him [Alberto] *then* Greek letters while he rested from reading theology." At Carpi Marcus translated Alexander of Aphrodisias' commentaries on Aristotle's *Topics*: Cranz, 101.

[63] See G. Mercati, *Codici Latini Pico Grimani Pio* (Vatican, 1938) 62, who says that (perhaps on Aldus' advice and in the aim of publication) Alberto's library of Greek manuscripts was acquired through purchase of the famous Venetian collection of the humanist Giorgio Valla (d. January 1500). Mercati believes that in his capacity as "secretary," Musurus very likely made a catalogue of the library (pp. 58–74, esp. 73). On the Greek manuscripts of Alberto see also J. Heiberg, "Beiträge zur Geschichte Georg Vallas und seiner Bibliothek," *Centralblatt für Bibliothekswesen*, XVI (Leipzig, 1896) 106ff. Musurus too copied manuscripts: on his MSS among the Codices Palatini graeci see A. Biedl, in *Byz. Zeit.*, XXXVII (1937) 36–38.

[64] Mercati, 50. Also on Montesdocca see Nicolao Antonio, *Bibliotheca hispana nova*, I (Madrid, 1783) 745ff.

[65] See especially Semper, *Carpi*, 20, 22. According to Firmin-Didot, *Alde Manuce*, 147, Alberto had a kind of "academy" of savants around him at Carpi, which served as a model for the academy that Aldus had the idea of forming — an important statement if true.

[66] Letter (undated) in Legrand, II, 316–19. Firmin-Didot, 30, dates it a little before the establishment of the Aldine press (1494–95). But Denissoff, *Maxime le Grec*, 90, objects, saying that Gregoropoulos had probably only recently arrived in Venice at the time of a letter sent to him by Michael Trivolis (dated 1499 or, at the latest, probably 1498) and that the earliest letters to Gregoropoulos are dated only 21 August 1497, and 1 October 1497. But this seems wrong now: cf. Manousakas, "Gregoropoulos Correspondence," 172, who dates the first letter to John in Venice in 1495.

bored with the life at Carpi and desires to return to Venice, the one difficulty being his employer's reluctance to lose him.

Sensing Marcus' growing dissatisfaction, Alberto, with the consent of the papal vicars at Bologna, made him the gift of an ecclesiastical property, the land of which was worked by a peasant and operated on the basis of a half-share. The location of the property, away from the city and the tumult of the court, gave Musurus some measure of relaxation and privacy. Musurus was especially pleased, he says, because he was not obliged to submit to ecclesiastical regulation, the property being a benefice that could be held by one in orders or not.[67] Evidently feeling a sense of guilt, he notes that his fellow Greeks may criticize him for having "deserted" his family and homeland. He himself is not earning the money of other Greek teachers in Italy — money that enables them to provide for their families still in Greece. Nevertheless, he feels that his position is not without honor: he is not a servant and lives in close association with a pious prince who admits him to his own table. Moreover, he is loved and respected by all.[68]

In other exchanges between Musurus and Gregoropoulos Musurus excuses himself for not yet visiting Gregoropoulos in Venice, blaming the fact on his lack of resources, especially inability to sell his wheat ("To come to Venice without money is folly"), and also on the condition of Alberto, who has fallen ill during the recent pre-Lenten festivities. Musurus, now openly expressing eagerness to leave Carpi, adds that he hopes soon to find a suitable reason for departure, and requests that future letters be sent to him via Aldus, whose delay in transmitting to him various manuscript sheets puzzles him.[69]

While Musurus was residing at Carpi, he remained in close contact with developments in Venice, which in these years were of

---

[67] According to Legrand, I, p. cx, it was possibly possession of this property and obligation to recite certain prayers every day that inspired Musurus to enter minor orders, but we have no indication of when he might have taken such a step. (Cf. Musurus' statement, in this same letter, that assisting daily at prayers and spiritual exercises was somewhat wearisome to him.)

[68] French translation in Firmin-Didot, 34.

[69] Information drawn from three letters (1) dated 4 April, probably of 1500 (see Legrand, II, 314-15; Firmin-Didot, 509-11, and trans., 511-13); (2) dated 14 March, probably of 1500 (see Firmin-Didot, 513-14, trans. 514-16; Legrand, II, 315); (3) dated April, probably of 1500 (see Firmin-Didot, 507-508, trans. 508; Legrand, II, 316).

significance for the growth of the Greek press and Greek scholarship. In late 1500 Calliergis, for primarily financial reasons, had to suspend publication.[70] Thereupon, at Aldus' urgings, Gregoropoulos, and in all likelihood other Cretans thrown out of work by the closing of Calliergis' press, accepted employment with Aldus.

Probably soon after Aldus' hiring of these skilled Cretan workers — and possibly even in part contingent upon it — there occurred a capital event for the propagation of Greek learning in the West, the formation of the Aldine Academy. Realizing that his ambition of printing the Greek classics was impossible of achievement without the collaboration not only of skilled printers but of men learned in the field of Greek letters, Aldus gathered round him a group of scholars and, in what was soon to become the fashion of the age, created an academy. In conjunction with two friends, Scipio Carteromachus of Pistoia (also known as Forteguerri) and the Cretan John Gregoropoulos, Aldus founded his *Neakademia* (New Academy), the prime function of which was to select the Greek authors to be printed and to seek solutions to the various philological and literary problems involved.[71] Although virtually every important Italian city of the later Renaissance was to possess one or more academies, that of Aldus alone was dedicated entirely to Greek studies.[72] Its constitution (*Neakademias nomos*), which was drawn up in Greek, provided for the exclusive use of that language at all sessions, and in the event of a violation of this rule a fine had to be paid to Aldus.[73] With the money collected, periodic banquets were held in imitation of the Platonic symposia.

In order to aid in the exigencies of the publishing process, the Academy was divided into several sections, with a group of proof

[70] The latest dated publication of Calliergis at this time was the Galen, October 1500. See Firmin-Didot, 562, and below, Chapter 7.

[71] That the Academy members helped in selecting works to be printed seems evident from the inscription often found in Aldine publications "ex academia nostra." Also in many of his prefaces Aldus mentions the names of various persons who suggested works for printing.

[72] Of course the circle of Bessarion in Rome in the mid-fifteenth century had also been devoted to Greek studies, but there Latin translation from the Greek — not publication — was the aim. Moreover, in contrast to the Aldine circle, exclusive use of the Greek language was evidently not prescribed. On the academies see J. Sandys, *Harvard Lectures on the Revival of Learning* (Cambridge, Eng., 1905) 100.

[73] Greek text in Firmin-Didot, 435ff., who says solecisms were not fined! Cf. Erasmus, *De recta pron.* (Basle, 1528), who implies *all* errors were fined.

readers, including a chief reader and a corrector (John Grego-ropoulos headed the correctors) belonging to each. Though each section was carefully organized, the Academy as a whole operated on a rather informal basis. Membership was apparently not fixed, and changes in the roster seem to have been not infrequent.[74] It included some very famous names, the more important of which may here be listed: Prince Alberto Pio of Carpi, Scipio Cartero-machus, Fra Urbano Bolzanio, Battista Egnazio,[75] Girolamo Alean-dro (the "true" founder of the teaching of Greek in Paris, before whom, in his capacity of papal nuncio, Luther would be arraigned at Worms),[76] Pietro Bembo (later secretary to Pope Leo X and cardinal),[77] and Fra Giocondo — all Italian humanist-scholars; Andrea Navagero,[78] Daniele Ranieri, Marino Sanuto (whose famous *Diarii* are a mine of information for the period), and Paolo Canale — Venetian statesmen and nobles;[79] Giovanni da Lucca and Ambrogio Leoni — Italian physicians; and, finally, a large

[74] As is evident from P. de Nolhac, "Les correspondants d'Alde Manuce," *Studi e documenti di storia e diritto*, VIII (1887) 255-99, who includes letters to Aldus from former or absent Academy members.

[75] The Franciscan Urbano Bolzanio of Belluna (b. 1440), tutor of the later Pope Leo X, had traveled in the Greek East and was the author of the first Greek grammar written in Latin (cf. A. Renaudet, *Erasme et l'Italie*, in *Travaux d'Humanisme et Renaissance*, XV [Geneva, 1954] 84, who says it was in Italian) and taught Greek in Venice to a large number of scholars. See Nichols, *Epistles of Erasmus*, I, 441, and G. Tiraboschi, *Storia della letteratura italiana* (Florence, 1809) VI, 1606. Egnazio, a Venetian by origin, was for many years professor of rhetoric at Venice (Nichols, I, 441). There is a good deal on Carteromachus in P. de Nolhac, *La bibliothèque de Fulvio Orsini* (Paris, 1887). See also S. Ciampi, *Memorie di Scipione Carteromaco* (Pisa, 1811). Carteromachus has left us an oration in praise of Greek learning in Venice, given on the inauguration of his public Greek lessons in 1504 (see Menge, "Vita Marci Musuri," 10-11, and esp. Ciampi, 20ff.).

[76] See J. Paquier, *L'humanisme et la réforme: Jérôme Aléandre de sa naissance à la fin de son séjour à Brindes* (Paris, 1900) esp. 37. François Tissard of Amboise had preceded Aleandro by a year in teaching Greek at Paris, but had abandoned his efforts on Aleandro's arrival in 1508. See Paquier, 36-37, and Renaudet, *Préré-forme et humanisme à Paris pendant les premières guerres d'Italie (1494-1517)* 501-503, 509ff. Cf. A. Tilley, *Dawn of the French Renaissance* (Cambridge, Eng., 1918) 262, which is now somewhat dated.

[77] J. Schück, *Aldus Manutius und seine Zeitgenossen in Italien und Deutschland* (Berlin, 1862) 75 and others list Bembo as an Academy member.

[78] On Navagero see Botfield, *Praefationes*, p. xxv, and bibliography in M. Cer-menati, "Un diplomato Naturalista del Rinascimento Andrea Navagero," *Nuovo Archivio Veneto*, XXIV (1912) 164-205. Navagero succeeded Sabellico as librar-ian of the library of St. Mark.

[79] On these three men see especially Firmin-Didot, *Alde Manuce*, 468-70 and 447-48. Also Renaudet, *Erasme et l'Italie*, 82.

group of Greeks: Demetrius Ducas (who, as will be observed, subsequently went to Spain and helped to produce the Greek version of Cardinal Ximenes' famous Polyglot Bible), John Gregoropoulos, and possibly Arsenios Apostolis — all of whom were from Crete,[80] Justin Decadyos of Corfu, and the Constantinopolitan Janus Lascaris, who had assumed Bessarion's role as "protector of the Greeks" and at this time held the high office of French ambassador to the Republic of Venice. Many celebrated names in Western intellectual as well as political history are to be found here.

It is significant that of a total of what have been estimated as some 36 to 39 more or less permanent members,[81] more than a dozen were Greeks, refugees or exiles from the ruins of the Byzantine world, and of these about half were from the island of Crete.[82]

In addition to regular membership, the *Neakademia* on occasion would confer a kind of honorary status on distinguished foreign visitors, who were thus enabled to attend its meetings during the course of their stay in Venice and subsequently return home the richer for their experience. Such was the case of the English physician-humanist Thomas Linacre,[83] and of Erasmus of Rotterdam, whose Venetian experiences constitute the subject of a later chapter of this book. There is reason to believe that other Greeks from the East, and Latin scholars as well, whose names have hitherto been hardly known to historians, were also associated with the Aldine milieu, such as Andreas Anesinus of Corfu and Giovanni Bembo, who in 1502 ate at the table of Aldus and Carter-

---

[80] On Cretan scholars, especially calligraphers, see Firmin-Didot, 579-86, Omont, *Fac-similés des manuscrits grecs des 15ᵉ et 16ᵉ siècles*, and esp. Chapter 2, above. On the question of Arsenios Apostolis, see below, Chapter 6, esp. text and note 60. On John Rhosos' supposed membership see above, page 54f., note 5.

[81] Authorities disagree on the exact number. Firmin-Didot, 148, names 39, the largest number. Renouard, *Annales*, III, 36-38, with 36 names objects, believing probably justifiably, that not every associate of Aldus was an "Academician." Schück, *Aldus Manutius*, 69-84, tends to agree with Renouard, yet their lists are hardly smaller than that of Firmin-Didot. M. Gilmore, *The World of Humanism* (New York, 1952) 190, notes that almost half of the total number were Greek.

[82] Cf. H. de Simons, "Erasmo y sus impresores," *Humanidádes*, XI (1925) 313-19 (a popular article), who says that thirty Greeks lived in the Aldine household. Most of the Academy compositors were Cretans, the head corrector, as noted, being John Gregoropoulos of Crete (Firmin-Didot, 151).

[83] Firmin-Didot, 129-31, and esp. 150.

omachus. Andreas, accredited envoy of Venice, was the good friend of the Venetian noble Giovanni Bembo (not related, evidently, to Pietro Bembo), who made voyages to the Greek East to gather inscriptions for his work, and who studied Greek, probably in Venice, with Arsenios Apostolis and in Corfu with John Moschus.[83a]

Despite Legrand's hesitation, it is probably safe to include Musurus as a regular member of this Academy. The argument that Musurus' residence in Carpi, and later in Padua, precluded such membership collapses when one considers that Musurus was able to leave Carpi on a number of occasions. In 1502, for example, we know that he visited Lascaris in Milan and Pavia,[84] and indeed often accompanied Pio on various journeys. Aldus himself indicates that Musurus was frequently in Venice. In his prefatory epistle to Musurus in his publication of Statius (dated August 1502), Aldus says, "We are publishing the index to the work under your name, most learned Musurus, because you have participated with me in so much work when you came into our academy from Prince Alberto of Carpi, whom you were teaching Greek." [85] When one recalls in addition the cases of Janus Lascaris, Aleandro, and Alberto Pio — all of whom did not reside continuously in Venice but are generally accepted as "commuting" members of the Academy — there seems little reason to exclude Musurus.[86]

[83a] See Bembo's letter to Anesinus, dated 1536 (ed. Th. Mommsen), in *Sitzungsb. d. bayerischen Akad.*, 1861, 584ff., where it is published as an autobiography of Bembo. Cf. below, Chapter 6, note 39a. Previously published in extract form and commented upon, with many errors, by I. Morelli, *Operette di Iacopo Morelli*, II (Venice, 1820) 37–59. For the MS see C. Halm and G. Meyer, *Catalogus codicum latinorum Bibliothecae regiae Monacensis*, II, pt. 1 (1874) 164. I am very grateful to the assistant director, Dr. Ferrari, of the Marciana library in Venice for kindly pointing out this work of Bembo to me.

[84] That Musurus went to Milan and Pavia in July and August 1502 and saw Lascaris is attested by Aldus' letter to Lascaris included in the Aldine edition of Sophocles (August 1502) (see Botfield, *Praefationes*, 261). See also Firmin-Didot, 212, and cf. Knös, *Janus Lascaris*, 96, n. 1, who places this visit rather in 1501. For Legrand's objection to Musurus' Academy membership see *Bibliographie hellénique*, I, p. cxii.

[85] See Aldus' letter to Musurus in Statius, in Menge, "Vita Marci Musuri," 18, 21. Also French translation in Firmin-Didot, 213–14 and 147. Sathas, *Neohellenic Philology*, 80, Denissoff, *Maxime le Grec*, 211, n. 5. All of these authors believe that Musurus was a member.

[86] In his preface to the *ed. prin.* of Sophocles (edited by Musurus, August 1502) Aldus writes about "those cold foggy days when we were seated around the fire in a half-circle with the members of our New Academy among whom

From the beginning the Aldine Academy was granted important privileges by the Venetian Senate, which enjoined anyone from reprinting Aldus' works or making use of the Greek characters he had developed.[87] The prohibition was not entirely successful, and for this reason Aldus sought new privileges from the Senate and the Doge. On November 13, 1502, it was even forbidden for anyone in Venetian territories to develop his own Greek type under penalty of forfeiting all his publications. Musurus too was singled out by the Venetian government and, probably in 1503, appointed by the Senate to preside over an office entitled *publica Graecarum literarum officina* (literally, "public workshop of Greek letters") as a kind of public censor of Greek works appearing in the city. As Musurus himself was later to write:

I have already been careful lest, from the public office of Greek letters — over which, through the liberality and beneficence of the Venetian Senate, I have now presided for thirteen years — proceed books which display foolish knowledge contrary to custom, or recommend themselves for sale because of irreverence.[88]

For the work of public censorship Musurus probably received some kind of stipend from the government. But his holding of the

by chance (*forte*) was Marcus Musurus" (Botfield, 261, and Menge, 21; cf. Firmin-Didot, 212). Legrand, I, p. cxii, believes that the word *forte* indicates that Musurus was not an Academy member, but it might well mean that since Musurus was then teaching in Padua he was not present at all meetings but happened to be at this particular one.

[87] For text see colophon to Aldine *Organon* of Aristotle. For modern criticism of the quality of Aldine characters see C. Bühler, "Aldus Manutius: The First Five Hundred Years," in *The Papers of the Bibliographical Society of America*, XLIV (1950) 205–215, esp. 207, who says that "Aldus was not a great printer in the sense that Nicholas Jenson . . . or even his father-in-law Torresano were masters of the art and technic of bookmaking. His press work was indifferent and his types were poor. It has been said . . . that his Greek types set back the study of that tongue for 300 years" (cf. above, note 39). Then he praises Aldus as a publisher and innovator and for his first printing of Greek texts. But one should emphasize, however, the great popularity of Aldus' works in enormously stimulating the study of Greek.

[88] From Musurus' preface to the *Orationes* of Gregory of Nazianzus (Renouard, *Annales*, I, 179–80), printed in 1516 (Firmin-Didot, 463, says 1506, which is obviously an error). See Legrand, *Bibliographie hellénique*, I, 136. There is a question over the precise meaning of "public office of Greek letters." Renouard, III, 42 and I, 180 (also Firmin-Didot, 147) believes that what is meant by Musurus' statement is the task of *literary* censorship only over Aldine publications. But Brown, *Venetian Printing Press*, 64–65, refers the position to censorship of *all* Greek works appearing in Venice and distinguishes among the various types of Venetian censorship.

post did not necessitate continuous residence in Venice, for we know that during his tenure of office he made frequent trips outside Venice and also taught in Padua.

An auspicious change occurred in the career of Musurus with his appointment, in July of 1503, as professor of Greek at the renowned University of Padua. As we have seen, the cities of Padua and Venice formed essentially a single center of culture. And the atmosphere of intellectual freedom fostered by the Venetians, together with the growing reputation of the Paduan faculties of letters and medicine, served to attract many students from northern Europe — from Germany, England, France, Poland, and Hungary — as well as from Italy. Of the Paduan chairs in letters, that of Greek had now attained considerable prestige. First occupied by the Athenian scholar Demetrius Chalcondyles (1463–1471), it was held by a number of successors whose names and periods of tenure are somewhat uncertain but among whom are evidently included several Greeks. Musurus' immediate predecessor was the Italian Lorenzo Camerti, better known as "the Cretan" because of his seven years of study in Crete. When Camerti was appointed Venetian envoy to Portugal, his place at Padua was filled temporarily by Musurus, and upon Camerti's death in 1505 the latter became permanent holder (*ordinario*) of the chair.[89]

Musurus' movements during the few years preceding his appointment at Padua are not entirely clear, but it was very probably this appointment that occasioned his departure from Carpi. Now firmly ensconced in one of the leading chairs of Greek in Italy, Musurus abandoned whatever thoughts he had of returning to his homeland. And summoning his father from Crete (his mother does not then seem to have been alive), he fixed his abode in Padua, along the Borgo Zocco, in the house of a bookseller named Fran-

---

[89] On the successors of Chalcondyles see Menge, "Vita Marci Musuri," 23–24, Ferrai, *L'ellenismo di Padova*, 29, Foffano, "Marco Musuro," 461–62, and cf. Papadopoli, *Historia gymnasii patavini*, I, 294. Molmenti, *Venice*, pt. 2, vol. I, 261 says that (the Italian) Giovanni Calfurnio followed Chalcondyles. I follow Facciolatus, *Fasti gymnasii patavini*, pt. 1, p. lv. Legrand, I, pp. cxiii and cxv, prints the senatorial order appointing Musurus to succeed Camerti. Musurus' initial salary of 100 florins offers a striking contrast to the 400 florins paid Chalcondyles forty years before! See Chapter 1, text and note 83. But cf. Sanuto, *Diarii*, VII, col. 661, who notes that on Nov. 4, 1508, the Venetian government voted to raise Musurus' salary from 60 to 100 florins a year.

Demetrius Chalcondyles.

DEMETRIUS CHALCONDYLES
(1423–1511)

cesco.[90] With more tranquillity of mind than before, Marcus Musurus now gave himself entirely to his beloved studies and teaching.

The six-year period of Musurus' instruction at Padua constitutes an important milestone in the development of Greek studies in Western Europe. Indeed, the success and widespread influence of his teaching — which has been largely unappreciated except by specialists in Renaissance philology — is perhaps comparable only to that achieved by the celebrated Manuel Chrysoloras in Florence a century before, and shortly thereafter by Guarino Veronensis in Ferrara. Merely to call the roll of the students of Musurus is to enumerate many of the most famous Hellenists of the age. Among the Italians were Lazaro Bonamico, who was later to teach Greek and Latin at Padua and in Rome and to have connections with Spain; Bernardino Donati of Verona; [91] Raffael Reggio, the septuagenarian and long-time professor of Latin at Padua, who faithfully arose each morning at seven in order to arrive at his colleague Musurus' lectures on time; also Girolamo Negri, secretary to several cardinals, and the Neapolitan Girolamo Borgia.[92] More important were the famous Girolamo Aleandro, who studied with Musurus from 1504 to 1507 and then went on to Paris, where he helped to inaugurate public instruction in Greek; [93] the learned poet-statesman of Venice Andrea Navagero, who subsequently became a valued editor of Latin works for the Aldine press; and Gaspar Contarini, who as a cardinal was to play a prominent part

[90] See Mercati, *Pio*, 73–74. Calliergis somewhat later may have resided with Musurus. See Chapter 7, note 36, on Calliergis. Also cf. Firmin-Didot, *Alde Manuce*, 525–26, for a letter of Calliergis to Gregoropoulos directing his letters to be sent to the Borgo Zocco. Today the Borgo Zocco (Zucco) is called Via Aristide Gabelli. Probably in 1497 John Gregoropoulos was living in Venice in the monastery of SS. John and Paul. See L. 6, Manousakas, "Gregoropoulos Correspondence."

[91] On Bonamico (who had studied in Venice with Calfurnio) see G. Marangoni, "Lazaro Bonamico e lo studio padovano," *Nuovo Archivio Veneto*, I–II (1901) 16off., Papadopoli, *Historia gymnasii patavini*, I, 307, and Hutton, *Greek Anthology*, 180; on Donati, see Papadopoli, II, 300 and Firmin-Didot, 467.

[92] See Nichols, *Epistles of Erasmus*, I, 449–450, and Marangoni, "Lazaro Bonamico," 126f. Raffael delivered the funeral oration on Aldus.

[93] See note 76. Also see A. Virgili, "Girolamo Aleandro," *Archivio storico italiano*, XXXI (1903) 400; and Nolhac, "Les correspondants d'Alde Manuce," no. 53, letter from Aleandro to Aldus in March 1506 referring to his study with Musurus.

in the papacy's struggle with the rising Lutheran movement in Germany.[94]

The reputation of Musurus as a teacher spread rapidly, and his lectures soon began to attract students from all parts of Europe. Germany was represented by the Dominican John Conon, "the true founder of Greek studies in Germany," according to certain modern scholars, who consider him to have surpassed even Reuchlin in his method and knowledge of Greek.[95] Curiously, we have surviving what purport to be notes of Conon's taken from a Paduan lecture of John Gregoropoulos on Aristophanes and on Sophocles' *Electra*. (Gregoropoulos was evidently at the time substituting for his friend Musurus.) [96] An example of a French scholar who studied under Musurus at Padua is Germain de Brie (previously a kind of servant-pupil to Janus Lascaris in Venice when the latter was the envoy of France to the Serenissima), who came to Padua in the specific aim of studying Greek with Musurus. After further study in Rome, de Brie eventually returned to his homeland, where he entered the service of the Cardinal Louis of Amboise and subsequently became secretary to the Queen of France.[97]

The best known of the northerners who profited from Musurus' teaching was the Dutch Erasmus. Though not formally enrolled as a pupil of Musurus, he doubtless attended the latter's lectures dur-

[94] On Navagero see note 78. On Contarini see A. Chacon, *Tiara et purpura veneta ab anno 1379 ad 1759* (Brescia, 1761) 378: "quam Patavino in Lyceo, Marco Musuro praeceptore usus puer didicerat"; and see G. de Leva, *Della vita e delle opere del Card. Gasparo Contarini* (Padua, 1863). Nardi, *Aristotelismo padovano*, 367, also names as a pupil of Musurus at this time Count Ludovico Nogarola of Verona, who later studied with Pomponazzi at Bologna.

[95] See especially A. Oleroff, "Conon et Grégoropoulos," 104–107. Also M. Meyer, "Ein Kollegheft des Humanisten Conon," *Zentralblatt für Bibliothekswesen*, LIII (1936) 281–84, who calls Conon the "founder of Greek studies in Germany" and regrets that we do not know more about his stay in Italy. He notes that Conon studied with Aldus, Musurus, Carteromachus, and John the Cretan [Gregoropoulos]. In the autumn of 1505, Conon went to Germany to seek (vainly) the protection of the Emperor Maximilian for the Aldine Academy. See Allen, *Epistolarum Erasmi*, I, 410, n. 19; also H. von Kleehoven, "Aldus Manuzio und der Plan einer deutschen Ritterakademie," *Bibliofilia*, LII (1950) 169–77. Further see L. Donati, "La seconda Academia Aldina ed una lettera a Aldo Manuzio trascurata da bibliografi," *Bibliofilia*, LIII (1951) 54, mentioning a letter of Aldus to the German humanist Conrad Celtis and referring to Aldus' hope of founding an Academy in Germany and thereby rendering the latter "a second Athens."

[96] See Oleroff, "Conon et Grégoropoulos," 105.

[97] Allen, *Epistolae Erasmi*, I, 447, n. 212.

ing his sojourn at Padua. On at least one occasion we know that Erasmus was a guest in Musurus' home; [98] moreover, Erasmus' pupil and biographer Beatus Rhenanus relates that whenever Erasmus encountered a difficult Greek passage he would consult Musurus, whose learning and kindness he was wont to praise to his friends.[99] In Erasmus' own words Musurus was "a Greek . . . marvelously skilled in the Latin language, an accomplishment attained by scarcely any Greek except Theodore Gaza and Janus Lascaris." [100]

We have little information on the specific courses conducted at Padua by Musurus, his methods of instruction, or the conditions under which he taught. But from out-of-the-way statements of various contemporaries or from such sources as the prefaces to Aldine editions, some facts can be gleaned. Musurus' curriculum no doubt included the teaching of grammar — a subject which, according to Menge, he taught his students in the morning, reserving the evening for instruction in the Greek poets, Homer, Hesiod, Theocritus, and the rest.[101] A marginal notation from a surviving document unknown to Menge informs us that Musurus also gave lectures on the *Greek Anthology*, his notes for which are believed to be the first scholia of any importance written on the epigrams contained therein.[102] Menge also affirms the probability of Musurus' having lectured on Aristotle, and in virtue of Padua's reputation as a center of Aristotelian studies this seems very likely. However, as special instruction in the original Greek text of the philosophic works of Aristotle had already been instituted in 1497 by Leonicos Thomaeus (under the influence of the anti-scholastic Ermolao

---

[98] See Allen, V, 244 (transl. in J. J. Mangan, *Life, Character, and Influence of Desiderius Erasmus of Rotterdam*, 2 vols. [New York, 1927] I, 259), for an incident in Padua involving Musurus, his father, and Erasmus. Cf. above, note 9.

[99] See translation of Beatus' life of Erasmus (inserted as preface to an edition of Origen) in Mangan, II, 379. Rhenanus also cites Carteromachus as giving advice in Greek to Erasmus.

[100] See Erasmus' letter to Gaverus in Allen, V, 244. In Nichols, *Epistles of Erasmus*, I, 256, Rhenanus is quoted as saying that Musurus had read everything and knew antiquity very well. On Erasmus see Chapter 9, below.

[101] Menge, "Vita Marci Musuri," 27, citing Varillasius (who is probably to be identified with Antoine Varillas). Cf. below, note 126, for definite evidence that Musurus taught Greek poetry only a few years later in Venice.

[102] See Hutton, *Greek Anthology*, 155, and n. 2, quoting a marginal notation of Aldus' brother-in-law, Francesco d'Asola, that in 1506 he had heard Musurus lecture on the *Greek Anthology*. It is interesting that the sole surviving lecture of Janus Lascaris in Florence was also on the *Greek Anthology*. Musurus, as noted, had been Lascaris' student in the Tuscan capital.

Barbaro, who, incidentally, was the first humanist to translate a
Greek commentary on Aristotle, that of Themistius),[103] it seems
likely that Musurus' lectures on Aristotle were restricted, or in the
main devoted, to that author's nonphilosophic works. This view
is perhaps strengthened by a statement of Musurus' fellow Cretan
and Aldine associate Demetrius Ducas, who advised him to teach
at Padua not only Aristotle's rhetoric but that of Hermogenes as
well.[104]

The teaching provided by Musurus in the Greek language and
literature sought to instruct the student in literary and philological
problems via the translation of classical Greek works into Latin and
vice versa. Although several Greek grammars had already appeared
(in 1494 that written in Greek by Constantine Lascaris with a
Latin translation by Crastoni,[105] and in 1497 one composed in
Latin by Urbano Bolzanio), the most widely accepted method of
teaching Greek in the period was that of providing the student
with both Latin and Greek versions of a work in order that he
might look to the Latin for the Greek words unfamiliar to him.
The measure of a good teacher, accordingly, was the ability to turn
Greek into Latin and the reverse. Here Musurus excelled, for he
could translate not only accurately but with great celerity and
even refinement of style.[106] To assist in this widely utilized method
of instruction, Aldus had taken care to publish Greek texts provided
with Latin translations, for example, those of Musaeus, Philostratus,
the poems of Gregory of Nazianzus, and Aesop's *Fables*.[107]

A vivid, albeit rhetorical, bit of evidence on the success of
Musurus' instruction at Padua, and on the dissemination of his
teaching as well, is provided by Demetrius Ducas' prefatory epistle
to Musurus contained in the first volume of the Aldine *Rhetores
Graeci* (published in November 1508):

[103] P. Kristeller, *Studies in Renaissance Thought and Letters* (Rome, 1956) 343.
On Thomaeus see also A. González Palencia and E. Mele, *Vida y obras de
Don Diego Hurtado de Mendoza*, I (Madrid, 1941) 289f. Cf. Chapter 1, note 61.
[104] See Menge, 27, and cf. below, Chapter 8 on Ducas, text and note 16. On the
teaching of Aristotle at Padua see Weiss, "Learning and Education in Western
Europe," 100.
[105] See Firmin-Didot, *Alde Manuce*, 63–64.
[106] Attested to in statement of L. G. Gyraldi, *Dialogi duo de poëtis nostrorum
temporum* (Florence, 1551) 63, and of Aldus in his edition of *Athenaeus* (a. 1514).
[107] See Chapter 8, note 60.

It is through your efforts, Musurus, in the celebrated and very renowned city of Padua where you teach publicly from the chair as from the height of a throne, that one sees depart each year from your school, as from the flanks of the Trojan horse, so many learned pupils that one could believe them born in the bosom of Greece or belonging to the race of the Athenians.[108]

Musurus was very conscientious in his instruction. Indeed, Paolo Giovio, the contemporary biographer of prominent Italian Renaissance personalities, informs us that he took only four days' vacation in the entire year. In 1508 the Venetian Senate recognized Musurus' services by raising his salary from the initial modest stipend of 100 florins to 140, at the same time declaring that he "lectures with immense satisfaction and profit for the students, especially the Venetian nobles who devote their time to the study of Greek" [109] — further evidence of the intellectual interests of the Venetian aristocracy.

Meanwhile, in spite of his many activities, Musurus continued, when he could, to attend sessions of the Aldine Academy. Not only did he offer advice on works to be printed, but there are indications that he was still able to help edit important Greek texts for Aldus. Thus in February of 1504 the Aldine press published its valuable edition of the plays of Euripides, which we know now, through the evidence of an epigram written by Janus Lascaris, definitely to be the work of Musurus.[110] In a letter unknown to Menge and Legrand, written probably in 1509 to Aldus in Venice, Musurus wrote (in Italian): "I shall do what I can and the time that remains

[108] Legrand, *Bibliographie hellénique*, I, 85-88. Firmin-Didot, 315 (French trans.).
[109] On Musurus' vacation see Paolo Giovio (Iovius), *Elogia doctorum virorum* (Antwerp, 1557). For his salary increase see Facciolatus, *Fasti gymnasii patavini*, I, p. lv; and on his commendation for his lectures see Sanuto, *I diarii di Marino Sanuto (1496-1533)*, ed. R. Fulin, F. Stefani, N. Barozzi, G. Berchet, M. Allegri (Venice, 1879-1903) vol. VII, col. 661, and Ferrai, *L'ellenismo*, 83. Cf., however, Sanuto, *Diarii*, VII, col. 661ʳ (November 4, 1508), which says the Venetian government raised his salary 40 florins, from 60.
[110] Legrand, I, pp. cxiiif., not aware of the evidence from Lascaris, rightly minimized the point raised by other authorities that Musurus was not even mentioned in Aldus' dedication of the volume to Demetrius Chalcondyles. But now see A. Turyn, *The Byzantine Manuscript Tradition of the Tragedies of Euripides* (Urbana, 1957) esp. 375 (where he mentions an interesting epigram of Lascaris praising Musurus' edition of Euripides) and 201, 259n (mentioning that Musurus catalogued an important Euripidean manuscript in Alberto's library at Carpi and himself later gained possession of it).

to me I shall devote willingly to that enterprise [the projected edition of Plato?]. But I certainly hope that during these holidays of the carnival I shall have nothing to do, and will therefore provide you with the Topics" [111] — evidently referring to the *Commentaries of Alexander of Aphrodisias on the Topics of Aristotle*, printed by Aldus in September of 1513.

With Demetrius Ducas, who was probably chief editor and supervisor of the work, Musurus aided in preparing for the press the extremely important *Rhetores Graeci* (the first volume of which appeared in November 1508, and the second in June, 1509). For a number of the works included in this collection, the Aldine is still the only edition which exists. As Aldus flatteringly addressed Musurus in his Latin preface to the second volume:

If there is anyone, most learned Musurus, to whom Greek books published by our care may be dedicated, it is you. For not only have you always been helpful in the past and continue to aid us in this our difficult task,[112] but you also teach Greek letters in the very famous school at Padua to so numerous an assembly of students of Greek letters that all marvel. Whence, through your teaching, many already within a few years have come forth skilled in the Greek tongue. This fact may soon prove of great benefit both to Latin letters, which flowed from the Greek, and to the liberal arts themselves, which have been transmitted from the Greek. We may understand therefore that already in our age almost all, in spite of barbarism, come to learn Greek no less than Latin, not unmindful of those lines of Horace: "Turn over the Grecian models both night and day," nor of those lines from the *De officiis* of Marcus Tullius Cicero addressed to his son Marcus, "I have, however, always combined Greek and Latin studies for my improvement, not only in the study of philosophy but for my training in oratory. I recommend that you do the same so that you may be equally versed in both languages." You accomplish this above all others, Marcus Musurus, as if he had written this advice to you as to his son Marcus, because you are able to join Greek to Latin with such skill that you not only have become adept in both languages but have become an outstanding philosopher — not in the eyes of barbarians but in those of the learned. We therefore dedicate to you these commentaries of Syrianus, Sopater, and Marcellinus on the *Rhetoric* of Hermogenes and the *Progymnas-*

[111] Letter in Nolhac, "Les correspondants d'Alde Manuce," 229–30. On date cf. Foffano, "Marco Musuro," 464.

[112] On the question of the editorship of this work (the *Rhetores Graeci*), see Chapter 8, text and note 12. And for the opuscules included see Renouard, *Annales*, I, 128.

mata of Aphthonius, about whose erudition and ability we would have
written a few words, as is our custom, in order to exhort students to
study, if a quiet mind had been ours. For at this time we can truly
say: "Having broken the laws, neighboring towns wage war against
each other, and impious Mars frightens the entire world." Farewell.[113]

Musurus' activities were not devoted exclusively to Greek scholarship. He also directed his attention, on occasion, to Latin translations from the Greek, an activity important in the period for the
general diffusion of Greek literature. Cardinal Mercati has identified the handwriting of a Latin translation of the Byzantine John
Philoponos' important *Commentaria in Aristotelis libros de genera-
tione et corruptione* (done in Padua in July or August of 1505) as
that of Musurus.[114]

The leisurely scholarly life of Padua, so much to the taste of
Musurus, was suddenly jarred by the impact of international politics. What Aldus himself had referred to in the last words of the
dedication to Musurus just quoted was the gathering war clouds
now threatening the very existence of the Venetian state. As a result
partly of the Turkish threat to Venetian possessions in the East
and partly of economic factors in Italy, Venice had sought since
even before the Turkish conquest of Constantinople in 1453 to
expand her territory on the Italian mainland. Most directly threatened by her encroachments were the nearby states of Milan, Ferrara, little Carpi, and especially the papal territories. In the opening
years of the sixteenth century political alliances shifted rapidly
until there crystallized in 1508 a great anti-Venetian coalition,
jealous of the power and wealth of Venice. It was this almost pan-
European league, the principal powers of which were France, the
Papacy, Florence, the Holy Roman Empire, and Spain, that now
threatened Venetian security. Involved in a great war, faced indeed by invasion, the Venetians had to turn all thoughts to the defense of their homeland. In view of the impending military opera-
tions, study at the nearby University of Padua was of course
disrupted — the school was probably closed, though some professors continued instruction on their own — and many of the

---

[113] For (Latin) text see Botfield, *Praefationes*, 277-78.
[114] Mercati, *Pio*, 57, n. 3.

students and professors had to flee from the city to return to their homelands or to scatter to nearby areas.[115]

Sometime after June of 1509 [116] Musurus too left Padua, to withdraw to Venice, with its more secure position in the lagoons. At the same time his friend Aldus closed his publishing house and betook himself to central Italy in order to safeguard his possessions there from the depradations of invading armies.[117] As the threat to Venice itself began to increase, Musurus looked for still another asylum and so wrote to Aldus, now in Ferrara, to secure him a safe conduct to that city. The authorization was received, but it is doubtful if Musurus actually left Venice.[118]

The next seven years, 1509 to 1516, were passed by Musurus in Venice, but for the first three of these we have sparse notices on his activities. With the whole Venetian state being increasingly geared to war and with the resultant disruption of scholarly activities, Musurus found himself with a good deal of time on his hands. It was in this period that he seems to have worked on the text of his celebrated edition of Plato.[119] At the same time he seems to have been employed as translator, officially or otherwise, by the Venetian government.[119a]

In 1510 Venice finally capitulated to the pope, and the dissolution

[115] See Foffano, "Marco Musuro," 465 and Pastor, History of the Popes, VI, 247-315. Also Marangoni, "Lazaro Bonamico," 121.

[116] The last evidence of Musurus' residence in Padua is the date (21 May 1509) of the letter constituting Aldus' preface to the Rhetores Graeci cited above. See Legrand, I, p. cxv, who shows that Musurus had definitely come to Venice by 10 July 1511 (on the basis of a note on a manuscript used for the same edition of the Rhetores).

[117] See Bühler, "Aldus Manutius," 212. Aldus went to Ferrara in 1509 and returned to Venice in 1512.

[118] There are letters unused by Menge and Legrand in Nolhac, "Les correspondants d'Alde Manuce" 79. Foffano, "Marco Musuro," 466, shows that Musurus also considered Pordenone as a place of refuge but denies the affirmation of other scholars that he went there with Navagero, Fracastoro, and other men of letters.

[119] See below, text and note 142. The statement of Giovio, Elogia, 72, that he also worked in this period on his famous poem to Plato may be false, as Leo X, prominently referred to therein as pope, was not elected to the office until early 1513.

[119a] To judge from an unused passage in Sanuto, dated Sept. 1510. Here Musurus, termed "optimus grecus," translates a letter, in Greek, addressed to the Venetian Signoria by the Turkish ruler Bayazid (Sanuto, XI, col. 419). Perhaps Musurus acted as translator in his capacity of "public censor" of Greek books. Cf. below, note 125.

of the anti-Venetian coalition of Cambrai brought peace once more to Venetia. The government now sought to recall the professors and students dispersed by the war. But the great Paduan university could only with difficulty recover its scattered elements, and it would be years before studies would be restored to their former luster.[120] As a beginning it would be easier and more expedient to re-establish the educational facilities of Venice itself. Thus the Senate provided for an appointment to the Greek chair in Venice, which had been vacant since the departure in 1506 of the Ferrarese scholar Nicola Leoniceno.[121]

This chair had originally been established in Venice so that those desirous of learning Greek would, in the initial stage of their training, not find it necessary to go to Padua. More important, the chair, which was attached to the Ducal Chancery school, provided for the training of civil servants of the Venetian chancery and for those officials who would be stationed in the many possessions of Venice in the Greek East. It was this public professorship of Greek that Musurus, now unemployed, was able to obtain, in January of 1512,[122] through the intervention of Francesco Faseolo, a jurisconsult and Grand Chancellor of the Venetian Senate. Musurus must have felt a certain satisfaction at this turn of events, since eight years before, in a competition for the post, he had been passed over in favor of Leoniceno.[123]

From the beginning Musurus was highly successful in his new position — his Paduan reputation no doubt standing him in good stead — as is indicated by Aldus' epistle to Faseolo inserted at the beginning of volume I of the Aldine *Rhetorum Graecorum Orationes* (dated April–May, 1513):

Venice at this time can truly be called a second Athens (*Athenae alterae*) because students of Greek letters gather from everywhere to hear Marcus Musurus, the most learned man of this age, whom you

[120] Padua did not reopen in 1509 as is sometimes stated, though the Venetian government quickly turned its attention to its reorganization. Molmenti, *Venice*, I, pt. 2, 258.
[121] Date of Leoniceno's (Lonigo's) departure given in Sanuto, *Diarii*, VI, col. 433 (cf. Legrand, I, p. cxvi).
[122] Exact date revealed by a document found by Foffano, "Marco Musuro," 466 (and Appendix, doc. I). Musurus' position was approved by the Senate on February 17 (Sanuto, *Diarii*, XIII, col. 486).
[123] On the competition see Sanuto, VI, 117 (cf. Legrand, *Bibliographie hellénique*, I, p. cxv).

have zealously brought by public stipend, and to whom you show many favors.[124]

The amount of Musurus' annual salary in Venice is not known, but may be estimated to be at least as much as the hundred gold pieces received initially by his successor Vittore Fausto in 1517. According to custom, the amount was increased by the senate after a few years, and Musurus at the same time received additional fees from private students whom he was instructing in Greek. With his colleague Gregorio Amaseo, who taught Latin, Musurus was required to rent a house near the basilica of St. Mark, and there, we are told, after the daily lesson conducted in an assigned public place, he would listen to the students repeating what they had previously learned.[125] Unfortunately we know less about Musurus' pupils in this Venetian phase of his teaching than about those he had instructed at Padua. Though still numerous and assembled from widespread areas, his students now seem to have required a more elementary presentation. One explanation for this may be that whereas his Paduan classes had consisted essentially of full-time students eager to master the refinements of Greek grammar and literature, his classes now included Venetian men of affairs who applied themselves to the study of Greek primarily to aid in their administrative duties and only secondarily to enrich their own culture.[126]

Among Musurus' non-Italian students was the French ambassador to Venice, Jean de Pins. Another was Janus Vertessy (called Pannonius),[127] a leading Hungarian humanist, to whom in 1514

[124] Menge, "Vita Marci Musuri," 32, quotes the preface of Aldus in the original Latin, Firmin-Didot, *Alde Manuce*, 334, in a French translation.

[125] See document of Foffano, "Marco Musuro," 467. Musurus was still serving as translator for the Venetian government. See Sanuto, *Diarii*, XIV, col. 414, dated June 23, 1512, saying that Musurus translated from Greek into Latin a letter from the Turkish Sultan, brought by his ambassador Ruis (Chiaus).

[126] Foffano, 457–58, however, thinks that Musurus also taught his pupils in the difficult art of poetry. This seems probable, to judge from the evidence provided by a letter from Filippo Pandolfini to Euphrosinus Boninus, saying that Pandolfini was sending to the latter, for publication by the Giunta press, a manuscript of Theocritus corrected by Musurus and used by the latter in his teaching in Venice (text quoted in Legrand, I, 125).

[127] Not to be confused with the better known student of the elder Guarino, Janus Pannonius, on whom much has been written. See, for example, Legrand, I, p. liii. On de Pins see below, note 154. Another pupil of Musurus was Hieronymus Vicchius, who later accompanied Alberto Pio on his ambassadorship to Rome (Menge, 40).

Aldus dedicated his *editio princeps* of the *Deipnosophistae* of the second century Greek writer Athenaeus. Part of Aldus' letter of dedication deserves quotation not only for its mention of Musurus but because of its indication of Venetian influence on the development of Greek studies in Hungary.

I could not congratulate you enough, Janus, and also your Hungarian compatriots and Hungary itself on your progress in Greek letters, although it is less than a year that you have had lessons in Venice from Musurus the Cretan . . . You know what a debt of gratitude you have contracted toward Venice and toward Musurus for the learning with which Musurus enriches you and for the examples Venice can offer you.[128]

Still another of Musurus' students in this period may have been the later famous Venetian cardinal Marino Grimani, though Mercati believes it equally possible that he may have studied under Musurus earlier at Padua. One of Musurus' better pupils at Venice was Pietro Alcionio, who tried unsuccessfully, on the death of Musurus, to secure the latter's Venetian chair and finally went on to assume the chair of Greek at Florence.[129] Also, from Prague there came the young Gelenius, who after studying with Musurus in Venice went in 1524 to Basle, where he produced editions of Callimachus and Aristophanes as well as the Planudean Anthology, and the first editions of several minor Greek geographers.[130]

According to Schück, it was while occupying the Greek chair of Venice that Musurus acted as librarian of Bessarion's collection of Greek manuscripts. This view is to be considered, since Sanuto in his *Diarii* reports that on May 5, 1515, the Venetian Senate decided to entrust the 800 manuscripts of Bessarion to Musurus and Battista Egnazio. It was then also decreed that a library to house them be constructed "above the piazza di San Marco." [131]

[128] Text in Botfield, *Praefationes*, 301, French translation in Firmin-Didot, *Alde Manuce*, 380. See Nolhac, "Les correspondants d'Alde Manuce," for Aldus' correspondence with scholars of Hungary regarding Greek manuscripts.

[129] On Grimani see Mercati, *Pio*, 14 and 74. On Alcionio see Mazzuchelli, *Gli scrittori d'Italia*, I, pt. 1, 376–83.

[130] Sandys, *History of Classical Scholarship*, II, 263–64.

[131] Schück, *Aldus Manutius*, 78; and Ferrai, *L'ellenismo*, 76, note, and 80, note. Sanuto, XX, cols. 176–78. But Menge, 32, lists the St. Mark librarians for the period: first Sabellicus, to 1506, and immediately thereafter Andrea Navagero, to 1529. His conclusion thus seems to be that there was no time for Musurus to have held the position, a view with which Foffano, "Marco Musuro," 462, appears to concur. The

In the year 1512, at the urgings of Andrea Navagero, Giovanni Giocondo of Verona and Musurus, Aldus reopened his press in Venice. The first work to be published was a second edition of Manuel Chrysoloras' much-printed Greek grammar, the *Erotemata*, upon the recommendation of Musurus, who may well have needed it for the use of his students. Incorporated in the volume was a second grammatical treatise of Chrysoloras, one of Demetrius Chalcondyles, another of Theodore Gaza, and moral sayings of various poets.[132] Musurus may have suggested, if he did not entirely edit, the *editio princeps* of the Greek text of Pindar (published in January 1513), an author about whom the West had hitherto only a rather vague notion.[133] The *Orations* of Isocrates also appeared at this time.[134] Musurus' collaboration with Aldus seems for a time to have been limited to advice. But in the summer of 1513 he assumed a more active role at the press. In July Aldus published a Latin work, Cicero's *Epistolarum ad Atticum, ad Brutum, ad Quintum fratrem xxi libri*, with a Latin translation of the interpolated Greek passages, in the rendering of which he was aided by Musurus. As Aldus wrote in his preface dedicated to Philip More de Coula, Hungarian envoy to Venice:

> For all these [interpolated Greek] terms we have given a rapid but careful interpretation with the aid of the most learned Musurus, my excellent collaborator, whose constant aid in the correction of texts is so precious to me that, if Greece had produced two more of his merit as counselors of mine, I would not despair of giving before long

---

building housing today's Marciana collection was not built until 1559, by Sansovino. For a letter of Marcus' to Navagero (1517) in which he mentions Bessarion's books, see P. Paschini, *Domenico Grimani* (Rome, 1943) 141 and elsewhere.

[132] See Firmin-Didot, 328.

[133] On Pindar see Aldus' preface to Navagero, translated in Firmin-Didot, 365. There is difference of opinion as to whether Musurus actually edited the Pindar. Turyn, *Pindari carmina* (Cracow, 1948) attributes to Musurus the corrections to the Aldine Pindar; cf. J. Irigoin, *Pindare*, 400–401, who says Musurus probably checked the text, though he probably did not edit it. Musurus himself owned two manuscripts of Pindar (Irigoin, 378, 176). (The Greek monasteries of south Italy had possessed manuscripts of Pindar befor 1500.) It is customary to attribute to Marcus Musurus specific readings of the Aldine Pindar.

[134] See Aldus' dedicatory epistle to Egnazio, in vol. 2 of *Rhetorum Graecorum Orationes* (trans. in Firmin-Didot, 337). The *ed. prin.* of Isocrates had appeared in Milan in 1493.

to people of taste, in very correct editions, the best works of both literatures [Greek and Latin].[135]

While Venice was struggling to recuperate from her disastrous defeat at the hands of the League of Cambrai, Rome was enjoying a period of peace and prosperity. And with the accession of the Medici Pope Leo X in 1513, the impetus to humanistic studies fostered so successfully by his family in Florence was now transferred to Rome. Whereas Leo's predecessor, the dynamic Julius II, had sought to consolidate and develop papal authority through a policy of force, especially as regards the Italian territories of the church, Leo focused his attention principally on the promotion of humanistic studies, which he sought to further through liberality and clemency. Following in the steps of his great-grandfather Cosimo, who had sponsored the establishment of the Platonic Academy in Florence, Leo now conceived the idea of starting a Greek institute at Rome for the purpose of instruction in the Greek language.

To carry out this plan the Pope summoned to the Holy See the most widely respected of the Greek émigrés, Janus Lascaris, and placed him in charge of the school. Lascaris, familiar with the achievements of his former student Musurus in Padua and Venice, desired his collaboration in the enterprise. And it was doubtless at Lascaris' suggestion that a papal communication was now sent to Musurus.[136] "I want as much as is within my power to restore (restituere) the Greek language and learning now close to destruction," wrote Leo to Musurus. And he requested the Cretan to call from Greece ten or twelve young men (or whatever number he might recommend) of good education and character to constitute a seminar of liberal studies in Rome "from whom the Italians may derive a direct acquaintance with and knowledge of the Greek tongue."

Responding favorably to the papal request, Musurus, as he informs us in a later letter, instituted a search for students in Crete, Corfu, and the maritime areas of the Peloponnese — students with

[135] Original Latin in Legrand, I, p. cxxiv, French translation in Firmin-Didot, 341.
[136] For Leo's letter drawn up by the Papal secretary Pietro Bembo, see Legrand, II, 321 (cf. I, p. cxvi) and Menge, "Vita Marci Musuri," 37–38. English translation in Roscoe, Leo X, II, 238–39.

Ioannes Lascares.

JANUS LASCARIS
(c. 1445–1534)

energy and a desire to learn, and, as he puts it with a certain psychological insight, "who had suffered spiritually." Musurus laments that some of the young Greeks, living under a slavery of many years, showed evidence not only of forgetting their ancestors but of becoming almost indifferent to education." [137]

It was in September of 1513 that Musurus produced under the Aldine imprint what was at once his most creative literary and his most significant philological work — the first edition of the complete works of Plato, to which he prefixed a long poem of his own entitled "Hymn to Plato." In this period when Platonic philosophy, along with the well-established Aristotelian currents of the north Italian Universities, had become one of the most formative elements in the thought of the Western Renaissance, this publication of Plato was of inestimable value. To be sure, a translation into Latin of all the Platonic dialogues had been made several decades before under Medici patronage by the Florentine Marsilio Ficino. But Musurus' edition now made readily available, for the first time in print, the original Greek text. The importance of Musurus' work in establishing an accurate text of Plato and in the wider dissemination of this author's influence has not always adequately been appreciated by intellectual historians in their concentration on the contribution of Ficino.

The Aldine Plato was dedicated to the new pope, Leo X, and, according to Aldus' encomiastic preface, the realization of the edition was in large part rendered possible by the humanist interests of Leo's father, Lorenzo il Magnifico. Lorenzo, as noted earlier, had

---

[137] From Musurus' preface to the Aldine *Pausanias*, in which he also praises Lascaris' role in the foundation of the school. See Legrand, I, 144ff. and p. cxviii; also discussion in Knös, *Janus Lascaris*, 140ff. See further, below (text for note 144), Musurus' poem to Plato in which he mentions at some length the bringing of Greek sons to Rome for study. On the basis of this passage, Foffano, "Marco Musuro," 468, thinks it probable that the hymn to Plato was sent to the Pope *before* publication of the entire edition of Plato and that therefore perhaps *Musurus* should get the credit for conceiving the idea of founding the school. For a list of Greek students at the Academy in Rome see E. Rodocanachi, *La première Renaissance: Rome au temps de Jules II et de Léon X* (Paris, 1912) 165: Nicholas Sophianos, Matthew Devaris (later secretary to Bembo), Christopher Contoleon, Constantine Rhallis, possibly Hermodoros Lestarchos, George Corinthios (nephew of Arsenios Apostolis), and George Balsamos (cf. Legrand, I, p. cli, n. 2). Sophianos later, when attached to Cardinal Ridolfi, helped to catalogue the latter's rich library of Greek manuscripts, which included many of Janus Lascaris. For manuscripts copied by these former Greek students, see Nolhac, *La bibliothèque de Fulvio Orsini*, 159ff.

sent Lascaris on a mission to the East. And it was during one such journey that Lascaris had discovered a number of manuscripts of Plato on Mount Athos.[138] By dedicating the work to Leo X, Aldus doubtless envisioned that he might in some manner win the patronage of the pope for his *Neakademia*, or, to quote his own words, he hoped that Leo would "re-establish the same Academy in Rome, where it would indeed more than ever prove profitable to learned men, among whom, in the first rank, figurês Musurus the Cretan, whose judgment is as sure as his intelligence is great . . . Like us it is peace that he desires, and like us he prays the Academy may be consolidated under your liberal protection." [139]

Whether Aldus actually intended to transfer his printing activities to Rome in the event that Leo could be prevailed upon to establish an academy there is a debatable question.[140] But the recent events disrupting the internal life of Venice, in particular the War of Cambrai, must have loomed large in his thinking. From 1506 to 1512 only eleven editions of any kind had issued from the Aldine press, compared to thirteen in the single year of 1497, or sixteen publications in 1502.[141] Moreover, in view of the well-known interest of the Medici family in humanistic endeavors, the enthronement of Leo X would augur well for the development of Greek studies in the papal capital. Aldus, finally, must have been aware of Rome's lack of a Greek press.

A more impressive tribute to Leo than Aldus' preface was Musurus' stirring "Hymn to Plato." So highly regarded was this poem by contemporaries, according to the sixteenth century writer Paolo Giovio, that it merited comparison with the works of antiquity itself. The modern authority Emile Legrand is equally lavish

[138] See Botfield, *Praefationes*, 286–90, also Firmin-Didot, *Alde Manuce*, 342. Aldus' subscription at the end of the second volume of the Plato speaks of the use of "very old and trustworthy manuscripts." See Menge, "Vita Marci Musuri," 33.

[139] Botfield, 289; Legrand, *Bibliographie hellénique*, I, 101–106; French trans. in Firmin-Didot, 346–351; English trans. in Roscoe, *Leo X*, II, 249–251.

[140] We know that in the fall of 1505 the German student John Conon had gone to Germany to seek (unsuccessfully) the support of the Emperor Maximilian for Aldus' Academy. See Allen, *Epistolae Erasmi*, I, 410, n. 19. Cf. Oleroff, "Conon et Grégoropoulos," 105. See also Aldus' preface to his publication of *Strozii poetae pater et filius*, dated 1513, calling on Lucrezia Borgia, Duchess of Ferrara, to establish an academy (Renouard, *Annales*, I, 141). Cf. Chapter 7, note 48a.

[141] Bühler, "Aldus Manutius," 221, who also calculates eleven editions for each year, 1513 to 1515.

in his praise, declaring that not for a millennium had a son of Greece spoken in language so noble and lofty.[142]

Let us summarize the contents of this two-hundred-verse-apostrophe to the "Divine Plato." Exhorting Plato to descend from heaven and accept the offering of his poem, Musurus urges him to go to Rome, where he will find in Pope Leo X not a cruel Sicilian tyrant but a clement prince. There, among the avid group of Platonists, Plato will encounter Janus Lascaris and Pietro Bembo, who will guide and introduce him to the Pope. Musurus asks Plato to persuade the Pope to recall the Christian world to peace so that, united, the nations may effectively wage war against the Turk for the recovery of Constantinople and Greece. In the meantime, Plato should urge, may the Pope extend his favor to the perishing liberal arts, further an interest in poetry, and in particular encourage the study of Greek through the creation of professorships in that language and the establishment in Rome of an Academy on the model of ancient Athens; thus glory may accrue to Leo equal to that of his great father Lorenzo and the other Medici. Were Plato to speak thus, affirms Musurus, the pope could not fail to be moved.[143]

The poem reflects the grace, elegance, and sweep of phrase characteristic of Musurus' style. Moreover, it is composed in the correct classical prosody and in the classical elegiac distichs. In content it constitutes a moving appeal to the spirit of Plato so to inspire the western European nations with love for the heritage of the ancient Greeks that they will speedily go to the aid of their descendants, whose harsh lot Musurus eloquently portrays in a lamentation on the destruction of liberty. Thus, aside from its literary merit, the poem may also be considered a unique contribution to the historiography of the last phase of the crusades, which sought unsuccessfully to rescue the Greek East from the Turkish oppressor. Almost all the Greek exiles in the West, especially Bessarion, at one time or other had produced works appealing for succor for their downtrodden people. But most of these writings have been

---

[142] P. Giovio (Iovius), *Le iscrittioni poste sotto le vere imagini degli huomini famosi* (Florence, 1552) 63, also Legrand, I, p. cxvi. Cf. opinions of Firmin-Didot, 352 and Papadopoli, *Historia gymnasii patavini*, I, 295.

[143] For original Greek text of poem see Legrand, I, 106-12, and Firmin-Didot, 491-98. The English translation, used in part below, is that of Roscoe, II, 241-47. I have, however, eliminated some of his archaisms such as lov'd and low'r.

neglected by Western scholars, though amid the excess of rhetoric some literary and historical worth can sometimes be discerned. Of all these, the work of Musurus is probably the most important as literature. We quote below selections from his poem in the sole translation done in English, the old version of Roscoe, which manages only very inadequately to capture some of the beauty of the original:

"Then [O Pope, says Plato] turn the tide
   of war on Turkey's shores,
And curb the wolf-like, unbelieving band,
Whose tyrant Empire fainting Greece deplores: . . .
On Asia's shores let warlike myriads gleam.
There let the Gaul, in mailed armour bright,
Spur his proud steed, conspicuous from afar; . . .
Germania's giant offspring too be there,
And, loved of Mars, Brittania's hardy race . . .
And Venice there her countless fleets shall send;
Imperial Venice mistress of the flood.
Spain's floating battlements, of mountain size,
Towards the wide Hellespont their course shall steer,
And whilst their towering masts salute the skies,
Each warlike prow the healing cross shall bear.
Then over Byzantium's towers, if once again
The light of freedom dawn; if then, represt
By thy victorious arms, on Graecia's plain
The poisonous dragon lower his hateful crest,
'Tis all achieved — for then, from bondage freed,
Achaia's sons their ancient fires shall feel;
Beneath their hands the barbarous foe shall bleed,
Or fly before their swift avenging steel . . .
And shouts of triumph, and victorious songs,
And grateful anthems, shall to heaven arise;
And whilst around thee crowd the conquering throngs
All Asia's wealth shall glitter in thine eyes . . .
And all mankind, beneath thy [the papal] equal reign
Enjoy the lasting peace by thee restored . . .

"From Graecia's shores, from fair Italia's clime,
Call thou their noble sons impatient forth;
Ingenuous youths, who feel the glow sublime,
Of native genius, or paternal worth.
And amidst thy Rome a calm retreat provide,
Hid from the crowd; but near the sheltered home

Let the fair Naiads roll their constant tide;
So may it emulate the far-famed dome
Of Grecian Academe where once it was mine,
To pour instruction amidst the youthful band;
Imbue the generous breast with truth divine
Retracing all that early culture planned.[144]
These now no more remain — yet still survive.
The latent sparks of learning's holy flame;
O let thy breath the genuine glow revive,
Till each young bosom catch the lucid beam.
On Tiber's banks Athenian bands shall rove
Nor mourn to quit Ilyssus' favoured strand;
Surrounding thousands shall thy toils approve,
And give thy name to every distant land . . .

"Too oft, forgetful of their trust divine,
Have former pontiffs burnt with warlike rage [145]
But by paternal maxims taught, it is thine
To heal the wounds of war, and meliorate the age."

Thus by thy strain, Immortal Plato! fired,
Shall mighty aims engage his ardent mind;
Such once his father's glowing breast inspired,
The friend of peace, the legate of human kind . . .
[Then] awhile in pleased attention shall he bend,
And to thy precepts yield a willing ear:
But now thy destined hour arrives — ascend
And join the triumph of the heavenly sphere.

The immediate reaction of Pope Leo to this noble literary offering is not known. There are no indications that he favored the establishment of the kind of academy suggested by Aldus and Musurus. Nor, however sympathetic Leo felt toward the Greek scholar-exiles, was he spurred by Musurus' lament for the lost Byzantium to launch a military expedition against the Turks. The age of Crusades had passed. Nevertheless, the dedication of Plato with its splendid encomium to the Medici helped to fix firmly in Leo's mind the double image of a talented Greek and a master printer. Thus on November 28, 1513 the pope recognized the work of the Aldine press by issuing a papal bull granting to Aldus the exclusive

[144] Foffano, "Marco Musuro," 468, bases on these lines his view that Musurus first suggested the foundation of Leo's Greek school in Rome.
[145] Pope Julius II, for example.

privilege of reprinting and publishing, for fifteen years, all Greek and Latin books already printed or to be published by Aldus, including those printed in the Italic characters which he had invented.[146]

Completed in the same month as the monumental Aldine Plato was another work edited by the indefatigable Musurus, the *editio princeps* of Alexander of Aphrodisias' *Commentaries on the Topics of Aristotle*. This text, one of the most important ancient commentaries on Aristotle, which was to become very influential in the interpretation of Renaissance Aristotelianism, did not appear until February 1514.[147]

Several months afterwards, in August of 1514, the Aldine press published what is undoubtedly Musurus' second most important textual edition — the *Lexicon* of the fifth or sixth century Alexandrian writer Hesychius. The volume was dedicated by Aldus to a noble Mantuan, Giacopo Bardellone, whose manuscript had been borrowed for the edition. In Aldus' prefatory words:

> We wish to publish, therefore, this book under your name, most learned Bardellone, so that scholars will be indebted to you — and we expect it will be more dear to you since Musurus, the common father (*compater*) of both of us, has edited it as accurately as he could in view of his other duties (*per occupationes*), and rendered it, so to say, better than the original [manuscript]. One can easily recognize the great number of emended passages if he compares the printed text with the manuscript.[148]

Musurus' work is of particular value because the manuscript of Hesychius he utilized is the only one known to have survived from the ancient world; moreover the work of Hesychius evidently had been unknown to the West before this time. Some modern critics have justifiably excoriated Aldus, and Musurus even more, for utilizing the Hesychius manuscript as printer's copy, thereby

---

[146] For summary of this privilege see Roscoe, II, 253. Earlier, Julius II had issued a somewhat similar bull in Aldus' favor.

[147] On the delay see Firmin-Didot, 367–68, and also Legrand, I, p. cxvi and 99–100; also cf. Renouard, *Annales*, I, 150. On Alexander's importance for the current interpretation of Aristotle, especially for getting away from the medieval scholastic interpretations of that author, see Kristeller, *Classics*, 40–41.

[148] Text in Botfield, *Praefationes*, 307, French translation in Firmin-Didot, 379. For the latest edition of Hesychius, see K. Latte, *Hesychii Alexandrini Lexicon* (Hauniae, Munksgaard, 1953) I, and the useful work of M. Schmidt, *Hesychii Alexandrini Lexicon*.

mutilating the codex with technical directions to the compositors. But this procedure was a not uncommon one in the period. Nor, we are told, did Musurus have much time available for work on a manuscript so faulty that it swarmed with errors.[149]

Musurus' edition of Hesychius has been criticized on other grounds. Some philologists have censured him for making unnecessary alterations in the text while neglecting to correct what they consider to be obvious errors. However, the science of philology was still in its infancy, and the modern canons of collation and criticism had not yet been formulated. In the sphere of textual criticism Musurus lacked forerunners, and was in fact largely self-taught. He did not have at his disposal really adequate equipment for his work — satisfactory dictionaries, grammars, and reference works with proper indices. Moreover, the useful technique of correlating analogous references from other lexica had not been developed. And with only a single manuscript of Hesychius at his disposal there was of course no basis for the comparison of readings. It is therefore unfair to compare his edition with those of modern philologists. Nor indeed was his aim, like that of most of today's classicists, confined to establishment of the purity of the original text. His ultimate objective was broader and at the same time perhaps more lofty — the preservation and diffusion of the ancient masterpieces so that both his own countrymen and the Westerners could read, easily and unhindered by innumerable difficulties.

Remarkably enough, in the very same month (August 1514) the Aldine Press was able to issue Musurus' *editio princeps* of the Greek author Athenaeus' *Deipnosophistae* (*Banquet of the Learned*), a kind of encyclopedia of miscellaneous information which drew on the accumulated scholarship of Athenaeus' age, the second to third century A.D. Prepared from an incomplete manuscript, the work was dedicated by its publisher Aldus to Musurus' Hungarian student, Janus Vertessy. (From this dedication we have already quoted.) According to Aldus' dedicatory epistle, Musurus not only corrected the "myriads of errors" with which the manuscript abounded, but replaced the missing first two books of the

---

[149] See Menge, "Vita Marci Musuri," 54-55, and cf. Brown, *Venetian Printing Press*, 45.

original with the corresponding sections from an epitome of the work.[150]

In February of 1515 the world of humanism suffered a severe loss, with the death of Aldus at the age of sixty-three. The passing of this leader in the task of restoring Greek letters, however, did not mark the end of Aldine publication, for his father-in-law and partner Andrea d'Asola, a first-rate printer in his own right (having originally purchased the printing equipment of Nicholas Jenson, he had entered the profession even before Aldus) took over the business. Nor did Musurus, deeply moved by the death of his friend, sever his connections with the Aldine Press, despite an offer of employment from the noted Florentine printers and rivals of Aldus, the Giunta. Founders of a flourishing press in Florence with a branch in Venice, the Giunta did succeed briefly in persuading Musurus to cooperate on the textual edition of Oppian's *Halieutica* (*On Fishing*), published in July of 1515.[151] This essay of collaboration was viewed with considerable displeasure by d'Asola — a feeling probably inspired by professional jealousy. Previously, in 1513, the Giunta had objected to the privileges granted to Aldus by Pope Leo X, and on January 10, 1515, Filippo di Giunta had published in Florence an edition of Theocritus. (This publication, interestingly enough, was evidently a reproduction of a manuscript of Theocritus that Musurus had corrected for the instruction of his classes in Venice.) [152] Moreover, the Giunta were second only to the printers of Lyons, France, in making counterfeit editions of Aldus' publications.

What may be considered Musurus' eulogy of Aldus appears in Musurus' publication in November 1515 of Aldus' Greek grammar,

[150] Legrand, I, p. cxviii and 121–22. Cf. Firmin-Didot, 379–83, who has garbled the meaning of this passage. See the recent edition of A. Desrousseaux and C. Astruc, *Athénée de Naucratis, Les Deipnosophistes* (Paris, 1956) p. xliiif.

[151] See Menge, 34 and especially Legrand, I, 126ff. and p. cxviii, for the letter of Bernardo di Giunta dedicating the *Halieutica* to Musurus and noting that Musurus had corrected the work from several manuscripts including three of his own (the passage is not entirely clear). On the Giunta family see Renouard, *Annales*, appendix, and A. M. Bandini, *De Florentina Juntarum Typografia et Juntarum Typog. Annales*, 2 vols. (Lucca, 1791).

[152] See Legrand, I, 128, for mention of d'Asola's publication (in 1517) of a version of Oppian in which he made very disparaging remarks about the earlier Giunta edition. On the objection of the Giunta to Leo's privileges, cf. Pastor, *History of the Popes*, VIII, 259. On the Florentine Theocritus of the Giunta see Legrand, 125–26 and cf. above, note 126.

the text of which, along with the explanatory material, was printed in Greek. Before his death Aldus had expressed the desire that the work be completed and published by Musurus, and it was therefore a kind of legacy of Aldus to his friend. To quote the simple but touching words of Musurus contained in the prefatory epistle he addressed to the French humanist Jean Grolier — a statement so different from the often bombastic Renaissance eulogy:

Aldus was an admirable man who placed public interest above his own. Sparing no expense, shunning no work, he devoted his money and his life to the welfare of scholars. I had often taken up my pen with the intention of recording these virtues, but whenever I did so my wound of sorrow, caused by Aldus' death, was reopened.

Noting that Aldus, a good father, had commended his children to the care of his father-in-law d'Asola, Musurus continues that the book, however, had been entrusted to him:

This Greek grammar, then (for this is the name of the little daughter), which Aldus, prevented by premature death, could not feed with additional nourishment of learning, I entrust to you [Grolier], sorrowful and shy that it is . . . Receive it hospitably, love, protect, and guard it.[153]

In the early part of 1516 Musurus, like others of the Greek exiles, turned his attention at least momentarily to ecclesiastical writings. Working from several manuscripts, he corrected for the Aldine press sixteen orations of the fourth century father of the Eastern church, Gregory of Nazianzus. Musurus himself wrote the preface to this *editio princeps*, and the volume was dedicated to his pupil, the French ambassador to Venice, Jean de Pins, Bishop of Rieux. De Pins (who was later to be attacked by Erasmus for his "Ciceronianism") procured many manuscripts for King Francis I, which were to form part of the collection of the royal library at Fontainebleau.[154]

Returning to the classics, Musurus now saw through the press the important first edition of the second century Greek traveler

---

[153] Legrand, I, 131–33. Faulty French translation in Firmin-Didot, 407–409.
[154] On this edition of Gregory see Menge, 34, and Legrand, I, p. cxviii, and for the preface, in the original, Legrand, 136–43. On de Pin's manuscripts see H. Omont, *Catalogues des manuscrits grecs de Fontainebleau sous François I et Henri II* (Paris, 1889).

Pausanias, which, along with his own lengthy preface written in Greek, he dedicated to Janus Lascaris. Saluting Lascaris as the "true representative (*proxenos*) . . . of the Greeks," Musurus affirms that the primary aim of Lascaris' life is the deliverance of Greece from bondage. The undertaking of a crusade against the Turks, which is desired by all the world and is constantly on men's lips, Janus works for ceaselessly. But it has not yet taken place, Musurus says, because of the petty quarrels of Western princes over one or another unfortunate little town and especially over Italy. In the meantime, as he puts it, other far more important areas are being abandoned to the Infidel!

Musurus praises his friend for his many services to the Greeks of Venice. In Rome especially, writes Musurus, Lascaris is now universally venerated and admired; he is considered the great patron of all the Greeks everywhere (*koinos hapantachou ton Hellenon prostates*), and in every way possible he seeks to aid his compatriots who come to Rome. Musurus lauds Janus' love of letters, his activity in public affairs, his honesty and humanity, particularly his refusal to cast blame on those who attack him unjustly.[155] However rhetorical his language, Musurus' sincere admiration for and devotion to his friend are obvious.

The final phase of Musurus' career took place in Rome, to which he seems to have moved toward the latter part of 1516.[156] The reasons for his departure from Venice are not entirely clear. One opinion is that he left in answer to a summons from the Medici Pope Leo X to come to Rome to aid personally in the direction of his Greek college; another, that Musurus saw in the papal capital an opportunity for material advancement of his career.[157] Lacking

[155] Preface in Legrand, I, 144–50; also in Botfield, *Praefationes*, 312–17. See Menge, 34; also Knös' summary, *Janus Lascaris*, 148–51. Musurus' edition was done from faulty manuscripts.

[156] Musurus wrote from Venice to Lazaro Bonamico, in July and September, that he was making plans to go, on the first of October, to Pesaro by boat and thence by horse to Rome; the letters are printed in Marangoni, "Lazaro Bonamico," 172 (see also preceding letter). Cf., however, another letter of Musurus written from Rome in June of the same year (see Mercati, *Pio*, 72, n. 2, and cf. note 160, below). Probably Musurus visited Rome briefly in about June, returned to Venice, to depart permanently for Rome in the latter part of the year.

[157] See for example, Legrand, I, p. cxviii; C. Börner, *De doctis hominibus graecis litterarum graecarum in Italia* (Leipzig, 1701) 225; also Papadopoli, *Historia gymnasii Patavini*, I, 204, who (alone) says that Musurus earlier, under Pope

definite evidence as to his motives, we may assume that several factors were involved. With the accession of Leo X and the economic and political decline of Venice, Medici Rome was now rapidly becoming the leading center of humanist scholarship, and its intellectual attraction, together with the presence of several good friends, must have figured prominently in Musurus' thinking.

Musurus' friends in Rome included persons of considerable influence at the papal court: Cardinal Pietro Bembo, the Latinist and former member of the Aldine circle who then held the post of papal secretary; Musurus' old pupil Alberto Pio, now the legate of the King of France; and Scaramuzza Trivulzio, Bishop of Como.[158] Moreover, Musurus' former colleague Zacharias Calliergis had, in 1515, established the first Greek press in Rome,[159] while his old mentor Janus Lascaris had become director of the newly founded Greek institute. We must not overlook Musurus' connections with Pope Leo himself. To him Musurus had dedicated his "Hymn to Plato," and at his request he had summoned pupils from Greece for the papal Greek school.

Musurus did not cut himself off from Venice, however. From a Venetian senatorial document,[160] we learn that Musurus obtained only temporary leave from his post. Indeed, he even promised his friends — and they included many Venetian noblemen of the highest rank — that he would soon return, and had left some of his books behind in Venice in the care of Carlo Cappello (who was later to become the Venetian envoy to Florence and still later to England). But the warm reception and papal honors accorded Musurus in Rome were until his death to hold him on the banks of the Tiber.[161]

Julius II, had come to Rome and broken into the following of John Cardinal Medici (Leo X).

[158] In Musurus' dedicatory letter to Trivulzio (see below, text and note 170) Musurus thanks the Bishop for aid extended to him in his nomination as archbishop (also cf. Legrand, I, pp. cxix–cxx). On Trivulzio see further Pastor, *History of the Popes*, VIII, 458, and Roscoe, *Leo X*, III, 128.

[159] See Chapter 7, text and notes 49ff.

[160] On the Venetian document see Don A. Calogera, *Raccolta d'opuscoli*, XXIII (Venice, 1728–1757) 29–31. Note especially the mention of many Venetian nobles ("bon numero de nostri zentilomini") studying Greek with Musurus in Venice. On Cappello see Mercati, *Pio*, 72, n. 2. Also see a letter of Musurus in Foffano, "Marco Musuro," 469.

[161] Legrand, I, p. cxviii. Kalitsounakis, in "Matthaios Debares," 84, holds that Musurus did *not* go to Rome. In an unused passage from Sanuto (*Diarii*, XIII, col. 293), dated Dec. 5, 1511, it is stated that (in Venice) Alberto Pio visited

Closely tied to the problem of his departure for Rome is the question of his appointment by the Pope to the Latin archbishopric of Monemvasia in Greece.[162] This appointment of Musurus to ecclesiastical office need not surprise us. If we recall the conditions under which he held an ecclesiastical benefice at Carpi, he may already have been in orders before his assignment to the see of Monemvasia. Moreover, nomination of humanists to high religious office was not uncommon during the Renaissance period. Several Greeks residing in the West had in fact already attained ecclesiastical preferment, among them Bessarion, who on two occasions had almost been elected pope. And earlier, in 1409, the Cretan scholastic and professor at Paris Petrus Philarges had actually attained the supreme office (as Alexander V) during the Council of Pisa.[163] It was not impossible that there now lay before Musurus a career similar to those of his illustrious compatriots.

The city of Monemvasia, a Venetian possession since 1464, as a consequence of the proclamation of union at the Council of Florence had acquired a Catholic (Uniate) archbishop as well as a Greek one.[164] And it was to this Catholic post that Musurus, by papal decree, was named on June 19, 1516.[165] Leo at the same time appointed him to the Cretan bishopric of Hierapetra and soon afterwards conferred on him the Cretan see of Herronesou (near Candia). Not content with these marks of favor, the Pope granted him

Sanuto in company with Alvise Bembo, Daniel Barbarigo, Carlo Capelli, other nobles, and also Marcus Musurus, lecturer in Greek.

[162] And not Ragusa, as formerly thought. While this book was in proof I found a letter (Allen, *Epistolae Erasmi*, II, 547) of Nicholas Sagundinus saying clearly that Pope Leo called Musurus to Rome to name him Archbishop.

[163] On Alexander V there is an inadequate work by M. Renieris, Ὁ "Ελλην πάπας Ἀλέξανδρος Ε' (Athens, 1881).

[164] On the situation in Monemvasia see W. Miller, "Monemvasia," *Journal of Hellenic Studies*, XXVII (1907) 238–39; also Legrand, I, p. clxviii. But Legrand (based on Giovio, *Elogia*, 67, made a false assumption — that Musurus was preceded in the see of Monemvasia by the Greek Manilius Kavakes Rhalles, an assumption which has confused many scholars. See now Manousakas, "Ἀρχιερεῖς," 122ff., who clarifies this situation. For more detailed treatment see below, Chapter 6.

[165] See G. Gerola, *Per la cronotassi dei vescovi Cretesi all'epoca Veneta* (Venice, 1914) 57. Bühler, "Aldus Manutius," 215, quotes as the date May 26, on the basis of a discovery of G. K. Boyce, but he does not so far as I know adduce the evidence. Cf. Mercati, *Pio*, 74, n. 3, who refers to June 19. In his preface to the Aldine Pausanias (May 1516) Musurus did not mention his elevation; and the preface of d'Asola (dated July of that year) notes that Musurus has *recently* ("nuper") been named archbishop. Cf. Manousakas, Ἀρχιερεῖς, 120.

additional ecclesiastical revenues in Crete and Cyprus.[166] The bestowal of all these honors reveals not only Leo's high regard for the Greek exile but, more important, his desire to insure Musurus a steady income so that he could live undisturbed and continue his scholarly endeavors in Rome. As we shall observe in a later chapter, Musurus' appointment to the bishopric of Monemvasia aroused the antagonism of another fellow Cretan, Arsenios Apostolis, his former teacher, who had aspirations of his own to the post.

Musurus was never more than the titular archbishop of Monemvasia. He never set foot in his see, remaining instead in Rome, detained among other things by the affairs of Leo's Greek school, which from the year 1516 had begun effective operation. Leo established professorships of Greek and Latin for the benefit of the young Greek students, with Lascaris and Musurus both teaching Greek and the well-known poet Lampridio of Cremona instructing in Latin.[167] It was the aim of the school to retain its Greek students in Italy as apostles of Hellenism, but some, their studies completed, desired to return to their homeland. (A few non-Greek pupils were also accepted, such as the Frenchmen Lazare de Baïf and Jean de la Forest, and the Fleming Christophe de Longueil.) [168]

In Rome Musurus was able to enjoy the intimacy of a number of prominent ecclesiastical officials. Foremost among these (as we are informed by one of the very few extant letters of Musurus in Italian, dated May 18, 1517) was the cousin of Leo X, Giulio Cardinal de' Medici, the later pope Clement VII.[169] Another friend and

---

[166] See Legrand, 399–402 and Sathas, 81, for documents showing that Musurus authorized his nephew Manoussos Sakellarios to retain authority over these new properties in Crete and Cyprus.

[167] See Legrand, I, p. cxix, and Rodocanachi, *Première Renaissance*, 165, who base their opinion that Musurus taught Greek in Rome on lines from a poem (in French) of Jean-Antoine de Baïf: "he [de Baïf's father] went up to Rome to see Musurus of Candia . . . that he might hear and learn the Greek of the ancient authors and thereby make himself learned . . ." But Menge, "Vita Marci Musuri," 41, is uncertain about this, believing it unlikely that an archbishop would lecture publicly — a view which is not necessarily true for the period. See below, Chapter 7, note 63, for example, the case of the Bishop of Nocera Varinus Favorinus; also see note 174, below, in which Musurus indicates his desire (though a bishop) to return to teach in Venice. On Lampridio of Cremona see Irigoin, *Pindare*, 409, n. 4.

[168] See T. Simar, *Cristophe de Longueil, humaniste* (Louvain, 1911) 52, and Rodocanachi, 127. In the letter mentioned in the next note Musurus writes that the Greek academy of Lascaris was flourishing, being full of young students.

[169] See letter in Legrand, II, 319, referring to his patron, the Medici Cardinal.

patron was the aforementioned Bishop of Como, Scaramuzza Trivulzio (shortly to be named a cardinal), for whom Musurus executed his only work in Rome as editor. At the request — indeed insistence — of Janus Lascaris, Musurus translated into Latin a small rather insignificant Greek treatise on gout (De podagra), which was offered to Scaramuzza, who like Lascaris was suffering from arthritic pains. The finished work was published on April 1, 1517, and reprinted a half-century later by the great French printer Henri Estienne (Stephanus).[170] This was to be the last scholarly work undertaken by Musurus.

Wearied perhaps by years of intensive, unremitting scholarly endeavor and long hours of teaching, Musurus died on October 17, 1517, at the early age of about forty-seven.[171] No details are available regarding his passing except the statement of Sanuto in his famous Diarii that he had been sick for two months and had become consumptive ("lo episcopo Mussuro . . . è stato amalato do mexi, era venuto eticho").[172] He was buried in the Roman Church of Santa Maria de la Pace, and over his body a tomb was erected with an epitaph by Antonio Amiterno, professor of rhetoric at the University of Rome.[173] The only other information we have on the last days of Musurus is a curious report of the same Sanuto that a few weeks before his death Musurus had written a letter to Venice informing the government of his approaching return. Evidently he cherished the hope of combining his Venetian teaching duties with those of his ecclesiastical office.[174]

[170] See dedicatory epistle in Legrand, II, 397–98. The work is reprinted in vol. 2 of Estienne's Medicae artis principes (1567). Firmin-Didot, Alde Manuce, 464, says the authorship is anonymous, but Legrand, I, p. cxx, notes that the treatise is attributed to Demetrius Pepagomenos. On Trivulzio see especially Renazzi, Storia dell' Università degli Studi di Roma, II (Rome, 1806) 77.

[171] There has been much discussion on his date of death. Legrand says "in the autumn," calculating the date from a letter of Bombasio to Erasmus dated 6 December 1517 (Legrand, I, p. cxx). Mercati, Pio, 74, n. 3, says death occurred before 4 November 1517: see A. Mercati, "Le spese private di Leone X nel maggio-agosto 1513," Atti della Pontif. Acc. Romana di Arch., ser. 3 Memorie, II (1928) 110. But now see Sanuto, Diarii, XXV, col. 66, who gives the exact date, 17 October, 1517.

[172] Some authorities (e.g. Menge, "Vita Marci Musuri," 41) say he died of dropsy.

[173] Epitaph quoted in Legrand, I, p. cxxi; see also Janus Lascaris' epigram on him, in Knös, Janus Lascaris, 161–62. On Amiterno see Renazzi, Università di Roma, II, 238. For contemporary encomia written about Musurus see Legrand, I, p. cxxi f.

[174] Sanuto, XXIV, col. 669, dated 10 September 1517: "[Musuro] voleva venir

As typically happened in the Italian Renaissance, a story subsequently arose as to the cause of his death. To Paolo Giovio is
first attributed the report that Musurus died of envy and disappointment at not being named to the cardinalate. Driven by insane
ambition which led him to an archbishopric, Musurus, according
to the story, aspired overhastily to the cardinalate. Musurus often
complained, continues Giovio, that none of the Greeks, to their
great shame, had achieved this high office, despite the fact that in
one particular day Leo X had raised thirty men of many different
nations to the sacred college. (Musurus, of course, was presumably
referring to his own generation, since he could not have overlooked
the examples of Bessarion and Isidore of Kiev, and still earlier of
Pope Alexander V.) So chagrined was Musurus by this, the account goes, that his body rapidly wasted away and he died.[175]

The only other contemporary to allude to the story is the more
circumspect Lilio Gyraldi, who adds, significantly, that what gave
rise to the report was the envy of others, who concocted the tale
as the sole means of defaming "this most learned and modest person." "But," Gyraldi continues, "they are of ill repute who spread
abroad this story of a man, who, wherever he was living, was well
spoken of by all. And he left behind a great many pupils distinguished in every discipline of letters and conduct (*totque . . .
discipulos insignes in omni literarum et morum disciplina*), who
by their words and acts prove them [the story mongers] to be
liars." [176]

In this period when so many humanists like Poggio and Filelfo
were characterized by braggadocio, laxity of moral standards, and
greed, not to speak of an attitude of mere lip-service to Christian-

---

a Venezia a lezer, ma li bisogna prima expedir alcuni brevi per benefici . . . et
sara a Venezia al principio di Studio."

[175] Giovio, *Elogia*, 67 (and *Le iscrittioni*, 63). Also see G. P. Valeriano, *De
litteratorum infelicitate* (Venice, 1620) 11. Papadopoli, *Historia gymnasii Patavini*,
I, 294, repeats the story almost *verbatim*. Cf. Menge, 42–43, and Sathas, *Neohellenic
Philology*, 84, who believe the story to be absolutely false. It is curious that according to another report Musurus actually did become a cardinal (P. Freher,
Theatrum virorum eruditione clarorum [Nurenberg, 1688] 25). Janus Lascaris, we
know, turned down an offer of appointment to the Cardinalate.

[176] L. G. Gyraldi, *Dialogi duo*, 63–64. Recent scholars agree with Gyraldi; see
Legrand, I, p. cxx; and Menge, 43. I have recently discovered several new documents in the Vatican and Venetian archives which I hope to publish soon and
which should further clarify the matter of Musurus' death and presumed aspirations to the cardinalate.

Marcus Musurus.

MARCUS MUSURUS
(c. 1470–1517)

ity, Musurus stands out sharply. He was remarkably free of his compatriots' general attitude of intellectual arrogance vis-à-vis the Latins, and of the rivalry that often marked the relations of the Greeks with one another, for example, of George of Trebizond and Michael Apostolis. Unlike many learned men of the age, Musurus never became involved in altercations with other scholars and, aside from a fervent interest in the crusade to the East, seems to have had no particular ambition to participate in political affairs. From what we have observed, then, of Musurus' character, we may conclude that he was essentially a man of honor, of sincere religious conviction and genuine modesty, quick to recognize his scholarly indebtedness to others Any disappointment he may have felt at Leo's failure to confer a cardinal's hat on a Greek was probably motivated less by personal vanity than by a feeling that there would be no Greek spokesman in the Curia to champion the objective so dear to him and to all Greeks — the liberation of the Greek East. The charge against Musurus of soaring ambition may therefore be considered another worthless, defamatory story typical of the contentious, less noble spirit of the Italian Renaissance, and, indeed, it may have been given easy credence because of his Greek background.

The many accomplishments of Musurus have not yet been accorded the recognition they deserve by intellectual historians, although, to be sure, several philologists familiar with his work of textual editing have little hesitation in ranking him as the most skilled scholar of the Greek language during the Renaissance.[177] There can be no doubt, of course, of the vast importance to classical scholarship of the remarkable number of first editions he produced — of eleven or twelve major Greek authors. But his work as teacher of Greek at Padua and Venice is, in view of the inspiration he provided for a large and important group of Western humanists, of hardly less significance. And it is both these activities combined that entitle Musurus, near the close of the Renaissance period, to

---

[177] Professors A. Turyn and A. Pertusi inform me that they would agree. Musurus' worth as a philologist has tardily been recognized because only beginning with the more systematic philological methods of the nineteenth century have scholars been able accurately to determine which works of editing were actually his. Musurus' talents were doubtless greater with respect to poetry than prose. See below, Conclusion, text and note 12.

take his place alongside the first great Byzantine scholar going to the West, Manuel Chrysoloras, as one of the two or three most influential Hellenists in the entire history of the revival and dissemination of Greek letters in western Europe.

In the hope that Musurus would return from Rome, the Venetian magistrates charged with public instruction had at first been reluctant to replace him. But a few months after his death a decree was published calling for applicants to fill the vacancy. A competition was to be held, and after the public presentation of Greek readings the best candidate would be selected.[178] News of the competition elicited what may be considered a supreme, though indirect, tribute from the leading humanist of the age, Erasmus, who was certainly not quick to praise the scholarship of any rival:

I do not think any one among us, either Gaul or German, is so rash as to want to put forth his candidacy in that theater or to enter into competition with the Italians, the posterity of Musurus . . . For what except hisses and laughter could such a one receive? [179]

[178] See document in Don A. Calogerà, *Raccolta d'opuscoli*, XXVIII, 29–31 (quoted also in Legrand, I, p. cxxii).

[179] Allen, *Epistolae Erasmi* (quoted in Legrand, II, p. cxxiii). Musurus' successor was Vittore Fausto, on whose close association in Spain with another Greek exile, Demetrius Ducas, see below, Chapter 8, text and note 72. An unsuccessful aspirant, as noted, was the Venetian pupil of Musurus Petrus Alcyonius (on whom see Firmin-Didot, *Alde Manuce*, 441; Mazzuchelli, *Gli scrittori d'Italia*, I, 377, and Nolhac, *La bibliothèque de Fulvio Orsini*, 448).

Chapter 6

ARSENIOS APOSTOLIS

Cretan Cleric and Philologist in Venice, Florence, and Rome

ARSENIOS (or Aristovoulos)[1] Apostolis, whose scholarly achievement has tended to be clouded for Western historians by certain unsympathetic traits in his character, is another Cretan deserving of more attention for his part in the transfer of Greek learning to the Western world. Son of Michael Apostolis, he is the most conspicuous example in the period of a Greek literatus who, after lengthy residence in Italy, returned to live in the East. As in the case of Musurus, his Western activities are closely bound up with the flowering of Greek studies in the three major centers of Italian humanism — Medici Florence, the Aldine milieu of Venice, and the papal court of Leonine Rome. Legrand has included a sketch of Arsenios' life in his *Bibliographie hellénique*. But re-examination of the sources is necessary in order to amplify Legrand's admittedly incomplete account, to clarify many questions relating to Arsenios' career and publications, and especially to establish Arsenios' place in the larger pattern of Western intellectual development.[2]

---

[1] On his name see below, text and notes 7 and 50.

[2] An early account of Arsenios is that of I. A. Fabricius, *Bibliotheca Graeca*, XI (Hamburg, 1808) 189-190, 580, etc.; see also Sathas, *Neohellenic Philology*, 126-130, with brief biography; A. Moustoxides, "Arsenios" (in Greek), Πανδώρα, VI (1855-56) 493ff., who published some of his letters; and especially Legrand, *Bibliographie hellénique*, I, pp. clxv-clxxiv. For Arsenios' letters, see Legrand, II, 337-46, 418. Salaville's summary on Arsenios Apostolis (or Apostolios) in *Dict. d'hist. géog. eccl.* III, cols. 1027-30, seems to be based on Legrand. The brief sketch by Firmin-Didot in *Alde Manuce* contains many errors, as will be noted below. Useful for chronological references to Arsenios is the article of Manousakas, "Gregoropoulos Correspondence," and for an important treatment of the question of Arsenios' assumption of the archbishopric of Monemvasia, see

It has generally been accepted that 1465 was the year of Arsenios' birth, but a somewhat later date may be the correct one. While the evidence for 1465, a note in a Vienna manuscript, indicates that Arsenios died in 1535 after living "about seventy years," an overlooked passage in a letter from his father Michael to Bessarion, dated by Noiret as late 1469, informs us that Michael had recently become the father of "still another infant (*neognon*) . . . Aristovoulos [Arsenios] by name." This reference to Arsenios indicates that in 1469 he had probably just been born or was at most not more than one or two years of age. Hence his date of birth may probably with greater accuracy be fixed as 1468 or 1469.[3]

Arsenios' birthplace was Candia (Herakleion), the flourishing Venetian capital on the island of Crete, where his father Michael had taken refuge after the fall of Constantinople. Arsenios' mother, the daughter of Count Theodosios of Corinth, whose family had originally come from Monemvasia, was the second wife of Michael. We know nothing of Arsenios' boyhood and early education, but it is likely that he received his first training from his father.[4] From the senior Apostolis, in fact, Arsenios inherited many characteristics, notably a similarity of intellectual interest. But he also acquired certain less attractive qualities — a readiness to flatter in order to secure his ends and a disposition to complain about the misfortunes of his life. Yet to say that he was simply a replica of

---

his "Prelates of Monemvasia," 104-45. Finally, see M. Manousakas' just-published work, "'Αρσενίου Μονεμβασίας τοῦ 'Αποστόλη ἐπιστολαὶ ἀνέκδοτοι (1521-34)," 'Επετηρὶς τοῦ Μεσαιωνικοῦ 'Αρχείου, VIII-IX (1958-59) 5-56, for eleven unpublished letters of Arsenios found in Rome's Biblioteca Vallicelliana. This work containing valuable data on the last years of Arsenios' career came to me when the present book was in press, but I have been able to incorporate its material in the book. Manousakas' work is referred to below as "Arsenios . . . Unpublished Epistles."

[3] For the Vienna manuscript see Legrand, I, p. clxxii. Michael's letter to Bessarion is printed in Noiret, *Lettres*, p. 113, no. 92, ll. 4-5. Note a passage in the same Vienna manuscript (Legrand) which implies that Arsenios was bereft of his father at an early age (ἐλείφθη δὲ ὀρφανὸς πάνυ ἐκ πατρός).

[4] Cf. Crusius, *Turcograeciae*, 90 (also Sathas, *Neohellenic Philology*, 123), who quotes Theodosios Zygomalas as saying that Arsenios was taught by Matthew Camariotes; but it would seem to me that this view is probably incorrect, for in Legrand, II, 109, l. 10, there is a letter of Maximos Margounios saying that Camariotes died shortly after Constantinople's fall, at a time when Arsenios had not yet been born. (Is it possible therefore that reference is made here rather to Arsenios' father, Michael Apostolis?). According to the Vienna manuscript (see preceding note) Arsenios, because of the early death of his father, was largely self-taught.

his father is inaccurate. For with the bitter experience of the latter ever before his eyes he was able with impunity in the early phase of his career to avoid emulating the more passive qualities of Michael. But, as we shall see, what led to his undoing in his later years was his overweening ambition and an inability to control his temper, with the result that in the end he alienated everyone.

Having at an early age acquired a love of letters, Arsenios, in the fashion of so many other Cretans, earned money by the copying of Greek manuscripts, either for the Venetian noblemen of Crete interested in ancient literature or for scholars of Italy proper.[5] And in fact, gathering together a group of students, he seems to have instituted a school for manuscript copying on the island, of which he was the leading spirit.[6] From the numerous manuscripts transcribed by himself and his associates we are able to glean a certain amount of information on his life. Thus the first concrete evidence about him after childhood is his own subscription, dated March 1489, to a manuscript of the *Argonautica* of Apollònius of Rhodes. The same codex informs us that this was not the first manuscript he copied and that at this time — already, it would appear at the age of twenty-one or -two — he had been ordained a deacon at Candia,[7] probably of the Uniate rite, following the predilections of his father.

In imitation of the elder Apostolis, Arsenios early began to teach. A pupil of his at this time was certainly John Gregoropoulos,[8] later to become a leading member of the Aldine circle. Among other students of Arsenios was very probably Gregoropoulos' good friend Marcus Musurus, for in a letter to Gregoropoulos Musurus

---

[5] See the catalogue of his manuscripts in Vogel and Gardthausen, *Die griechischen Schreiber*, 42–44. There are certainly to be found in European libraries other manuscripts copied by him (and the other scholars treated in this book) which are not listed in Vogel-Gardthausen's lists of MSS.

[6] Cf. Wittek, "*Scriptorium* de Michel Apostolès," 290–97.

[7] Signed Ἀριστόβουλος Ἀποστολίδης [Apostolides in Byzantine style = son of Apostolis, a form used by Arsenios in the early manuscripts he copied] (ἱεροδιάκονος θείᾳ χάριτι) μισθοῦ χάριν καὶ ταύτην τὴν βίβλον ἐν Κρήτῃ ἐξέγραψα. Μάρτιος 1489. See Legrand, *Bibliographie hellénique*, II, 418; cf. H. Omont, *Catalogue des manuscrits grecs de la bibliothèque royale de Bruxelles* (Gand, 1885) 26.

[8] There are three pieces of evidence for this: (1) a letter of John to Arsenios, dated 5 December 1499, terming the latter διδάσκαλος (Legrand, II, 267; cf. Manousakas, "Gregoropoulos Correspondence," 192); (2) a letter to John, in which the writer, John's father George Gregoropoulos, speaks of ὁ ὑμέτερος διδάσκαλος ... Ἀριστόβουλος (Legrand, II, 269); (3) see text for next note.

asks whether "our teacher when we were children, the deacon [Arsenios] . . . is still in Venice." [9]

According to what may be deduced from a recently discovered document, in June of 1492 Arsenios appeared in Venice seeking authorization to collect all the revenues of his predecessor in the office of deacon, the Cretan George Vranas. The claim was disallowed by the Doge. But Arsenios' unsuccessful journey to Venice may perhaps have been what spurred him to proceed to the Medici court of Florence,[10] where subsequently we find him copying important Greek manuscripts.

Certainly connected with Arsenios' appearance in Florence is the name of the famous Byzantine scholar Janus Lascaris. For Arsenios' name is listed on a Cretan document dated April 3, 1492, as a witness in a transaction involving the purchase of manuscripts by Lascaris, who himself had been sent to the East by Lorenzo de' Medici to search for Greek codices.[11] Legrand is of the opinion that when Lascaris subsequently departed from Crete he took with him to Italy the young Arsenios (possibly in accordance with a charge of Lorenzo to seek out and bring back to Florence talented young Greeks trained in the trade of a scribe). But though Lascaris undoubtedly played some part in inducing Arsenios to come to Florence — witness Arsenios' own statement in a later letter to Pope Leo X, "That philhellene, the high-minded Lorenzo, then attracted me, too, to Florence through the instrumentality of the very wise Lascaris" [12] — we know from a document recently printed that Arsenios had already come to Italy of his own volition in order to take care of personal business before the Doge of Venice.

Lorenzo the Magnificent died in the summer of 1492, shortly before Arsenios' arrival in Florence in the fall of the same year. And in his stead his son and successor, Piero de' Medici, became Arsenios' patron. Arsenios, appropriately enough, now occupied him-

---

[9] Letter printed in Renouard, *Annales*, III, 284. (Also see Manousakas, "Gregoropoulos Correspondence," e.g., 193, n. 3, 176, 185, 201). The slight difference in age between Musurus and Arsenios is not a serious objection to the theory of Musurus' study with the latter.

[10] See Manousakas, "Βενετικὰ ἔγγραφα," no. 21, and esp. pp. 211–12.

[11] Contract printed in Legrand, II, 326. Cf. Knös, *Janus Lascaris*, 49–50.

[12] See Walz, *Arsenii Violetum*, 2–3. Also preface printed in Legrand, II, 340–42.

self with copying for Piero the manuscripts Janus Lascaris had brought back from the East.[13]

According to Arsenios' own testimony his days at Piero's court were very pleasant.[14] Florence was still, intellectually, the most brilliant foyer in Europe. Along with such celebrated Italian scholars as Marsilio Ficino and Angelo Poliziano, there were to be found there a number of noted Greek intellectuals, including Janus Lascaris, Demetrius Chalcondyles, and, as we have seen, Arsenios' compatriot the young Marcus Musurus, then a student of Lascaris'.[15] It was probably now that Arsenios made the acquaintance of Giovanni de' Medici,[16] later Pope Leo X, at this time a youth of seventeen.

Arsenios next appears in Venice, where we find him, in 1494, at work for the publishing firm of Aldus Manutius. Why he left Florence is not clear, but one may speculate that his departure, like that of Musurus, was related to the collapse of the Medici regime in the face of imminent French invasion, the attraction of Venice for Cretan expatriates, and, not least, the practical factor of an opportunity for employment. Whatever his motives, Arsenios' name appears as an editor of one of Aldus' very first publications, the curious Greek poem *Galeomyomachia*. As Arsenios notes in his preface to the volume, he was ignorant of the author of the poem (who is now known to be the twelfth century Byzantine writer Theodore Prodromos).[17] In his preface Arsenios also makes

[13] On Arsenios' arrival in Florence, see his (one extant) letter to Leo, in Walz, 2 (Legrand, II, 341): τοῦ ἀοιδίμου τότε πατρὸς ὑμῶν πρὸ ὀλίγου εἰς χοροστασίας ἁγίων ἀποιχομένου. Also, Ἰωάννης ὁ Λάσκαρις . . . τὰς (βίβλους) μὲν ἐκγράφων ἐγὼ Πέτρῳ τῷ μεγαλοπρεπεῖ . . . τὰς πλείους γὰρ ἐκείνων δι' ἐμοῦ ἀνεκαίνισε. (For a list of the manuscripts brought back by Lascaris, see E. Vogel, "Litterarische Ausbeute von Janus Lascaris' Reisen im Peloponnes um's Jahr 1490," *Serapeum*, XV (1854) 154–160. But for the definite date of his arrival, in the fall of 1492, see Manousakas, "Βενετικὰ ἔγγραφα," no. 21, and esp. p. 212.

[14] See Arsenios' words of gratitude to Leo X for the favors extended to Arsenios by Leo's brother Piero, in Walz, 3 (Legrand, 341).

[15] See above, Chapter 5.

[16] Walz, 3: ὅπου (in Florence) καὶ τὴν σὴν ἔγνων μακαριότητα.

[17] See K. Krumbacher, *Geschichte der byzantinischen Litteratur* (Munich, 1897) 751; Legrand, *Bibliographie hellénique*, I, 19, and n. 2; and G. Fumagalli, "Saggio bibliografico sulla Galeomiomachia di Teodoro Prodromo," *Rivista delle biblioteche*, II (1889) 49–56, who says that the manuscript revealing Prodromos' authorship was among those given to Venice by Bessarion. The *Galeomyomachia* lacks both place and date, but is attributed to Aldus on the basis of the type font (Legrand, I, 18, and Scholderer, *Catalogue of Books Printed in XV Century*, V,

a rather elaborate announcement of his intention to publish, shortly, the collection of proverbs compiled by his father Michael, called *Ionia*.[18] This promise, as we shall see, Arsenios was never able to carry out.

Arsenios certainly worked on other Aldine projects in this period.[19] And the publication of one, in August of 1496, suggests that he may still have been in Venice on that date. This work, *Thesaurus Cornucopiae et horti Adonidis*, is a collection of thirty-four extremely important Greek and Byzantine grammatical treatises originally collected by the Italian Hellenist Varinus (Guarino) Favorinus of Camerino and Carolus Antenoreus of Florence, with the help of the famous teacher of Favorinus, Angelo Poliziano. Aldus Manutius and his friend, the Franciscan Urbano Bolzanio, reworked, added to, and edited the work for publication. A charming quatrain on the Muses by Arsenios was included in the work, together with other epigrams composed by Aldus, Carteromachus, and Angelo Poliziano.[20] The *Thesaurus* is of great interest to classicists because it also contains fragments from ancient Greek poets which cannot elsewhere be located, the manuscript sources for which are now lost.[21]

In October of 1497 we find Arsenios in Crete for the second time within a year. For this we have three pieces of evidence — two epistles directed to John Gregoropoulos in Venice, the first from his father George Gregoropoulos, and another from Arsenios, addressed to his friend and former pupil. The third, a document (overlooked by Legrand and others) which refers to Arsenios' arrival in Crete, probably at the end of 1496, is a manuscript of

553, who says the *Galeomyomachia* was probably printed for private publication). On the date of Aldus' first editions see Chapter 5, note 28.

[18] For preface see Legrand, I, 18–19. Arsenios later did publish certain sayings (*Apophthegmata*) he had collected. See below notes 70ff. Cf. above, Chapter 4, text and notes 103–105.

[19] See below, text and note 26, mention of his work on Alexander of Aphrodisias.

[20] Renouard, *Annales*, I, 20–21; Firmin-Didot, 83; also Roscoe, *Leo X*, II, 262, note b and 263. Legrand makes no mention of the work of Favorinus or Arsenios. On Favorinus and the *Thesaurus* see E. Mestica, *Varino Favorino Camerte* (Ancona, 1888) and A. Lemke, *Aldus Manutius and his Thesaurus Cornucopiae of 1496* (Syracuse, 1958) 1ff. Cf. Chapter 7, text and notes 77–78. The *Thesaurus* included treatises of Aelian Dionysius, Eustathius' Commentary, Herodian, Choeroboscus, John the Grammarian.

[21] Cf. Reitzenstein, *Griechische Etymologika*, 260. Analysis of the *Thesaurus*' sources is a good subject for research.

Sophocles with scholia, dated in that year. Arsenios had copied the manuscript for the Florentine monk Pietro Candido, a member of the Medicean circle in which Arsenios had moved while in Florence.[22] Scholars have ventured no opinion as to the reasons for the frequency of Arsenios' voyages between Crete and Venice in this period. But a passage from one of his letters indicates the possibility of a business relationship, possibly a commission for Arsenios to obtain manuscripts for Aldus. It is perhaps in this context that the following words of Arsenios addressed to John Gregoropoulos should be understood: "Until now I have been awaiting the book I ordered from Kyrios Aldus, so that in return I can send him those he has requested." [23]

Arsenios was still in Crete in late 1498, as is disclosed by still another letter of his to John Gregoropoulos, requesting the dispatch of both the Aldine *Lexicon* of Crastoni (published in December of 1497) and the Aldine edition of Aristophanes (which appeared July 15, 1498).[24] Only a short time later, at the end of 1498 or beginning of 1499, Arsenios' relationship with Aldus was broken off as the result of a difference between the two over a financial matter. Evidently the quarrel — details of which are not entirely clear — was carried on through the mail and without the presence of Arsenios in Italy. Western historians have tended to blame Arsenios for the falling-out, citing the incident as one more evidence of his contentious disposition. An impartial scrutiny of the sources, however, may indicate a basis for a less adverse judgment.

[22] Arsenios returned to Crete sometime after publication of the *Thesaurus* (August, 1496) and we find him still in Crete on January 22, 1497, the date on which he finished copying the manuscript of Sophocles (see Vogel and Gardthausen, *Die griechischen Schreiber*, 42). On the basis of a letter of George Gregoropoulos directing his son John to inform Arsenios of the good health of his mother (which Manousakas, "Gregoropoulos Correspondence," 174-75, dates 1497; cf. Legrand, II, 269, dated only February 13), we know that Arsenios left Crete for Venice between January 22 and February 13 (1497) and he must have returned to Crete *after* August 21, 1497 (Legrand, II, 295 and Manousakas, 179 — letter of George Karandenos to John) and *before* October 1 of the same year (see Arsenios' letter, from Crete, to John in Venice dated October 1, 1497; Legrand, II, 337) from which it is clear that Arsenios was again in Crete. Candido belonged to the monastery of Santa Maria degli Angeli in Florence.

[23] Legrand, II, 337: Ἐς τόδε προσεδόκων τὰς βίβλους ἃς παρήγγειλα τῷ κυρίῳ Ἄλδῳ πέμψειν, ἵνα καὶ ἡμεῖς ἀντιπέμψωμεν ἃς παρήγγειλε. See below, text and note 40, for another possible reason for Arsenios' desire to return to Crete.

[24] Letter printed in Legrand, II, 338, without date or addressee. Cf. Manousakas, "Gregoropoulos Correspondence," 185.

The issue was first raised by Aldus, who wrote to Arsenios [25] demanding repayment of a loan of ten and a half ducats which, two years before, Aldus had made to Arsenios, possibly in the form of books. Arsenios replied that he owed nothing to Aldus inasmuch as the sum was covered by his work for Aldus in Venice. He claimed that he had spent two months copying the text of Alexander of Aphrodisias, an important ancient commentator on Aristotle. (Volume One of the remarkable Aldine edition of the Aristotelian commentaries was not to appear until 1503).[26]

Aldus refused to accept Arsenios' version and, through his agent, appealed to the Venetian courts in Crete, taking an oath that he had not received the sum from Arsenios even in the form of work. The court ruled in Aldus' favor and Arsenios was directed to make restitution of the sum in question. The sole source of information for this litigation is an undated letter of Arsenios addressed to John Gregoropoulos.[27] The letter is worth quoting not only because it has seldom been cited but because it offers a somewhat different picture of Aldus from that of the selfless patron commonly portrayed by historians. Arsenios wrote: [28]

Aldus, who is called the philhellene but in reality is the opposite, asks me to return, via a certain Fra Paolo, the ten and a half gold ducats for the books which, as you know very well, I repaid in the form of copying and labor, which I did in correcting the books printed by him. But I, on my part, request from him the pay for about two months and [for copying] the ten quaternia of Alexander [of Aphrodisias'] commentary on Aristotle's Physics, of which the total pay comes to more than the ten and a half gold ducats he demands. Since his agent has refused to accept my version, and inasmuch as the agent, according to Aldus' letter, has not taken care to secure an oath from him (for alas Aldus continues to deny all these things), it was ruled by the judges here (*entautha*) that I have to hand over the said gold pieces, Aldus

[25] That Aldus raised the issue is known only from Arsenios' letter; the pertinent passage is κατὰ τὴν τοῦ Ἄλδου γραφήν. For entire passage see below, text and note 29. Legrand makes only brief reference to the trouble between Aldus and Arsenios.
[26] See Renouard, *Annales*, I, 24.
[27] Since Gregoropoulos was then in Venice with Aldus, Arsenios evidently wrote to John in order to present his side of the story.
[28] Cf. E. Robertson, "Aldus Manutius, the Scholar-Printer (1460–1515)," *Bulletin of John Rylands Library*, XXXIII (1950) 68, who translates a preface of Aldus which also presents Aldus in a none too sympathetic light.

having sworn an oath that he has not received the money in the said manner . . .[29]

With few details at our disposal (and these from only one contestant) it is difficult to evaluate the merit of either side in the quarrel between Arsenios and Aldus. Arsenios' opinion of Aldus as expressed here ("Aldus, who is called the philhellene but in reality is the opposite") is of course an exaggeration. But one cannot help forming the impression that, however much Aldus idealized the ancient Greeks and their literature, his attitude toward their Byzantine cultural heirs, like that of many other Italian humanists, was conditioned less by sympathy for their plight as exiles than by his own need to exploit their literary talents in his publishing activities.[30] The positions of the two, moreover, with regard to the Venetian administration were certainly unequal. Aldus was a highly respected citizen whose publications added luster to the reputation of Venetian intellectual life (as we have seen the Senate had granted him a monopoly with respect to the Greek books he produced).[31] Arsenios, on the other hand, was a colonial. Hence it is understandable that in a Venetian court of law it would not have been easy for him to make a strong case against Aldus. And even if the Cretan employees of Aldus may have sympathized with their compatriot in this altercation, dependent as they were on Aldus for employment and in some cases even their subsistence, they were not likely openly to express sympathy for Arsenios.[32]

Very probably relating to the dispute between Aldus and Arsenios is a letter sent to Arsenios from Ferrara by a friend Gregory Helladios, possibly a Greek from Corfu.[33] Though not referring to Aldus specifically by name, Gregory urges Arsenios to forget his recent troubles and to be reconciled with his former employer,

[29] See Legrand, *Bibliographie hellénique*, II, 338, for the (undated) letter.
[30] Cf. the letter of Bessarion to Michael Apostolis, printed in Mohler, *Aus Bessarions Gelehrtenkreis*, no. 33, p. 481, in which the sentiment of Latin jealousy of the Greek exiles is expressed.
[31] On the Venetian system of monopoly see F. Norton, *Italian Printers 1501–1520*, p. xxvii.
[32] One cannot but note the repetition of certain cryptic but suggestive remarks in the letters passing back and forth among the Cretans of the Aldine establishment — phrases such as "I can't write anything openly about this," and "tear up this letter after reading it."
[33] The name Helladios, like the Byzantios adopted by Michael Apostolis, may have been assumed. Sathas, *Neohellenic Philology*, has nothing on Gregory.

whom Gregory includes among those he derisively alludes to as "merchants" (*emporoi*) [34] — meaning, of course, those who capitalize on scholarship! Gregory's justification for his advice is that

it is necessary to tolerate these difficulties from such people, even to return and to come to new terms with them despite the fact that you have already been deceived many times. For what can an ordinary person accomplish without the businessman? In my opinion the merchants are a necessary evil of city life, for we can live neither with them nor without them.[35]

Striking is the phrase "you have been deceived many times." Though it may refer to nothing of any real significance, one wonders whether Arsenios (and possibly Gregory) had had other unpleasant experiences with Aldus.[36]

His friend's suggestion evidently had little influence on Arsenios. He did not return to Aldus' employ. Rather we find him remaining in Crete, where he was to reside for the next six or seven years, from the last part of 1497 to the end of 1504.[37] A letter of George Gregoropoulos to his son John suggests that for at least part of this period Arsenios lived with his half-sister Penelope and her husband, and we know that Arsenios' mother was then still alive.[38] Evidence shows that in 1500 (July 26) Arsenios was named an executor of the will of Andreas Damoros, *protopapas* of Candia, who bequeathed to Arsenios, for use during his lifetime, a valuable manuscript containing the commentary of John Chrysostom on St. Paul's epistles. For reasons unknown, Andrew, in a codicil to his testament dated September 1, 1503, revoked the donation.[39]

Arsenios' activity in Crete during these years entailed, it would

[34] Τί γὰρ ἄν τις τῶν πολιτικῶν δρώῃ ἐμπόρων χωρίς.
[35] Entire letter in Legrand, II, 339; Firmin-Didot, *Alde Manuce*, 534–36.
[36] See Robertson, "Aldus Manutius, the Scholar-Printer," 65, who quotes Aldus himself as saying that on four occasions he had had trouble with his employees, who had conspired against him "prompted by avarice." Aldus may perhaps have driven his employees too hard.
[37] See letter in Legrand, II, 337, indicating Arsenios' presence in Crete in October, 1497. Also Manousakas, "Gregoropoulos Correspondence," 200, n. 1.
[38] On Penelope see Noiret, *Lettres*, 17. For Gregoropoulos' letter see Legrand, II, 269, 267, 270 and 272 (where George says Arsenios is living with his whole family: πανοικί). On Arsenios' mother, see Legrand, II, 269. Cf. Manousakas, "Gregoropoulos Correspondence," 175.
[39] For the testament see C. Sathas, *Bibliotheca graeca medii aevi* (Venice, 1877) VI, 674–75. Also on Damoros see the informative note of Manousakas, "Gregoropoulos Correspondence," 183 and 185, and his "Βενετικὰ Ἔγγραφα," nos. 18–20.

seem, mainly the copying of manuscripts and a certain amount of teaching.[39a] At the same time it seems that he held a benefice from a Cretan monastery (perhaps St. Pelagia in Candia) to which as *hierodiakonos* he belonged and where he was accustomed to celebrate the liturgy. In an undated letter of George Gregoropoulos, addressed both to his son John and to Arsenios, who was then in Venice "because of certain affairs," we read: "Know [Arsenios] that the *hegoumenos* [abbot of the monastery] died on February 16 and that at once wolves appeared to seize your monastery and to expel you. And among these . . . is the rascal (*skotendytes*) Mesourios with the aid and assistance of his uncle Makrós Mousourareon . . . With the help of God, however, and the efforts of your faithful brother-in-law they were repulsed." [40] If Mesourios (a not uncommon variation of Musuros or Mousouros) is to be identified with Marcus Musurus,[41] this might well mark the origin of the antipathy between Musurus and Arsenios that was to become so pronounced in the later phase of Arsenios' career. Arsenios' letters to Venice always included greetings to be conveyed to his many friends there, including the Greeks Janus Lascaris and Justin Decadyos as well as certain Italians. But, perhaps significantly, no such reference is ever made to Musurus or Aldus.

It was evidently in this period that Arsenios first conceived the design of gaining control of the archiepiscopal see of Monemvasia,

[39a] Arsenios, we are told (cf. Chapter 5, text and note 83a), taught Greek to the Venetian humanist Giovanni Bembo. Bembo also reports that during his Eastern travels he visited Crete, where he saw his teacher, Arsenios, who was sick in bed with the gout and who said that he wanted to die not in Crete but in Venice or Rome. ("Ibi [Candia] salutavi doctorem meum litterarum Graecarum Aristobulum Milessiae Epidaurique archiepiscopum in lecto podagrantem qui mihi dixit se nolle mori Cretae, sed Venetiis aut Romae.") See Mommsen ed., p. 595; Mommsen dates Bembo's journey in 1505 (p. 592).

[40] Legrand, II, 270. Manousakas, "Gregoropoulos Correspondence," 176, dates the letter after February 16, 1497. (Yet, compare Legrand, II, 267, where John writes to Arsenios in Crete to inform Musurus' parents that Musurus is well). Legrand's opinion (I, p. clxvi) that Arsenios returned to take possession of the benefice seems wrong, since George Gregoropoulos, in the same letter, says he has foiled the "usurpers and that there is no need to return."

[41] See Legrand, II, 270, n. 1 and now Manousakas, "Gregoropoulos Correspondence," 176 and n. 3. See also Gerland, "La noblesse Crétoise," 232. Musurus seems to have returned to Crete at this time (Legrand, I, p. cix and Manousakas, 180). The act of usurpation mentioned in the letter above does not, however, seem compatible with Musurus' character. The ending -us, of course, in Musurus, is the Latinized form.

the implementation of which was to become the overriding ambition of the remainder of his life. Monemvasia, a town situated on a huge rock off the southwestern coast of the Peloponnese, had seen many masters since the thirteenth century. Its economic and strategic importance had early attracted the Venetians who took possession of it after the Fourth Crusade of 1204. In 1260 Monemvasia was restored to the Byzantine Emperor Michael VIII Palaeologus,[42] under whose descendants (termed "Despots of the Morea") it was able to maintain its independence even after the Ottoman conquest of Constantinople in 1453. Sometime during the years 1460 to 1464 it was bequeathed by the Despot Manuel Palaeologus to Pope Pius II, who was eager to launch a crusade against the Turks. But in 1464 the Venetians recovered the city, and it thereafter remained in their possession until 1540, at which time it finally succumbed to the Turks.[43]

The ecclesiastical situation in Monemvasia during the Venetian occupation was somewhat different from that obtaining in other Venetian colonies of Greece. The majority of the population was Orthodox, owing allegiance to the Greek patriarch at Constantinople. There were also, though fewer in number, a group of Greek Uniates recognizing papal jurisdiction, and of course the Roman Catholic members of the Venetian administration. But what complicated the situation was the remarkable fact that the Venetians permitted the town to have at once both a Latin and a Greek archbishop.[44]

It was the Orthodox throne of the city to which Arsenios now aspired. For his audacious scheme he needed not only the support of the Venetian government but the tacit sanction of Rome and of course the approval of the Orthodox patriarch of Constantinople. Implementation of his plan would be in the Venetian interest because with a Venetian-controlled prelate, a "crypto-Catholic," as it were, on the Orthodox throne of Monemvasia, there would no

[42] See Geanakoplos, *Michael Palaeologus*, 154–55.
[43] On Monemvasia see the recent very sketchy work of E. Kalogeras, *Monemvasia, the Venice of the Peloponnesus* (in Greek) (Athens, 1956), which garbles some of the facts on Arsenios. On the Morea see the work of D. Zakythinos, *Le Despotat grec de Morée*, 2 vols. (Paris, 1926 and 1953).
[44] Miller, *Essays on the Latin Orient*, 241. I have found the names of only three Latin archbishops for the entire period. See episcopal lists in B. Mystakides, " Ἐπισκοπικοὶ κατάλογοι," Ἐπετηρὶς Ἑταιρείας Βυζαντινῶν Σπουδῶν, XII (1936) 200.

longer be any problem regarding the ordination of the Orthodox clergy of nearby Crete.[45] In view of the political and religious implications, the success of Arsenios' undertaking would require a large measure of diplomatic finesse and tact.

And so, shortly after the autumn of 1504, Arsenios appeared in Venice before the Council of Ten to present his plan. After winning Venetian support (as we shall observe, during his career he was to have amazingly little difficulty in persuading the Venetian government to go along with most of his schemes), he set out for Monemvasia. The first step in the plan, his ordination to the Orthodox priesthood, was achieved without undue opposition. But for his election as metropolitan by the Orthodox clergy and people he had to resort to documents provided him by the Venetian government — documents which threatened severe measures to be taken against any persons who might deign to oppose his nomination.[46] And a storm of disapproval was aroused by his attempt to have himself consecrated archbishop. He had been, after all, a Uniate, and Orthodox consecration could be received only at the hands of Orthodox bishops acting on the approval of the Patriarch of Constantinople.[47] But despite these formidable obstacles Arsenios, utilizing all the artifice, cajolery, and threats at his command, was able to prevail. His installation as archbishop took place at the end of 1506,[48] one of the prelates officiating being the former Orthodox bishop of Monemvasia himself, Cyril, who, as we are told by a letter of Arsenios, had only recently "resigned" his throne because of illness or old age.[49] It was at this time, on the occasion of his con-

[45] See above, Chapter 2, text and notes 7ff., for mention of this problem.

[46] See Manousakas, "Prelates of Monemvasia," 108.

[47] See document no. 4 published in Manousakas, "Prelates of Monemvasia," 70-73.

[48] See the epigram of Arsenios, dated 1506-1508, written in Crete (where he went soon after his consecration) and in which he terms himself Archbishop of Monemvasia. (Cf. above, Chapter 2, text and note 33, on Donato). Also cf. Manousakas, "Prelates of Monemvasia," 114-15, citing Sanuto, *Diarii*, VII, col. 714, referring to Arsenios as Archbishop of Monemvasia. All the above points are at variance with Legrand, I, p. clxviii, who affirmed that Arsenios' consecration to the Archbishopric of Monemvasia did not take place until 1514. This has misled a number of modern scholars (cf. also the earlier works of Roscoe, *Leo X*, II, 248, and H. Hodius, *De doctis hominibus* [London, 1742] 293). But Legrand did not use the letters of Arsenios published in I. Lamius, *Deliciae eruditorum seu veterum ἀνεκδότων opusculorum collectanea* (Florence, 1740) (cf. Manousakas, "Prelates of Monemvasia," 106ff.).

[49] See Manousakas, "Prelates of Monemvasia," 109-10, n. 41, and document no.

secration to the archiepiscopal dignity, that Arsenios, following the practice of the Eastern church, changed his name from Aristovoulos to Arsenios — a fact that has caused a good deal of trouble to several important scholars, who have mistakenly believed that the two names refer to two different persons.[50]

Arsenios' apparent success notwithstanding, the patriarch of Constantinople balked at his enthronement, considering it an absolute usurpation, especially since Arsenios immediately entered upon a policy of ordaining to the priesthood new candidates favorable to himself. Nor would the Orthodox population of Monemvasia accept the validity of his acts. The result was that the entire see was torn by upheaval.[51] The attitude of the Orthodox to this curious but enlightening episode in the affairs of Venetian-dominated Greece is revealed in the following account of the Greek writer Manuel Malaxos, in his *Patriarchal History of Constantinople*: [52]

During the patriarchate of Pachomius, there lived the uncanonical Arsenios, of the family of Apostolis, who obtained the throne of . . . Monemvasia illegally and contrary to the ecclesiastical canons . . . This same Arsenios was a deacon, and he came from Venice to Monemvasia with the great authority of the Venetian government which then controlled the city. And it was decreed by the Venetian authorities and the legate of the pope, that, once consecrated bishop, he should occupy unhindered the see of Monemvasia, and if any clergyman or layman should oppose and refuse to accept him, that person would be punished severely and exiled for his entire life . . . The legitimate metropolitan of Monemvasia, canonically consecrated by the most holy Great Church of Christ [that of Constantinople] was still in good health. And so in order that the Venetians might control his throne, they expelled him . . . And while the true prelate was still living, this illegal Arsenios obtained his see with the support of the Latins, thus adulterating the church of Christ-God.

The *History* continues with the statement that the Greek patriarch then dispatched an epistle to Arsenios censuring the latter's

---

6, pp. 142ff. The sources of information on the consecration differ. Legrand follows that of Manuel Malaxos (the writer of the *Patriarchal History*) in Crusius, *Turcograeciae*, and in the Bonn edition, but we also have the report of Arsenios himself, which must also be considered.

[50] See Legrand, *Bibliographie hellénique*, I, p. clxv, n. 1. Also Omont, *Facsimilés de manuscrits grecs des 15ᵉ et 16ᵉ siècles*, 10, and Firmin-Didot, *Alde Manuce*, 150, who term Arsenios and Aristovoulos brothers! Hodius and Renouard were also misled by the two names.

[51] Manousakas, "Prelates of Monemvasia," 116.

[52] *Historia Patriarchica* (Bonn ed.) 141-43.

manner of consecration as well as his anti-Orthodox activity in Monemvasia and inviting Arsenios to resign his office. Arsenios thereupon made an attempt to placate the patriarchal ire by dispatching to him a clever letter appealing to ancient authors (including Aristophanes — for whom Arsenios seems to have had a particular fondness) and, more important, containing an Orthodox profession of faith, from which was pointedly omitted the *filioque* clause so abhorrent to all the true Orthodox. (As an example of the partisanship evoked even among modern scholars by the career of Arsenios we might point out that Legrand, in direct opposition to Salaville, condemns "this prelate appointed by the pope and now boldly declaring himself a son of the Greek church by omitting the *filioque* from his profession of faith.") [53]

Arsenios' verboseness and honeyed words were not without some effect, to judge from the patriarchal response which was composed by Manuel Corinthios, the Great Rhetor of the patriarchal court (who may possibly have been a relative of Arsenios on his mother's side). But the patriarch was not really mollified, and in the end Arsenios accomplished nothing. Indeed the patriarch, in June of 1509 (and not in 1504 as Legrand has believed), in an encyclical issued to all the Greek communities of the Venetian possessions, announced sentence of excommunication against the "false Bishop Arsenios who uncanonically and unworthily ascending to that office . . . for the sake of the Latins stirs up and unsparingly launches excommunications against them [the Orthodox]." [54]

To judge from the evidence available, it is clear that in the face of this excommunication Arsenios was forced to leave Monemvasia, evidently to retire to Crete.[55] His withdrawal may be taken not only as evidence of the hostility toward him of the large part of his Monemvasiote flock but probably as an indication of the attitude of the Venetian authorities, who preferred his departure to further alienation of their Orthodox subjects.

Exiled from Monemvasia, Arsenios now seems to have remained

[53] For Arsenios' letter see Legrand, II, 344, and Salaville, *Dict. d'hist. géog. eccl.*, III, col. 1027, and esp. 1030, where he emphasizes the sincerity of Arsenios' Catholic confession.

[54] For text, see S. Lampros, " Ὁ κατ᾽ Ἀρσενίου τοῦ Ἀποστόλη ἀφορισμὸς τοῦ Πατριάρχου Παχωμίου Α᾽," Νέος Ἑλληνομνήμων (1906) III, 56–58. Also Manousakas, "Prelates of Monemvasia," 117, and 137–38.

[55] See *Historia Patriarchica*, 147–48, which seems wrong in saying that Arsenios then went immediately to Rome.

for some ten years in Crete. During this decade he supported himself as a scribe and as a teacher of Greek,[56] though as he himself informs us he also received a small income of thirty-six ducats from the Venetian government.[57] It was during this period, evidently between 1506 and 1508, that he greeted, with choice verses written for the occasion, the arrival of the humanist patron Girolamo Donato, newly appointed governor of Crete. Later (March 1513), on the occasion of the ascent of his old friend Leo X to the throne of St. Peter, Arsenios, together with the Latin and Uniate clergy of Crete, headed by the island's Venetian archbishop Jerome Landi, participated in a joyous celebration, marked by the lighting of thousands of torches and the pealing of church bells.[58]

Little other information has been available on this early period of his life, even from the manuscripts he copied, most of which are undated.[59] Several recently discovered documents, however, reveal the very interesting fact that at the end of 1508 at the latest Arsenios found himself again in Venice (as evidenced by a decision of the Venetian Senate dated June 8, 1509), and that at that time he knew and associated on friendly terms with the great humanist Erasmus. Whether this meant the two met in the Aldine milieu or elsewhere is not clear, although it is doubtful that Arsenios had become reconciled with Aldus. But in any case Arsenios himself relates in a later letter to Erasmus (dated September 30, 1521, from Florence) that he was sending to Erasmus, as a "small token of mutual friendship . . . at the time when the wise Muses brought us together in Venice," a copy of his book *Apophthegmata*, which he had recently published in Rome.[60]

---

[56] Legrand, I, p. clxxiv, refers to a manuscript (the *Anthology*) copied by Arsenios, which bears a notation showing that Arsenios, after his excommunication, returned to Crete. Legrand takes this to mean that Arsenios opened a school in Crete. We do know definitely that Arsenios taught John Zygomalas and Franciscus Portus in the Peloponnese (Monemvasia): E. Legrand, *Notice biographique sur Jean et Théodose Zygomalas* (Paris, 1889) 71, 104.

[57] Lamius, *Deliciae eruditorum*, XV, 135-37.

[58] See the long passage in *Violetum*, esp. 3-4: Ἰωάννην τὸν Λάντον . . . πυρσοὺς μυρίους, ἐν τοῖς κωδωνεῶσιν ἀνῆψε, κώδωνας ἠχεῖν τοῖς ἐπ' αὐτὸ τοῦτο τεταγμένοις . . . ἐν ἡμέραις ὅλαις ὀκτὼ οὐκ ἐπαύσατο. Also Legrand, II, 341. On Donato's skill in Greek and Latin see documents quoted by G. degli Agostini, *Notizie istorico-critiche*, II, esp. 217.

[59] See Manousakas, "Prelates of Monemvasia," 120 and esp. n. 2, mentioning a Cretan scholar George Kalyvas who had connections with Arsenios.

[60] For Arsenios' letter to Erasmus see Manousakas, "Arsenios . . . Unpublished

Arsenios' days in Crete were not serene. Though rejected by the Greeks of Monemvasia, he could not, it seems, banish from his mind the thought of his lost throne. Now, however, he directed his gaze not to the recovery of the Greek but toward the securing of the Catholic throne. This Latin post had been assigned, in 1514, by Pope Leo X to the Italian Andrea Minuti, who at the same time had been awarded the Cretan bishopric of Hierapetra and shortly afterwards, as an expectative benefice, the episcopal see of Herronesou, also on the island.[61]

The following year Andrea died, and it was Arsenios' hope that Leo, the son of his former patron Piero de' Medici and a proved devotee of Greek learning, would now confer on him the Latin archbishopric of Monemvasia to compensate for the loss of the Greek. But Arsenios found his hopes deceived. For Leo instead favored another Cretan, the eminent teacher of Greek in Venice and formerly at Padua, Marcus Musurus, who in his youth had even studied with Arsenios. The appointment of Musurus to the see of Monemvasia took place, according to papal decree, on June 19, 1516, and the assignment to Hierapetra a few weeks later.[62] Arsenios at once complained to the Pope at being supplanted by "a Cretan" and entreated Leo to call him personally to the Curia so that "as before in Florence when I was a deacon and served the brother of your lordship, Pietro of blessed memory, so now in Rome I may also serve your divine and holy lordship." [63] As we have seen, Marcus Musurus' acceptance of the Catholic archbishopric of Monemvasia was to retain him in Rome until his death in 1517.

Leo did not appoint a successor to Musurus until March 5, 1520. The appointee was still another Greek, the seventy-year-old Uniate, Manilius [Emmaneul] Kavakes Rhalles of Sparta, who had

---

Epistles," no. 1, especially Πέμπομεν δέ σοι δι' αὐτοῦ καὶ βιβλίον ἐν τῶν "'Αποφθεγμάτων," ἃ ἐν 'Ρώμῃ ἔναγχος ἐτυπώσαμεν, τῆς πρὸς ἑκατέρους φιλίας δεῖγμα μικρόν . . . ἀφ' οὗπερ ἡμᾶς 'Ενετίαζε συνήγαγον αἱ σοφαὶ Μοῦσαι. For the Venetian senatorial decree see Manousakas, "Prelates of Monemvasia," 144 and annex, doc. no. 1.

[61] See Gerola, *Vescovi Cretesi*, 5. Cf. Manousakas, "Prelates of Monemvasia," 120. The Bishop of Hierapetra was Niccolò dal Monte and it was in expectation of his death that the post was awarded to Minuti.

[62] Manousakas, "Prelates of Monemvasia," 145. Cf. above, Chapter 5.

[63] See Arsenios' dedicatory letter to Pope Leo X in Walz, *Arsenii Violetum*, 5. Also Legrand, II, 341–42.

achieved a considerable reputation as a poet of Latin verse in Italy, where he had lived for years in association with an even better known Greek humanist poet and companion of Lorenzo de' Medici, Michael Marullus Tarchaneiotes.[64] Rhalles was in the service of Leo's cousin Cardinal Julius de' Medici (later Pope Clement VII), and it was evidently through Julius' intercession that he secured the post at Monemvasia. Thus for a second time the ambitions of Arsenios were thwarted. From a letter of Arsenios (the preface to his edition of the scholia of Euripides) we learn that sometime before or during 1519, and in response to an earlier request on his part, he was now granted permission by Leo to come to Rome.[65] A plausible explanation of Leo's invitation might well be the status of the affairs of the papal Greek school, which after the death of Musurus and the dispatch of Lascaris on several papal embassies (to France, for example, at the end of 1518) [66] required the services of a more permanent director. Arsenios himself wrote in a later letter to Lascaris that he (Arsenios) put forth efforts to revive the school (anazopurese). And we know definitely from a recently published document that Arsenios not only taught there but participated in various other activities of the school.[67]

It was in the year 1519, or possibly shortly before, that Arsenios edited in Rome one of his most important and influential works, a collection of apophthegmata drawn from various Greek philosophers, emperors, orators, and poets. This was published at the press of the Greek college in Rome, called that of Monte Cavallo [68]

[64] On Rhalles see Chapter 5, note 164. Also S. Lampros, "Λακεδαιμόνιοι βιβλιο-γράφοι," Νέος Ἑλληνομνήμων, IV (1907) 340, and Sathas, Neohellenic Philology, 77, n. 2, who notes that Poliziano described Rhalles as excelling in his knowledge of Latin. Finally, see A. Hatzes, Οἱ Ῥαούλ, Ῥάλ, Ῥάλαι (Kirchhain, 1909) 41ff.

[65] Dedicatory letter of Arsenios to Pope Paul III of Arsenios' Scholia of the Very Best Commentators on Seven Tragedies of Euripides (Junta, 1534): προμήθειάν τινα γραφῆναι προσέταχεν ἥτις ἐς τόδε μένει νεκρά (Legrand, I, 223). Cf. below, note 115.

[66] Knös, Janus Lascaris, 163.

[67] See Manousakas, "Prelates of Monemvasia," 124, document quoted. Also see the letter of Arsenios to Lascaris dated 27 October 1534 (Manousakas, "Arsenios . . . Unpublished Epistles," no. 9 and p. 53), where it is stated that Arsenios taught in the college after Lascaris' departure for France (in November or December of 1518) and also that Leo's subsidy to the college amounted to 1000 gold ducats per year.

[68] Actually Arsenios' work bears neither place nor date of publication but has been ascribed to Monte Cavallo (ca. 1519) by Legrand, Bibliographie hellénique, I, 169–71 ('Αποφθέγματα Φιλοσόφων καὶ Στρατηγῶν Ῥητόρων τε καὶ Ποιητῶν) and by

which had been under the general supervision of Janus Lascaris, who, in 1517 and perhaps with the aid of Arsenios, had initiated a series of publications beginning with the scholia on Homer.[69] The volume now published, entitled *Apophthegmata*, was actually only a part of Arsenios' enlarged version of his father's collection of proverbs, the *Ionia* (as Michael had originally termed it).[70] Arsenios may have begun the work of "gathering and selecting" new material years before in Florence (that is, between 1492 and 1494) when he was engaged in transcribing for Leo's elder brother, Piero de' Medici, the manuscripts brought back from the East by Janus Lascaris.[71] As we have seen, already in 1494, with the appearance of the Aldine *Galeomyomachia*,[72] Arsenios had announced as forth-

Norton, *Italian Printers, 1501–1520*, 98: *Praeclara dicta* . . . Also see Walz, *Arsenii Violetum* p. iii. Firmin-Didot, *Alde Manuce*, 569, says that the *Apophthegmata* was published by Calliergis in Rome before 1522 (cf. Firmin-Didot, 573).

[69] These are not the famous scholia of Eustathius, nor is Lascaris mentioned any place in the work, though Legrand, II, 154, attributes the work to Lascaris, "Arsenios . . . Unpublished Epistles," 53, in the light of the now corroborated theory that Arsenios actually taught in Leo's Greek college in Rome, raises the question as to the possible contribution of Arsenios also to the edition of the five books previously published in 1517–18 by the Monte Cavallo press and which are ascribed to Lascaris alone (and to his pupils).

[70] In his preface (to Leo X) Arsenios says he is publishing only part of the material he has collected (Legrand, I, 170). Arsenios never published his father's *Ionia*, which was first to appear in 1538 printed in Basle, and later in 1619 and 1653. See J. Graesse, *Trésor de livres rares et précieux au Nouveau Dictionnaire*, I (Milan, 1950) 167–68. The complete collection (i.e., his father's work plus his own additions) was printed in 1832 (Walz, *Arsenii Violetum*). In a letter to Cardinal Ridolfi dated 1532, Arsenios says that the complete collection had not yet been published. See below text and note 89 (Legrand, I, 214). The term Ionia was a fairly common one in the later Byzantine period.

[71] See Walz, 2: ὅπου (in Florence) τὰς μὲν ἐκγράφων ἐγώ . . . ἐρανιζόμην καὶ ἀνελεγόμην τὰ κάλλιστα, ὡς αἱ μέλισσαι τῶν ἀνθέων τὰ εὐωδέστατά τε καὶ ὡραιότατα. (Arsenios compares his collection and selection of the best works to the bees "that partake of the sweetest-smelling and most beautiful of the flowers.") It was possibly in Florence that Arsenios arranged alphabetically and copied scholia on Homer, which, however, he never published. See J. Cramer, *Anecdota graeca e codicibus Bibliothecarum Oxoniensium* (Paris, 1839–41) III, 371ff. A. Turyn, *The Byzantine Manuscript Tradition of the Tragedies of Euripides* (Urbana, 1957) 373, shows that Arsenios and Janus Lascaris copied certain manuscripts jointly, to which we can now add interesting evidence from Arsenios' dedicatory letter to Leo preceding his *Ionia* manuscript, in Walz, 2, where he mentions his work of copying manuscripts in Florence for the Medici.

[72] See above, note 17. It should be noted that Manousakas, "Arsenios . . . Unpublished Epistles," 6, points out that in the Greek manuscript containing the eleven unpublished letters, there is included a lexicon of unusual proper names and words compiled by Arsenios when he was reading the ancient literature. This work is to be differentiated from the famous *Ionia*.

coming the publication of his father Michael's collection. But in the *Galeomyomachia*, perhaps significantly, no mention was made of any work he himself had done to enlarge his father's collection. (What prevented immediate fulfilment of the project may well have been his quarrel with Aldus.)

Arsenios sent the complete collection compiled by his father and himself, in manuscript form, to Pope Leo X. From the dedicatory letter enclosed we may assume that the work of compilation was completed between May of 1516 and the fall of 1517, as evidenced by Arsenios' clearly implied reference therein to Musurus as Archbishop of Monemvasia.[73]

At about the same time as the appearance of his *Apophthegmata*, Arsenios published at the Monte Cavallo press another smaller work entitled Γέρας . . . σπάνιον τῶν σπουδαίων (*Precious Gift for the Scholars*), which included short treatises on various topics he had collected, together with a brief dialogue (written by himself) among a bookseller, a bookbuyer, and a book. In this treatise Arsenios, with an eye for publicity, took the opportunity to announce the forthcoming publication of his *Apophthegmata*.[74]

In 1518 or 1519, at the suggestion of Janus Lascaris, and for the benefit of Greek-born students, Pope Leo resolved to found, in Florence and Milan, two additional Greek institutes modeled after the original Greek college in Rome.[75] The school in Milan was placed in charge of Antonios Eparchos, a Greek from the island of Corfu, whose later gift to the King of France of more than thirty valuable Greek codices was to form part of the nucleus of the Royal French library at Fontainebleau.[76] Arsenios was entrusted

---

[73] Walz, 5: παρ' ἀνδρὸς Κρητὸς ἐν ῥώμῃ καὶ ταῦτα διάγοντος. This reference to Musurus makes Sathas' dating of the book (1515) impossible (*Neohellenic Philology*, 129).

[74] Firmin-Didot, *Alde Manuce*, 570, says this forms a second part of the other volume (*Apophthegmata*, above) but Legrand, *Bibliographie hellénique*, I, 166–68, says rightly that it constitutes a distinct work. See Norton, *Italian Printers 1501–1520*, 97–98 and now Manousakas, "Prelates of Monemvasia," 124, who believes the two works appeared at the same time.

[75] See Knös, *Janus Lascaris*, 155, 152.

[76] On Eparchos see Legrand, II, 360–61, for a letter from Eparchos to Arsenios from Venice (dated 1521 by Legrand; cf. I, p. ccxi, n. 4; cf. Lamius, *Deliciae eruditorum*, IX, 107). Also *Bibliothèque de l'école des Chartes*, LIII (1892) 95–110, and L. Delisle, *Le cabinet des manuscrits de la bibliothèque impériale* (Paris, 1868) 157. Finally, L. Dorez, "Antoine Eparque," *Mélanges d'archéologie et d'histoire*, XIII (1893) 281–364.

with the directorship of the school in Florence,[77] as a kind of compensation, it would seem, for his loss of Monemvasia. We have few details on his activities at the school aside from several letters exchanged by Arsenios and Lascaris,[78] and a bit of evidence provided by the Florentine humanist Antonio Franchini. Referring to Arsenios, "the Cretan Archbishop of Monemvasia," as "a man of great erudition and very acute judgment," Franchini states that Arsenios presided over an institute at Florence for those adolescents whom Pope Leo, "for the sake of restoring the Greek language, had gathered together from the heart of Greece." [79]

Arsenios was carrying on his educational duties in Florence when on December 1, 1521, Pope Leo, the school's founder and patron, died. With the cancellation of Leo's subsidy the College closed (as evidently did that of Rome), and for this reason and because little could be expected from Leo's successor, the austere Adrian VI, Arsenios soon afterwards seems to have departed for Crete. Before leaving Florence, however, he collaborated with Franchini in the latter's edition of Aristophanes, published in February of 1525 by the Giunta (the arch-rivals of the Aldine press), for which Arsenios edited the scholia.[80]

What spurred Arsenios to leave Italy was the new developments regarding the see of Monemvasia, the reacquisition of which was ever uppermost in his mind. Pope Leo, perhaps wishing to do

[77] Both directorships are known through the letter of Eparchos to Arsenios cited in preceding note, and one of Arsenios to Janus Lascaris, cited below.

[78] Cf. Manousakas, "Prelates of Monemvasia," 126. Also see his "Arsenios . . . Unpublished Epistles," no. 9 (dated by Manousakas the end of 1531) and p. 53, where it is revealed that Arsenios had taught in *both* the Greek colleges of Rome and Florence.

[79] See Legrand, II, 156. On Franchini (Francino) see also F. Inghirami, *Storia della Toscana*, XIII (Fiesole, 1844) 88-89. Cf. Eparchos' letter to Arsenios, dated September 1521, saying that Lascaris "established for the Greeks this public school in Florence over which you preside." (Manousakas, "Arsenios . . . Unpublished Epistles," no. 9 and p. 35.)

[80] See in Legrand, I, p. clxx, and II, 156-57. Francini's (Francino) dedicatory letter to Benedetto Accolti, Archbishop of Ravenna, dated 1525, speaks of Arsenios' collaboration in Florence and indicates that he was no longer in that city. I. A. Fabricius, *Bibliotheca Graeca* (Hamburg, 1791) 4th ed. of G. Harles, II, 381, says Arsenios' edition of the scholia was less important than the Aldine of Musurus. Also on Aristophanes cf. D. Lockwood, "Aristophanes in the 15th Century," *Transactions and Proceedings of the American Philological Association*, XL (1909). On Arsenios' whereabouts after leaving Rome, Legrand has provided no information, but see Manousakas, "Prelates of Monemvasia."

something for Arsenios [81] but yet not desirous of infringing on the
rights of the then archbishop of Monemvasia, Rhalles, had before
his death come to a decision: to unite the Orthodox throne of Monemvasia with the Latin, and after the death of one of the two archbishops (Rhalles or Arsenios) to utilize the income from the dissolved see for the establishment of a school enabling twelve students to study Greek letters.[82] Since Rhalles was a good deal older
than Arsenios, the decree was probably intended to favor Arsenios. But Rhalles, refusing to acquiesce, sought to negate the provisions by relinquishing his throne and rights thereof to another
candidate of his own preference, a Mantuan named Filippo Arrivabene. At this juncture Arsenios went to Venice and on August 13,
1521, appeared before the Senate appealing for execution of the
papal decree. But though the Venetian government was again favorable, even to the point of writing letters in his behalf to Monemvasia
and Crete, nothing definite could be done until the death of Rhalles.[83]

Arsenios was suddenly recalled from Crete by his old patron,
Janus Lascaris, who, in a letter to be dated probably the beginning of 1523, informed Arsenios of the death of the Archbishop
Manilios Kavakes Rhalles and urged Arsenios to hurry to Venice
in order to seek the aid of his Venetian friends for the recovery of
his see. "Haste is imperative," he added, because "someone from
Mantua [Arrivabene] is now also aspiring to the post." [84] Lascaris
urged Arsenios to seek out Arrivabene and through personal nego-
tiation to attempt a settlement of the matter.

The words of Lascaris produced their effect. Losing no time,
Arsenios immediately hastened to Italy and, in accord with Lascaris' suggestion, entered into negotiations with Arrivabene, whom
the death of Rhalles had now put in a rather difficult position. The

[81] Known from a letter of the Venetian Doge, printed in N. Iorga, *Notes et
extraits pour servir à l'histoire des croisades au XVe siècle* (Paris, 1899–1916) VI,
101 (cf. Manousakas, "Prelates of Monemvasia," 124).

[82] The papal order has been lost, but is known from Arsenios' letter to Pope
Paul III (see note 65, above, in which Arsenios speaks of a προμήθεια promised by
Leo X to him [Legrand, I, 222–23]).

[83] Sanuto, *Diarii*, III, cols. 277–78. Manousakas, "Prelates of Monemvasia," 125–
26.

[84] Legrand, *Bibliographie hellénique*, I, p. ccxix.

following settlement was agreed upon by the two prelates: Arrivabene would retain the Cretan bishopric of Hierapetra, and Arsenios was to recover the archbishopric of Monemvasia in addition to receiving each year from Arrivabene the sum of 100 ducats. This agreement was confirmed by the new Pope Clement VII, and, on January 20, 1524, ratified by the Venetian Senate.[85]

Following the approval of these depositions by all the parties concerned, Arsenios was able, at long last, to re-enter into possession of his see.[86] What reception he received from his old Orthodox parishioners on his return under the tutelage of the Latin church can only be surmised. At any rate, possibly to win them over to his new role, or because despite his fanatical devotion to his self-seeking ambition he very probably did have some feeling for his own race, he now evinced great concern for the general welfare of the people of the city.[87] Thus several years later (1527) we catch sight of him in Venice, where he appeared in his role of archbishop to voice before the authorities of the Republic a petition on behalf of his parishioners. The nature of his petition is known from several documents which relate principally to the defense and provisioning of the city in the face of the continual Turkish danger and the depredations of corsairs. Also mentioned are commercial and legal questions involving the relations of Greeks and Venetians. Arsenios, perhaps not surprisingly, included a request of his own that the income from a certain church within the walls, which had

---

[85] According to Sanuto, XXXV, col. 363: "don Arsenio . . . et domino Filippo Arivaben de Mantoa . . . essendo concordà per via del Legato che l'ditto Arseni habbi il possesso di Malvasia et pension ducati 100 a l'anno dal ditto domino Filippo, qual habbi il vescova' di Gierapetra." Cf. Manousakas, "Prelates of Monemvasia," 128, and n. 1. The bishopric of Herronesou went to another, Francesco Dandolo! (Manousakas, 132, and notes, mentions Venetian senatorial documents ratifying the settlement). Miller, Latins in the Levant, 503, years before had realized that this kind of agreement had been reached between a Greek and Italian prelate.

[86] Date of return to Monemvasia estimated as before 1525, since we know that he left Florence before publication of Francini's Aristophanes (1525). See above, text and note 80. For documentary evidence that Rhalles was the immediate successor of Musurus, see Sanuto, XXV, 64, 66; cf. 120, 502; also Pastor, History of the Popes, VIII, 262, note.

[87] Arsenios wrote a letter to Justin Decadyos (see Manousakas, "Prelates of Monemvasia," 28) referring to the funds he says he spent in behalf of the Monemvasiote citizens.

formerly been paid to his mother, now be restored to her. Arsenios' petition was accepted by the College of Ten in its entirety.[88]

At the beginning of 1531 Arsenios undertook a similar mission to Venice, as we read from a later letter of dedication he wrote to his patron, the Cardinal Niccolò Ridolfi (included in his two-volume edition of various works of Michael Psellus):

I have come to Venice from Monemvasia in the Peloponnese now for the second time, most Holy Cardinal, partly in order to request from the most high Senate of the Venetians whatever may improve the public welfare of the Monemvasiotes, partly also to secure something for myself from the most Holy Church, from the shepherd of shepherds and father of fathers — a small portion of the paternal inheritance. For I too am a member of the Catholic church and not at all, by the grace of God, decrepit. But I am wasting away (*tekomai*) from hunger and poverty; alas, because of our sins, the revenues of my bishopric have been alienated by the Turks . . . Indeed, I have fallen into such destitution that I have no idea what I shall live on. For these two abominable wives of mine, podagra and poverty, have completely devoured even the few provisions which I brought with me in order frugally to feed this body. But these two creatures while plaguing me have also consoled me . . . and we have come together in an act of love to give birth to my two very beautiful daughters . . . who have now attained marriageable age [i.e., readiness for publication]. To one I have given the name *Ionia* and the other I call *Ascetic Garden*; for they are full of maxims and advice and instructions on various matters, the one of pagan, the other of Christian savants . . .[89]

The plight of the people of Monemvasia, as disclosed by the letter, was indeed serious. For the adjacent mainland areas of the Morea upon which the city depended for supplies had, in 1503, fallen to the Turk,[90] and the city, situated on what was virtually an island, could now be provisioned only from the sea. Arsenios' depiction of his own situation, however, is probably somewhat exaggerated. Indeed his rhetorical use of metaphor to stress his poverty, hunger, and rheumatic pains is not a little reminiscent of his father's way of writing. The information, on the other hand, af-

---

[88] For the documents regarding petitions and responses see Sathas, *Documents inédits*, IV, 228–235. Also see notice of Sanuto, XLIV, col. 475.

[89] Arsenios' letter of dedication is printed in Legrand, I, 212–13. Cf. a similar letter in Lamius, *Deliciae eruditorum*, XV, 39–41. On Arsenios' edition of Psellos and on Ridolfi, see below, text and note 101.

[90] Miller, *Essays on the Latin Orient*, 240.

forded here on his composition of the *Ascetic Garden* — a fairly common title in the Byzantine period referring to works written for the spiritual guidance and edification of monks — is not available elsewhere. The *Ionia* of course we know about. But the true purpose of the letter cannot be understood until we examine Arsenios' activities in the meantime.[91]

Arsenios' ambition was still not satisfied with regaining his Monemvasiote chair: he coveted also the see of Hierapetra and, like his father, desired to preside over a Greek school in the West — in Arsenios' case as a kind of re-establishment of Leo's old schools at Rome and Florence, which Arsenios had never forgotten. In order to execute his aim of acquiring Hierapetra, he took steps to approach not only the Pope and the Venetian government but, with little hesitation, it would appear, even the Orthodox patriarch of Constantinople! Thus from Venice in September of 1531 he wrote a mollifying letter to Constantinople seeking ratification of his old consecration to the Orthodox throne of Monemvasia. His letter is of particular interest on account of its indication that because of his excommunication and propapal views the "Orthodox" Greeks of Venice (as he calls them) abhorred and altogether avoided him.[92]

But the Constantinople patriarch, well informed as to the conduct of Arsenios, was not easily persuaded to grant the forgiveness requested. Arsenios meantime wrote a spate of letters to whatever persons he thought might look sympathetically on either of his objectives. In one letter to Lascaris dated October 15, 1531, he begged the latter to appeal in his behalf to Pope Clement (as formerly he had to Leo X) to carry out and confirm the papal pledges that had been made to Arsenios.[93] It was at this time that Arsenios

[91] The following episode on Arsenios' intrigues to secure the see of Hierapetra has been revealed by Manousakas, "Prelates of Monemvasia," but he does not there discuss Arsenios' intellectual activities.

[92] Printed in Lamius, IX, 109–12. Reprinted in Πανδώρα, VI (1855–56) 493–94 (cf. Manousakas, "Prelates of Monemvasia," 130).

[93] Lamius, XV, 41–43 (cf. 132–34). Cf. remarks of Manousakas, 131. Now see also another letter from Arsenios to Lascaris dated before 3 October 1531 in which the same thing (establishment of a Greek school to be supported by revenues from Hierapetra in Crete) seems to be referred to and in which Arsenios also asks Lascaris to undertake to teach his pupil George Balsamon, whom Arsenios is sending to Rome. Lascaris' response reveals acceptance of Balsamon as his

presented to Clement VII an old Bible manuscript with a lengthy dedication in which, after calling on the Pope to save Greece from the Turk, he entreated his aid also in his own behalf.[94]

What Arsenios was by implication referring to here (as he had in earlier letters to Ridolfi) was the foundation of another Greek academy, to be maintained by the income of the Bishopric of Hierapetra which, in accord with Leo's proposal, was to be awarded to Arsenios. Other epistles, similar in purpose, were written to Cardinal Ridolfi, and to another humanist Cardinal Egidio Canisio.[95] The new claim of Arsenios to Hierapetra, in obvious contradiction to his settlement with Arrivabene, can be explained only by the return of the latter to Mantua from his see of Hierapetra.[96] Astonishingly enough, the Venetian government (in a letter dated December 28, 1531, addressed to its agent in Rome) supported Arsenios' proposal for the recovery of Hierapetra (even while its rightful occupant was still alive!) and blandly directed the agent to request the Pope to assign Arrivabene to another post.[97]

After hearing the plea Clement seems to have summoned Arsenios' patron Cardinal Ridolfi to the Curia (Ridolfi was then in residence at his Bishopric of Vicenza). But the end result was unfavorable to Arsenios, since the only satisfaction he received was empty promises. Henceforth Arsenios did not cease to write everywhere seeking the execution of the pledges and dramatizing his need, which now had become more pressing than ever.[98]

---

student (both letters printed in Manousakas, "Arsenios . . Unpublished Epistles," nos. 2A and B). On Balsamon, see Manousakas, 39.

[94] The manuscript is today Cod. Laurent. plut. VI, 2. The dedication is printed in A. M. Bandini, *Catalogus codicum manuscriptum Bibliothecae Mediceae Laurentianae*, II (Florence, 1764) 85–87.

[95] For an epistle to an anonymous Roman cardinal (obviously Ridolfi) on the same matter, see Lamius, 36–38, and Manousakas, "Arsenios . . . Unpublished Epistles," no. 4. For the complete text of that to Canisius see Manousakas, "Arsenios . . . Unpublished Epistles," no. 3. From this letter we see that Arsenios was one of the sixteen Uniate Cretan priests given a yearly allowance from the (Latin) patriarchal estates of Crete, a practice instituted by Bessarion. On Cardinal Egidio Canisio see G. Signorelli, *Il Card. Egidio da Viterbo, Agostiniano, umanista e riformatore* (Florence, 1929) esp. 85–103.

[96] See Manousakas, "Prelates of Monemvasia," 132.

[97] Cf. Sanuto, *Diarii*, LV, col. 296. Also Manousakas, 132.

[98] Sanuto, LV, cols. 436–37, is the source for all this. In a letter written to Cardinal Ridolfi, dated probably in 1532 (Manousakas, "Arsenios . . . Unpublished Epistles, no. 5) Arsenios exaggeratedly writes that he has been forced by poverty to sell all his books. See also letters exchanged by the Corfiote Justin Decadyos (written from Constantinople, probably in 1532) and by Arsenios (probably

After his second appeal to the Venetian Senate, Arsenios did not again return to Monemvasia. With evidently little to look forward to in Greece (and perhaps thinking that his affairs required his presence in Italy), he spent the last four years of his life in Venice. But these years, whatever his living conditions may have been, were certainly prolific; despite old age he guided through the press a number of editions of important Greek authors.[99] The Aldine press was still flourishing, now under the direction of the heirs of Aldus, but Arsenios did not renew his association with that firm. Instead, in 1532, the lesser-known press of Stefano da Sabbio published Arsenios' edition of the *Introduction to the Six Modes of Philosophy* by the eleventh century Byzantine Neoplatonist historian, Michael Psellus. And in December of that year the same publisher produced his edition of a second volume of Psellus' works, *An Abridgment of Psellus' System of the Four Mathematical Sciences, Arithmetic, Music, Geometry, and Astronomy.*[100] Psellus' division of the mathematical sciences into four parts was similar to the medieval quadrivium. In both Byzantine and Latin cultures this quadrapartite division was to be distinguished from the literary and rhetorical classification of the trivium.

These two volumes of Psellus Arsenios dedicated to his patron, the famous Cardinal and bibliophile Niccolò Ridolfi, the grandson of Lorenzo the Magnificent and nephew to Pope Leo X, who was later to acquire much of the rich manuscript collection of Janus Lascaris. Arsenios was instrumental in purchasing manuscripts for Ridolfi, as we know from at least one letter he addressed to the Cardinal at his see in Vicenza. It had been probably through his earlier connections with the Medici that Arsenios first met the Cardinal, whose family had amassed great wealth in the wool trade and owned banks in France and England, as well as Italy.[101]

---

dated 1533) mentioning Arsenios' penury (nos. 6A and B in "Arsenios . . . Unpublished Epistles").

[99] See, for example, Arsenios' phrase, in Legrand, *Bibliographie hellénique*, I, 210: "recently we [Arsenios] published the mathematics of Psellus." Probably Arsenios published other editions that we are as yet unaware of.

[100] See Legrand, I, 212. Also on the da Sabbio family see Norton, *Italian Printers 1501–1520*, 150. Legrand has placed in reverse order the two works of Psellus (see Legrand, I, 210, for Arsenios' own words as to the order of publication).

[101] On the Ridolfi family see G. Moroni, *Dizionario di erudizione storico-classica*, LVII (Venice, 1852) 208–209; *Enciclopedia Italiana*, XXIX 283; and Roscoe, *Leo*

Continuing his interest in Byzantine works, Arsenios, in March of 1533, published an edition of the poetry of Manuel Philes, *Iambic Verses on the Qualities of Animals*.[102] Arsenios may well have felt a personal identification with this thirteenth century Byzantine writer whose life had also been one of extreme misery. Perhaps emulating Philes (who like other Byzantines of the Palaeologan period would stoop to any sort of flattery to gain his objectives),[103] Arsenios now dedicated his work to no less a dignitary than the Holy Roman Emperor Charles V. In his dedicatory epistle Arsenios, after explaining various characteristics of animals that might serve as examples to humans, concludes by sycophantically addressing the Emperor: "I am your dog and you are my sweet master. So I bark and beg for something to eat"[104] — words surpassing in their servility even those directed by his father, as we have seen, to Charles' grandfather the Emperor Frederick III.

A few months later (probably on September 9, 1533) Arsenios addressed a letter to Pope Clement VII, whose friendship with Arsenios dated from the latter's early days in Florence. The importance of the letter (which may not actually have been sent) lies in its mention of two annotated works which Arsenios declares he has recently published, but which have apparently not survived even in manuscript form: Homer's description of the shield of Achilles and Hesiod's of that of Heracles. In the same letter, as well as in a similar one sent to Cardinal Ridolfi, at whose expense the two works were presumably printed, Arsenios suggests that the "Shield of Heracles" be sent to the Emperor Charles V and that of Achilles to the French King Francis I, on the occasion of the marriage of Francis' son to Catherine de' Medici. Arsenios' presump-

---

X, III, 126. On the Ridolfi library, formed partly from the famous library of Janus Lascaris, see H. Omont, "Un premier catalogue des manuscrits grecs du Cardinal Ridolfi," *Bibliothèque de l'Ecole des Chartes*, XLIX (1888) 313-24; G. Mercati, "Indici di manoscritti greci del Cardinal N. Ridolfi," *Mélanges d'arch et d'histoire*, XXX (1910) 51-55; and R. Ridolfi, *La biblioteca del Cardinal N. Ridolfi*, in *Bibliofilia*, XXXI (1929) 173-93. Also references in Turyn, *Byzantine Manuscript Tradition of Euripides*, 88, 372.

[102] Legrand, I, 215-18.

[103] On Philes see Krumbacher, *Byzantinischen Litteratur*, 774-80, and *Vasiliev, History of the Byzantine Empire*, 706.

[104] For the passage see Legrand, I, 216-18, esp. 218. Cf. also the article of G. Zoras, "Charles V of Germany and Efforts for the Liberation (of Greece)" (in Greek) Νέα Ἑστία, LIII (1953) 755ff., which includes a Peloponnesian poem appealing to this same Charles to liberate Greece from the Turkish yoke.

tion in offering advice to Europe's crowned heads is excusable
when we realize that the primary aim of both letters was evidently
"to push these two great lords of Europe to a common expedition
against the Turk . . . and to restore liberty to the scattered Greek
people." Only thus, affirms Arsenios, can the Greeks live peace-
fully as a Christian people; he closes his letters with a plea to God
to bring an end to the schism of the churches.[105] Like those of his
father before him and of the other Greek exiles, Arsenios' appeal
for a crusade fell on deaf ears: this was the period of Suleiman the
Magnificent and an apogee of Turkish power. But we may note
that even the self-seeking Arsenios was imbued with the same feeling of patriotism as the rest of his compatriots.

It was probably in this same period that Arsenios made still
another attempt to influence Charles V. He published and dedicated to Charles what was evidently an encomiastic oration ex-
tolling the military successes of that Emperor. This work, as Arsenios informs us, he printed in 500 copies so that not only the
Westerners but the Greeks too could learn of Charles' character
and exploits.[106]

Some months after the appearance of Philes' verses, but still in
the same year, Arsenios is supposed to have published (in Greek)
a work entitled *Genealogical stemmata of some illustrious Byzantine families from the most ancient up to the present period.* Of all
Arsenios' scholarly endeavors this would most directly have concerned the history proper of Byzantium. But the diligent Legrand
has shown that the work is an imposture and that it should be attributed to the fabrication of D. Rhodocanakis, who is typical of
several nineteenth century Greek historians whose scholarship with
reference to the learned Greek exiles is today rather suspect.[107]

Arsenios very likely played a significant part in the publication
of other important Greek literary works, about which, however,
we have little or no information. Besides his probable contribution
to the early works of the Monte Cavallo press mentioned above,

[105] The two letters are printed in Manousakas, "Arsenios . . . Unpublished
Epistles," nos. 7–8 and pp. 51–52.

[106] See Manousakas, no. 11 and pp. 55–56. Also see A. Morel-Fatio, *L'historiographie de Charles Quint,* I (Paris, 1913). Such encomia were not rare, though Arsenios' work (which has not survived) was then one of the first of its kind.

[107] Legrand, I, pp. vii–viii; and see especially the same author's *Dossier Rhodocanakis* (Paris, 1895) 6.

we now know that at least two years before his death in 1535 he
projected the publication of the celebrated scholia on Homer of
Eustathius, the twelfth century Byzantine Archbishop of Thessalonica. As Arsenios relates in a letter addressed once more to his
great patron Cardinal Ridolfi, he had laid the groundwork for the
edition by preparing for the press two works (neither any longer
extant) compiled from Homer and other orators and poets, which
he had entitled *Homeric Catena*, probably the so-called chain
commentary (Ὁμηρικὴ σειρά) and *Series of Proverbs* (Παροιμιακή).
Arsenios emphasized that he had already prepared the manuscript
of Eustathius' scholia and was sending it to Ridolfi.[108] But Arsenios' edition of Eustathius was not to appear in print, the monumental edition of the scholia in fact not being published until later in
Rome, beginning in 1542 with the collaboration of the Greek
secretary of Cardinal Ridolfi, Matthew Devaris, who also compiled the index to the fourth volume.[109] Nonetheless, in Arsenios'
abortive effort to print Eustathius we have still another example of
the noteworthy services of this indefatigable prelate to the advancement of classical scholarship in the West.

The wretchedness of Arsenios' living conditions was somewhat
mitigated when, on March 30, 1534, a decree of the Venetian Council of Ten appointed him preacher at the church of San Giorgio
dei Greci in Venice. This appointment of a "Catholic" prelate
(he was still titular bishop of Monemvasia) [110] was considered a
most unwelcome intrusion by the Greek congregation of the
church, which, in spirit at least, was Orthodox and was energetically striving to preserve its independence of action from the mo-
lestations of the local Venetian clergy. (A half century after this
event, as we have earlier observed, the Greeks ultimately triumphed

[108] Letter printed in Manousakas, no. 10 (n. d.) and p. 54. A catena (chain)
commentary consisted of a series of comments from various authors.
[109] See Legrand, *Bibliographie hellénique*, I, no. 101, pp. 237–38. In H. Omont,
Catalogue des manuscrits grecs de G. Pélicier (Paris, 1886), Pélicier reports that
he found a Greek manuscript of Eustathius' scholia in Arsenios' hand. Manousakas,
"Arsenios . . . Unpublished Epistles," 55, says that two Greek manuscripts in
Arsenios' hand contain Eustathius' scholia. See also L. Dorez, "Le Cardinal Marcello Cervini et l'imprimerie à Rome," *Mélanges d'archéologie et d'histoire*, XII
(1892) 289–303, 291–301: *Le commentaire d'Eustache sur Homère*. Also J. Kalitsounakes, "Ματθαῖος Δεβαρῆς καὶ τὸ ἐν Ῥώμῃ Ἑλληνικὸν Γυμνάσιον," Ἀθηνᾶ, XXVI
(1914) 81–102 (cited hereafter as "Matthaios Debares").
[110] According to a chart in Kalogeras, *Monemvasia*, 41, the Greek (Orthodox)
Archbishop of Monemvasia, in the years 1529–1540, was named Ioasaf.

and the Greek clergy and its flock in Venice were able effectively
to place themselves under the jurisdiction of the Patriarch of Constantinople.) [111] But the Council of Ten evidently believed that
the benefits to be derived from the preaching of this learned partisan of union would outweigh any disturbances that might ensue.[112]

On May 29, 1534, the Council of Ten, in consultation with Arsenios, issued a second decree, ordering the consecration of two
priests (to be named by Arsenios in the presence of the Venetian
patriarch) who were to act as Arsenios' assistants in the services
of San Giorgio. Against this decree and what they considered an
attempt to force Catholicism upon them, the members of the Greek
colony reacted violently and, if we may believe the very Orthodox
Patriarchal History of Constantinople, "There was a great commo-
tion and disturbance in the Church of the Greeks, St. George's, and
many Greeks ran the risk of death as a result of the oppression of
Arsenios." [113]

One wonders what motivated the fanaticism of Arsenios. Was
he, as Salaville contends, actuated by a sincere desire for ecclesiastical union? Or was he seeking so to ingratiate himself with the
Venetian civil and ecclesiastical authorities that they could not refuse to help in furthering his career? In attempting to answer this
question one must take into account certain other aspects of Arsenios' conduct at this time: his renewed profession of attachment
to the Roman church which he included in his letter, quoted above,
to Cardinal Ridolfi [114] and also his dedication to the new Pope,
Paul III, in December of 1534, of his edition of the scholia on
Euripides (*Scholia of the Very Best Commentators on Seven Tragedies of Euripides*), published in Venice by Luca Antonio Giunta.[115] This *editio princeps* is of fundamental significance for subsequent Euripedean scholarship. Arsenios, who certainly knew
what to look for, drew his material from several sources, among
them a manuscript from Bessarion's collection in Venice containing
hitherto unused Byzantine scholia, a Planudean paraphrase of Euripides.[116] While in his dedicatory letter to Paul, Arsenios took occa-

[111] See above, Chapter 3. Also Fortescue, *Uniate Eastern Churches*, 138.
[112] Legrand, I, p. clxxi, and Salaville, *Dict. d'hist. géog. eccl.*, III, col. 1029. Cf.
also Veludo, *Greek Colony*, 56–60.
[113] *Historia Patriarchica* (Bonn) 148.
[114] See Legrand, I, 213.
[115] See Legrand, I, 219.
[116] See esp. Turyn, *Byzantine Manuscript Tradition of Euripides*, 19, 66ff., 158.

sion to complain about Venetian rule in Greece, it is certainly revealing that at the same time he sought to further his own ambition in the Church. The letter to the Pope is well phrased, indeed rather eloquent, and is of interest to us not only because it exposes clearly Arsenios' personal ambitions but because of its insight into the rather pathetic attitude of many of the émigré Greeks who felt that their intellectual contributions and manifest devotion to the Roman church deserved emoluments equal to those received by their Western-born colleagues. Nevertheless, however appreciative some Western men of letters and dignitaries may have been of the services of the Greeks, the centuries-old prejudices separating East from West were still too strong to be entirely bridged.

Let us examine more closely the letter of Arsenios to Pope Paul III: Arsenios complains about Western rule in Greece and laments the misery to which the sad political situation and the action of "certain Westerners" (especially Latin prelates whom he compares to the publicans) had reduced the Greek bishops. After making an unequivocal profession of the Catholic faith he complains that the unfortunate (Uniate) Greeks are not given even "their small part of the paternal heritage. Are we not, we too," he writes "Christians? Are we not faithful to the Holy Roman Church? Do we not proclaim you as supreme pontiff, pastor and father, and ecumenical doctor? Why do you deprive us of our paternal inheritance as if we were bastards? We do not demand the purple," he adds, suggestively, about a point that certain scholars believe may also have preoccupied Musurus; "still it would not be out of place to include one or two Greeks among so great a number of cardinals of all countries . . ."[117] We do not ask for rich dioceses, wealthy bishoprics or abbacies; I would be satisfied with only a little."[118]

G. Dindorf, *Scholia graeca in Euripidis tragoedias* (Oxford, 1863), has collected the scholia of the Arsenios edition. Euripides, of course, wrote more than seven plays. The Aldine Euripides (edited by Musurus in 1503) did not include the scholia. Turyn kindly informs me that the view, sometimes expressed, that Arsenios found Euripidean scholia in Cretan monasteries (cf. Arsenios' preface to the Venice, 1534, ed. in Legrand, *Bibl. hell.*, I, 223) is probably incorrect.

[117] Earlier, on June 26, 1517, Leo X had in one day created thirty-one new cardinals, many from among his own friends and close relatives, including Niccolò Ridolfi. See Roscoe, *Leo X*, III, 124–29. Cf. above, Chapter 5, text and note 175.

[118] See letter in Legrand, I, 220–24, esp. 222.

The need Arsenios felt to induce (or to appear to induce) the Orthodox Greeks to conform to Western beliefs [119] is once again evidenced in his relations with the Corfiote monk, Joannikios Kartanos. The latter, in the preface to his book *Selection of Stories from the Old and New Testament* (published in Venice in 1536) says, cryptically, that he was denounced and imprisoned by Arsenios because of a "single word" he had uttered to the latter. (The word, according to Legrand, was "apostate.") It must be noted, however, that Kartanos' book, based on the Apocrypha, then much read in Greece, was rather extreme in its views, giving a pantheistic, even fantastic, interpretation to many of the accepted ecclesiastical dogmas.[120]

The final publication of Arsenios of which we have record was the *Didactic Discourse of Alcinous on the Doctrines of Plato*, which was printed in Venice by Stefano da Sabbio in March 1535, and dedicated to the Italian Paul Renaldus.[121] Publication of this work (the *editio princeps* had already appeared) added another edition to the growing list of commentaries on Plato and Aristotle that, under the influence of the Greek exiles, were becoming so important for the philosophic thought of the period.

Meantime, none of Arsenios' requests to the Pope seem to have been answered. (Paul was not the friend to humanism — or to the Greeks — that the two Medici popes had been.) And so alone and embittered over what he considered were the many persecutions he was made to undergo, Arsenios died. We have no information about his last days except for a notation on a Greek manuscript disclosing that his death occurred in Venice on April 30, 1535, and that he

[119] In a letter to Justin Decadyos, dated probably 1533, Arsenios excoriates the Greek (Orthodox) clergy for what he says is their lack of interest in education and declares that it was on this account that he was induced to live among the "wise" Italians who respect and admire him (!). Yet at the same time, he affirms, he loves his own country and his flock at Monemvasia (see Manousakas, "Arsenios . . . Unpublished Epistles," no. 6B, p. 21).

[120] Legrand, I, 231. Cf. Sathas, *Neohellenic Philology*, 147. Kartanos was not a Uniate but was considered a heretic and ultimately excommunicated by the Orthodox Constantinopolitan patriarch for his "blasphemies and heterodoxical beliefs." See B. Stephanides, *Ecclesiastical History* (in Greek) (Athens, 1948) 658, and also *Dict. theol. cath.*, II, cols. 1805–06.

[121] Legrand, I, 225. I can find no other information on Renaldus. Alcinous is thought to be the same person as the Platonist Albinus of the second century A.D. See J. Freudenthal, *Der Platoniker Albinos und der falsche Alkinoos* (Berlin, 1879) and, more recently, R. Witt, *Albinus and the History of Middle Platonism* (Cambridge, 1937).

was buried in the courtyard of the (provisional) church of San Giorgio dei Greci.[122] His nephew and pupil, the humanist Count George Corinthios, erected a monument to him, the Latin inscription of which has been preserved in a manuscript of the period:

To Arsenios Apostolis, Bishop of Monemvasia, who with his erudition blessed sacred letters and the two languages, George Corinthios, his nephew, erected this.[123]

According to the Orthodox author of the *Patriarchal History*, Arsenios died "unrepentant and still under excommunication. And his soul went to join those of the heretic Nestorius and the rest. His miserable cadaver was found [intact] after a time, black and swollen, and all who saw it were fearful and trembling." This is a striking commentary on the Orthodox view toward what was considered his apostasy. For conservation of the body of a heretic after death was for the Orthodox proof of certain reprobation. As for the contemporary Western sources they take almost no notice of the death of Arsenios.[124] Indeed, his fanatical, self-seeking aggressiveness had probably only corroborated the view already growing in the minds of many Western humanists, that the Greek exiles had now outlived their usefulness. Thus this learned and opportunistic philologist-cleric, who despite ceaseless embroilment in ecclesiastical intrigue contributed much to the service of Greek scholarship (witness his important editions of both classical and Byzantine authors, the pupils he instructed, and the numerous manuscripts he copied), ended his days not only despised by most of his Greek compatriots but, what would doubtless have been more galling to him, virtually ignored by the Latins.

[122] Cf. a note (referring to his approximate age and date of death) in the Vienna MS. Philol., no. CXXVIII; also Legrand, I, p. clxxii.

[123] Latin version printed in Legrand, I, p. clxxiii. The inscription is preserved in the archives of St. Augustine of Padua. On Corinthios see Legrand, I, 252, and for a list of manuscripts belonging to him see H. Omont, *Notes sur les manuscrits grecs du British Museum* (Paris, 1882) 17; H. Stevenson, *Codices manuscripti Palatini Graeci Bibliothecae Vaticanae* (Rome, 1885) 215 and 236. Four manuscripts of his are in the Bibliothèque Nationale of Paris (see Nolhac, *La bibliothèque de Fulvio Orsini* 162, n. 4). On Corinthios, see also Manousakas, "Arsenios . . . Unpublished Epistles," 39.

[124] Legrand, I, p. clxxiii (and Salaville, *Dict. d'hist. géog. eccl.*, III col. 1030), suggests that the remains of Arsenios were later exhumed and that they disappeared at the time the church of San Giorgio was reconstructed.

Chapter 7

ZACHARIAS CALLIERGIS

Cretan Calligrapher and Founder of the Greek Press in Medici Rome

PUBLICATION of Greek books was, as we have seen, effectively initiated with the appearance in Milan of the *Erotemata* of Constantine Lascaris, published in 1476 by Demetrius Damilas the Cretan. Venice followed soon after, in 1484 with the *Erotemata* of Chrysoloras (printed by Peregrino da Bologna) or in 1486 with the *Batrachomyomachia* of the so-called Homeric school, executed by Laonikos the Cretan.[1] But Rome, despite its early introduction of a Latin press (1467) and the ecumenical significance of the city as the seat of the papacy, saw the publication of no Greek work until as late as 1515. The lag in the emergence of a Roman Greek press was at least partly due to the absorption of the energetic pope Julius II in political and military affairs and artistic endeavors to the exclusion of more literary pursuits.[2] It was the different atmosphere created through the efforts of the humanist pope, the Medici Leo X, that intensified the revival of Greek letters in Rome and attracted to that city the man who set up its first Greek press — Zacharias Calliergis.[3]

[1] On Chrysoloras' *Erotemata*, see above, Chapter 3, text and note 16. On the "Homeric School" see Schmid-Stählin, article in *Geschichte der griechischen Literatur* (Munich, 1929) I, pt. 1, 230. For the *Batrachomyomachia* see Homer, *Opera*, ed. T. Allen, V (Oxford, 1912) 168–183. Also cf. Chapter 3, text and note 18.

[2] See Scholderer, *Catalogue of Books Printed in the XV Century*, pt. V, 9.

[3] Aside from the sketch of Legrand, *Bibliographie hellénique*, I, cxxv–cxxx, the useful but now outdated account of Firmin-Didot, *Alde Manuce*, 544ff., the three-page sketch in Sathas, *Neohellenic Philology*, 120–23, and the references to Calliergis in Lobel, *Greek Manuscripts of Aristotle's 'Poetics,'* (cf. A. Moustoxides,

Calliergis was born in the Cretan city of Rethymnon.[4] The evidence commonly cited for the date of his birth is a casual reference made by Erasmus, on the occasion of a dinner held in 1508 at the home of Musurus in Padua, to "a remarkably learned youth named Zacharias." If Erasmus' statement does in fact refer to Calliergis, all we can deduce from it and from an additional remark of his, playfully alluding to himself as an "old man," is that Calliergis was considerably younger than Erasmus, who was then about forty-one years of age.[5] More reliable testimony, hitherto overlooked, seems afforded by Calliergis' first publication, the *Etymologicum Magnum*, which appeared in 1499 after some six years' preparation. If we assume that at the time Calliergis first undertook the work he was at the very least twenty years of age, his birth should then be fixed at no later than the year 1473.[6]

Together with Janus Lascaris and Demetrius Ducas, Zacharias seems to have been one of the few Greek scholars residing in the West able to claim descent from the old imperial Byzantine dynasties.[7] From the thirteenth century on, the Calliergis family had played an important role in Cretan political life, one branch supporting Venetian domination, the other actively opposing it. In the late fourteenth century a member of the pro-Venetian branch, George Calliergis, as a reward for service against Genoa in the War of Chioggia, was raised to the patrician class and even admitted to the Venetian Grand Council.[8] We do not know to which line of the

Hellenomnemon, I, 328–36), no detailed systematic account exists of Calliergis' life.

[4] Birthplace known from subscription of his publication of Agapetus, published May 1509 (see below, text and note 44). Legrand, I, p. cxxv and 95.

[5] For the incident see P. S. Allen, *Opus Epistolarum Des. Erasmi Roterodami*, V, no. 1347, p. 245 (transl. in J. Mangan, *Life, Character, and Influence of D. Erasmus* [New York, 1927] I, 259). For Erasmus' age see Mangan, 3, and on Musurus, Chapter 5 above.

[6] On the *Etymologicum Magnum*, see Musurus' preface to the work, translated in part below, text and notes 13 and 22.

[7] See Gerland, "La noblesse Crétoise, "221, 224–27, 234, where he says, surprisingly, that Phokas was the ancient Byzantine name of the Calliergis family.

[8] Gerland, 208–9, 224; Thiriet, *La Romanie vénitienne*, 455. On the rebellions led by the Calliergis family see especially Xanthoudides, *Venetian Crete*, 55–74, 74–78, 99–110; and Gerland, 225; also M. Manousakas, Ἡ ἐν Κρήτῃ Συνωμοσία τοῦ Σήφη Βλαστοῦ (Athens, 1960) 51–52. On the form of Calliergis' name, whether Callergis or Calliergis (or even Phocas) see Gerland, 234. Important too is Gerland's *Das Archiv des Herzogs von Kandia, in Königlische Staatsarchiv zu Venedig* (Strasbourg, 1899), which is concerned with family archives. Calliergis himself spelled his name variously.

Calliergis family Zacharias belonged. But there seems little doubt that for several generations before his birth, his immediate forebears had been on favorable terms with the Venetian government.

No details are available on the early years of Zacharias' life, nor do we know the date of his arrival in Venice. Like Musurus, however, he probably came to Italy at an early age, not as a refugee seeking asylum but as a voluntary expatriate, attracted by the increasing importance of the Greek community in the economic and cultural life of the Venetian Empire.[9]

An epistle dated simply in May, directed to Zacharias from his friend the Mantuan Hellenist John-Jacob Arrigoni, possibly a bookseller, reveals several details about Zacharias' personal life: that his parents were with him in Venice, that he was married, and that he was keenly interested in the copying of Greek manuscripts.[10] Calliergis' reputation for elegant calligraphy is, of course, well known, but the information provided about his immediate family is unavailable elsewhere. The suggestion of Firmin-Didot that a certain Anthony, cited in a letter of Musurus as a Venetian bookseller in 1499, is Zacharias' brother, is probably correct. However, the Cretan Peter Calliergis, mentioned by the same author as aiding Zacharias financially, appears to belong to a different generation.[11]

There are major gaps in our knowledge of Calliergis' life at almost every point. We know absolutely nothing about his education — whether he received it in Crete or Venice or in both places

---

[9] Firmin-Didot, *Alde Manuce*, 545, makes the rather romantic statement that Zacharias' expatriation was motivated by a deep devotion to Hellenism.

[10] Specifically mentioned in the letter are works of Rufus, Oribasius (the Greek medical writer of the fourth century A.D.), and Strabo, and a Latin work, Virgil's *Georgics*. See Legrand, II, 298–99. (Lobel, *Greek Manuscripts of Aristotle's 'Poetics'*, 51, is doubtless correct in surmising that Calliergis copied manuscripts before 1499.) Lobel would change the reading "Mantua" to "Padua," but we know that Arrigoni was from Mantua (Legrand, I, p. xcix, and II, 306; also Firmin-Didot, 529–30).

[11] On Anthony see Legrand, II, 312, for a letter to Zacharias in care of Anthony's book shop. Cf. Chapter 5, note 50, and Firmin-Didot, *Alde Manuce*, 516–17, where he puts in brackets: Anthony [Calliergis]. Cf. also Lobel, 50. A probably later letter (written on Sept. 26, 1500, according to Manousakas, "Gregoropoulos Correspondence") from John's father indicates that John Gregoropoulos was then living with John (should this be Nicholas?) Vlastos. For references to Peter Calliergis see Noiret, *Lettres*, 46, who cites Michael Apostolis' letters to a rich man of this name. Roquefort, in Michaud, *Biographie Universelle*, VI, 411, lists a certain George Calliergis, professor of Greek at Venice in the early sixteenth century and a learned Hellenist.

— nor who his teachers were. Indeed, we have fewer biographical data on Calliergis than on any other scholar under discussion in this book. Our first definite knowledge of Calliergis is in connection with the press he set up in Venice. This was, if not the first Greek press of Venice in point of time, certainly the most important printing establishment owned and operated by Greeks in the city.[12] Though even the date of its foundation is uncertain, certain details may be gleaned from Musurus' dedicatory preface inserted in Calliergis' first publication (1499), the magnificent *Etymologicum Magnum*, the largest of the existing medieval Greek dictionaries and a typical example of the scholarship of the medieval Byzantines. From Musurus' statement in the preface that "success has now rewarded the efforts of those who six years ago undertook this printing in Greek characters," it would seem that the initial steps for setting up the press were taken as far back as 1493.[13] Given the complexities of printing Greek incunabula, Calliergis may well have experimented with trial editions before producing the *Etymologicum*.

According to Firmin-Didot, who may well be right — though his remarks are often inexact, exaggerated, or undocumented — Calliergis had conceived the idea of printing all the important Greek works of classical antiquity as early as Aldus and possibly even before him.[14] Unlike the Aldine press, however, that of Calliergis was devoted exclusively to the printing of Greek works. Aldus also printed Latin classics and, on occasion, even works in the vernacular (Bembo's editions of Dante and Petrarch, for example). But it was Calliergis' intention, from the very outset, to print Greek works alone.

Calliergis founded his press with the support of a wealthy, aristo-

[12] Cf. above, Chapter 3, text and notes 18–19. Also Kontosopoulos, "The Greek Press in Venice," 292, who omits mention of Laonikos and Alexander. Cf. Brown, *Venetian Printing Press*, 43.

[13] On the preface see above, Chapter 5, text for note 58; it is reprinted in Firmin-Didot, 553–55. Fumagalli, *Lexicon Typographicum Italiae*, 478, puts the founding of Calliergis' press ca. 1494. See Proctor, *Printing of Greek*, 119, for lavish praise of the printing achievement of the *Etymologicum*.

[14] Firmin-Didot, 546–48. Cf. Legrand, I, p. cxxvi. Legrand has not utilized all available material on Calliergis; for example, he publishes a letter (II, 297) of Calliergis which is lacking in Firmin-Didot (and which explicitly mentions Padua), but nowhere does he use this information. The letter is unsigned but the handwriting is certainly that of Calliergis.

cratic fellow-Cretan from Rethymnon, Nicholas Vlastos. On the basis, largely, of a subscription at the end of the *Etymologicum* ("the impression of this *Grand Etymologicum* has been executed, thanks to God, at the expense of the noble and illustrious Nicholas Vlastos of Crete"), certain scholars have regarded Vlastos as merely a Maecenas in the enterprise.[15] But the appearance of Vlastos' mark side by side with that of Calliergis on the final pages of the *Etymologicum* seems rather to point to some kind of partnership arrangement, probably with Calliergis responsible for the actual typography, Vlastos providing most of the funds, and both sharing in the risks and profits. To reinforce this view we may cite a patent issued to Vlastos in 1498 by the College or Cabinet of Venice for his "model of very beautiful Greek letters, united with their accents — something never before executed so well or so beautifully."[16]

Like Musurus, Calliergis prided himself on his Byzantine ancestry. In a letter to Gregoropoulos he signed himself simply "Zacharias the Roman," that is, the Byzantine.[17] His printer's mark itself was Byzantine, being the imperial double-headed eagle with a shield superimposed — shown on the title page of this book — a symbol he would later continue to use in Rome.[18]

Moreover, his partner and workmen were all Cretan compatriots from the Greek colony in Venice, John Gregoropoulos acting as press overseer.[19] It is clear that in founding his press Calliergis was motivated to a high degree by ethnic pride and a love for Hellenism. One may recall here the lines of the poem describing the press of

[15] For instance, Firmin-Didot, 547. Cf. Legrand, I, p. cxxvi and 55–58. From indications in Vogel and Gardthausen, *Die griechischen Schreiber*, 346, we know that Vlastos, like other Cretans, copied manuscripts. On the Vlastos family, see C. Kerofilas, *Une famille patricienne crétoise: les Vlasto* (New York, 1932), and Manousakas, Ἡ ἐν Κρήτῃ Συνωμοσία, 26–28, and bibliography cited.

[16] Original Italian text in Brown, *Venetian Printing Press*, 55. Cf., however, above, Chapter 5, text and note 59, for Musurus' poem on the Cretan role in printing, where he terms Vlastos merely *choregos* (patron).

[17] Legrand, II, 297–98 and Firmin-Didot, 526. Firmin-Didot is puzzled by the term "Roman" applied here to Calliergis. But the Byzantines always termed themselves Romans, since their empire was the direct continuation of the ancient Roman Empire, technically at least.

[18] Legrand, I, 56–58, prints the mark along with that of Vlastos.

[19] Legrand, II, 264. Also see Manousakas, "Gregoropoulos Correspondence," 192, n. 2. It was while working for Calliergis that John was evidently living at the home of Vlastos, or possibly of Vlastos' father (since *John* Vlastos is mentioned in the letter rather than Nicholas). See Manousakas, 195 and 197.

Τόπος, ϖαρὰ τὸ τύπος. ἕκαστος γὰ͂ Τόπος, ἰδίῳ τύπῳ
κέχηται. ἢ ϖαρὰ τὸ τάφος. πᾶς γὰρ τόπος, ἔστ ταφὴν
Τοσαῦτα, ὄνομα πτώσεως αἰτιατικῆς ⟨ἐπιτήδειος.
τῶν πληθυντικῶν. ην̄ δὲ καὶ ϖαραγωγὴν ἐκ τοῦ Τόσα.
ϖαραλήγουσαν ἔχον τὴν αω̄τ. καὶ ὡς Γαρέστὶ ὁ λέγων,
ὅτι ὡς τῶν της τῆς ϖαραγωγῆς τῆς ͽ γενικῇ ἀριθμοῖς
ϖροϊούσης, ἢ ϖρό τέλους συλλαβὴ βούλεϊ ἔχειν τὸ
μῦ τοῦ ἐπ τῆ λικούση φωνήεντος. ἔστιν οὖν τῆ μος. τὸ
τημοῦρος ϖαράγωγον ἔξ τ υ τὸ ο ϖρόκειμ͂. ὁμοίως τὸ
τηνίκα τηνικαῦτα, οὕτω κὴ ηʼρʼθα ϗθεν ἐντεῦθεν. τὸ
ἀλλό κὴ ωʼ τ τόσος γρου ͽρος. τόσα γρουͼαῦͼαι γρουͼαῦ—
τα. καὶ ἀ γεην γὰρ καὶ ἀριθμοῖς ἀι ϖαραγωγαὶ Γίνον͂ͼ.
οἱ, τηλίκος, τηλικοῦͼρος. τηλίκα, τηλικαῦͼα. τρὶ
η, ρὶ η νὴ τι ωʼφ ͽλον εῖναι. δὴ ἐπειδὴ καὶ ὡς ἔστι ὁ λέγων
οὐκ ἔστιν ἐπιγοῆσαι τὸ η κὴ ͽ υ ἐν μιᾶ συλλαβῆ καὶ τὰ
ὅμοια, τούτου χάριν γʼ ἐπεὶ τὸ η ͽσα, κὴ γʼ γι αὐτη.
Τόφρα, ἐπὶ γρου ͽην. οἷον, Τόφρα Σʼ αῦτ ρʼ ὡς απʼ ὑπ͂θει
κράτος ὀφρʼ αν ἀχαιοί. ἔτι καὶ ἀπὸ δυ τι κὸμ ἐʼ ͽʼ ῥῆμα.
Ἰστέον ὅτι η μίκα γʼ κρᾶσίς ἐν ἀρμονῆ διὸ λέξεων, ἴθε η
κορωνίς. οἷον τὸ ἐμοῦ τοῦ μὲν. τὰ ἐμὰ, τὰ μά. ϖρόε
σπ, ϖροῦσπ. ϖρόοπλον, ϖροῦπλον. ἢ δὲ γʼ φανερόν. η νι
κα δὲ μὴ Γίνεϊ κρᾶσῆς ἐν ἀρμονῆ διὸ λέξεων, οὐ τίθεϊαι
κορωνίς. οἱ νόος γοῦς. δημοθένεος δημοθένοις· ϖρός
κεϊ ͽαι ἐν ἀρμονῆ διὸ λέξεων, διὰ τὸ ἡρακλέης ἡρακλῆς·
τοῦ γʼ ἐκ διὸ λέξεων ὂν, ὅμως οὐκ ἔχει κορωνίδα,
ἔπει οὐκ ἐγένετο ἐν ἀρμονῆ διὸ λέξεων ἡ κρᾶσις, ἀλλʼ
ἐν τῷ μέσω τῆς δευτέρας λέξεως. ἡ ͽ ἀρμογῆ τῶν διὸ
λέξεων, μεταξὺ τοῦ α καὶ τοῦ η κη ͽ.

GREEK TYPE USED IN CALLIERGIS'
Etymologicum Magnum, VENICE, 1499

Calliergis written by his close friend and collaborator Musurus, which exalt the role of the Cretans in the establishment of the art of Greek printing.[20]

The Greek font cut by Calliergis differed considerably from those of Aldus, and is considered superior to his, although it too was based on the cursive writing hand of the period.[21] Zacharias' books were printed in red and black, and many of his pages compare favorably with leaves of a richly illuminated Byzantine manuscript. In a letter he addressed to Vlastos, Musurus (who, as we have seen, aided Calliergis in editing the *Etymologicum*), lauded the type produced by his friends, justifiably feeling a sense of national pride in the accomplishment:

Although the types recently invented in this city seem to have left to posterity no hope of surpassing them in beauty, you were not discouraged — either by the knowledge that equaling them was difficult to consider or by taking such excuses as a valid pretext for laziness . . . and you hoped that . . . you would succeed and achieve your goal, leaving to posterity a work which will contribute both to your glory and to the common benefit of our people.[22]

Inevitably Calliergis' press, because of its careful and elaborate work, soon became a rival of the Aldine. Yet, unlike much humanist behavior, there seems to have been no jealousy to mar the friendship of the two printers. As observed elsewhere, Aldus even advertised the works of Calliergis in his own catalogues. (Whether Calliergis returned the favor — or even issued catalogues — we cannot say.) Thus in a letter to John Reuchlin (one of the earliest and most famous Hellenists of Germany), dated October of 1502, Aldus listed several publications of Calliergis and noted particularly that he was transmitting to Reuchlin a copy of the *Etymologicum Magnum*. Later in 1505 Aldus was requested by the German monk

[20] See above, Chapter 5, text for note 59. Note that the subscription at the end of Calliergis' volume (Legrand, I, 55) reads that the work was printed "at the urging of the Byzantine Princess Anna Notaras." Since Anna, daughter of the last Byzantine "prime minister," was very wealthy, she may well have contributed financially to the project. (On Anna see above, Chapter 3, note 26.) Musurus' poem, however, does not mention Anna, though he refers to Vlastos.

[21] Aldus' type may have been modeled on a specimen provided by Musurus, but comparison shows the differences from his own hand. Cf. Chap. 5; n. 39.

[22] See Firmin-Didot, 522, for Greek text, especially εἰς κοινὴν τοῦ γένους ὠφέλειαν. John Gregoropoulos also included a quatrain in this work.

Henry Urban to send to the latter, via the Fuggers, various books, including the *Etymologicum*.[23]

Zacharias was at this time living with the bookseller Anthony (his brother?), who may perhaps have helped in the founding of his press, as no doubt he must have done in the circulation of his books.[24] Zacharias' plans for future publications are indicated by the letter of Musurus to him mentioned earlier, recording Musurus' aim of purchasing for Calliergis several manuscripts, including one of Galen, from the well-known doctor Leoniceno of Ferrara.[25]

Only little more than three months after the appearance of Calliergis' first publication, he issued the *editio princeps* of the *Commentary of Simplicius on the Categories of Aristotle*. In this period when there was a growing emphasis on the nonscholastic interpretation of Aristotle, this first publication of a Greek text of a commentator on the philosopher was to have considerable influence.[26] Embellished with the usual Calliergian ornamentation, the text was evidently printed from a manuscript copied by Calliergis himself for Vlastos,[27]

The next two works to be issued appeared under the name of Vlastos alone. First to be printed was the *editio princeps*, dated May 22, 1500, of Ammonius Hermeiae's *Commentary on the Five Voices of Porphyry* [28] — another work of philosophic commentary — and in October of that year there followed the *Therapeutics* of Galen.[29] It is interesting that the Galen manuscript, secured by Musurus from Leoniceno, had originally been copied by Musurus himself during his student days in Florence.[30]

[23] Firmin-Didot, 235 and 291. Reuchlin had studied Greek with the Byzantines John Argyropoulos, Chalcondyles, and Contoblachas. See L. Kukenheim, *Contributions à l'histoire de la grammaire grecque, latine, et hébraïque à l'époque de la Renaissance* (Leiden, 1951) 9, n. 10.

[24] See above, text and note 11.

[25] On whom see Chapter 5, text and note 48.

[26] On the importance of Simplicius in this period, see Kristeller, *Classics*, 26, 41.

[27] Legrand, I, 62. Vogel and Gardthausen, *Die griechischen Schreiber*, 125.

[28] On this work and the problems of chronology involved, see Legrand, I, 74–75, and I, p. cxxviii. Note that the book's subscription refers to Venice as the "Queen of Cities," a title applied by the Byzantines to Constantinople.

[29] Legrand, I, 74–75. Cf. Sathas, *Neohellenic Philology*, 120–23, who evidently alone does not include the Galen as a work of Calliergis. Calliergis' double-headed eagle is, to be sure, missing from the Galen as well as from the Ammonius Hermeiae. Moreover a letter of Musurus (Legrand, I, 75) to Gregoropoulos at this time mentions Vlastos and says nothing of Calliergis' participation.

[30] Letter of Musurus to Calliergis (Legrand, II, 312).

Despite the absence of Calliergis' name and mark from the last two publications, Legrand and Firmin-Didot are of the opinion that the collaboration of the two Cretans did not cease and that both works were still their joint product.[31] There are indications, however, that the partnership was dissolved soon after the appearance of the Simplicius. In view of a total lack of evidence for Calliergis' residence in Venice from October 26, 1499, to April 12, 1501, it may well be that Calliergis traveled during the period to Crete. Documentary evidence, in fact, attests that on the latter date he returned to Venice from some kind of journey in the aim of moving his family to Padua, to the Borgo Zocco.[32] On the basis of articles he brought back with him for his friend John Gregoropoulos (socks and a *charaka* — both very possibly the gift to John of his fond parents in Crete, who, we know from other letters, were in the habit of sending him wine, sausages, ham, grapes, and even ink),[33] it is not unlikely that Calliergis had just returned from his homeland. To quote from the letter then left by Calliergis for John Gregoropoulos:

Kyr John, dearest friend, I came to Venice yesterday in order to take my family with me to Padua. I came here to Aldus' house, to his print shop, to talk to you, but not finding you there [John was now working for Aldus] [34] I left your socks and the ruler (*charaka*) in care of Bartholomew to give you. I also wanted to meet on certain business matters Kyr Benedict, called by some Pilate, but since I could not find him either, I left the enclosed letter, which I beg you, please, to give to him. Goodbye now. Be of good health and keep well, as thank God we are well.[35]

---

[31] Legrand, I, p. cxxviii and Firmin-Didot, *Alde Manuce*, 562. Legrand, I, 75, bases his view that Calliergis was still with Vlastos on two letters of Musurus discussing the purchase of a Galen manuscript for the edition. But both letters are *previous* to the publication date of Simplicius, and the second letter does not make any mention of Calliergis in connection with the manuscript. Legrand, I, 75, notes that the Giunta press in Florence acquired some of Calliergis' typographical materials after publication of the Galen.

[32] See below, notes 35–36. See also Denissoff, *Maxime le Grec*, 90.

[33] See letters in Manousakas, "Gregoropoulos Correspondence," 179, 186, 201.

[34] See a letter of Musurus to John, dated April 5, 1500 (in Legrand, II, 316), referring to the forwarding of John's letters by Aldus; hence John must have left Vlastos even *before* completion of the Ammonius Hermeiae edition (May 22, 1500). A quarrel may have occurred at this time among the Greeks, for we know that George Moschus was fired as corrector (letter in Legrand, II, 313).

[35] This letter (dated April 12, 1501) is ascribed to Zacharias by Legrand, II, no. 1, 297 (also by Lobel, *Greek Manuscripts of Aristotle's 'Poetics'*, 50) because

In another letter dated less than a month later, Zacharias queries John about the arrival of their friend Musurus (whom he here affectionately terms "my brother"), and instructs John to address his letters to "Zacharias the Roman at the Borgo Zocco opposite the well." [36]

If we may assume that Calliergis was absent from Venice from October 1499 to April 1501, what may we say about Vlastos in the meantime? Some scholars believe that the absence of Vlastos' name on publications after the Galen (1500) indicates that his death occurred soon afterwards, with consequent detrimental effect on the financial resources of the press. In the light of overlooked evidence from Sanuto's *Diaries*, however, we know that Vlastos was still living in 1503 and indeed was wealthy enough to loan funds to the Venetian bank of Lipomano in order to save it from bankruptcy. As late as 1514, in fact, we learn that Vlastos inherited some property from a certain "Madona Anna Matara," doubtless the Byzantine princess Anna Notaras, for whom he had acted as agent in the preceding years. [37] After 1500, however, there seems to be no further indication of Vlastos' connections with Calliergis.

Legrand has made no attempt to describe Calliergis' activities during the interval after the appearance of the Galen. But it seems safe to say that during this period, following upon the dissolution of his association with Vlastos, Zacharias supported his family, at least in part, by the traditional method of Cretan intellectuals, the copying of manuscripts. As evidence of his work we have two signed but undated manuscripts written in Padua. [38] Two others, unsigned and undated, apparently are also to be assigned to his Paduan residence, since for both he had the collaboration of a

---

of the handwriting. "Kyr Benedict" may possibly refer to Benedetto Ramberti, a member of Aldus' household and librarian of St. Marks. See Firmin-Didot, *Alde Manuce*, 466–67.

[36] Legrand, II, no. 2, 297–98; Firmin-Didot, 525–26. It is dated simply May 9. Cf. above, Chapter 5, note 90, on the Borgo Zocco, today, I am informed, named Via Aristide Gabelli.

[37] See Sanuto, *Diarii*, IV (1880) col. 822. Also Kerofilas, *Les Vlasto*, 79–112, and C. Mertzios, "Ἡ διαθήκη τῆς Ἄννας Παλαιολογίνας Νοταρᾶ," Ἀθηνᾶ, LIII (1949) 17–21. Cf. Manousakas, "Gregoropoulos Correspondence," 203n.

[38] Paris, gr. 2823 and Bonon. 2302 (see Lobel, *Greek Manuscripts of Aristotle's 'Poetics'*, 50).

Greek named Constantine Mesobotes, who we know definitely was in Padua in 1508.[39]

With Padua only some twenty miles from Venice, Zacharias was able to maintain close contact with his Venetian acquaintances. We may quote from another of his many notes to John Gregoropoulos, in which he mentions their mutual friends Aldus and the Venetian humanist Pietro Bembo, and provides further corroboration for his activities as a scribe:

I have received the very beautiful papers of our Giovanni Pietro [Bembo] and I am very grateful to him. As for the money you have spent, our priest Battista [Egnazio?] will return it to you if he has sold the Musaeus; otherwise I will repay you soon when I see you. Greet for me the wise and learned Gabriel,[40] and tell him the manuscripts (*tetradia*) have been copied. Greet also our Scipio Carteromachus and all the members of the *Neakademia*, and especially its chief and leader.[41]

Like Venice, Padua had its circle of learned Hellenists, and we may be sure that Calliergis mingled with them. His friend Marcus Musurus in 1503 was named professor of Greek at the University of Padua, and there began to gather around him a large group of students from all parts of Europe. A letter of Erasmus gives us a glimpse of Paduan camaraderie on the part of the Greek exiles and Western scholars — with Erasmus and Calliergis dining at the home of Musurus and his elderly father and bantering with one another about their respective ages.[42]

In 1509 Calliergis resumed publication with the issuing in Venice on April 14 of a very slim volume of sixteen leaves, even the title of which (*Exepsalmata*), until Legrand's researches, was uncertain.[43] Nothing is known of the circumstances of this publication. It was followed less than a month later (May 11, 1509) by the ap-

[39] See Lobel, 50. On Mesobotes see "Hands and Scribes," *Classical Quarterly*, XXII (1928) 202, n. 3, which suggests he was a Paduan.

[40] This, I think, may refer to Gabriel Braccio of Brisighella, who with two friends had applied in Venice, in 1498, to print in Greek and Latin with new type. They published Aesop and other works, and he subsequently became a member of Aldus' Academy. See Brown, *Venetian Printing Press*, 43.

[41] Legrand, II, no. 3, 298, and Firmin-Didot, 527-28, with French translation. The fact that the letter is addressed to Aldus' printing shop and mentions the Academy places it after 1500.

[42] See Chapter 5, text and note 9; and this chapter, text and note 5. See also Chapter 5, text and note 83a.

[43] Legrand, I, 94 and p. cxxviii. Also Norton, *Italian Printers 1501-1520*, 133.

pearance of the *De officio regis* of the Byzantine Deacon Agapetus, a work consisting of advisory chapters on kingship addressed to the Byzantine Emperor of the sixth century, Justinian.[44]

The small size of these two volumes may partly have been due to Zacharias' inability to find adequate financial support. The expense of his next work, a charming, well-executed prayer book called *Horologion*, published on August 23, 1509, was met by one Jacopo de Pontio of Lecco.[45] This book, likewise of small format, was printed in the usual red and black of Calliergis (though without his printer's mark) and, as has recently been established by Cardinal Mercati, was based on a manuscript contained in the library of Alberto Pio.[46] The increasingly severe competition in the printer's trade led Calliergis to secure from the Venetian authorities a privilege guaranteeing the work against those who might pirate the edition.[47]

In a preface to the work Calliergis announces to the reader his new objective. Realizing, he writes, that many of the classic Greek philosophic and poetic works have already been put into print (a reference doubtless to Aldus' accomplishments), he intends now to emphasize the publication of Greek religious works, which, as we know, had been of little concern to Aldus. Thus he makes appeal to all "Orthodox Christians" (referring probably to all Greeks in general) to support his project of printing a series of books used in the performance of the Greek liturgy — works now becoming rare "because of the bitter misfortune of our nation." Like all the Greek exiles, Calliergis could not forget the fate of his compatriots in the East and the servitude to which the Greek race had been reduced.[48]

---

[44] Legrand, I, 95, and p. cxxviii. Firmin-Didot, 563. Cf. Sathas, *Neohellenic Philology*, 122, who lists this wrongly as a Rome edition. The Agapetus work is often found bound with the *Exepsalmata*. Printers of the period did not bind their books themselves but sent them elsewhere. Agapetus' work influenced the development of the monarchic ideal in both Russia and France.

[45] Legrand, I, 96 and p. cxxix. Legrand was unable to identify Pontio, but he is cited in Brown, *Venetian Printing Press*, 61, under the name Jacomo di Penzi (Pentius) of Lecco, who printed in Venice from 1495 to 1527. He is listed also in Norton, 146.

[46] Mercati, *Pio*, 64.

[47] Firmin-Didot, 562.

[48] See Legrand, I, p. cxxix. Passage quoted in I, 97. The Uniates used the same liturgical texts as the Orthodox.

The unsettled political conditions and economic depression in Venice resulting from the War of the League of Cambrai seem to have been responsible for the closing of Calliergis' press, as had likewise happened in the case of Aldus. And for six years, Calliergis disappears from sight, not to reappear until 1515 in Rome. Like other scholars of Venice, Calliergis may well have been attracted to the papal capital by Leo X's promotion of humanistic learning, in particular by Leo's foundation of a Greek school headed by Janus Lascaris, and, more important, by the opportunity to establish a Greek press where none as yet existed. The latter point would seem to be supported by an interesting letter, hitherto unused, dated May 15, 1511, written by Angelo Colocci, the famous humanist and secretary to several popes, to Scipio Carteromachus in Venice or Bologna. After requesting the dispatch of several classical authors, Colocci writes: "Shortly Jacomo Mazzocchio, formerly Mercurio, desires to bring the Greek press to Rome (*vol condurre la stampa graeca in Roma*); already he promises to print Eustathius on Homer and wants to bring compositors. Giovanni Antonio Marostico says that he can make use of that Zacharias who did the *Etymologicum* (*di quello Zacharia che fece lo Ethymologicon*). Inform yourself about him, for when the (papal) court is reassembled I want you and me to bring to Rome the *Neakademia*, with its emphasis on Greek; nothing, however, can be done without you." [48a]

Whether anything actually came, then or later, of the plans of Colocci is not clear. We do know definitely, however, that when Calliergis arrived in Rome and set up his new press he had the financial support of the wealthiest individual in all Italy, the Sienese banker Agostino Chigi, who permitted Calliergis to set up his typographical equipment in one of his numerous homes in Rome. Though not himself well educated, Chigi had become the patron of a large number of eminent humanists then at the papal court, such as Leo's secretary Pietro Bembo, Paolo Giovio, Cornelio

---

[48a] Letter in "Les correspondants d'Alde Manuce," *Studi e documenti di storia e diritto*, VIII (1887) 297, no. 43. Marostico was later appointed professor of Greek at Padua in 1517, with the re-establishment of that chair. Mazzocchio is probably Jacobus Mazochius, a bookseller-printer of the University of Rome, listed in Norton, *Italian Printers*, 101-2, who printed a translation of Isocrates in 1509. Evidently it was planned to move Aldus' Academy to Rome.

Benigno, and Pietro Aretino, not to mention such famous artists
as Raphael, who was then living in Chigi's home. Because of various
loans he made to the government of the Serenissima, Chigi often
visited Venice, at which times, we are told, he was accorded the
place of honor next to the Doge.[49] And there on some such occasion
he may have met Calliergis.

How far Rome lagged behind Venice in the printing of Greek
works may be gathered from the fact that Calliergis' initial publication in Rome (August 13, 1515) constituted the very first Greek
book to appear in that city. This was the celebrated edition of Pindar [50] containing the pioneer edition of the important scholia. The
editio princeps of Pindar's text had, to be sure, already appeared under the Aldine imprint in January of 1513, but the manuscript now
followed by Calliergis in his edition of the work was, in the view
of modern scholars, essentially superior, as was the philological
progress made. So important was this edition, in fact, that it would
stand for three centuries as the vulgate version of both the text and
scholia.[51]

The Greek colophon of the Calliergian Pindar reads as follows:

This collection of the poems of Pindar — the Olympians, the Pythians,
the Nemeans, and the Isthmians — has been printed and finished with
God's aid, at Rome the queen of cities, in the house of the magnificent
Augustino Chigi, at his personal expense, and at the urgings of the
learned Cornelio Benigno of Viterbo, and by the labor and skill of
Zacharias Calliergis of Crete, in the year A.D. 1515, 13 August, in the
pontificate of Leo X.[52]

The Benigno whose name is mentioned here was an Italian with
an intimate knowledge of Greek who, along with Carteromachus
and others, had, in Rome in 1507, revised and corrected (but with-

[49] Pastor, *History of the Popes*, VIII, 116–17; and Roscoe, *Leo X*, II, 256. According to Rodocanachi, *Première Renaissance à Rome*, 264, Chigi (who had
gained his wealth from the papal salt and alum mines) was not merely a patron
but a businessman. We know that he lent Benigno 400 ducats to print the Pindar
and later reclaimed them! See below, note 52.
[50] See Firmin-Didot, 364; Legrand, I, p. cxxix; and Roscoe, II, 257–258.
[51] See Irigoin, *Pindare*, 412, esp. n. 5, on Calliergis' use (he was the first to do
so) of Vatican manuscript B; also A. Turyn, *De codicibus pindaricis* (Kraków,
1932). On the work's significance and Calliergis' role see Irigoin, 420.
[52] Colophon printed in Legrand, I, 130. Irigoin, 408–409, quotes the Pindar dedication, which, notably, is to Benigno and not to Chigi. Cf. note 49 above, showing that Benigno bore the expense of printing the Pindar.

out printing) the influential geographical work of Ptolemy.[53] In the production of the Pindar, Benigno, despite the emphasis of the colophon, would seem to deserve much more credit than Chigi. For the dedicatory verses addressed to Benigno by the humanist Benedetto Lampridio indicate that Benigno aided Calliergis in the actual work of editing. And from other records we learn that Benigno later returned to Chigi a sum of money he had borrowed from the latter for the purpose of printing the Pindar.[54]

Rome in this period, as Pastor has well described, was what Paris was to become centuries later — the center of European culture. To dwell in Rome was the height of good fortune for every intellectual of the age. Pope Leo had gathered around him, in part through liberal distribution of pensions, a large and impressive group of learned humanists, scholars, and artists (as well as certain second-rate playwrights and musicians). They came from all over Europe, including Venice, which, since its humiliation at the hands of the League of Cambrai, had begun to lose to Rome its exalted position as leader in Greek studies.

The circle of literati surrounding Pope Leo included Latinists as well as Greek scholars: Pietro Bembo and Jacopo Sadoleto,[55] the papal secretaries; Jacopo Sannazaro, Paolo Giovio (who wrote biographies of many members of Leo's court), and others. Also a number of prominent political figures, including the old student and patron of Aldus and Musurus, Alberto Pio, Prince of Carpi, now the diplomatic representative in Rome of the King of France, Francis I.[56] Alberto had transported to Rome his rich library of manuscripts, many of which had been originally purchased from the humanist Giorgio Valla [57] and had subsequently served as the basis for various important Aldine publications of Greek works.[58]

[53] Roscoe, *Leo X*, II, 257. The Greek *editio princeps* of Ptolemy came out in 1533 in Basle with Erasmus as editor, according to Sandys, *History of Classical Scholarship*, II, 105.

[54] See Irigoin, 409–10. Also C. Gallavotti, *Theocritus* (Rome, 1946) 310. Lampridio was Latin professor in Rome at the Greek College of Lascaris (see above, Chapter 5, text and note 167). On Chigi's loan to Benigno, see note 49 above.

[55] See R. Douglas, *Jacopo Sadoleto, 1477-1547: Humanist and Reformer* (Cambridge, Mass., 1959) 14–28.

[56] Pastor, *History of the Popes*, VIII, 138.

[57] On Valla see especially Mercati, *Pio*, 59.

[58] See Mercati, 59. Cf. Lobel, *Greek Manuscripts of Aristotle's 'Poetics'*, 9, who says some of Alberto's Greek manuscripts remained in Carpi after Alberto was expelled and were brought to Rome sometime before 1531.

When Calliergis arrived in Rome, the Greek school established by Leo under the direction of Lascaris had already been organized. Papal munificence, in fact, soon permitted the setting up in the school's buildings, situated in the house of the Colocci on the Quirinal, of a special press called that of Monte Cavallo for the printing of Greek texts to be edited by Janus Lascaris and his pupils. But its first work of publication, the scholia of Homer, did not appear until 1517.[59] There seems to have been no formal connection between the press operated by Calliergis and that of the Greek school, though the common interests of Calliergis and Lascaris must have drawn them together on more than one occasion.[60]

To establish a more permanent basis for the development of humanistic letters in Rome, Pope Leo reformed the existing municipal university of the city, erecting new buildings and inviting many eminent scholars to join its teaching staff. The splendor of the University rested on its eighty-eight professorships, of which, in 1514, three were reserved for lectures in the Greek language.[61] The latter received a maximum salary of 300 florins, a sum which compares very favorably with the yearly compensation received in the same period by Musurus in Venice.

The first professor of Greek appointed by Leo was Basilios Chalcondyles, the half-Italian son of the celebrated Athenian scholar Demetrius Chalcondyles, with whom Leo himself had studied as a youth in Florence. After the lamented early death of Basilio, his colleague the Italian scholar Augusto Valdo continued Greek instruction. Valdo, we are told, was so enamored of Hellenism that after a long sojourn in Greece he continued to wear the Greek cos-

---

[59] Pastor, VIII, 259–60 and 262. This press also issued a new edition of Porphyry and the very important first edition of the scholia on Sophocles. See Norton, *Italian Printers 1501–1520*, 97, and Turyn, *Manuscript Tradition of the Tragedies of Sophocles*. On the possible connection of Arsenios with the early works of the Monte Cavallo press see Chapter 6, note 69. It is interesting that Angelo Colocci, who became head of the Roman Academy, is named as the printer of the first texts issued by Monte Cavallo (Norton, 97). On Colocci see G. Lancellotti, *Poesie italiane e latine di M. Angelo Colocci* (Iesi, 1772) 36.

[60] We may recall that the Monte Cavallo press published the two little works of Arsenios, *Apophthegmata* and Γέρας (undated). The works of Calliergis' press and of Monte Cavallo are sometimes confused by scholars, but Norton, 97, distinguishes between the two presses.

[61] Pastor, *History of the Popes*, VIII, 272–73. See Renazzi, *Università di Roma*, II, 76–78. Also below, Chapter 8, text and notes 106–10.

tume in Italy.[62] Another holder of a Greek chair at Rome was Varinus Favorinus of Camerino (also called Guarino), a Benedictine monk who had studied with both Janus Lascaris and Poliziano and possessed a remarkable knowledge of Greek. In 1512 Varinus had been named director of Leo's private library in Rome, and still later he was appointed by Pope Leo, his former pupil, to the bishopric of Nocera.[63]

The premature death of young Chalcondyles was more than compensated for by the appointment at the University of Rome of the illustrious Janus Lascaris. Pope Leo was evidently not desirous of restricting the benefits of Lascaris' teaching to the young students of his Greek school, and had therefore appointed him to the vacant Greek chair.[64]

Owing to the dearth of competition from other Greek presses in Rome and, of course, to the advantages offered by Leo's court, Calliergis found less difficulty than at Venice in finding patrons to support his work. Hence his publications now appeared with greater regularity. Turning to Greek lyric poetry and mythology, Calliergis on January 15, 1516, issued an edition of the Greek pastoral poet Theocritus with scholia. It was Calliergis' collaborator on the Pindar, Cornelio Benigno, who now provided the funds for the printing of Theocritus. At the beginning and end of the book there are two printer's marks — the usual double-headed eagle of Calliergis and a new one, the *kerykeion* (the rod carried by Hermes, herald of the gods) surmounted by a star.[65] Interesting that Calliergis chose to combine the classical symbol of Hermes, the god of letters, with his Byzantine printer's mark!

As in the case of the Pindar, Calliergis' Theocritus had been preceded by earlier editions, that of Milan in perhaps 1480, the Aldine of 1495, and the Juntine of 1515. But the edition of Cal-

[62] On Basilio and Valdo see Renazzi, II, 76–77. Also on Valdo, see L. Dorez, "L'exemplaire de Pline l'ancien d'Agosto Valdo de Padoue et de Cardinal Marcello Cervini," *Revue des bibliothèques*, V (1895) 14ff.

[63] On Favorinus see Renazzi, II, 77; Legrand, *Bibliographie hellénique*, I, 178; Roscoe, *Leo X*, II, 261; and Mestica, *Varino Favorino Camerte*, 38ff. Also see below, text and note 77.

[64] Renazzi, II, 77. Kalitsounakes, "Matthaios Devares," 86. As noted, the Greek school was closed in 1521 at the death of Leo X.

[65] Legrand, I, 134 and p. cxxix; Firmin-Didot, *Alde Manuce*, 564; Norton, *Italian Printers 1501–1520*, 96. Might the two symbols indicate that Calliergis had a new partner?

liergis was the first to include the scholia; it contained several yet unprinted poems of Theocritus; and it is considered by modern scholars to be a more accurate edition than any of its predecessors.[66] As Calliergis himself writes in his preface: "I found the scholia scattered in many manuscripts and with much trouble I collected them." And he tells us that among the new poems he incorporated are those on the young Hercules, Hercules the lion-slayer, the Bacchantes, the Distaff, the Lovers, the Caristys, nineteen epigrams on various subjects, and four poems written by Simmias of Syracuse.[67]

Calliergis continued publication with the issuance on March 4, 1517, of a text by the fourteenth century Byzantine writer Thomas Magister, *Dictionary of Attic Locutions.*[68] This work is of great importance because of its wealth of information on Byzantine lexicographical and stylistic research of the Palaeologan era. The volume is dedicated to Michael Sylvius, "ambassador of the very pious and invincible Emmanuel, King of Portugal." Calliergis, in his dedication, thanks Sylvius for his generous aid and good will, "for batted on the sea by the storm and the waves it is near you that I have taken refuge as in a safe and accessible port, near you a true philhellene and generous supporter, the liberal patron of this work of publication so beneficial to the public." [69] Thus a representative of distant Portugal, of whose culture humanism had not yet become an essential part, was able to participate in the revival of Hellenism in Rome.[70] Very shortly thereafter (on July 1, 1517) Calliergis'

[66] The earlier edition of Aldus had not had available all the poems printed by Calliergis. Gallavotti, *Theocritus,* 309–313, thinks the improvements of Calliergis' edition may well be attributed to certain manuscript corrections made by Musurus in Padua already in 1503–1509.

[67] See Legrand, I, 136. There is difference of opinion as to the *editio princeps:* Sandys, *History of Classical Scholarship,* II, 104, cites Milan, 1493 — Sathas, *Neohellenic Philology,* 122, Milan, 1481 — but Graesse, *Trésor de livres rares et précieux,* VI (1900) 113, says Milan, 1480. On the origins of the first "incunabolo" of Theocritus "which served as the basis of the Aldine edition, then the Florentine of Giunta, and that of Calliergis," see C. Gallavotti, "Da Planude e Moscopulo alla prima edizione a stampa di Teocrito," *Studi Italiani di Filologia Classica,* XIII (1936) 46–59.

[68] Legrand, I, 150 and p. cxxix.

[69] Greek version in Firmin-Didot, *Alde Manuce,* 566–67 (note the inaccurate French translation, 568). Following the dedication are two pieces of verse in honor of Sylvius (and mentioning Calliergis) by Lactantius Ptolemaeus of Siena. On Sylvius see A. González Palencia and E. Mele, *Vida y obras de Don Diego Hurtado de Mendoza,* I (Madrid, 1941) 263–66.

[70] See Weiss, "Learning and Education in Western Europe," 125. Cf. M. Bataillon, *Etudes sur le Portugal au temps de l'humanisme* (Coimbra, 1952) 97.

press issued the *editio princeps* of the Greek Sophist Phrynichus, a brief grammatical work of only twenty folio pages which is often to be found bound with that of Thomas Magister.[71] The importance of the Phrynicus is out of all proportion to its size, as it constitutes a significant contribution to our knowledge of Atticistic style and trends.

Once again a lacuna occurs in the sources, with the next publication of a volume of Calliergis' not reported until three years later, in 1520. A Greek religious work, evidently corrected by Janus Lascaris, the book contained hymns to the Virgin in eight modes. Hence the title *Octoechos*, a term well-known in Byzantine hymnography and referring, among other things, to a collection of songs for liturgical purposes.[72] While Legrand has doubted the correctness of the title of the publication, Cardinal Mercati has shown that the manuscript utilized in printing the *Octoechos* was contained in the library of Alberto Pio, the books of which were then located in Rome.[73]

From a record dated November 17 of the same year (1520) we can catch a brief glimpse of Calliergis' interest in the more practical aspects of the publishing business. The document, a contract between Calliergis and another printer, George de Rostogni, relates to the publication of Greek books to be sold at the Lausanne fair,[74] and implies that Calliergis' publications were being disseminated in northern Europe.

After a further interval of two years, Calliergis' press produced the *Erotemata* of Chrysoloras, together with a treatise of Demetrios Chalcondyles on the formation of verb tenses.[75] The numerous reprintings of Chrysoloras' *Erotemata* — first published in Florence at the end of 1483, then at Venice in the following year by Pellegrino da Bologna, and again, as we shall see, by Demetrios Ducas

---

[71] Legrand, I, 153 and p. cxxix; and Firmin-Didot, 569 (not listed by Sathas).

[72] On the term *octoechos* see E. Wellesz, *History of Byzantine Music and Hymnography*, 2nd ed. (New York, 1960) 31, 116ff.

[73] Legrand, I, 172–73, and p. cxxix; also Mercati, *Pio*, 64, n. 2, both of whom fix the date of publication at 1520. Mercati says Aldus printed the majority of the manuscripts of Alberto's library.

[74] See document in Rodocanachi, *Première Renaissance*, 426, and cf. 204–5.

[75] Legrand, I, 174 and p. cxxix. Cf. Firmin-Didot, 573, who says that the two works were actually published in Florence before 1500 by the printer Alopa. Cf. also Sathas, *Neohellenic Philology*, 123, n. 1; also Fabricius, *Bibliotheca graeca*, VI, 227.

at Alcalá, Spain, in 1514, to mention only a few editions — may serve as a kind of barometer to Europe's burgeoning interest in Greek literature in the original, for the study of which a mastery of Greek grammar was of course an absolute prerequisite. It is noteworthy in this connection that in the first four decades of the sixteenth century twice as many Greek grammars were published as had appeared in the entire half century of printing before 1500.[76]

Calliergis' last publication of which we have any record is the Greek dictionary of the learned Benedictine Hellenist Varinus Favorinus of Camerino (May 27, 1523). Favorino's lexicon, which during the sixteenth century was several times to be reprinted, has been considered by some scholars to have been a valuable scholarly tool in that it replaced the defective dictionary of Crastoni, which was probably edited, as we have seen, for the Aldine press by Marcus Musurus. But Favorinus' work, from the viewpoint of original scholarship, is hardly deserving of the praise lavished upon it. For it is simply a compilation of materials drawn from such Byzantine sources as the Suda lexicon ("Suidas"), the *Etymologicum Magnum*, Eustathius of Thessalonica, Manuel Moschopoulos, and Thomas Magister. And whatever value it possessed was based largely on the fact that it made more readily available to the West materials taken from works of these important but as yet insufficiently known authors.[77] Of these, the *Etymologicum Magnum*, the Suda lexicon, and Thomas Magister had already been published, in 1499, 1499, and 1517 respectively (the first and third by Calliergis himself and the second by Chalcondyles in Milan). Calliergis' edition of Favorinus' lexicon also contained several epigrams composed by Janus Lascaris, Carteromachus, and Poliziano, along with the reproduction of special privileges granted in behalf of the work by Pope Leo X.[78]

[76] See Kukenheim, *Contributions à l'histoire de la grammaire*, 44. Aleandro, the "true" founder of Greek studies in Paris, began to prepare a new edition of the *Erotemata* not long after his arrival in that city in 1508. See above, Chapter 5, note 76.

[77] The eminent classicist A. Turyn is of the opinion that the *Lexicon* of Favorinus does not contain one item that does not appear in the Byzantine sources cited. See also Krumbacher, *Byzantinischen Litteratur*, 577. Also see Rodocanachi for an exaggerated view of its importance. (Here Calliergis is termed "ad presens Romanie Curie impressor principalis"; evidently he had become officially employed by the papal court.) Finally, see Favorinus' biography by E. Mestica, *Varino Favorino Camerte* (Ancona, 1888) 73f.

[78] Legrand, I, 174ff., and p. cxxx. Also see A. Lemke, *Aldus Manutius and his Thesaurus Cornucopiae of 1496* (Syracuse, 1958) 1ff.

Though the productions of Calliergis' press seem to come to an end at this point, we have further evidence of his talents as a scribe in manuscripts now to be found in collections at Paris, the Vatican, and Oxford. According to Lobel we can follow the activities of Calliergis only up to 1524, the date of the last extant manuscripts copied in his hand.[79] After this date he disappears, and one can only speculate on his fate. Barring sudden death, it is possible that he may have departed from Rome, which, after the death of the great patron, Pope Leo, in 1521 and the unexpected enthronement of the pious antihumanist Pope Adrian VI, gradually ceased to be an important center of humanist endeavor.[80] Unwilling, or unable because of the state of papal finances, to support the large circle of humanists favored by his predecessor, Adrian turned his attention primarily to reform of the scandalous abuses increasing in the church. Artists and humanists of note, among them the learned, pious secretary of Leo, Jacopo Sadoleto, were made to feel unwelcome, and departed from the Curia to seek favor and employment elsewhere.

Alarmed at the threat to the West resulting from the fall of the Latin bastion of the Greek island of Rhodes to the Turks, Adrian sought to launch a new crusade in defense of Christendom. But even this aim did not predispose him to look with favor on the Greek expatriate scholars resident in the papal capital.[81] In the light of the drastic change in Rome's intellectual climate, one can readily understand Calliergis' cessation of publication or even his departure from Rome. As one bitter humanist opponent of Pope Adrian put it, with some exaggeration, his was the reign of "the deadly enemy of the muses, of eloquence, and of all things beautiful." [82]

Calliergis' name is not nearly so well known to historians as that of Aldus or the Giunta. In numbers alone, his editions cannot bear comparison with theirs. But Calliergis endeavored to publish editions of finer execution and higher quality, without the mass-production methods which not infrequently characterized the frantic output of even such craftsmen as Aldus. In view of his high stand-

---

[79] Lobel, Greek *Manuscripts of Aristotle's 'Poetics,'* 50; Legrand, I, p. cxxx; cf. Sandys, *History of Classical Scholarship*, II, 80, n. 2. Also Vogel and Gardthausen, *Die griechischen Schreiber*, 125-26.

[80] There was a partial revival, however, under the second Medici pope, Clement VII (1523-1534).

[81] Pastor, *History of the Popes*, IX, 72-83.

[82] See Pastor, IX, 224.

ards as a printer, his introduction of the art of Greek printing to Rome, his foundation of the leading Greek-owned press in Venice, and, not least, his work as editor and copyist of a number of valuable classical and Byzantine secular and ecclesiastical texts, Zacharias Calliergis deserves a higher place in the annals of both printing and Hellenic scholarship than has hitherto been accorded him.

Chapter 8

DEMETRIUS DUCAS

*Cretan Pioneer of Hellenic Studies in Spain and an Editor
of the Polyglot Bible*

A STRIKING EXAMPLE of the distance to which Greek letters
were diffused in the West through the mediation of Venice is to be
found in the career of Demetrius Ducas, Cretan collaborator of
Aldus Manutius and member of his brilliant Greek Academy. Ducas was summoned by Cardinal Ximenes to Spain, a country as yet
little affected by the humanistic outlook of Italy, where he published the first Greek books in the Iberian peninsula, took a leading
part in preparing the Greek text of Ximenes' celebrated Complutensian Polyglot Bible, and gave impetus to the systematic study of
Greek at the first Spanish humanist university, that of Alcalá.

References to Ducas in both Western and Greek sources are
sporadic and infrequent, and it is probably for this reason that the
most important study on the Greek men of letters who found their
way to the West, that of Emile Legrand, does not include a biography of Ducas. Xanthoudides' analysis of Cretan civilization under
Venetian domination fails even to mention him. Nor, since manuscripts in Ducas' hand are still unknown, is he referred to in such
significant publications as Vogel and Gardthausen's annotated list
of Greek scribes and manuscripts of the medieval and Renaissance
period.[1] Our task therefore is to piece together the scattered evi-

---

[1] Legrand, *Bibliographie hellénique*, though including no biography of Ducas,
makes sporadic references to him, and has printed documents relating to his
publications. Firmin-Didot, *Alde Manuce*, has very little on Ducas and in fact
confuses him with another Demetrius. Cf. Vogel and Gardthausen, *Die griechischen Schreiber*, and Xanthoudides, *Venetian Crete*. Nor is Ducas listed in Omont,

dence of the sources in order to present as coherent and connected a narrative of Ducas' career as possible.

To begin with, as in the case of several other Greek exiles in the West, there has even been difference of opinion as to the identification of Ducas. Often confused with this Cretan-born scholar is another Cretan, a copyist of manuscripts likewise named Demetrius, who occasionally signed himself simply "Demetrius the Cretan" but whose usual subscription was "Demetrius Damilas" or, more fully, "Demetrius Milanese the Cretan." (As the last signature implies, the family of this second Demetrius had originally come from Milan,[2] though he himself was born in Crete.) To Damilas goes the honor of editing the first dated, wholly Greek book to be printed anywhere, the grammar of Constantine Lascaris, which appeared in Milan in 1476.[3] Firmin-Didot, Delitzsch, and others have misled students by their confusion of the two Demetriuses, but Legrand correctly considers them different persons, and Bataillon emphasizes that Demetrius the Cretan, or Damilas, must have lived a generation before Ducas.[4]

Candia, the capital city of Crete (today called Herakleion), was probably the birthplace of Demetrius Ducas. The exact date is unknown, but it may be fixed, at the latest, as about 1480. The first mention of Ducas' name occurs in a will made in Candia on November 24, 1500, when he signed the testament of one John Costomires,[5]

Fac-similés des manuscrits grecs des 15ᵉ et 16ᵉ siècles, which, like Vogel and Gardthausen, focuses entirely on copyists of manuscripts. Though manuscripts copied by Ducas seem to be unknown, compare some emendations and variants in Ducas' hand in a Plutarch manuscript (no. 881 in A. Martini and D. Bassi, *Catalogus codicum graecorum Bibliothecae Ambrosianae*, II [Milan, 1906] 981f.). The manuscript is discussed by M. Treu, *Zur Geschichte der Ueberlieferung von Plutarchs Moralia* (Breslau, 1884) III, 15.

[2] See Legrand, I, 2, n. 3. Demetrius Ducas on occasion signed himself "Demetrius Ducas the Cretan."

[3] Registered in Legrand, I, 1ff. Cf. Sandys, *History of Classical Scholarship*, II, 104, who omits this work from his chart of Greek first editions. On other disputed predecessors of this work see Chapter 3, note 17.

[4] See Firmin-Didot, 43, n. 1, who wrongly ascribes to Demetrius Ducas the first Greek book published in Italy and attributes to Ducas also the famous edition of Homer, of 1488, in which the editor signs himself "Demetrius the Cretan." Both works were actually done by Damilas. (See the mention of a certain Nilos Damilas, in Tomadakes, *Iosef Bryennios*, 89). On Damilas' brother, Antonius, see below. See also F. Delitzsch, *Studien zur Entstehungsgeschichte der Polyglottenbibel des Cardinal Ximenes* (Leipzig, 1871) 26; Legrand, I, 194; and M. Bataillon, *Erasme et l'Espagne* (Paris, 1937) 21, n. 3.

[5] Ἐγώ, Δημήτριος λεγόμενος Δούκας μάρτυς εἰμί. In Sathas, *Bibliotheca graeca*

drawn up by the Candiote notary Antonios Damilas, brother of the above-mentioned Demetrius Damilas. From the fact that Ducas acted in the capacity of witness to such a personal declaration we may deduce two pieces of information — that he had for some time been resident in the area, and, that he had already attained legal age — in other words, that he was then at least eighteen or possibly twenty-one years old.

Practically nothing is known of Ducas' early life in Crete. Sometime, however — plausibly in early manhood — he may well have visited Constantinople. The suggestion of such a journey is to be found in the following overlooked passage, very probably composed by Ducas, which constitutes part of the Greek preface to Cardinal Ximenes' famous edition of the New Testament:

The ancient Greeks were wont to write without such accent marks above their characters. This fact is plain and does not need proof, being manifested clearly in many old manuscripts such as the poems of Callimachus and the Sybilline oracles, and *in some ancient inscriptions on stone in Constantinople* which are inscribed simply with letters [without accents] . . .[6]

The vividness of the italicized phrase would lead one to believe that the author had seen the inscriptions of Constantinople *in situ*, since that Christian Roman capital would not ordinarily be cited in connection with ancient pagan monuments and inscriptions. One may, of course, speculate at length about the possibility of a journey by Ducas to Turkish-occupied Constantinople. But we know with certainty that scholarly interests drew Janus Lascaris, Michael Apostolis, and other Greeks of the period to this traditional center of the Byzantine world [7] to search for ancient manuscripts.

Whether or not Ducas visited Constantinople, we find him definitely established in Venice by the first decade of the sixteenth century. Why he came to Italy is unknown but, like other Cretans,

---

medii aevi, VI, 676–77; and see Legrand, I, 194, n. 2. Note that Ducas here signs Doúkas, though his usual signature is Doûkas.

[6] Preface printed in Legrand, I, 116–17 (and, of course, in the original Complutensian Bible). For Ducas' probable authorship of this preface, see below, text and notes 77–80.

[7] For journeys to Constantinople after 1453, see above, Chapters 4 and 5 on Michael Apostolis and Musurus. Of course Ducas might have been told by a friend about Constantinopolitan inscriptions, but in that case he would probably have mentioned this. In any event, a trip to Constantinople was not unusual then.

he was probably attracted by the reputation of Venice as a center of refuge and opportunity for Greeks from the East, especially those with a sound knowledge of classical Greek.[7a]

Our first explicit reference to Ducas in Italy occurs in November of 1508, in the Aldine edition of the first volume of the *Rhetores graeci*, an extremely valuable collection of Greek treatises on rhetoric which included the first edition of Aristotle's *Poetics*. From this source we gather that Ducas had already become a valued member of the Aldine circle and as such had been entrusted with responsibility for the editing of this celebrated work. As a kind of preface, there is attached to the book a letter of Demetrius addressed to his Cretan colleague Marcus Musurus, in which he extols Aldus for his accomplishments. Ducas writes:

Aldus, however, to whom all scholars owe much gratitude, salvages the wreckage (*ta nauagia*) of Greek books which were in danger of being entirely lost and sunk; and of those manuscripts remaining, he multiplies each many times over and instead therefore of one manuscript — and this one at that being very rare — he provides a thousand for the philologists, utilizing that very useful artifice (*sophisma*) of the press, which invention, had the Gods granted it in antiquity, would not have permitted us now to be deprived of any of those many admirable books.[8]

Although the aptness of Ducas' metaphor on Aldus' preservation of Greek works is striking, in view of other remarks that have elsewhere been quoted there is nothing exceptional about his praise of the Aldine achievements. Nor is Ducas' closing statement as to the loss of many ancient texts surprising, for there was a widespread feeling among the humanists that with the Turkish capture of Constantinople in 1453, whatever manuscripts still existed in the East should be secured before they would perish from lack of care.[9]

[7a] It is possible that before going to Venice Demetrius appeared for a time in Carpi, for in several letters published by Nolhac, "Les correspondants d'Alde Manuce," there is mention of a certain Demetrius. See esp. no. 55, p. 212 (1888), dated end of November, 1507, from Aleandro in Motta to Aldus in Venice asking Aldus to greet Demetrius if he has yet come to Venice from Carpi ("Se Messer Demetrio e agiunto da Carpi salutatelo"). This could refer to Demetrius Moschus or the old Demetrius Chalcondyles, then residing in Milan. See also letter no. 8, p. 262, and no. 42, p. 295, also referring to Demetrius.

[8] Letter in Legrand, I, 85–86. Other sections quoted above in Chapter 5, text and note 108.

[9] On the Turkish treatment of Greek manuscripts at the time of Constantinople's sack in 1453, see above, Chapter 4, text and note 64. Also cf. Babinger,

Indeed, as late as 1514 the Venetian ambassador to France, Bernardo Navagero, could appeal to the Pope for the launching of a new crusade against the Turks, less for the welfare of Christendom than (as he affirmed) in the hope of recovering lost Greek and perhaps Latin writings.[10] It is remarkable to find the suggestion for a crusade prompted not by anti-Muslim feeling or even the hope of religious union between East and West but solely with a view to advancing the cause of humanistic learning! [11]

To return to the Aldine edition of the *Rhetores graeci*: while it would seem that Ducas deserves chief credit for the over-all editing of this important work [12] — Renouard calls it the most valuable of all the Aldine editions [13] — it is clear that in one section [14] consisting of the *Rhetoric* of Hermogenes (a third century B.C. Alexandrian work which was highly influential in the development of Renaissance rhetorical literature), he had as collaborator his employer Aldus. This is manifest from a passage of the same prefatory letter of Ducas cited above: "And that Rhetoric of Hermogenes, O Musurus, printed at our friend Aldus', I corrected together with the wise philhellene and friend of yours Aldus." [15]

In the same letter Ducas advises Musurus, then teaching at the University of Padua, to include in his lectures, "besides the *Rhetoric*

Mehmed der Eroberer und seine Zeit (Munich, 1953) 119, which indicates that Mohammed II had some interest in collecting a library which included some classical manuscripts.
[10] Statement found in Andrea Navagero's preface to his *Ciceronis Orationes* (published by Aldus in 1514).
[11] In 1531 the Venetian nobleman Pietro Bembo made a remarkable speech to the Venetian Signoria lamenting the grave loss of important treasures of Greek literature. Quoted in Ferrai, *L'ellenismo di Padova*, 9; also see version published in *Memorie dell' R. Istituto del regno Lombardo-Veneto* (Milan, 1821). Bembo's speech describes the then miserable condition of the enslaved Greek people and affirms that it was proper for the Venetians to be the custodian of Greek literature because many Greeks lived in their city and the Venetians controlled various Greek areas with their numerous Greek teachers. Cf. below, Conclusion, text and note 1.
[12] View of Menge, "Vita Marci Musuri," 31; Firmin-Didot, *Alde Manuce*, 448–49; and Sathas, *Neohellenic Philology*, 85. (See above, Chapter 5, text and note 112.) This is a disputed point.
[13] Renouard, *Annales*, I, 128.
[14] One should distinguish between Aldus' publication of the above-mentioned *Rhetores graeci*, which incorporated rhetorical works on *how* to compose and deliver speeches, and Aldus' *Oratores graeci* (2 vols., printed in 1513), which included, besides the lives, the actual orations of Aeschines, Lysias, et al.
[15] Greek text in Legrand, I, 87.

of Hermogenes, the rhetorical treatises of that genius (*tou daimon-iou*) Aristotle, whom to praise and recommend is, it seems to me, superfluous, lest I too hear that saying of Brasidas, 'Who criticizes Hercules?' [16] Who does not exalt Aristotle, who made his own every aspect of wisdom from the greatest to the smallest — the man in whom nature revealed its complete power. For that which Aristotle did not know is outside the realm of human knowledge." [17]
The high praise of Aristotle expressed here is a striking manifestation of the continuing admiration for Aristotle in the north Italian universities (of Padua and Bologna in particular), despite the great enthusiasm kindled in Florence several decades before for the philosophy of Plato. Though the *Rhetoric* of Aristotle had certainly been known to the Western medieval world, it had long been neglected by the professional rhetoricians. But because of the emphasis of the Italian humanists on rhetoric and style, it was, so to speak, rediscovered, and during the sixteenth century came to exert a strong influence on the humanist rhetoricians.[18]

Actually a good deal of the credit for the renewed emphasis on the Aristotelian writings in general which became characteristic of the fifteenth and sixteenth century Italian universities, should go to the Greek exiles who (as Ducas advised Musurus) imbued in their Italian pupils a desire to study Aristotle in the Greek original in preference to the older medieval translations of the scholastics. In this connection one may recall that in 1497 Leonicos Thomaeus, as a result of the efforts of the Venetian noble Ermolao Barbaro, had begun to lecture at Padua on the original text of Aristotle.[19] In the light of this emphasis one can readily understand that any Aristotelian exegesis at that same university on the part of the uni-

[16] Brasidas was King of Sparta and her best general in the first part of the Peloponnesian war.
[17] Legrand, I, 87.
[18] See Kristeller, *Classics*, 40. The medieval scholastic philosophers had considered Aristotle's *Rhetoric* as an appendage to his *Ethics* and *Politics*.
[19] On Renaissance Aristotelianism see Kristeller, *Classics*, chap. 2, esp. p. 39; and Nardi, *Aristotelismo padovano, passim*. Kristeller, *Studies*, 575–76, emphasizes that at Padua Aristotelianism was linked with the teaching of medicine rather than theology, as was the case, say at Paris. On Ermolao Barbaro see above, Chapter 1. Also Ferrai, *L'ellenismo di Padova*, 25, and Molmenti, *Venice*, I, pt. 2. On Leonicos Thomaeus see Chapter 5, note 103. P. Kibre, *The Library of Pico della Mirandola* (New York, 1936) 30, interestingly enough, shows that the manuscripts of Aristotle in Western libraries of the later fifteenth century always outnumbered those of Plato.

versally admired Cretan humanist Musurus, even on works other
than Aristotle's philosophic writings, would now be eagerly received.

Following his work on the *Rhetores*, Ducas, in March of 1509,
supervised at the Aldine Press the first edition of certain works of
Plutarch, principally ethical, which together are commonly known
as the *Moralia*. A huge volume of more than 1,100 pages, the edition was based on manuscripts of Plutarch which Cardinal Bessarion in 1468 had bequeathed to the Venetian library of St. Mark.[20]
To help in the reading and collation of manuscripts for the *Moralia*
— a difficult task for which diverse codices were used [21] — Ducas
had the assistance of two rising Western scholars, Erasmus and
Girolamo Aleandro,[22] both of whom were later to surpass him in
their influence on the intellectual life of Western Europe. As was
the customary practice of editors, Ducas inserted his own preface
to the volume, in part reading: "Aldus the Savior of the Greek language (*ho soter tes Hellenidos phones*), without sparing either pain
or expense, gave to us this intellectual treasure that is Plutarch." [23]

A lacuna occurs at this point in our sources for the life of Ducas.
As with several scholars previously discussed, this may be partly
attributed to the dislocation of Venetian life resulting from the
city's involvement in the War of the League of Cambrai (1509).
Aldus himself, as we have seen, left Venice to retire to Ferrara.[24]
Demetrius Ducas, on the other hand, vanishes completely from
sight, not to reappear until four years later in Spain, at the University of Alcalá, in the employ of the famous Spanish cardinal and
prime minister, Francesco Ximenes.

In the opening years of the sixteenth century, Spain, only recently united politically, lagged far behind Italy in humanistic endeavors and particularly in Greek scholarship. Indeed, Spain seems

[20] Bessarion (d. 1472) pledged the manuscripts in 1468 to Venice, and they
were moved there the following year (cf. above, Chapter 5, text and note 33).
On Bessarion's manuscripts utilized by Ducas, see Firmin-Didot, 317.

[21] The latest edition of Plutarch's *Moralia* is that of W. Paton and I. Wegehaupt, *Plutarchi Moralia*, I (Leipzig, 1925), with a preface by M. Pohlenz. Pohlenz
says (p. xii) that the Aldine edition was done with great difficulty from various
manuscripts, with Ducas as the chief editor. On Ducas' work see also above, note
1, especially Treu, *Ueberlieferung*.

[22] See Firmin-Didot, 317. Cf. below, Chapter 9, text and note 88.

[23] For Greek text see Legrand, I, 92.

[24] See above, Chapter 5, text and notes 116-17.

to have had little of that contagious enthusiasm for Greek studies
that one finds, say, in Florence on the arrival of the Greek teacher
Chrysoloras, in Padua and Venice when Musurus assumed the professorship of Greek, or even in Paris with the initiation of public
lectures by Girolamo Aleandro.[25] During this period, in fact,
knowledge of Greek in Spain was virtually the possession of a
privileged few among the high clergy, great nobles, and scholars.[26]

What interest in Greek there was in Castile had evidently been
stimulated by a few individuals, who at the end of the fifteenth century had studied or traveled in Italy and subsequently returned
home. Such was the case of Ayres Barbosa,[27] actually a Portuguese
who had studied in Florence under Poliziano (himself the pupil of
the Byzantine John Argyropoulos) and then returned to become
professor at the famous Castilian University of Salamanca. More
noted is the Spaniard Antonio de Lebrija (or Nebrija), who, after
many years of study in Bologna, with, among others, the Constantinopolitan refugee Andronicos Callistos, held the chair of rhetoric
at Salamanca.[28]

Despite the activities of these individuals, Castilian interest in
Greek remained relatively small. A considerable number of Greek
manuscripts, some very rare, had been gathered in Spain, it is true,
as a result of Aragonese connections with Sicily and southern Italy
and the contact of the Spanish Borgia popes with Rome. And we
know that in Aragonese Naples Alfonso, drawing partly on his

[25] On Aleandro in Paris (in 1509), see above, Chapter 5, note 76. Janus Lascaris had previously, in 1496, taught Greek in the French capital, but privately
(Tilley, *Dawn of the French Renaissance*, 257-58; cf. Sandys, *History of Classical
Scholarship*, II, 169).
[26] For a rather old analysis of the state of early Greek scholarship in Spain, see
C. Graux, *Essai sur les origines du fonds grec de l'Escurial* (Paris, 1880) 1ff. On
the restriction of Greek to the Spanish elite classes, see Graux, 9. It is to be noted
that the example of the fourteenth century King of Aragon, John I, who had a
passion to learn Greek and amass Greek books (see Setton, "Byzantine Background," 65-68), seems to have been a rather unusual case and did not lead to
any really significant development of Greek humanist studies in later fifteenth
century Aragon (cf. Weiss, "Learning and Education in Western Europe." 125).
[27] On Barbosa see Nicolao Antonius, *Bibliotheca hispana nova* (Madrid, 1783)
I, 170. (Graux, 9, notes that his name is hardly known.)
[28] On Lebrija's study with Callistos, see below, Chapter 9, note 75. Also on
Lebrija see P. Lemus y Rubio, "El Maestro Elio Antonio de Lebrixa," *Revue hispanique*, XXII (1910) 478. Other Spaniards who studied in Italy or Sicily are J.
Sepúlveda (on whom see below, notes 102-103, and L. Ranke, *Zur Kritik neuerer
Geschichtsschreiber* [Leipzig, 1874] 107ff.), and the Spaniards Francisco de Men-
doza and Fernando Nuñez, on whom see below, text and note 93. Also see
Weiss, 123.

realm's Byzantine tradition, favored many scholars, including some Hellenists like Constantine Lascaris.[29] Thus we may say that in Castile at the close of the fifteenth century at least the beginnings of interest in Greek studies were apparent, while in Aragon proper after the early fifteenth century the outlook for Hellenism was only potentially encouraging.[30]

Of the small group of Spanish proponents of Greek studies, the most significant, of course, is Cardinal Francisco Ximenes, who is generally considered to be the central figure in the emerging Spanish humanist movement. But, as was typical of militantly Catholic Spain, his interests lay not like those of the true humanist in classical antiquity per se, but in the more practical benefits that could be derived from a knowledge thereof. It was his aim above all to inculcate in his clergy a knowledge of a language basic for the origins of Christianity, without which biblical and patristic texts would be almost a closed book. A knowledge of the original Greek text of Aristotle in particular could be used to effect in the conversion of the Moors, whose texts of that respected author were generally read in the Arabic (Averroist) version.[31]

Because of his deep interest in Greek, then, for the development of an educated reform clergy, Ximenes took care to provide, at his new University of Alcalá, which he had founded near Toledo in 1508, for a chair of the Greek language, along with others in Hebrew and Arabic.[32] Who the original holder of this Greek professorship was is not certain, owing to the vagueness of most of the data available on the foundation of Alcalá University. But one name that appears, however briefly, in virtually all the sources is that of Demetrius Ducas.[33]

[29] He was later in Messina; on earlier Catalan humanism see Introduction, note 11.

[30] The problem of the origins of Spanish humanism still needs research.

[31] The knowledge of Aristotle in the Arabic version (i.e., Averroism) could best be opposed by knowledge of Aristotle in the original Greek.

[32] The Arabic chairs were evidently never filled, probably because Ximenes was primarily interested in the biblical languages and perhaps because teachers of Arabic were easily accessible. See Bataillon, *Erasme et l'Espagne*, 21.

[33] On the obscurity of the sources and mention of Ducas, see in particular Bataillon, esp. 21, one of the most authoritative scholars on the development of Spanish humanism. As for the views of other modern scholars on the distribution of the work at Alcalá, they are not at all clear: see, for example, K. Hefele, *The Life and Times of Cardinal Ximenes*, 2nd ed., trans. J. Dalton (London, 1885) 125, who says that at the opening of Alcalá University in 1508, all 42 professorial chairs were occupied, including 4 in Hebrew and Greek, and, moreover, that both

The most concrete indication of Ximenes' views on the way in which a knowledge of Greek could serve the Church is provided by his grandiose plan to print, for the first time, the entire Bible, incorporating the original Greek and Hebrew texts of the New and Old Testaments along with the Vulgate Latin version. For this project the University of Alcalá was to provide the personnel, and it is as a member of the faculty of this institution that Demetrius Ducas next comes into our view.

According to his own statement Ducas came to Spain at the invitation of Ximenes "because of my knowledge of Greek." [34] Why the Cardinal singled him out from more widely known Greeks in the West, including the many other talented Hellenists of the Aldine Academy, is unclear.[35] Aside from the rather unlikely explanation that Ducas himself expressed a wish to visit Spain, he might have been recommended by his employer Aldus Manutius, who would doubtless have preferred not to lose the services of his most valued editor and close friend, Marcus Musurus. Of the other learned Greeks in the Aldine milieu, Ducas was probably at once the most competent in philology and the most experienced in the complex processes of printing Greek texts.[36] Even more important may have been Ducas' keen interest in patristic studies, an attitude that would coincide well with the predilections of Ximenes. For however often the Cardinal has been portrayed as attracted by the "New Learning," in the last analysis he viewed it more as a revival of the ideals of ancient Christianity than as a harbinger of a humanist philosophy of life.[37]

Nuñez and Ducas taught philology. Ducas could hardly have been at Alcalá in 1508, since he was then in Venice editing the Aldine *Rhetores Graeci* and Plutarch (published 1508-9).

[34] See below, text and note 47.

[35] Ximenes had himself been in Rome during the period 1459-1465. Evidently he made no subsequent trips to Italy; at any rate there is no record that he met Ducas there. See below, text and notes 89-90 for another suggestion regarding Ximenes' selection of Ducas.

[36] According to Oleroff, "Conon et Grégoropoulos," 106, the Aldine Greek, John Gregoropoulos, had probably died earlier in 1505. Another important Greek of the early Aldine circle had been John Rhosos, who was noted for his beautiful handwriting. Why Ducas would abandon the stimulating environment of Venice for the relative backwardness of Spain is not clear.

[37] See Alvar Gómez de Castro, *De rebus gestis a Francisco Ximenio Cisnerio*, in *Hispaniae illustratae Scriptores* (Frankfort, 1603-1628) 933; and Benito Hernand y Espinosa, "Cisneros y la fundación de la Universidád de Alcalá," *Boletín de la*

Definite evidence that Ducas, in 1513, was occupying a chair of
Greek at Alcalá [38] is provided by a list of the salaries paid at that
time to the Alcalá professors, and also by a notice of one of his
pupils, Diego Sigeo. In the words of the latter, as recorded in his
rare book entitled *On the Reason for Accents* (*De ratione ac-
centuum*): "My teacher in the classroom (*viva voce*) in the school
of Complutum [Alcalá] was Demetrius Ducas, Greek of race and
Cretan by birth." [39] The amount of Ducas' salary, one of the
meager details known about his employment, was 200 florins, a sum
which he considered inadequate and which evoked his complaints. [40]

Spanish historians quickly pass over the role of Ducas as instructor of Greek at Alcalá, but this phase of his activity is of some
importance. To be sure, the curriculum of Salamanca, the earliest-
founded and most famous medieval Spanish university (dating from
the early thirteenth century),[41] had included Greek probably since
at least the latter part of the fifteenth century, in accordance with
the decree of the Council of Vienne (1311–1312) prescribing, for
ecclesiastical reasons, the institution of Greek chairs at Rome, Paris,
Bologna, Oxford, and Salamanca.[42] The names of the Portuguese

Institución libre de Enseñanza, XXII (December, 1898), who emphasizes the
religious aspects of the humanism of Alcalá. Also Hefele, *Cardinal Ximenes*, 136.
Even the constitution of the University read: "Ut melius verbum Dei disseminare
possint." See A. de la Torre y del Cerro, "La Universidad de Alcalá; datos para
su historia Catedras y Catedraticos," *Revista de Archivos, Bibliotecas y Museos*,
ser. 3, XXI (1909) 51, n. 6.

[38] View also of Bataillon, *Erasme et l'Espagne*, 21. Fernando Nuñez is often
believed to have been teaching at Alcalá at the time of Ducas or even before, but
P. Groussac, "Le commentateur du 'Laberinto,'" *Revue hispanique*, XI (1904) 224
and 179, n. 3, says that Nuñez' name is absent from the first list of the faculty of
the University, whose foundation he dates in 1508. Nuñez may then have held
the chair of rhetoric rather than of Greek. Cf. Sandys, *History of Classical
Scholarship*, II, 158, who refers vaguely to Nuñez as teaching Greek at Alcalá.

[39] See de la Torre, "La Universidad de Alcalá," 262, and Bataillon, 22. Also
Barbieri, in *Boletin Histórico*, I (1880) 54: "Et vivae vocis praeceptorem meum in
schola Complutensi Demetrium Ducam natione Graecum, patria Cretensem."
Sigeo's work was published in Lisbon in 1560.

[40] See de la Torre, "La Universidad de Alcalá; datos para su historia," 262, and
also 443, where it is noted that 200 florins were equal to about 1,558 *reales*. The
salary of 200 florins evidently covered both Ducas' teaching and work on the
Bible. Compare Ducas' salary at Alcalá with the salary of 300 florins paid the best
professors at the University of Rome by Pope Leo X. See Chapter 7, on Calliergis.

[41] See T. Davies, *The Golden Century of Spain* (London, 1937) 25.

[42] The Vienne decree was adopted at the insistence of Ramón Lull of Majorca.
See R. Weiss, "England and the Decree of Vienne on the Teaching of Greek,

Ayres Barbosa and of Antonio de Lebrija have already been cited in connection with Salamanca. While it is quite clear, therefore, that Ducas did not initiate the study of Greek in the Iberian peninsula, to him evidently goes the honor of being the very first professor of that language at the pioneer humanist or, more accurately, Christian humanist university of Spain, Alcalá. By virtue of the position he occupied, Ducas was afforded an opportunity to influence members of the Spanish intellectual class, who were now attending that university in increasing numbers.[43]

Unfortunately, we have almost no details on the actual teaching of Ducas — what his course of instruction consisted of, and so forth. But among his activities there is one achievement that is certainly worthy of note, his undertaking of the publication of the first two Greek books to be issued in that country.[44] Although the art of printing had been introduced into Spain as early as 1470 or 1474, and a press established at Alcalá in 1502,[45] no Greek works had yet been published, and their importation from abroad was still very limited. Ducas evidently recognized the need for adequate texts so that his students could acquire systematic training in the rudiments of grammar and syntax. Thus he undertook, at his own expense, the printing of these two Greek books. The first of the two volumes — published at Alcalá on April 10, 1514 — consisted of a predominantly Byzantine collection of grammatical treatises. These were entitled: (1) *The Erotemata of Chrysoloras*, (2) *On the Formation of Tenses from the Works of Chalcondyles*, (3) *The Fourth Book of the Syntax of Theodore Gaza*, (4) *On Irregular Verbs*, (5) *On Enclitics*, and (6) *Monostich Sayings of Various Poets*.[46]

Arabic, Hebrew and Syriac," *Bibliothèque d'Humanisme et Renaissance*, XIV (1952) 1, and Bataillon, 20.

[43] See Hefele, *Cardinal Ximenes*, 127. Also H. Thomas, *Periods of Typography: Spanish Sixteenth-Century Printing* (London, 1926) 10, who remarks that Alcalá was the leading center for the printing of Spanish books in that century. A perusal of entries in E. Legrand, *Bibliographie Hispano-grecque* (New York, 1915) gives the same impression.

[44] Neither Hefele nor, astonishingly, Graux, *Essai*, mentions these two books (Thomas, 29, indicates one of the two). Legrand, *Bibliographie hellénique*, I, 118–20, and Bataillon, 21, are among the few who make brief reference to them.

[45] According to A. Palau y Dulcet, *De los origines de la imprenta y su introducción en España* (Barcelona, 1952) 12–13, the first Spanish press was established in 1470 in Seville. Thomas, 6, cites 1474 as the date. On the beginning of printing at Alcalá, see Thomas, 10.

[46] Listed in Legrand, I, 118.

On the state of Greek studies at Alcalá before Ducas' arrival, we are fortunate to have his own statement. In the next to last folio of the same work there is the following illuminating notation:

Demetrius Ducas the Cretan to the scholars of the Academy of Complutum [Alcalá], best wishes. Summoned by the most reverend Cardinal of Spain because of my knowledge of Greek, I came here, and, finding a great want of Greek books, or rather, so to say, a desert (*eremia*) in this respect, I printed and offered to you, to the best of my ability, some texts on grammar and poetry, using letters [characters in Greek type] which I found here. No one has shared with me the great expense of publication nor the labor of correction, but I alone, day by day, was barely able to complete the work of reading, copying, and correcting the manuscripts. It is up to you now to receive appreciatively what I have accomplished with sweat, sleeplessness, and expense, and to thank me. I, however, shall say I have received your thanks if through studying these books you become proficient in Greek letters. Farewell.[47]

In view of the Renaissance tendency toward hyperbole, one may perhaps question Ducas' statement as to "a great want of Greek books or rather, so to say, a desert" with regard to this foremost humanistic institution of Spain. (Actually a primary aim of Ximenes in founding the University of Alcalá was less to provide a haven for the new humanistic interests than to establish a school for expounding the scholastic philosophy of Scotism, instead of that of Thomas Aquinas to which the older University of Salamanca was so attached.[48] Corroborative evidence, however, for the general tenor of Ducas' remarks is provided by an inventory of the library of the college of San Ildefonso, which constituted the very heart of Alcalá University. According to this record, in 1512, two years before Ducas published his textbooks, the library contained only fourteen Greek works, as follows: [49] *Vocabularium grecum* [Greek

---

[47] My translation from the Greek printed in Legrand, I, 119. The accuracy of Ducas' reference to "letters which I found here" is supported by J. Catalina Garcia López, *Ensayo de una tipografía complutense* (Madrid, 1889) 11, and Thomas, 29, who state that Ducas' books used the Greek type (largely in imitation of uncial letters) cast for Ximenes' Polyglot New Testament.

[48] On the two schools see G. Reynier, *La vie universitaire dans l'ancienne Espagne* (Paris-Toulouse, 1902) 110; Weiss, "Learning and Education in Western Europe," 123; and for documents on Salamanca see E. Esperabé y Arteaga, *Historia pragmática e interna de la Universidád de Salamanca* (Salamanca, 1914) *passim*.

[49] Catalogue listed in Bataillon, *Erasme et l'Espagne*, 22, n. 2. Most of these seem to be printed works.

vocabulary]; *Cornucopia grecum* [sic] [Greek anthology]; [50] *Vocabularium grecum Cirili; Suidas grece;* [51] *Etimologicus magnus* [sic] *grece;* [52] *Ars* [= grammar] *Greca Urbani;* [53] *Ars greca Constantini;* [54] *Evangelia grece; Apocalipsis et Evangelium Mathei grece; Psalterium grecum; Chrysostumus super Matheum grece et Chrysostumus in Genesim grece; Vite sanctorum grece:* five volumes of the Aldine edition of Aristotle; [55] *Manli* [Manilii] *astronomicon et Arati phenomena latine et grece.*

The poverty of this list contrasts sharply with the wealth of such fifteenth century Italian collections as that of Bessarion, whose library included about 500 Greek manuscripts; of Giorgio Valla, with 151; and of the Duke of Urbino with 93.[56] One may note in the list cited of San Ildefonso the inclusion of Christian writings along with Aristotelian and classical grammatical texts to the exclusion of secular literary works — a circumstance consonant with the emphasis of Ximenes on the use of philosophy and philology for the furtherance of theological aims.[57]

On the recto of the last folio of Ducas' first volume, there are printed certain Latin verses directed to readers of the work and written by one Laurentius Martinus Bradyglossus (Greek for stutterer) de Lillo, who is undoubtedly to be identified with the

[50] *Cornu copiae* (sic) was a common Renaissance title; for example, Aldus had printed a *Cornu copiae grecum.*

[51] *Vocabularium . . . Cyrili* refers probably to the lexicon of Cyrillus of Alexandria, a fourth century A.D. lexicographer. See partial edition of A. Drachmann, *Die Ueberlieferung des Cyrillglossars* (Copenhagen, 1936). "Suidas" (now more accurately called the Suda lexicon) was published first in Milan in 1499 by Chalcondyles (Graesse, *Trésor de livres rares et précieux*, VI, 525, and Legrand, I, 63; Sandys, *History of Classical Scholarship*, 104, wrongly says in Venice).

[52] See Chapter 7 on this work, which was printed in Venice by Calliergis in 1499.

[53] Probably the Aldine edition (1497) of the Greek grammar of Urbano Bolzanio, the first to be written originally in Latin.

[54] Probably the grammar of Constantine Lascaris.

[55] Published between 1495 and 1498, this was one of Aldus' very first works and constituted the *editio princeps* of the Greek text of Aristotle. It was an aim of Ximenes to republish a complete but much better Aristotle and to include the old as well as a new Latin translation. He had entrusted the task to Juan Vergara, but it was never finished. See Hefele, *Cardinal Ximenes*, 176.

[56] On these libraries see Kibre, *The Library of Pico della Mirandola*, 23–24; also see above, Chapter 1, text and note 78, and Chapter 5, note 33. Also Mercati, *Pio, passim.*

[57] There was in the town of Alcalá also the private library of Hernán Nuñez, who, according to Bataillon, *Erasme et l'Espagne*, 22, n. 22, lived there from 1514 to 1517 "en marge de l'Université."

Spanish humanist and pupil of Ducas, Lorenzo Balbo (Balbus in Latin means stutterer).[58] Composed in the style and meter of a classic Latin lyric, this bit of poetry seems a little incongruous in Alcalá's environment of Christian humanism, and is more typical of contemporary Italian writing of the period. The poem, however, provides a very rare example of Spanish praise for Ducas' endeavors. The first half of the poem reads: [59]

> Thymbraean Apollo, singing, with his Phorian lyre raised sweet songs from the mount of the Virgins [Muses]
> And Amphio erected Penthean [Theban] walls with his divine lyre, and with his song softened Ismenus.
> Sweet Demetrius adorns the Western shores [Spain] whom bright Calliope [the muse of epic poetry] favors greatly
> Since none of the ancients has sung with greater splendor, whoever they may have been and however eagerly they sought to sing.
> Lo! Apollo leads this man where the blue wave washes the tired, fiery-footed horses of Tethys and where night makes the wandering Phoebe [the moon] sink into the waves.
> So the name of Demetrius shines throughout the whole world.

The second volume published by Ducas and dated the same year (1514) contains a famous late classic work often used by Renaissance students as an elementary Greek reader, Musaeus' *Poem on Hero and Leander* [60] (which we have earlier mentioned as published by Aldus). As a commentary on the enduring qualities of this poem, Ducas included in the book a few verses of his own:

> Phoebus granted only to poets the privilege of rendering the big small and the small big and taught them how to do so.
> The virgin Hero and Leander, though mortal, become immortal through songs that gladden the heart.
> If then a Musaeus would sing of my death I should want to perish at once in order to obtain immortality.[61]

[58] See Garcia López, *Tipografía complutense*, 11. A. Gómez de Castro, *De rebus gestis a Francisco Ximenio Cisnerio* (Alcalá, 1569) (as cited in de la Torre, *La Universidad de Alcalá*, 64), calls Balbo one of the best students of Ducas and Nuñez.

[59] Original Latin text in Legrand, *Bibliographie hellénique*, I, 120 (my translation is used here).

[60] Musaeus' poem, as we have seen, was one of Aldus' first publications and was produced with a Latin translation flanking the Greek, so that the reader could refer back and forth. See Chapter 5, text and notes 40–41.

[61] Greek text reproduced in Legrand, I, 121.

At the end of the work Ducas inserted the following note: "This was printed by the skill of Demetrius Ducas the Cretan in the Complutensian Academy, which the most reverend Francisco Ximenes, by divine providence Cardinal of Spain and Archbishop of Toledo, has created and which Academy he has exalted with men very learned in all manner of wisdom." [62]

The printer for both volumes was Arnaldo Guillen de Brocar, whom the Cardinal had brought to Alcalá from his printing establishment in Logroño, Spain, to help in producing his Polyglot Bible.[63] There is no reason to doubt Ducas' affirmation, as quoted above, that his first volume was issued at his own expense. For besides the fact that the volume lacks dedication to a patron, a pertinent passage of a documentary report contained in the Alcalá University archives under the year 1513–14 informs us that 300 *reales* from the wages of "el dicho Demetrio" were to be credited to Guillen de Brocar.[64]

While Ducas was teaching at Alcalá, his talents were put to further use by Cardinal Ximenes in the great enterprise of publishing the Polyglot Bible. Fired with the idea of printing for the first time the original Greek text of the New Testament, together with the Hebrew of the Old and the Latin Vulgate version,[65] Ximenes, starting in 1502, had begun to assemble at Alcalá both learned scholars and ancient manuscripts. These scholars, virtually all of whom were Spaniards, were summoned from the universities or intellectual centers of Paris, Salamanca, and Italy and organized into what has been termed a small Academy of Biblical studies.[66] The group customarily held its meetings in the Cardinal's own palace.[67] Into this circle Ducas would be made welcome not only

[62] Legrand, I, 120.
[63] On Guillen de Brocar see D. B. Updike, *Printing Types, Their History, Forms, and Use* (Cambridge, Mass., 1961), II, 46f. and 64f.; also Thomas, *Spanish Printing*, 28f.
[64] Quoted in Bataillon, *Erasme et l'Espagne*, 22, n. 1: "Para en cuenta de ciertos libros grecos que ha de haser para el dicho Demetrio." One wonders if Ducas might have been financially well off in view of the fact that he published these works in Spain at his own expense, as he did also later in Rome for Sepúlveda. On the other hand, he complained of his wages at Alcalá (see above, text and note 40).
[65] For the genesis of this see Hefele, *Cardinal Ximenes*, 120.
[66] Hefele, 125; cf. Bataillon, 39–41.
[67] Bataillon, 26. A. de la Torre, "La Casa de Nebrija en Alcalá," *Miscellanea Lebrija*, I (1946) 199–200, says that during the years 1515–16 and 1516–17 Ducas

because of his thorough knowledge of Greek grammar but also because of his considerable experience in the editing of Greek texts — a skill which was as yet entirely undeveloped in Spain.[68]

Historians have found it difficult to define the exact role of Ducas in the project of the Polyglot Bible. Nor, in fact, is it easy to tell from the accounts of the sources precisely what part each of his Spanish collaborators played in the enterprise.[69] Spanish historians, contemporary as well as modern, speak glowingly of this magnificent product of Spanish humanism. But amid the general praise lavished on the Spanish participants, the contribution of Ducas has been virtually ignored. The discussion which follows attempts to determine the part played by Ducas in establishing and editing the original Greek text of the New Testament, one of the most important undertakings of the entire Polyglot Bible, regarding which the evidence has not yet been closely examined.[70]

In the first place, though Ducas is always listed as a participant in the work of the New Testament Greek text, authorities disagree on the names of his collaborators. Five men seem to have participated — besides Ducas, Nicetas Faustus and the Spaniards Hernan Nuñez (Pincianus), Juan Vergara, and Bartolus de Castro. At least these are the five whose dedicatory verses to Ximenes are inserted in the volume after the colophon — an inclusion in this period normally indicating participation in publication. Certain scholars also list as a collaborator the name of the most famous Spanish humanist of the epoch, Antonio Lebrija. But it is clear that early in the venture Lebrija broke with the Cardinal over the method of

---

lived at Alcalá, in the "calle de la Imprenta, en la tercera casa contando desde la de la esquina inclusive."

[68] Graux, *Essai*, 20–23.

[69] See, for example, Bataillon, 24–25, who in this connection sternly criticizes the work of the intimate friend of Ximenes, Juan de Vallejo (see Juan's *Memorial de la vida de Fray Francisco Jiménez de Cisneros*, ed. A. de la Torre [Madrid, 1913]), for his vague reports. Also see C. Tischendorf, *Novum Testamentum Graece*, III (Leipzig, 1894) 206, n. 1, who says Tregellino is wrong in affirming that Stuniga (Zuñiga) was chief editor of the New Testament Complutensian Bible.

[70] We pass over Ducas' work on the Old Testament, for which less evidence is available and about which all kinds of conflicting statements have been made by modern scholars: for instance, Hefele, 139, says that Ducas (along with Zuñiga and Nuñez) occupied himself with a *Latin* version of the Septuagint. Bataillon, 42, is doubtless right in assigning Ducas rather to the Greek Septuagint version of the Old Testament.

establishing a correct text (he said he would refuse to risk his reputation as a humanist on this point), insisting, in a strikingly modern approach, that even the Latin Vulgate version must be corrected by reference to the original Greek and Hebrew texts.[71]

According to Legrand (who not infrequently cites Greek sources overlooked by other Western authorities) it was Ducas and Fausto that were responsible for preparing the Greek text, a view, however, for which he offers no explanation. Fausto was evidently Venetian (despite the affirmations of Hodius and even the learned M. Bataillon that Nicetas Fausto was "definitely" Greek by birth). Probably a pupil of Ducas', Fausto's first name was really Vittore (or Victorio), the Italian equivalent of the Greek Nicetas. It was Fausto, as we have noted elsewhere, who was later to succeed Marcus Musurus in the Greek chair at Venice.[72]

The editors working on the Polyglot were permitted by Ximenes to compose prefaces to their respective sections of the publication. Thus at the beginning of the New Testament volume there is inserted an unsigned prefatory essay, the authorship of which has not yet been determined.[73] That the author of this piece was also the chief editor of the Greek version of the New Testament volume we are persuaded to believe from the careful pains taken to explain the method followed in the work of establishing the text. Anticipating the reader's questions as to the differences in the Greek type utilized in the printing of the Old and the New Testament volumes, the editor carefully explains why it was chosen to employ Greek characters without accents. (Actually it would be more accurate to say that a peculiar system of accentuation was employed, the acute accent alone being used and only on polysyllabic words, while aspirates were entirely omitted.) [74] The editor also offers

[71] See especially Bataillon, 40–41, who says that the main reason Ximenes called Lebrija to Alcalá in 1513 from Salamanca was to revise the Latin Vulgate. On page 43 he also notes that the exact role of Zuñiga, often considered an author of the interlinear version of the Septuagint, is "impossible to determine."

[72] See H. Hodius, *De Grecis illustribus* (London, 1742) 321; and Bataillon, 42. On the Greek chair of Venice see Legrand, *Bibliographie hellénique*, I, p. cv. We know that in 1522 Fausto published in Venice, and at the expense of Andrew Kounades, a Greek from Patras, the *Parakletike*, a type of Greek religious book of hymns to the Virgin.

[73] For the Greek original of the preface, see also Legrand, I, 115–17.

[74] In the vocabulary to the New Testament accents and aspirates were used, however. See E. R. Gregory, *Textkritik des Neuen Testamentes*, II (Leipzig, 1902) 924.

σεις ἰδίασ, Τὰ ὁπωσοῦμ ϖαρεμπίϖτομτα εἰς ὀυκ ἐ
ϖιβάλλουσαμ θέσιμ, ἐλέγχουσιμ Διὰ Τῆς παρ᾽ ἑαυ=
τῶμ ἀκολουθίας. Τῶμ Τοίμυμ Τοῦ λόγου μερῶμ,
ἃ μὲμ εἰς ἀριθμοὺς καὶ γέμη καὶ ϖτώσεις μετασχη
ματιζόμεμα, ἃ Δὲ εἰς ϖρόσωπα καὶ ἀριθμούς, ἃ Δὲ
μηθὲμ ἐϖιΔεχόμεμα Τοιοῦτόμ Τι, ἀλλὰ καθ᾽ ἕμα μό
μομ σχηματισμὸμ ἐκφερόμεμα. Ταῦτα Δὴ μεταληφ
θέμτα ἐξ ἰΔίωμ μετασχηματισμῶμ εἰς Τὰς Δεούσας
ἀκολουθίας ἀριθμῶμ ἢ ϖροσώπωμ ἢ γεμῶμ, Τῆ
Τοῦ λόγου συμτάξει ἀμαμεμέρισται εἰς ἐϖιπλοκὴμ
Τοῦ ϖρὸς ὃ φέρεσθαι ἕκαστομ Δεῖ. Ὁιομ, ἐι ὅυτω Τύ
χοι ϖληθυμτικὸμ ϖρὸς πληθυμτικὸμ κατὰ Τὴμ Τοῦ
ἀυτοῦ προσώπου παρέμπΤωσιμ· γράφομεμ ἡμεῖς.
μαμθάμουσιμ ἄμθρωποι. Τὸ γὰρ ἐμ μεταβάσει Τοῦ
ϖροσώπου ὀυ ϖάμτως ἀπαιτήσει Τὸμ ἀυτὸμ ἀριθ
μόμ. ἔστι γὰρ φᾶμαι, καὶ Τύϖτουσι Τὸμ ἄμθρω=
πομ, καὶ Τύπτουσι Τοὺς ἀμθρώπους. κατὰ ϖτῶ
σιμ. ὁ ἀυτὸς Δὲ λόγος κἀπὶ Τῶμ κατὰ γέμος ἢ πΤῶ
σιμ ἢ ϖρόσωπομ λαμβαμομέμωμ. ἔτι γὰρ καὶ Τὸ ἐμ
μεταβάσει ἀΔιαφορεῖ. ἡμῶμ ἀυτὸς ἀκροᾶται. καὶ
ὀυμ ἐι συμέλθοι κατὰ Τὴμ ἀυτὴμ ϖτῶσιμ, ὑποπεσεῖ
ται εἰς Τὸ ἀυτὸ πρόσωπομ. ἡμῶμ ἀυτῶμ ἀκροῶμ=
ται. ἐιμὴ ϖαρέμπτωσις συμΔεμικὴ Τὸ ϖρόσωπομ
Διαστήσει. ἡμῶμ καὶ ἀυτῶμ ἀκροῶμται. κατὰ γέ
μος. ὡσαύτως Δὲ κἀϖὶ Τῶμ γεμῶμ. ὅυτοι ὁι ἄμ=
Δρες. Τούτους Τοὺς ἄμΔρας. ϖάλιμ γὰρ Τὸ ἐμ μετα
βάσει Τοῦ ϖροσώϖου ἀΔιαφορήσει καὶ κατὰ γέ=
μός, καὶ κατὰ ἀριθμόμ. Τούτους γυμὴ ὕβρισεμ.
κατὰ ϖρόσωϖομ. καὶ ἐϖὶ ϖροσώπου. ἐκεῖμοσ
ϖατὴρ ὠμ ἐϖιμελεῖται Τοῦ ϖαιΔός, ἀλλὰ Δὴ καὶ
σοῦ καὶ ἐμοῦ · ἔιϖερ ὄυμ μὴ ἐϖισυμβαίμοι Τῆ
λέξει Τὸ Τὴμ Διάκρισιμ Δυμάμεμομ φαμερῶς

GREEK TYPE DESIGNED FOR CARDINAL XIMENES' COMPLUTENSIAN POLYGLOT
NEW TESTAMENT, AS USED IN DEMETRIUS DUCAS' EDITION OF THE *Erotemata*
OF CHRYSOLORAS, ALCALÁ, 1514

corroboration for the sometimes disputed view that certain manuscripts on which the Greek edition was based were sent to Ximenes by Pope Leo X. We might note parenthetically that it now seems well established that Leo dispatched these manuscripts to Ximenes from the Vatican on his own initiative and even before he ascended the papal throne. Unfortunately we do not know conclusively which manuscripts were used in the edition,[75] but since the type cast seems closely to have imitated the uncial letters of ninth to thirteenth century Byzantine codices, it has very plausibly been suggested that the manuscripts date from that period.[76]

It is noteworthy that the author of this preface generally employs the term "we" (ἔδοξε καὶ ἡμῖν), though in contrast at one point (where he evidently wished to provide particular emphasis) he instead uses the singular "I" (λέγω).[77] The difference in usage between singular and plural forms may perhaps be meaningless, but since in the Latin version of this preface which follows the Greek text the "I" is replaced by "we",[78] the use of the "I" may well indicate that one person was mainly responsible for editing the Greek text.

In another passage of the same preface, as we have earlier noted, the author refers with a certain familiarity to "some ancient inscriptions on stone in Constantinople."[79] Of the four men that we know were associated with Ducas in the New Testament enterprise,

---

[75] So say Hefele, *Cardinal Ximenes*, 173; Bataillon, *Erasme et l'Espagne*, 45; and Tischendorf, *Novum Testamentum Graece*, III, 206. Cardinal G. Mercati, however, in *Opere minori*, II (Vatican, 1937) 418, says two Vatican Greek manuscripts (330 and 346) lent to Ximenes by Leo X, *motu proprio*, are referred to in the Archivio Segreto, Diversiorum Cameralium, t. 63, f. 116.

[76] See Proctor, *Printing of Greek*, 144; Hefele, 174. Cf. T. H. Darlow and H. F. Moule, *Historical Catalogue of the Printed Editions of Holy Scripture in the Library of the British and Foreign Bible Society* (London, 1911) II, 3, who date the manuscripts in the thirteenth century. Thomas, *Spanish Printing*, 29, distinguishes between the "evil" Aldine characters (which were cursive) and what he considers the superior Alcalá Greek uncial characters.

[77] For expression "we" (ἡμεῖς) see Legrand, I, 115, l.1 and 116, l.17; also 117, l.8; and for "I" (λέγω) see 116, l.24.

[78] For the Latin preface see the original Complutensian Bible (the Latin version is omitted from Legrand). It is also noteworthy that the Latin version is simpler in its wording (which may perhaps mean it was translated from the Greek).

[79] See above, text and note 6. The Latin version mentions Rome instead of Constantinople. (Actually the reference in the Greek text is to "the city" [ἡ πόλις], which, to a Greek, could only mean Constantinople.) Rome, in any case, is hardly known for its Greek monuments and inscriptions.

none, except for Ducas himself, seems ever to have set foot in the Greek East. Now if to the several pieces of evidence already adduced we add the fact that the language employed seems to be that of one intimate with the nuances of Greek style, and, finally, the very striking circumstance that the dedicatory poems of Ducas and Fausto are alone written in Greek (the other three being in Latin), it would seem justifiable to affirm that Ducas was not only the author of this preface but primarily responsible for editing the Greek text of the New Testament volume.[80]

On January 10, 1514, the printing of the New Testament was completed. Although it was the first volume to appear, in the entire Polyglot of six volumes it would constitute number five, the first four being devoted to the Old Testament. The New Testament publication contained both the Greek and the Latin Vulgate versions. But in order to permit the reader to compare both texts closely, the two versions (as explained in the preface of the work) were printed so as to advance together line by line on each page, with small gothic reference letters inserted to designate the corresponding words in both texts.

It was in the last part of the volume and after presentation of the four Gospels, St. Paul's Epistles, the Acts of the Apostles, and the Apocalypse, that the five poems or epigrams dedicated to Ximenes were printed. It is probably no coincidence that that of Ducas is printed first. Ducas' text reads: "Demetrius Ducas the Cretan: If holy acts and a holy life can lead mortals to Olympus which is the land of the blessed, then the archpriest Ximenes should be divine, because his works — such as this Bible — are fitting gifts to mortal men." [81] The epigram of Fausto, also composed in Greek, but in a more labored style than that of Ducas, refers, interestingly enough to Zeus' "divine" appointment of Ximenes as his instrument for promotion of the acceptance of the Greek cultural inheritance in Spain. The verses of the three other collaborators express the same kind of laudatory sentiment. Most interesting are those of Juan Vergara, "Master of Arts of Toledo," which are cast in the form of a dialogue between the Polyglot itself

---

[80] Bataillon, *Erasme et l'Espagne*, 42, agrees but also offers no explanation. Cf. Firmin-Didot, *Alde Manuce*, 44, n. 1.
[81] Printed in Legrand, I, 115.

and the reader. The verses of Bartolus de Castro, here termed "Magister . . . Burgensis" (Master of Burgos), obliquely praise the New Testament volume by lamenting the darkness into which biblical studies had fallen before the appearance of the present publication.[82] For the use of its readers there was included at the end of the volume a very brief summary of Greek grammar with explanatory material in Latin, together with an index of the Greek words that appear in the New Testament.

With the completion of the New Testament the staff spent the next three and one-half years in preparing the Old Testament for publication. In the editing of the Greek Septuagint text of the Old Testament it is generally agreed by scholars that Ducas made a very important contribution. Four versions of the Old Testament were involved in the publication, Greek, Latin, Hebrew, and Chaldaic (Aramaic), the first three being printed in parallel columns, with the Latin Vulgate version in the middle. Ximenes compared this arrangement of the three texts to the collocation of Christ between the two thieves. But according to certain modern authorities what he actually referred to was rather the situation of the Roman Church between the Greek Church and the Jewish synagogue.[83]

In view of the lamentable state of biblical scholarship in western Europe before the publication of Ximenes' Polyglot, the work constitutes a great landmark in scriptural studies. Indeed the Greek New Testament should really rank as the *editio princeps*,[84] an honor, however, that cannot be accorded to the Old Testament, inasmuch as the first complete printed version of the Hebrew Bible had already been published in 1488 by the Soncino family at the Lombard town of the same name.[85]

[82] On Vergara, who, as noted above, was assigned by Ximenes to do a Greco-Latin edition of Aristotle, see Bataillon, 23, and n. 3. Also A. Bonilla y San Martin, *Clarorum Hispaniensium: Epistolae Ineditae*, in *Revue Hispanique*, VIII (1901) 226ff. Further, Legrand, *Bibliographie hispano-grecque*, 57, shows that Juan's brother Francisco, in 1524, was in his third year of a professorship of Greek at Alcalá. Note, by the way, that like Ducas, Francisco here complains about the scarcity of books.

[83] See Hefele, *Cardinal Ximenes*, 151 and Darlow and Moule, *Historical Catalogue of Holy Scriptures*, II, 4.

[84] The first published edition of the *entire* Greek Bible (evidently Septuagint as well as New Testament) seems to have been that of Andrea d'Ásola, Aldus' father in law, dated 1518, Venice. Erasmus' Greek New Testament was published first.

[85] See Hefele, 136 (according to whom the editor was the Jew Abraham Ben

Owing to the death of the Cardinal (November 8, 1517) and the delay in obtaining papal approval for publication, the Polyglot, which had been entirely completed already in July of 1517, did not circulate until as late as 1521.[86] It seems that papal approval was withheld because the famous humanist Erasmus had, in the meantime, secured both papal and imperial rights to publication of the Greek Testament. Erasmus had begun his own edition at the insistence of his opportunistic publisher Johannes Froben, who had heard of the excitement being engendered by report of the Alcalá edition. And on April 17, 1515, he had written to Erasmus, then in England, urging him to come to Basle as soon as possible in order to discuss the publication of an edition of the Greek New Testament under his imprint.[87]

Erasmus' work, it is true, circulated several years before that of Alcalá, but in scholarship it is inferior. For Erasmus' edition, completed and seen through the press in the astonishingly brief period of less than a year, was based on a much smaller number of manuscripts and, of course, did not include the Old Testament. In Erasmus' own words his edition was "precipitated rather than edited" (*praecipitatum fuit verius quam editum*).[88]

Though scholars have often discussed the respective merits of the Alcalá and Erasmian editions, it should be noted that before the appearance of either work Aldus had already conceived the design of printing a Polyglot Bible. And in 1504 he had even produced one printed page of Genesis, presenting in parallel columns the Greek, Latin, and Hebrew texts. In a letter to the German humanists Conrad Celtis and Vincent Longinus, dated three years before (1501), Aldus had written that "the Old and New Testaments in Greek, Latin, and Hebrew have not yet been printed but will

---

Chajim); also *Enciclopedia Italiana*, XXXII, 138. Before this Spain had been the home of many famous redactors of the Hebrew text. Cf., however, Graesse, *Trésor de livres rares et precieux*, I, 383, who says the first edition of the Hebrew Bible appeared in 1487.

[86] Bataillon, *Erasme et l'Espagne*, 46, shows that after Ximenes' death his property and possessions became the object of much litigation.

[87] See Gregory, *Textkritik des Neuen Testamentes*, II, 928 and Tischendorf, *Novum Testamentum Graece*, III, 208. Cf. J. Lyell, *Cardinal Ximenes, Statesman, Ecclesiastic, Soldier, and Man of Letters* (London, 1917) 35, who says that Erasmus had secured an exclusive privilege.

[88] See Erasmus' epistle dedicating his work to Pope Leo X, quoted in Gregory, 929.

be." [89] The work, however, never came to birth. It is not impossible, in view of our lack of knowledge regarding Ducas' career before 1508, that Ducas might have had something to do with this proposed Aldine edition and that perhaps for this reason he may have first come to the attention of Ximenes.

We may recall that some years before the appearance of his New Testament Erasmus had spent most of the year 1508 at the house of Aldus in Venice. While there he participated actively in the affairs of the Greek Academy and printing establishment, and, as we have observed, assisted Ducas in revising the text for the edition of Plutarch's *Moralia* (published in March of 1509).[90] What Aldus' influence with respect to biblical scholarship and publication may have been on Erasmus is of course difficult to judge, though in view of the liberal exchange of ideas among members of the Aldine circle it is clear that such projects may well have been the subject of conversation. In the last analysis, however — though in another sense — even Aldus was not entirely original in method. For as far back as the third century A.D., the Eastern church father Origen, in his famous *Hexapla*, had produced a manuscript edition of the Old Testament embodying in parallel columns six different versions of the text in Hebrew and Greek characters.[91]

Of Ducas' further activities in Spain after completion of the Polyglot Bible we know virtually nothing, except, as we learn from an archival document of Alcalá, that the date of his last remuneration from that university was May 13, 1518 — a payment which covered the six-months' period from May to October, 1517.[92] Whether Ducas then departed from Spain or stayed on for a time is unclear. In any case he may have chosen to leave because of termination of the Polyglot and the death of his patron, circumstances which must have made the intellectual climate of Spain

[89] On Aldus' single page (with Greek text in the middle), see facsimile in Renouard, *Annales*, III, 44–45, and also Aldus' letter, 273–74. See, too, I. G. C. Adlerum, "Das erste gedruckte Stück des griechische N.T. vom Jahre 1504," *Eichhornium Repertorium*, XVIII (1786) 150–57 (unavailable to me). Firmin-Didot, *Alde Manuce*, 178–80, prints a French translation of Aldus' letter.

[90] Legrand, I, 89ff: and cf. above, note 22, and Chapter 9, text and note 88.

[91] The *Hexapla* is now lost, but we have clear evidence for its existence.

[92] See de la Torre, "La Universidad de Alcalá," 263. In another article "La Casa de Nebrija en Alcalá," 200, de la Torre says Ducas quit teaching in October 1517.

seem even less stimulating than ever. On May 8, 1519, we know that his professorship of Greek was assumed by his Spanish associate Nuñez de Guzman, who liked to be called "El Comendador griego" ("Greek commander," or, as a recent scholar would render it, "Greek commentator").[93]

Once again there is a gap in our information on the career of Ducas. He is not mentioned in any source until fully eight years later, in October of 1526, when his name appears as editor of a Greek book published in Rome, *The Divine Liturgies of St. John Chrysostom, of Basil the Great, and of the Presanctified of the Archbishop Germanos*. Ducas was doubtless the printer as well as the editor of this work, since in the colophon we read the words, "[executed] by the skill of Demetrius Ducas the Cretan," a phrase then commonly employed by printers, Calliergis for example, in their publications.[94] From Ducas' prefatory letter we learn that he was aided in the edition by two high-ranking ecclesiastics with Eastern sees, the Archbishop of Nicosia (Cyprus), Livio Podocataro, and the Metropolitan of Rhodes. Podocataro, a Venetian born of a Cypriote family, had studied at Padua; the latter is probably to be identified with the Franciscan Leonardus de Balestrinis.[95]

The same volume contains a preface of which the following passage is of the most interest:

To Orthodox Christians[96] everywhere, Demetrius the Cretan sends

[93] See "La Universidad de Alcalá," 422–23, for document of Nuñez' nomination, on 8 May 1519. See also Reynier, *La vie universitaire dans l'ancienne Espagne*, 151. On the interpretation of "Comendador griego" as "Greek Commentator," see especially P. Groussac, "Le Commentateur de 'Laberinto,'" 201, n. 1, who denies the usual view that Nuñez was a commander of the order of St. James. This interpretation of the word seems unlikely.

[94] See in Legrand, I, 192ff. Moreover, see Sadoleto's letter (below, text and note 104), where he says Ducas "undertook to emend and to print some Greek books not yet published" (*libros graecos nonnullos, qui, nondum impressi, . . . emendandi et imprimendi . . . curam susceperit*).

[95] Legrand, I, 193, n. 1 and 194, n. 1. On Podocataro see also Mas Latrie, "Histoire des Archevêques Latins de l'île de Chypre," *Archives de l'Orient Latin* (1884) II, 320–24, and Fabris, "Professori e scolari greci," 125 and 133; and on Leonardo (who left Rhodes after the Turkish conquest in 1522 and died in 1524, before publication of Ducas' liturgies — hence his aid must have been given at least two years before the actual printing — see M. Lequien, *Oriens christianus* (Paris, 1740) III, col. 1054.

[96] Ducas was doubtless a Uniate (certainly the pious Grand Inquisitor Cardinal Ximenes would not otherwise have admitted him to Spain!). Yet the term "Orthodox Christians" here seems to refer to *all* Greeks, Orthodox and Uniate; both groups used the same language in the liturgy.

247

his greetings . . . Those who have published works which they consider to be of the highest quality or who have collected and restored to their ancient state of perfection the poems of those other [ancient] Greeks (whose manuscripts are old and were being devoured by worms and in danger of disappearing like shipwrecked vessels), thus rendering them accessible to philologists — these certainly do meritorious work but they do not devote their time to the highest type of learning which is theology. Whoever, then, has published, for those eager to read, the spiritual instructions of the Bible as well as the prayers and discourses of the holy fathers, by which our souls will be enabled to live together with the heavenly angels, has provided us with true nourishment for both the present life and that of the future.[97]

The sentiments expressed here by Ducas closely resemble those expressed by Calliergis some fifteen years earlier. Evidently Ducas felt that the emphasis hitherto placed on the printing of the Greek classics should now be extended to the Byzantine religious works, which in his view could provide spiritual as well as practical benefit and were therefore of a more enduring value for Christians. Ducas' views seem rather similar to the attitude of such contemporary Western Christian humanists as his former Aldine colleague Erasmus, for whom, as is well known, study of the classics was primarily a means for the realization of a higher Christian ideal. An even more succinct statement along the same lines had been incorporated into the Greek preface to the Complutensian New Testament, which, as we have shown, was probably the work of Ducas: "Those who have tasted of the sweetness of divine words put aside the rest of the sciences." [98]

Ducas' whereabouts in the years prior to his arrival in Rome are unknown to us. But though it is probably correct to assume that he left Spain in 1518 or shortly thereafter, are we to believe that he went directly to the papal capital? It is not likely that he returned to his circle of friends at Venice. For Aldus had died in 1515 and the members of his Academy soon after dispersed. Moreover, under the aegis of the fervent Hellenist Leo X, who ascended the papal throne in 1513, Rome had begun to displace Venice as the chief center of Greek studies. Already there, as we have seen, was the "protector of the Greeks," Janus Lascaris, former envoy of the

[97] See Greek text in Legrand, I, 193.

[98] Legrand, I, 117: τῆς γὰρ γλυκύτητος τῶν θείων λόγων γευσάμενοι τὰς λοιπὰς τῶν ἐπιστημῶν μακρὰν χαίρειν ἐάσετε.

French King to Venice, along with other Byzantines, including Marcus Musurus and Arsenios Apostolis. And we know that in 1515 Calliergis had established the first Greek press in Rome.[99]

The lavish literary patronage of the Pope inspired the emulation of a group of wealthy patrons connected with the Curia — cardinals, ambassadors, and bankers. Among these were Augustino Chigi, Italy's richest merchant-prince, Giulio Cardinal de' Medici (later Pope Clement VII), Alberto Pio, Prince of Carpi and ambassador of France to the Holy See, and Angelo Colocci, the wealthy secretary to Leo X, whose name appears on the productions of the Greek Monte Cavallo press, which had been set up in his own house on the Quirinal.[100] These are a few of the men who encouraged and supported the endeavors of painters and sculptors, of scholars and printing enterprises.

Like Janus Lascaris and probably Musurus, Ducas may have come to Rome at the explicit invitation of Leo himself in order to teach Greek. Certainly the name of Ducas must have been known to Leo, who had provided Greek manuscripts for the Alcalá Bible and to whom Ximenes in fact had dedicated the entire publication.[101] On the other hand, Ducas may not have arrived in Rome until shortly before publication of his *Liturgies* (1526), by which time, as we know, Leo had already been succeeded on the throne by the austere Adrian VI and then by Leo's cousin, Clement VII, the second Medici to wear the triple crown.

In February 1527, five months after the appearance of the *Liturgies*, a second book published by Ducas appeared in the papal capital, a Latin translation made by the erudite Spanish humanist Juan Sepúlveda of a very influential Greek philosophical work, the *Commentary of Alexander of Aphrodisias on Aristotle's Metaphysics*. Ducas dedicated this volume to the then Pope Clement VII, who was very much interested in the ancient commentators on

---

[99] On Rome under Leo X see Pastor, *History of the Popes*, VIII. Also Rodocanachi, *Première Renaissance à Rome*, and Roscoe, *Leo X*.

[100] See Norton, *Italian Printers 1501-1520*, 97. Also Legrand, I, 159, for Greek colophon of the Monte Cavallo scholia on Homer (1517); and Pastor, VIII, 185, 189, 260.

[101] See above, text for notes 75-76. Note also the lavish praise of Leo in the Alcalá New Testament preface (probably, as shown, done by Ducas). Mercati, *Opere minori*, II, 481, mentions the gift to Leo of a superb exemplar of the Polyglot.

Aristotle and had in fact requested the translation from Sepúlveda.[102] (Sepúlveda had studied philosophy at the University of Alcalá during the years 1511 to 1514, and although we do not know where he learned Greek, it seems probable that he had then known Ducas, who was in that period teaching at the university.) [103] Clement's epistle of response constitutes the last mention we have of Ducas and provides an important bit of information on his activities at this time. We quote from the letter:

To all people and individuals into whose hands this letter of ours may come, health and our apostolic blessing. Since our dear son Demetrius Ducas of Crete, public professor (*publicus professor*) of Greek letters in our bountiful city of Rome, has taken care to print or to have printed with diligence and labor and also at his own expense Alexander of Aphrodisias' treatise on the metaphysics of Aristotle turned into Latin, we deem it right that on account of the merits of his virtue and labors of this kind he obtain some recognition from us. We [therefore], under pain of sentence of excommunication and penalty of loss of all books, expressly restrain through the present letter individual printers of books, whoever and wherever they may be throughout Christendom, and in whatever manner they may exercise this art of printing or take care to have it exercised . . . that they may not presume to number among their books or to dare in any manner to print or cause to be printed the said Alexander of Aphrodisias, in order that this printing [of Ducas] may be offered for the period of six years from the time of this first impression . . .

Dated January, 1527, and drawn up by Jacopo Sadoleto [104] [papal secretary]

The document is nothing more than a kind of papal license granted to Ducas for the exclusive publication rights to the book for a

---

[102] See Legrand, *Bibliographie hispano-grecque*, pt. 2, 61–62, for reference to the dedicatory epistle (undated) of Sepúlveda to Pope Clement VII; and 61, where Legrand gives the name of the printer of Ducas' volume, Marcellus Silber, *alias* Franck (omitted from Legrand's *Bibliographie hellénique*), dated February 1527 and in which Legrand refers to Ducas as the "commercial editor" (publisher) of Sepúlveda's work. (Cf. A. Losada, *Juan Ginés de Sepúlveda* [Madrid, 1949] 273, which says Silber was editor.) Norton, *Italian Printers 1501–1520*, 102–103, remarks that some of the Silbers' works (father and son) are unsigned.

[103] Sepúlveda, a pupil of Pomponazzi, in Rome moved in the circle of Alberto Pio, Prince of Carpi. Erasmus considered Sepúlveda (who also translated Aristotle's *Politics* into Latin and later in fact became Pope Clement VII's official translator of Aristotle) the most illustrious writer of his time. See A. Morel-Fatio, *L'historiographie de Charles-Quint*, I (Paris, 1913) 43.

[104] Latin text in Legrand, *Bibliographie hispano-grecque* pt. 2, 62–63. Cf. Bataillon, *Erasme et l'Espagne*, 23, n. 2.

period of six years. Its value, however, lies in the fact that, along with a similar privilege granted to him the previous year by Clement after publication of his *Liturgies*, it provides our sole evidence for his appointment to a "public professorship" of Greek in Rome.[105]

The term "public professor" as applied here to Demetrius Ducas probably refers to an instructorship at the University of Rome, an institution formed by the merger of the older curial college of the papacy and the newer municipal university.[106] The term seems to have carried the implication of instruction to all students, laymen and ecclesiastics. Leo had only recently admitted the latter to classes at the Roman university (in civil law, for example), though at the same time he cautioned that the instruction should emphasize Holy Scripture and divine precepts more than grammar and rhetoric.[107]

At the time of Ducas' tenure the University of Rome was in decline. Having reached its peak early in the pontificate of Leo X, it gradually fell into debt as a result of that pope's employment of an overly large number of professors and the high salaries he paid. Already by 1519 the stipends of the faculty had fallen into arrears and the city council had to cast around for a source of immediate revenue. During the reign of Clement VII the University had even smaller funds at its disposal. Yet the institution was still flourishing enough to attract large numbers of students to the lectures given by the noted scholars in residence.[108]

The length of Ducas' period of instruction in Rome is uncertain. All we know is that he was definitely teaching there in 1526 and 1527. Some light on the circumstances of his instruction may by analogy be provided by a document of Leo X, dated a decade or so before, in 1514, which registers the names and duties of the entire University faculty, in the number of eighty-eight. Three names are listed as the professors of Greek for that year: Augusto Valdo, Basilio Chalcondyles (the talented son of the even better-

[105] See Legrand, *Bibliographie hellénique*, I, 193–94.
[106] See H. Rashdall, *Medieval Universities* (Oxford, 1895) II, pt. 1, 38–39; Renazzi, *Università di Roma*, I. It is not known exactly when the two schools were combined.
[107] Rodocanachi, *Première Renaissance à Rome*, 162. See also Renazzi, II, 76–77, who implies that Lascaris lectured to all.
[108] See Rodocanachi, 161–64, and Pastor, *History of the Popes*, X, 345.

known Demetrius Chalcondyles), and Varinus Favorinus of Camerino, formerly the teacher of Leo himself. Of these three the first
was to teach in the morning, the second in the evening, and Favorinus on holidays.[109] Although other sources inform us that in this
period Leo also appointed Janus Lascaris to the university's faculty
of Greek (in addition to the headship of his institute for Greek
students), it is clear that the various embassies undertaken by
Lascaris in behalf of the Holy See — for Clement VII in 1529, for
example — must have prevented him from teaching continuously
at the University.[110]

Only a few months after Ducas' publication of Sepúlveda's translation of Alexander of Aphrodisias, the war clouds that for long
had been gathering over Rome and were restrained by the astute
diplomacy of Pope Clement VII burst, and the Spanish and German
armies of his most holy majesty, Emperor Charles V, now entered
the splendid capital of the Medici popes. A notorious sack followed,
beginning May 6, 1527, and lasting three days, and it was this fate-
ful event which brought to a premature close Rome's period of
pre-eminence in the Renaissance. One may conjecture that with
the hurried exodus of many humanist scholars as a result of the
barbaric destruction wrought in the capital, Ducas too made his
escape, or, as is entirely possible, he may have been among the
many men of letters put to death by the mutinous troops.[111] In any
event, he vanishes completely from our sources, and until a further
manuscript or document bearing his name comes to light the story
of Demetrius Ducas' short but not uneventful career must come to
an abrupt end.

What may we say in conclusion about his significance for the
history of scholarship, in particular for the transmission of Greek
letters to the West? Ducas' work as editor of Aldine first editions

[109] See Renazzi, II, app. 2, 236–39. Cf. Pastor, VIII, 273. On the three scholars
see also above, Chapter 7, text and notes 61–64.

[110] On the Greek institute (which seems to have closed after Leo's death) see
above, Chapter 6. Also on Lascaris see Renazzi, II, 76–77; Pastor, X, 336, 343;
and esp. Knös, *Janus Lascaris*, 187ff.

[111] On the disastrous sack see the excellent description of Pastor, IX, 388ff. and
esp. X, 344–45. Giovanni Pierio Valeriano, *De litteratorum infelicitate* (Venice,
1620), a contemporary account which describes the fate of many scholars, does
not mention Ducas. Sathas, *Neohellenic Philology*, 227, says Ducas very probably
died in Madrid, but he is probably confused because he does not mention his
return to Italy after his Spanish sojourn at Alcalá.

has, to be sure, been given a certain recognition, and this alone would entitle him to a place in the history of Renaissance learning. But, as we have seen, the later phases of his career, in particular his activities in Spain and Rome, have been lightly passed over by scholars, who have generally failed to connect this phase with his activities at the Aldine press. The zeal of Spanish historians to provide a secure place for their country in the movement of the Renaissance, and especially to depict the development of Spanish humanism as the work of native Spaniards, has almost entirely obscured the accomplishments of Ducas, the Greek from Crete. To cite a few typical remarks of Spanish writers: Quintanilla y Mendoza, an early seventeenth century historian, in discussing the Polyglot Bible, makes lavish reference to Lebrija and alludes to Ducas only with the words "Demetrius the Cretan, Greek of nation." [112] So the *Historia* of another Spaniard, Thaunus (who mistakenly calls Ducas, Lucas!),[113] and the anonymous *Hispaniae Bibliotheca* published in 1608 both say that it was with Nuñez that "Greek letters were born in Spain" ("cum eo graecas litteras in Hispania natos").[114] Similarly, the Spaniard Alvar Gómez de Castro, a contemporary of Ducas and the chief biographer of Ximenes, records that "Spain owes to Lebrija almost all the glory of her classical knowledge" ("Cui Hispania debet quicquid habet bonarum literarum.") [115] Even the often-cited modern scholar Charles Graux, in the introduction to his basic work on the Greek manuscripts of the Escurial library, dismisses Ducas with a single brief footnote: "There came to Spain [in this period] some Greeks who occupied certain chairs in the Universities . . . for example, Demetrius Ducas"; while, in the same context, and in company with Delitzsch, Graux refers elaborately to Nuñez as "the introducer and father of Greek studies in Spain." [116]

While Ducas was not the very first to introduce the study of Greek to the Spanish peninsula — that honor evidently falls to Bar-

---

[112] In his *Archetypo de virtudes, espejo de prelados: el Venerable Padre y Siervo de Dios Fray Francisco Ximénez de Cisneros* (Palermo, 1653) 136.
[113] See Jacques Auguste Thaunus, *Historiarum sui temporis libri CXX* (Paris, 1606–1609) I, 322.
[114] Published in Frankfort, pp. 548–50. (Cited also in Graux, *Essai*, 23.)
[115] Gómez de Castro, *Francisco Ximenio Cisnerio* (Alcalá, 1569).
[116] Graux, 9, and n. 1 and Delitzsch, *Studien*, 25–26.

bosa, who in 1489 (or possibly a year later) began to teach Greek at Salamanca [117] — it would seem that he deserves at least as much credit as a pioneer in this respect as Nuñez. Indeed, six years prior to Nuñez' initial publication of his famous so-called juxtalinear translations of Greek works into Latin (1519), Ducas, as we have seen, was printing at Alcalá, and at his own expense, two instructional Greek texts aimed to fill a vital need in the education of his students, which made it possible to transmit Greek to a wider audience. Ducas' attitude stands in sharp contrast to that of Nuñez, who manifested utter indifference to so fundamental an aspect of Greek studies as the editing and publication of original texts. Though the possessor, for example, of a very rare manuscript of Themistius containing several yet unpublished speeches, Nuñez made no effort to publish these, and the printed editions of Themistius' orations thus remained for a long time incomplete.[118]

We have already discussed at some length the capital role of Ducas in the publication of the Alcalá Bible, especially in the preparation of the Greek text of the New Testament. But though admittedly we know little about his teaching at Alcalá, it is very possible that his chief influence on the development of Spanish humanism may in the last analysis lie less in his contribution to the Alcalá Polyglot than in his association with students and teachers of that university — in other words, in the interest he generated for further studies of Greek at this leading Spanish intellectual center of the sixteenth century. While seeking, however, to allot to Ducas his proper place in the Renaissance in Spain, we should be careful not to exaggerate the success of his efforts to propagate interest in Greek. For the temper of Spain in comparison with that of the more secular Venice, Florence, and even Rome, remained fundamentally ecclesiastical and thus all too often unreceptive to the study of the Greek language per se.[119] Many historians, in fact, believe that not long afterwards the further development of Spanish

[117] See especially Bataillon, *Erasme et l'Espagne*, 20, and n. 3; and 21, quoting Barbosa's pupil (Diego de Zuñiga) on this point. Also cf. Esperabé y Arteaga, *Historia de la Universidád de Salamanca*, II, 328.

[118] Graux, 21, shows that even after the appearance of the Aldine Themistius (*editio princeps*, 1534), Nuñez still did not publish the ten yet unedited speeches in his possession. In fact, four of these were not to be edited until 1614, in Leyden.

[119] See especially Graux, 20, who emphasizes the fact that the Spanish scholars of Greek were not true philologists.

humanism was hindered by the intense absorption of the country in combating the rising Protestant movement.

The activities of Ducas in Spain served to open the way for the subsequent arrival in that country of other Greeks, especially men of letters from his Cretan homeland. Several, like Anthony Kalosenas and Nicolas Turriano (or Della Torre), worked there as copyists and were responsible for cataloguing the great Greek manuscript collection of the Escurial, founded in the latter half of the sixteenth century by King Philip II.[120] Among the last and certainly the best known of the Greek émigrés to adopt Spain as their home was the celebrated painter El Greco, born the Cretan Domenicos Theotocopoulos. Like his predecessor Ducas, he left his birthplace to go to Venice, whence, his outlook broadened by the beneficent influences of that city, he found his way to Spain. The career of El Greco thus provides a parallel example in the artistic sphere to the intellectual influence we have been tracing of the Byzantine East on western Europe by way of Venice.

[120] On these and other Greeks and the Escurial, see especially Graux, 31, 48, 50, 110ff.; Legrand, I, 317; and Kyrou, " Ἡ πνευματικὴ ἀκμή," 310. In 1576 the Escurial library acquired the large collection of Greek manuscripts formed by Diego de Mendoza, the envoy of Charles V in Venice. The manuscripts had been gathered largely in Venice or as a result of two journeys to Mount Athos and the Greek East made around 1543 by the Corfiote Nicholas Sophianos at the commission of Mendoza. (See A. González Palencia and E. Mele, *Vida y obras Don Diego Hurtado de Mendoza* [Madrid, 1941] I, 253–57.) Sophianos brought back 300 manuscripts from the East!

Chapter 9

DESIDERIUS ERASMUS

Associate of the Greek Scholars of Aldus' Academy

W E have thus far concentrated on the careers of several Greek exiles important for their work in disseminating Greek letters in the West. The last figure to be considered is the celebrated Erasmus, whose personality dominated the development of European humanism in the first half of the sixteenth century. Though not a Greek, he is nevertheless included here because he is perhaps the outstanding example of a Northern humanist who, having profited from association with the Eastern émigrés, was able to "popularize" the classical learning in his writings and thus more effectively than any other scholar to reach a wide audience in northern Europe.

Erasmus' career has of course been the subject of a vast literature.[1] But the common emphasis on him as a Northern humanist has served to obscure the importance of his activities in Italy, a tendency further magnified by his own words denying any cultural indebtedness to that country.[2] The whole of Erasmus' visit to Italy, which took place between 1506 and 1509, has been the sub-

[1] A few of the more important general biographies of Erasmus are: Mangan's *Life of Erasmus*; P. Smith, *Erasmus* (New York, 1923); J. Huizinga, *Erasmus of Rotterdam* (London, 1952); A. Hyma, *The Youth of Erasmus* (Ann Arbor, 1930); F. Seebohm, *The Oxford Reformers* (London, 1914); R. Newald, *Erasmus Roterdamus* (Freiburg in Breisgau, 1947); K. Meissinger, *Erasmus von Rotterdam* (Berlin, 1948); R. Drummond, *Erasmus, His Life and Character as Shown in his Career and Books* (London, 1873) 2 vols.; E. Emerton, *Desiderius Erasmus of Rotterdam* (New York, London, 1899); and M. Phillips, *Erasmus and the Northern Renaissance* (London, 1949). Also see E. Nelson, "Recent Literature Concerning Erasmus," *Journal of Modern History*, I (1929) 88–102. Works on specific aspects of Erasmus' career will be cited below.

[2] See below, note 99.

ject of a recent essay, "Erasme et l'Italie," by the eminent French scholar, A Renaudet.[3] Despite the real excellence of his study in providing a composite picture of Erasmus' intellectual constitution, Renaudet has not sufficiently scrutinized or evaluated what seems, in certain respects, to have been the most formative phase of Erasmus' Italian sojourn — his nine months' association in Venice with Aldus and his Greek Academy, engaged in the publication of Greek texts. It is the purpose of this chapter to re-examine this vital phase of Erasmus' Italian visit in order to determine, as accurately as possible, what influence the scholars of Venice, in particular the émigré Greeks, may have had upon the northern savant.

When Erasmus arrived in Italy in September of 1506 he had, it is true, already achieved some recognition among European men of letters.[4] Through residence in Italy, however, he hoped to enhance his academic stature by obtaining a doctor's degree in theology, a requisite credential if his theological views were to receive the serious consideration of contemporary scholars.[5] More important, as several of his own statements explicitly attest, he went to Italy primarily to perfect his knowledge of Greek ("Italiam . . . adivimus Graecitatis potissimum causa").[6] Some proficiency in

---

[3] Published in *Travaux d'Humanisme et Renaissance*, XV (Geneva, 1954). Only ten pages of the essay discuss Erasmus in Venice. On Erasmus' stay in Italy in general, see also the rather brief studies of P. de Nolhac, *Erasme en Italie*, 2nd ed. (Paris, 1898) and the same author's *Erasme et l'Italie* (Paris, 1925), which is of somewhat less value. The general biographies of Erasmus cited above devote little space to his activities in Italy, and even Firmin-Didot, *Alde Manuce*, makes only brief references to Erasmus in Venice.

[4] What brought him initial recognition was the first publication of his *Adages* in Paris in 1500, followed by the *Enchiridion militis christiani* in 1504 (which also drew criticism). See Mangan, *Life of Erasmus*, I, 121ff.

[5] See Erasmus' statement, in P. S. Allen, *Opus Epistolarum Des. Erasmi Roterodami* (Oxford, 1906), hereafter cited as *Epistolae Erasmi*, I, 432 (English translation in Nichols, *The Epistles of Erasmus*, I, 418).

[6] Letter to Servatius of November 16, 1506, in Allen, *Epistolae Erasmi*, I, 433. Cf. Phillips, *Erasmus and the Northern Renaissance*, 45: "In 1506, Erasmus never wavered from his purpose, which was now to perfect his Greek"; and on page 56: "In Italy Erasmus had a clear conception of what he was working for, and the gap to be filled was still in the fuller knowledge of Greek." Tilley, *Dawn of the French Renaissance*, 287, 292, affirms that on Erasmus' arrival in Italy he was a "passable Greek scholar," and that he went there "chiefly for the sake of Greek." He also believes (290) that Erasmus did not make the most of his opportunities for Greek study in Paris, perhaps because of the increasingly theological tone of the University of Paris. Interestingly enough, Erasmus does not seem to have met the Byzantine Janus Lascaris (who had already helped Guillaume Budé with his Greek) in Paris. Erasmus and Lascaris met in Venice (Nichols, 447).

that language he had already acquired in northern Europe, partly
as the result of self-instruction and partly under various teachers,
among whom was George Hermonymus of Sparta, according to
Erasmus an instructor of little worth, under whom he had read in
Paris.[7]

To emphasize how essential Erasmus considered a knowledge of
Greek, one need quote only the now famous lines he wrote to his
patron Anthony of St. Bergen, "If you would drink deeply of the
wellspring of wisdom apply to Greek. We have in Latin at best
some small brooks and turbid pools; while the Greeks have the
purest fountains and rivers flowing with gold." And elsewhere he
wrote, even more pointedly, "Latin erudition, however ample, is
crippled and imperfect without Greek."[8]

On his arrival in Italy Erasmus' first step was to secure a degree
from the University of Turin. His original intention had been to
apply to the great University of Bologna, but to obtain a doctorate
from that institution necessitated the possession of other scholarly
titles which Erasmus had never found time to acquire.[9] After
securing the Turin doctorate,[10] evidently with a minimum of effort,
Erasmus proceeded to Bologna, where he was offered the hospitality of Paolo Bombasio, professor of Greek at the university there.
During a thirteen months' stay at the home of the latter, Erasmus
had an opportunity to meet a number of scholars and presumably
to pursue the study of Greek, perhaps through attending some of
Bombasio's lectures, certainly through engaging in informal discussions with his host.[11]

[7] On Hermonymus see H. Omont, "Hermonyme de Sparte, maître de grec
à Paris, et copiste de manuscrits (1476)," *Mémoires de la Société de l'histoire de
Paris et de l'Ile-de-France*, XII (1885) 65–98; J. Boissonade, *Anecdota Graeca*
(Paris, 1833) V, 420–26; and Sathas, *Neohellenic Philology*, 69, who wrongly says
that Melanchthon studied with Hermonymus. For Erasmus' opinion see Sandys,
History of Classical Scholarship, II, 169, n. 3, quoting from Erasmus' *Catalogue of
Lucubrations* prefaced to his *Opera Omnia*. I. Bywater, *The Erasmian Pronunciation of Greek and its Precursors* (London, 1908) 24, n. 8, states that Budé also had
scant respect for Hermonymus but thought well of his pronunciation.

[8] Allen, *Epistolae Erasmi*, no. 149, I, 352; cf. Nichols, I, 313; Smith, *Erasmus*,
46–47 (all with slightly different wording).

[9] Cf. also Mangan's explanation, I, 223, that a relative of the pope was chancellor at Turin while Bologna was then in the hands of enemies of the pope.

[10] See E. Major, *Erasmus von Rotterdam* (Basle, 1926) for a photograph of the
Turin diploma (conferring the doctorate of theology), dated September 4, 1506.

[11] According to a letter of August 15, 1536, written by Beatus Rhenanus (a
pupil and a kind of biographer of Erasmus) and included in Froben's *Origen*
(1536), Erasmus "when at Bologna . . . did not attend any lectures, but, con-

It was possibly Bombasio who induced Erasmus, intending to leave soon for Rome, to write a letter (on October 28, 1507) to Europe's foremost printer, Aldus Manutius, in which he requested publication of his Latin translation of two plays of Euripides, *Hecuba* and *Iphigenia in Aulis*.[12] Erasmus' letter, a skillful combination of respect, flattery, and humility, began by complimenting Aldus for his notable contribution to classical learning. Erasmus then struck a sympathetic note by mentioning reports that Aldus had received "no proportionate gain" for his labors, and expressed interest in Aldus' proposed Greek edition of Plato, while, strikingly enough, suggesting publication of the Greek text of the New Testament.[13] Subtly shifting his ground, Erasmus went on to say that though his two plays had already been printed in Paris (in September 1506) by Badius,[14] he had refused Badius permission to reprint them because, to quote him, "I fear lest, as the proverb of Sophocles puts it, he will mend one mischief with another. I should think my lucubrations secure of immortality [however] if they came out printed in your type, especially the minute type which is the most elegant of all." [15] What he referred to, of course, was the famous Aldine type, more widely known as *Italic*, which had been invented by Aldus.[16]

---

tented with the friendship of Paolo Bombasio . . . pursued his studies at home" (Allen, *Epistolae Erasmi*, I, 55, translated in Nichols, *Epistles*, I, 23). On Bombasio also see L. Simeoni, *Storia della Università di Bologna* (Bologna, 1947) II, 46–47, who says that the Bolognese Greek chair was instituted in 1455, the chair of Greek literature in 1610, and that Bombasio's successor in the Greek chair was one Peter Ipsilla, a Greek of Aegina. Bombasio is also mentioned in de Nolhac, "Les correspondants d'Alde Manuce," 230–32, 82–89. Also see G. Fantuzzi, *Notizie degli scrittori bolognesi* (Bologna, 1782) and Allen, *Epistolae Erasmi*, I, 443.

[12] This letter is among fifteen discovered by Nolhac in the Vatican in 1898. Four constitute the sole correspondence we have between Erasmus and Aldus. Printed in Allen, *Epistolae Erasmi*, nos. 207, 209, 212, 213, I, pp. 437–42, 447–49, translated in Nichols, *Epistles*, I, 428–30, 432–35. Mangan, I, 232, thinks Erasmus' letter to Aldus may have been due rather to the influence of Carteromachus, whom Erasmus had recently met in Bologna.

[13] On Aldus' intention of printing the Bible and his publication of one "polyglot" page of the Old Testament, see above, Chapter 8, note 89. The Aldine *editio princeps* of Plato appeared in 1513 (Chapter 5, above).

[14] Erasmus had left for Italy before then, but had previously deposited the translations with Badius on his return from London. See Tilley, *Dawn of the French Renaissance*, 292.

[15] For the letter see Allen, *Epistolae Erasmi*, no. 207, I, 439, and Nichols, *Epistles*, I, 430; cf. Mangan, I, 233.

[16] The old view was that the Aldine type imitated the hand of Petrarch (cf. Nolhac, "Les correspondants d'Alde Manuce," VIII [1887] 248, n. 2, who shows

We know from a second letter of Erasmus that Aldus' response — which has been lost — must have been favorable.[17] Indeed, Aldus may well have invited Erasmus to come to Venice, as may be surmised from Erasmus' plea of ill health. Nevertheless, Erasmus took care to send Aldus precise directions for the publication of his plays, the manuscript of which he now dispatched from Bologna to Venice.

In one month's time, by December 1507, the printing of the Euripidean plays was accomplished. At this juncture Erasmus, despite his originally stated intention to proceed to Rome, suddenly appeared in Venice. No letters explain the change in plan,[18] but it is probable that what persuaded Erasmus to make the journey was his desire to see published under the Aldine imprint one of his most cherished works, the *Adages*, a collection of proverbs gleaned chiefly from various classical authors, Latin and Greek. Erasmus had begun this collection shortly after his return from England in 1500, and in June of that year, at Paris,[19] it had been first printed by Jean Philippe as a slim volume entitled *Adagiorum Collectanea*. Already in Bologna Erasmus had devoted some little care to enlarging the work, but publication of a new edition at this time could afford considerable latitude for error, especially since he had not yet even finished his intended revision of the volume.[20] His presence, then, at Venice was imperative, and thus for a period of nine months, from January to September of 1508, Erasmus was to be a guest in the house of Aldus.

---

the lack of resemblance between the Aldine type and Petrarch's autograph). The generally accepted view today is that Aldus followed one of the two current book scripts of the late fifteenth century (which should most correctly be termed humanist cursive, not humanist chancery script). See B. Bischoff, G. Lieftinck, G. Battelli, *Nomenclature des écritures livresques du IXe au XVIe siècles* (Paris, 1954) 35-43, and now B. L. Ullmann, *The Origin and Development of Humanistic Script* (Rome, 1960).

[17] Allen, *Epistolae Erasmi*, no. 209, I, 440-442; Nichols, I, 432; cf. Nolhac, *Erasme en Italie*, 100-105.

[18] Beatus Rhenanus mentions a letter, now lost, of Erasmus to Aldus (see Nolhac, 30, n. 3), which would probably have shed light on Erasmus' change of plans.

[19] See Allen, no. 124, I, 287. The month of publication is not stated. Nichols, *Epistles*, I, 236. Smith, *Erasmus*, 41, and Emerton, *Erasmus*, 91, agree on June, while Tilley, *Dawn of the French Renaissance*, 291, and others favor July. In any case, by the time of Erasmus' arrival in Venice, the second edition of the *Adages* (published by Badius in Paris, January 1507; cf. Tilley, 292) had been out a year.

[20] See below, text for note 31, Erasmus' own statement; also testimony of Rhenanus, in Allen, *Epistolae Erasmi*, I, 55 (Nichols, *Epistles*, I, 23, 28; cf. Nolhac, *Erasme en Italie*, 24).

Whoever you are, Aldus earnestly begs you to state your business in the fewest possible words and be gone, unless, like Hercules to weary Atlas, you would lend a helping hand. There will always be enough work for you, and all who come this way.

This challenge, inscribed over the door of Aldus' print shop, con-fronted Erasmus when he presented himself at what then ranked as the leading publishing house in Europe.[21]

Before we discuss the activities of Erasmus in the Aldine environment it may be well to give some account of the living and working conditions of the employees and business associates of Aldus. Erasmus himself, in his colloquy *Opulentia Sordida* (*The Wealthy Miser*, as someone has aptly translated it), has left us what is generally accepted as a description of the Aldine establishment.[22] Virtually all the employees, some thirty-three in number,[23] lived in the same household, a building in the quarter of San Paternian which was the possession of Aldus' father-in-law and later business partner, Andrea d'Asola.[24] In these cramped quarters where Erasmus had to share a room with Girolamo Aleandro,[25] and where, moreover, all were accustomed to take their meals together, Erasmus, a chronic complainer, was evidently not exactly satisfied. In his colloquy Erasmus describes the household as miserly; the host, he says, crudely economized by serving only two meals a day, the first at one o'clock and the second on the master's — that is, d'Asola's — return, often after ten. The fare was extremely frugal, usually thin soup and bad wine (responsible, Erasmus claimed for

[21] Translated by E. Tatham in "Erasmus in Italy," *English Historical Review*, X (1895) 649. Cf. Nolhac, 32.

[22] Text in *Colloquies of Desiderius Erasmus*, trans. N. Bailey (London, 1900) III, 180–95. Also see Mangan, I, 247. For analysis, see especially P. Smith, "Key to the Colloquies of Erasmus," *Harvard Theological Studies*, XIII (1927), who identifies the pseudonyms used by Erasmus. He shows that Antronius (Greek for "ass") is d'Asola; Orthrogonus (Greek for "born at dawn") is Aldus Manutius; Verpius, the circumcised, is Aleandro. (Erasmus thought Aleandro was a Jew; see Mangan, I, 247. Cf. Firmin-Didot, *Alde Manuce*, 419, who says that Verpius refers to Musurus or John of Crete.) Also Strategus (Greek for "general") is Carteromachus; cf. Smith, *Erasmus*, 53.

[23] See Mangan, I, 248–49, for Erasmus' enumeration.

[24] On the relationship of Aldus and d'Asola (actually a younger man), see Ferrigni, *Aldo Manuzio*, 156, and Semper, *Carpi*, 24. Aldus' house and press had apparently been moved to San Paternian from Sant' Agostino, as evidenced by a will of Aldus' drawn up on March 27, 1506. Cf. Brown, *Venetian Printing Press*, 49, and Castellani, *La stampa in Venezia*, 56.

[25] On this, see especially the letter of Beatus Rhenanus (Nichols, *Epistles*, I, 30).

bringing on his first attack of the stone),[26] with the *pièce de ré-sistance* consisting of "a morsel of stony cheese and seven small lettuce leaves floating in a bowl of rancid vinegar." [27]

Most scholars agree that while this picture of the Aldine household contains certain elements of truth, it is at the same time grossly distorted. Actually the colloquy was written twenty-three years later as a defense against the scurrilous attack on Erasmus of the Ciceronian Julius Caesar Scaliger, who reproached him with "having escaped from a monastery in Holland in order to take refuge with Aldus, engaging himself as a corrector of proofs and drinking like a triple Geryon, but doing only half the work of one man." [28]

Whatever sentiments Erasmus may have expressed subsequently, there is no evidence of a rift between him and members of the Aldine circle during the period of his stay in Venice. Evidently the only person provoked by the 1531 satire was Aldus' old friend Alberto Pio, who later, in 1535, while an exile in Paris and himself involved in the conflict over Ciceronianism, scornfully accused Erasmus of ingratitude to Aldus and of working for the latter as a mere corrector of proofs rather than as an associate.[29] Actually, in the Aldine workshop the terms "corrector" and "editor" were virtually synonymous. Aldus himself, for example, insisted on reading all final proofs, and even such eminent Hellenists as Marcus Musurus and Demetrius Ducas on occasion served as correctors. The term, therefore, had no opprobrious connotation. Nevertheless, in view of the remarks of his detractors, Erasmus always was careful to maintain that he corrected only his own work and this after elimination of the obvious errors by another proofreader.[30]

---

[26] See Erasmus' *Apologia ad xxiv libros Alberti Pii* (in Nichols, *Epistles*, I, 447). Because of the stone, Erasmus asked d'Asola that he be allowed to prepare meals in his chamber.

[27] Translation of Mangan, I, 250.

[28] For the (disputed) date of Scaliger's work containing this statement and for a clear study of their complex controversy, see especially V. Hall, Jr., "The Life of Julius Caesar Scaliger (1484–1558)," *Transactions of the American Philosophical Society*, n.s., XL (1950) 99ff. Cf. Smith, *Erasmus*, 311, who dates it 1529. Also R. Christie, *Etienne Dolet, Martyr of the Renaissance* (London, 1899) 201, and Mangan, I, 256.

[29] On Pio see Semper, 21a. Excerpts from polemics of Pio and Erasmus are printed on pp. 27b–29, and esp. in n. 152. Scaliger repeated Pio's charge (Nichols, *Epistles*, I, 448). In Allen, *Epistolae Erasmi*, I, 462, Bombasio calls Musurus "Erasmus' enemy"!

[30] For Erasmus' defense see Nichols, *Epistles*, I, 446–47.

Immediately upon Erasmus' arrival in Venice, the work of publishing an enlarged edition of his *Adages* began. As noted, his revision of the volume was then far from complete. Indeed, to quote his own words, he had at the time "but the confused and undigested material of future work, and that compiled *only from authors already published*." [31] The closing phrase may be compared with a revealing statement Erasmus later made as to the unavailability of Greek manuscripts when, in 1500, he published the first edition of the *Adages* in Paris: "I had no supply of Greek codices, without which trying to write about proverbs is nothing else than trying to fly without wings, as Plautus says." [32]

Erasmus found the situation in Venice altogether different. Generous aid came from members of the Aldine circle, who supplied him with various manuscripts in their possession, including even texts of unedited authors. Aldus himself provided unpublished codices from his own library, which, Erasmus attests, was supplied better than any other, especially in Greek books.[33] In addition, Aldus permitted Erasmus access to letters of scholars from all over Europe with whom he was in correspondence regarding manuscripts and literary problems.[34] Specific acknowledgment of indebtedness was made by Erasmus in the famous adage "Festina Lente," where he wrote that "without the precious aid of these men my book would have been much less complete." [35]

Erasmus makes individual mention, in the same adage, of Janus Lascaris and Marcus Musurus, as well as the Italians Battista Egnazio and "Frater" Urbanus (Urbano Bolzanio).[36] All of them are

[31] "Idque ex evulgatis dumtaxat autoribus" (from 1526 edition, entitled *Adagiorum Opus* (Basle, 1526) chil. II, cent. 1, prov. 1, p. 340). Translated in Nichols, *Epistles*, I, 438.

[32] Remark printed in preface of Froben's 1515 edition of *Adages*; translated by T. Appelt, "Studies in the Contents and Sources of Erasmus' 'Adagia' with Particular Reference to the First Edition, 1500, and the Edition of 1526" (dissertation, University of Chicago, 1942) 14; and see Allen, *Epistolae Erasmi*, I, 523.

[33] See Nolhac, *Erasme en Italie*, 51, citing "Festina Lente." Also cf. Froben's 1526 edition, p. 339.

[34] For the correspondence see Nolhac, "Les Correspondants d'Alde Manuce," VIII (1887) and IX (1888), esp. IX, 250ff. and 253.

[35] See 1526 Froben ed., 339-40. Also the passage translated by Smith, *Erasmus*, 42: "Many learned men of their own accord offered me authors not yet published." That these passages appear later in the 1526 edition but not in the original Aldine makes them even more significant.

[36] All four are again mentioned by name in Erasmus' later work *Apologia* (in Nichols, *Epistles*, I, 447).

credited by Erasmus with the loan of rare manuscripts from their private libraries, including a large number of very important Greek works unprinted or inaccessible to him. Among the Greek manuscripts lent him were the dialogues of Plato (the Greek *editio princeps* issued from the Aldine press in 1513); Plutarch's *Lives*, and the *Moralia* (which, edited by Ducas, was at that very moment being printed);[37] Athenaeus' *Deipnosophistae;*[38] Aphthonius;[39] Hermogenes with scholia and the *Rhetoric* of Aristotle (both of which were included in the Aldine *Rhetores Graeci* printed in 1508–1509);[40] a complete Aristides with annotations;[41] scholia on Hesiod and Theocritus, as well as the even more valuable ones of Eustathius of Thessalonica on Homer;[42] Pausanias;[43] Pindar with (to quote Erasmus' own phrase) "carefully made annotations";[44]

[37] See 1526 Froben ed. of Erasmus' *Adages*, 340: "Moralia, quae sub finem operis mei coepta sunt excudi." Plutarch's *Moralia* was actually issued in 1509. The *Lives* were first printed in 1517 by F. Giunta of Florence. See Bandini, *De Florentina Juntarum Typografia et Juntarum Typog. Annales*, II, 122. The *Lives* were published in 1519 by Aldus (Renouard, *Annales*, I, 207).

[38] Its unavailability to the West is corroborated by C. Bühler, "Aldus Manutius and the Printing of Athenaeus," *Gutenberg Jahrbuch* (Mainz, 1955) 104–106. The *editio princeps*, edited by Musurus (see Chapter 5), was published by Aldus in 1514, although there exists a single page of a projected Aldine edition dating from 1499 to 1500.

[39] On Aphthonius, the fourth century A.D. Greek rhetorician, see Firmin-Didot, *Alde Manuce*, 312, and Graesse, *Trésor de livres rares et précieux*, I, 158. His *Progymnasmata* was evidently in press when Erasmus was with Aldus.

[40] The Hermogenes first became known in the West through the Aldine edition, which also included Aristotle's *Poetics* as well as his *Rhetoric*. Curiously, Erasmus affirms that the manuscript of Aristotle's *Rhetoric* lent him included the commentary of Gregory of Nazianzus ("Aristotelis rhetorica cum scholiis Gregorii Nazianseni," 1526 Froben ed., p. 340). However, Gregory does not seem to have written such a work, at least I can find no evidence of it. Cf. Nolhac, *Erasme en Italie*, 40, n. 4, Renaudet, *Erasme et l'Italie*, 85, and Appelt, "Erasmus' 'Adagia,'" 146, who cite Gregory's scholia, but without comment. Smith, *Erasmus*, 146, deliberately omits mention of Gregory's work, though he is quoting Erasmus' own words.

[41] Unknown to the West before this time, the *editio princeps* of Aristides was published in 1517 by Giunta at Florence (Graesse, I, 205). But Aldus published certain orations of Aristides in *Rhetorum Graecorum Orationes* in 1513 (Firmin-Didot, 334; cf. Graesse, I, 206).

[42] Eustathius' scholia were already known to the West through manuscripts of Bessarion, but the scholia were not published until 1542–1550 in Rome, edited by Mathew Devaris of Corfu, pupil of Janus Lascaris (Graesse II, 258; also Sandys, *History of Classical Scholarship*, II, 78).

[43] The *editio princeps* of Pausanius appeared in 1516, from the Aldine press (but after Aldus' death), edited by Musurus (see above, Chapter 5 on Musurus, text and n. 155); but the work was probably known to the West before this time.

[44] Pindar, 133, perhaps edited by Aldus himself (Schück, *Aldus Manutius*, 79,

a proverb collection ascribed to Plutarch [45] and also the sayings
compiled by Michael Apostolis (whose son, Arsenios, as we have
seen, was at one time on intimate terms with, if not a member of,
the Aldine group) [46] — and, as Erasmus concludes in the same
adage, "alia minuta." [47]

Even a cursory glance at this list reveals that it comprises some
of the most celebrated and influential works of Greek antiquity in
the fields of rhetoric, philosophy, ethics, geography, and epic and
lyric poetry. And the large majority of these — with the notable
exception of the writings of Plato, Aristotle, and Plutarch — were
virtually unknown to the West before their subsequent publication
by the Aldine Press. Through Erasmus' own words, moreover,
there is here revealed direct exchange between representatives of
not two but three cultural traditions — Byzantine, Italian, and, if
we may use the term, northern European — a fact of vital importance for the later development of Western intellectual thought.
Only in Venice, owing to the peculiar circumstances of its connections with the East, could Erasmus in this period have been
provided with such a rich variety of important and unexploited
Greek authors.[48]

---

says Musurus edited it), was issued in 1513 (Sandys, II, 104). See above Chapter 5
on Musurus, note 133. Calliergis' famous Pindar with scholia appeared in Rome in
1515. The author of Erasmus' "carefully made annotations" is not specified,
though it may well have been Musurus, who, we know, owned two manuscripts
of Pindar. See Irigoin, Pindare, 176 and 378.

[45] Some modern scholars cite the author as "a certain Plutarch," but since the
famous Plutarch of Boeotia did make such a collection, this probably refers to
him. The collection is referred to usually as that of Pseudo-Plutarch.

[46] It was evidently part of Arsenios' own enlargement of Michael's work,
Ionia, that Arsenios had printed around 1519 in Rome. See Walz, Arsenii Violetum,
p. iii. Cf. above, Chapter 6 on Arsenios, text and notes 19–25, for Arsenios' employment with Aldus and reference to his exchange of manuscripts with Aldus
from Crete. According to a document recently printed (Manousakas, "Prelates
of Monemvasia," 115–16, 144), Arsenios was definitely in Venice and knew
Erasmus during the latter's stay there. Now cf. also Manousakas, "Arsenios . . .
Unpublished Epistles," no. 1, for the letter of Arsenios to Erasmus. On all the
above, see also Chapter 6, note 60.

[47] All the above manuscripts, as noted, are listed in the slightly enlarged version
of the adage "Festina Lente" published in the 1526 edition of Adagiorum Opus
of Froben, p. 340. A considerable number of these manuscripts had probably been
brought from the Greek East originally by Janus Lascaris in 1492, at the time of
his journey commissioned by the Medici. See Legrand, Bibliographie hellénique, I,
p. cxxxvi, and above, Chapter 6.

[48] In Rome in the mid-fifteenth century, Pope Nicholas V had already collected
350 Greek manuscripts, but Bessarion's library, now deposited in Venice, included

For this magnificent aid Erasmus more than once expressed gratitude. In one place he records that he was assisted by certain ones "whom I knew neither personally nor by name." Notable is the contrast he draws, again in "Festina Lente," between the liberality of the Aldine scholars who strove to aid him, "an utter stranger," and what he terms the "selfishness" of the Northern savants.[49]

Incorporation of the mass of new material so increased the scope of the *Adages* that this Aldine edition of 1508, a folio volume of over 500 pages containing more than 3,000 adages, constituted in reality a new work.

While Erasmus set himself to write, Aldus began to print with that "deliberate rapidity" which Erasmus has helped to make famous in "Festina Lente" ("make haste slowly"), the adage in which he describes the Aldine printer's mark of an anchor entwined with a dolphin,[50] and praises Aldus' professional ideal of tempering swiftness with deliberateness.

It was the first time that Erasmus had essayed the role of writing at the same time that printing was in progress. What rendered his task even more difficult was the skill of the Aldine workmen, who printed with a rapidity extraordinary for the time. The first proof, we are told, was corrected by an employee named Serafino.[51] Erasmus then occupied himself with additions and what today would be termed author's corrections. The final copy was always corrected by Aldus himself. Aldus' meticulousness evoked a query from Erasmus as to why he took such pains, to which the reply was "studeo" ("I am learning").[52] The picture of the two scholars working together in a room filled with the noise of the press has remained classic in the annals of printing.

Publication of the *Adages* was completed by September 1508, after nine months of uninterrupted labor. The volume, which occupies a capital place in the development of humanistic learning,

---

about 500 (see above, Chapter 1, text and note 78). Indeed, in Venice Erasmus seems not to have used Bessarion's library so much as private collections like those of Janus Lascaris, Musurus, and Aldus, as he himself indicates (see text above).

[49] See 1526 Froben ed. of *Adages*, 340; also Nichols, *Epistles*, I, 438-39.
[50] For discussion of the origin of this mark see Nichols, *Epistles*, I, 437-40.
[51] See Erasmus' *Apologia* (in Nichols, *Epistles*, I, 446).
[52] Nichols, I, 446.

is essentially a vast congeries of proverbs, maxims, and pithy sayings gleaned from Greek and Latin authors. The idea of making such a collection was not new, for works of more or less similar type had already been compiled by the Byzantines, such as that of Michael Apostolis.[53] But the work of Erasmus is among the very first of its kind in the West.[54]

What made his volume particularly distinctive was not only the richness and variety of the proverbs included, but the fact that a predominant number were accompanied by instructive commentaries, the content of which, Erasmus admits, was in great part based on Greek materials given to him by, and analyzed in conjunction with, members of the Aldine circle.[55] Such a storehouse of ancient sayings with explanations would be invaluable to those desirous of improving their knowledge of the classics, and of even more practical use to the educated man, for whom elegance of style could be enhanced by graceful allusion to classical authors. The *Adages*, in fact, were to enjoy enormous popularity, especially in the North, and were utilized for over a century, not only as a Latin and Greek dictionary and grammar, but also as a commonplace book, journal, and history of travel all in one.[56] Not without

[53] Many other such works of compilation were produced in Byzantium, notably the so-called Suda lexicon (actually a kind of encyclopedia), at one time wrongly thought to be the work of an author named Suidas. The term "Suidas," to refer to a person, was evidently first used by Eustathius of Thessalonica in the twelfth century. See F. Dölger, "Der Titel des sogenannten Suidaslexikons," *Sitzungsberichte der bayerischen Akademie der Wissenschaften zu München, Philosophisch-historische Klasse* (Munich, 1936), 6, Appelt, "Erasmus' 'Adagia,'" 138, n. 2, wrongly refers to Suidas instead of using the correct form, ἡ Σοῦδα.

[54] According to Mangan, *Life of Erasmus*, I, 126, several other Westerners, including Polydore Virgil, anticipated Erasmus in this field, though Erasmus' work is of course much larger and in addition enriched with comments. But it is typical of Erasmus that he failed to mention his indebtedness to Polydore, which incensed the latter.

[55] See for example, Erasmus' adage, "Rana Gyrina Sapientior," from Plato's *Theaetetus*, as printed in *Opera Omnia* (first appearing in the edition of 1520, so far as I am aware), where Erasmus writes: "That I was able to interpret this passage more accurately was due to Girolamo Aleandro, a man . . . bound to me by an old friendship." (On Aleandro's study with Musurus, see above, Chapter 5, text and note 93.) Since Erasmus and Aleandro fell out after Erasmus left Venice, this passage should refer to their common residence in that city. This is a specific example of the kind of discussion that constantly went on in the Aldine group.

[56] See Drummond, *Erasmus*, 27. Cf. Appelt, 40, who regards this statement as slightly exaggerated because, in his view, the *Adages* lacked organization. However, though the earlier editions have no genuine index, only a list of contents, the Aldine 1508 edition (which Appelt does *not* use) contains not only an alpha-

justification has the book been termed the most popular work of the entire period.

In order better to explain the nature of the Aldine edition and especially the magnitude of the Greek material newly incorporated, two selections from the work, by the persons responsible for its production, are here presented in English translation.[57] First, the preface of Aldus in which he praises Erasmus to the reader, and, second, a similar passage by Erasmus from his adage "Festina Lente," wherein, as if in response to Aldus' preface, he extols the work of his printer and his contribution to letters.[58]

ALDUS TO SCHOLARS [59]

I wish nothing more, dear readers, than to be of service to you. On this account, therefore, when there had come into my hands this erudite work of Erasmus of Rotterdam, that most learned of men in the world [60] (this work containing adages of such variety and richness of content is worthy of being compared with the works of antiquity itself), I interrupted the publication of certain authors which I had been preparing in order that we might print this instead, believing that it would prove useful to you, both because of the great number of adages which the author has assiduously collected with a maximum of effort and solicitude from a large group of writers, Latin as well as Greek, and also because during the course of the work many passages in the writings of either language were judiciously emended by him or eruditely explained.

The work reveals how much one may profit from proverbs such as these — just think, in fact, how they can be accommodated to different uses. In this work about ten thousand verses from Homer, Euripides, and other Greek writers have been with fidelity and scholarliness translated into Latin utilizing the same meter as the Greek, in addition to numerous passages from Plato, Demosthenes, and other authors.

But whether I speak the truth, you shall judge from your own ex-

betical index but one carefully arranged by subject, which would be of much help to readers.

[57] The complete title of the Aldine edition is *Adagiorum Chiliades tres, ac centuriae fere totidem.* The date of publication is given as September 1508, "Venetiis in aedibus Aldi." My microfilm was obtained from the Bodleian Library, Oxford. I have also consulted a copy of the original Aldine edition in the Biblioteca Nazionale Centrale in Florence.

[58] Except for a part of Aldus' preface, this to my knowledge is the first time that the following two selections have appeared in English translation (the translations are my own). Neither is included in Botfield's famous *Prefationes.*

[59] The Latin original is shown in the illustration; it is also printed in Renouard, *Annales,* I, 125.

[60] "Hominis undecunque doctissimi."

ERASMI ROTERODAMI ADAGIORVM
CHILIADES TRES, AC CENTV-
RIAE FERE TOTIDEM.

ALD. STVDIOSIS. S.

Quia nihil aliud cupio, q̃ prodeſſe uobis Studioſi. Cum ueniſſet in manus meas Eraſmi Roterodami, hominis undecunq̃ doctiſs. hoc adagiorũ opus eruditum. uarium. plenũ bonæ frugis,
& quod poſſit uel cum ipſa antiquitate certare, intermiſſis antiquis autorib. quos pa-
raueram excudendos, illud curauimus imprimendum, rati profuturum uobis
& multitudine ipſa adagiorũ, quæ ex plurimis autorib. tam latinis, quàm
græcis ſtudioſe collegit ſummis certe laborib. ſummis uigiliis, &
multis locis apud utriuſq̃ linguæ autores obiter uel correctis
acute, uel expoſitis erudite. Docet præterea quot modis
ex hiſce adagiis capere utilitatem liceat, puta quẽ-
admodum ad uarios uſus accõmodari poſ-
ſint. Adde, q̃ circiter decẽ millia uer-
ſuum ex Homero. Euripide, & cæ
teris Græcis eodẽ metro in
hoc opere fideliter, &
docte tralata ha
bétur, præ
ter plu
rima
ex Pla-
tone, De-
moſthene, & id
genus ali
is. An
autem uerus ſim,
ἰδοὺ ῥόδος, ἰδοὺ καὶ τὸ πήδημα.
Nam, quod dicitur, αὐτὸς αὐτὸν αὐλᾶ.

Præponitur hiſce adagiis duplex index Alter ſecundum literas
alphabeti noſtri. nam quæ græca ſunt, latina quoq̃
habentur. Alter per capita rerum.

OPENING PAGE OF THE ALDINE EDITION OF ERASMUS' *Adages*,
CONTAINING ALDUS' PREFACE TO SCHOLARS, VENICE, 1508

perience. "Behold Rhodes, behold therefore where you must jump." [61]
For, as is often said, "He plays the flute best who plays himself." [62]

The two sayings in the last paragraph, it may be observed, are
evidently taken from the proverb collection of the Cretan Michael
Apostolis — a copy of which was presented to Erasmus by his
roommate Aleandro, who in turn probably secured it from Arsenios
Apostolis. [63]

[Erasmus' Encomium on Aldus] [64]

Indeed I do not believe that this mark [Aldus' printer's mark of the
anchor and the dolphin] was even more illustrious at that time when,
engraved on the imperial nomisma [the Byzantine coin], it was carried about to be effaced by the handling of merchants than it is now,
when everywhere in the world, in fact even beyond the limits of the
Christian Empire, it is spread abroad, along with books of both languages, to be recognized, held in esteem, and exalted by all who devote
themselves to the cult of liberal studies: particularly by those, who,
surfeited with that debased, barbarous, and dull learning, [65] aspire to
true and ancient erudition, for the restoration of which this man, as if
born for the task, seems made, indeed coined, so to speak, by the fates
themselves. With such ardent devotion does he aspire to this one end,
with such indefatigable zeal does he strive, that he has hitherto not shied
away from any task whatever in order that the material of literature
may be restored for scholars [and rendered] unimpaired, genuine, and
pure. How much, in fact, he has already achieved in this respect (although I should say almost in spite of unfavorable circumstances), his
work clearly indicates. Indeed if some god, the friend to worthy literature, would look with favor on the splendid and truly royal sacrifices

[61] For this famous proverb, for which Aldus cites no source, see Leutsch,
Paroemiographi Graeci, II, 149 (with a slight alteration in wording). Leutsch
cites Gregory of Cyprus (thirteenth century), who evidently took it from
Aesop, fable 30 (see Leutsch, 101, n. 86). The proverb is also included in
Apostolis' collection; see Walz, *Arsenii Violetum*, 302.

[62] See Leutsch, 149; also Walz, 85, for the proverb, in Michael Apostolis' collection. It is also included in the earlier ones of (pseudo) Diogenianus and
Macarius of Philadelphia.

[63] On Aleandro's presentation of the work to Erasmus, see the latter's words in
his "Festina Lente," Froben ed., 1526, p. 340: "Proverbiorum collectio . . . titulo
Apostoli, cuius libri nobis copiam fecit Hieronymus Aleander." On Arsenios' contribution, and his friendship with the Aldine group, see above, note 46. Also cf.
Chapter 6, text for note 60.

[64] This selection from the adage "Festina Lente" first appears in the Aldine
Adages, though Smith, *Erasmus*, 41–42, 44, states that the adage was not printed
until 1526. The single passage concerning aid rendered Erasmus by the Aldine
circle is lacking from the 1508 edition, but the adage proper is certainly included.

[65] A reference to medieval scholastic learning.

of our friend Aldus, and if ill fortune too will spare him for a few years, the result, I promise to scholars, will be that they will have completely restored and corrected whatever worthy authors exist in the four languages of Latin, Greek, Hebrew, and Chaldaean [Syriac] and indeed in every kind of discipline, and this will come about from the work of this one man alone, and, as a result no person shall find lacking any portion of literature. With this accomplished, it will be evident how great a store of valuable manuscripts have heretofore remained hidden or unknown through negligence, or suppressed by the foolish desire of those to whom only one thing is near to their hearts — that they alone may appear to have knowledge.[66] It will then be manifest to what degree the works of authors swarm with strange emendations, even those which now seem to have been satisfactorily edited. If someone, merely as an experiment, would care to compare the *Epistles* of Pliny,[67] which will soon be published by the Aldine press, with those of other, irresponsible editions, the difference to be found there, he can expect to find in respect to other authors as well. By God, it is a Herculean task and one worthy of a princely mind to restore to the world something divine which has almost completely foundered, to search for what is hidden, to bring to light what has been concealed, to imbue with life what has been extinguished, to reconstruct passages that have been mutilated, and to emend others distorted in countless ways through the fault especially of irresponsible printers, to whom the small profit of even one gold coin is of greater value than all of literature.

Now consider even further: as much as one may exalt the importance of those who protect or enhance the power of the state by their services, it must be remembered that these deal exclusively with profane matters, and only within circumscribed limits. But he, on the other hand, who revives literature that has been perishing, achieves rather a sacred and immortal result, for to restore literature is almost more difficult, in fact, than originally to have created it. Moreover, it should be noted that the latter acts not only for the profit of one single province, but for the benefit of all peoples everywhere and of all ages.

If one seeks to evaluate the accomplishments of princes, among these the greatest glory must be ascribed to Ptolemy [Philadelphus]. But his library was enclosed within the constraining walls of a building, while that of Aldus is delimited only by the ends of the world itself.

---

[66] The passage beginning "Indeed if some god . . ." is translated by Drummond, *Erasmus*, I, 287, who also translates the final sentence of the passage, "But his library . . ." (Cf. Smith, 44-45.) Aside from these minor excerpts, the selections have not been rendered into English.

[67] Pliny's *Epistles* were published by Aldus in November 1508 (Renouard, *Annales*, I, 126). Erasmus, according to Appelt, "Erasmus' 'Adagia,'" 145, cites Pliny the Younger twenty-six times in his *Adages*. (Appelt used the 1526 edition.)

A more precise method of measuring the extent of the influence of the Aldine group on Erasmus would be to establish the number of Greek passages added to the Aldine version as compared with those included in the edition produced in Paris immediately before his Venetian residence.[68] Though the *Adages* had already undergone various reprintings,[69] only this 1507 Paris edition, done by Jean Petit and Josse Badius, was actually a revision. And in this Paris edition, which bears the title *Adagiorum Collectanea* (*Collection of Adages*), there is an increase of merely 23 adages over the original edition, with only 332 paragraphs containing Greek.[70] In the vastly enlarged Aldine edition, however, of which the new title *Chiliades Adagiorum Tres* (three thousand adages) is extremely revealing, more than four-fifths of the proverbs are now entirely new or substantially altered in form. And 2,734, or no less than 84 per cent of the total, now contain Greek passages of two to six lines or more in length, along with greatly extended Latin elaborations of previous annotations.[71]

Although in subsequent editions the total number of proverbs in the *Adages* was ultimately to exceed 4,000,[72] it is evident that the greatest increase in the size of the volume occurred in the interval

---

[68] Such a comparison has not hitherto been made.

[69] On the various editions see F. Van der Haeghen, R. Van der Berghe, and T. J. Arnold, *Bibliotheca Erasmiana, Bibliographie des oeuvres d'Erasme: Adagia* (Gand, 1897). Though the original Paris edition entitled *Adagiorum Collectanea* was far slimmer than the Aldine *Chiliades*, publishers continued to print it. The *Collectanea* went through four editions (1500, 1507, 1509, and one undated) and thirty-one reprints. The *Chiliades* was published in fifteen editions (nine during Erasmus' lifetime) and thirty-six reprints.

[70] This Petit-Badius edition (1507) is generally cited as containing 838 adages, but three adages are misnumbered (for instance, two are sometimes given the same number); hence there are actually 841. In the Aldine edition I have also noted ten misnumbered adages.

[71] This percentage is based on a careful comparison of the two editions made by my assistant Catherine Byerly, who has determined that only slightly over half (463) of the adages in the 1507 edition were incorporated into the Aldine publication. Of these 463, passages in Greek were for the first time introduced into 129 of the adages in the Aldine edition, while in 103 others the amount of Greek was increased. The number of adages without Greek passages remained relatively static — 509 adages in 1507 and 537 in 1508. The conclusion to be drawn is that the over-all increase in size of the Aldine edition is due mainly to the addition of proverbs derived from Greek sources, that is, the manuscripts given him by members of the Aldine circle. It should be noted that the work of Appelt, "Studies in the Contents and Sources of Erasmus' 'Adagia,'" hardly considers the Aldine 1508 edition or the problem of Erasmus' debt to the Aldine circle.

[72] In the last edition published by Erasmus (Basle, 1536).

between the two editions in question, that is between the 1507 Paris edition and the Aldine of 1508. Aside from the contribution of Bombasio in Bologna — which seems to have been small and which Erasmus hardly mentions [73] — it seems clear that by far the largest share of credit for this tremendous increase in content, particularly in connection with Greek authors, should be ascribed to members of the Aldine circle, especially the Byzantine scholars, who lent rare manuscripts to Erasmus and discussed with him the meaning and significance of the material therein.

Erasmus' Venetian residence would have been profitable if marked only by publication of this enriched edition of the *Adages*. But there were other ways in which he benefited from the Aldine group. We may, for example, consider the problem of the so-called "Erasmian" pronunciation of ancient Greek, current today among scholars and commonly held to be the work of Erasmus.[74] Closer scrutiny reveals that this belief has little basis in fact and that the inspiration for the theory came, at least in part, from the Aldine circle.

Actually three other Western scholars preceded Erasmus in this field, Antonio de Lebrija, of Salamanca University in Spain,[75] the

[73] Appelt, "Erasmus' 'Adagia,'" 145, shows that in the 1526 edition Erasmus mentions Bombasio only twice as suggesting proverbs, while, for example, citing "Suidas" 325 times. I was able to discover only one mention of Bombasio in the entire Aldine 1508 edition (p. 65r).

[74] See Erasmus' treatise, *De recta latini graecique sermonis pronuntiatione . . .* (Basle, 1528). On the Erasmian pronunciation see, among others, E. Drerup, *Die Schulaussprache des Griechischen von der Renaissance bis zur Gegenwart*, vol. I (Paderborn, 1930); E. Egger, *Hellénisme en France* (Paris, 1869) I, 451–70; and H. O. Pernot and L. Hesseling, "Erasme et les origines de la prononciation érasmienne," *Revue des études grecques*, XXXII (1919) 278–301.

[75] From Salamanca University, Lebrija (1442–1522) went to Italy for ten years, where he studied Greek at Bologna under Andronicos Callistos and perhaps Constantine Lascaris and Demetrios Chalcondyles (see Drerup, I, 31, and Bywater, *Erasmian Pronunciation of Greek*; but cf. Cammelli, "Andronico Callisto," who does not mention Lebrija). Later at Alcalá in Spain he worked for Cardinal Ximenes on the Complutensian Polyglot Bible (see above, Chapter 8 on Ducas). Lebrija wrote on Greek pronunciation as early as 1503 (Bywater, 20), his work later being appended to the Alcalá edition of *Introductiones Latinae*. Interestingly enough, Lebrija lists certain "errores Graecorum" of the time (Bywater, 19). On Lebrija's life, but excluding his ideas on Greek pronunciation, see also Lemus y Rubio, "El Maestro Elio Antonio de Lebrija 1441?–1552," *Revue Hispanique*, XXII (1910) 459–508, and XXIX (1917) 13–120, esp. 91, which lists under the year 1563 a work of Lebrija, inaccessible to me, entitled *De litteris Graecis* (Saragossa, 1563).

Italian Girolamo Aleandro,[76] and Aldus himself.[77] Aside from Lebrija, who was not an Aldine but who seems to have studied Greek in Italy with at least one Byzantine scholar,[78] Aleandro was evidently only following in the footsteps of his employer and associate Aldus.[79] A small tract of Aldus on this very problem, *De literis Graecis, ac dipthongis et quemadmodum ad nos veniant . . . ,*[80] was evidently in press at the time of Erasmus' arrival at the Aldine establishment and during the initial stages of publication of his *Adages*. Granted the freedom permitted the eternally inquisitive Erasmus to browse in Aldus' library — even to the point of examining his personal correspondence — Erasmus could not have failed to read a tract published for anyone to see. But this raises an even more basic question: if we accept the inspiration of Aldus and what seems the anterior but more obscure influence of Lebrija on Erasmus' ideas of proper Greek pronunciation,[81] to whom should be attributed the original suggestion for such a reform? There is reason to believe that initial responsibility should rest with the Greek refugee-scholars themselves,[82] who were the most influential agents in reviving the study of Greek in the West. With ancient Greek a quantitative,[83] and Byzantine (as well as

[76] According to Bywater, 11, Aleandro had produced a short statement on Greek pronunciation in 1512, only several years after leaving Venice.

[77] Drerup, I, 39, also mentions a Dutch contemporary of Erasmus named Ceratinus, whom Kukenheim, *Contributions à l'histoire de la grammaire*, 19, shows to have produced a study on Greek pronunciation one year after Erasmus.

[78] See above, note 75.

[79] Bywater, 12–13. Drerup, 37, states that Lebrija first attempted to systematize a new method of pronunciation and dared to criticize the Byzantine pronunciation, but says that for Aldus and Aleandro the ideas remained theoretical.

[80] Listed in Renouard, *Annales*, I, 123. Bywater, 13, says this *fragmentum* of Aldus is lost.

[81] Bywater, 21, says Lebrija owed nothing to his contemporaries. Indeed, Lebrija himself remarked that he stood alone with regard to Greek pronunciation. Cf. note 75 on the early date (1503) of his writing on this problem.

[82] Pernot and Hesseling, "La prononciation érasmienne," 299–300, and Drerup, 37, believe that the Greek exiles first suggested changes in pronunciation or at least had views in agreement with, or later adopted by, Aldus and Aleandro. Bywater, 11, observes that the protest of Aldus and Aleandro against current Greek was "without a sign of apprehension that the new view might alienate their Greek friends or be resented by them as the suggestion of barbarians." In his own treatise, Aleandro wrote that "the Greeks of our day are no more happy in their pronunciation than the Latins in theirs" (see Bywater, 11). In Bywater's view, Aleandro must have been repeating what others, especially Musurus, told him. Drerup, 62, and Knös, *Janus Lascaris*, 160, n. 2, also count Lascaris among promoters of a new pronunciation (cf. Pernot and Hesseling, 301).

[83] Byzantine scholars must have been conscious of a difference between the ancient and their own pronunciation, because of the problem of meter in poetry.

modern) Greek an accentual, language,[84] the Byzantines must have suspected even before this period — and there is evidence to support this — that there existed certain differences between their own pronunciation and that of their ancient forebears, especially with respect to metrics in poetry.[85]

In reply to the obvious question why these Byzantines never attempted to implement their own ideas, the answer is probably that it would have militated against their national pride to try to alter a pronunciation traditional for centuries. One must remember that for this sensitive, subject people recently conquered by the Turks, almost the sole vestige of ethnic identity, apart from the Orthodox faith, was the heritage of the Greek language. Consequently, any attempt to tamper with the customary pronunciation, however theoretical, would have met with immediate opposition. As for Erasmus, though he must thus be stripped of the credit for originally conceiving the idea of a reformed or, more accurately, "restored" pronunciation, to him must go the credit of systematizing the theories already suggested by others into a full program of Greek pronunciation. In other words, it was his treatise which later served as the basis for a successful propagation of the new pronunciation.[86]

Erasmus relates that after publication of the *Adages*, he was persuaded by Aldus to remain a few weeks longer in Venice. During this period he discussed problems of rhetoric with Aldus, emended certain confused verses in manuscripts of Plautus, edited texts of Terence and Seneca,[87] and with Aleandro corrected the text of Plutarch's *Moralia*, which was then in press.[88]

We may cite in this connection Demetrius Triklinius and other fourteenth century Byzantine scholars who evidently knew about quantity, since they emended ancient texts correctly, in this regard at least.

[84] Or, to use a better term, isochronal.

[85] See above, notes 82–83.

[86] See Drerup, 47 and Bywater, 7. On the reception of the Erasmian pronunciation in Western Europe, see G. Anagnostopoulos, *Greek Encyclopedia* (in Greek), XI, 499 (with bibliography) and Sandys, *History of Classical Scholarship*, II, 130. Already opposing what became the "Erasmian" pronunciation and supporting the Byzantine was Reuchlin in Germany: hence the modern Greek (Byzantine) pronunciation is today often called Reuchlinian. Reuchlin, as noted, had studied with the Byzantines Argyropoulos in Florence and Contoblachas in Basle.

[87] See Erasmus' *Apologia* (in Nichols, *Epistles*, I, 445). Also Firmin-Didot, *Alde Manuce*, 414, n. 2.

[88] See Firmin-Didot, 317. Cf. statement of Rhenanus in Mangan, *Life of Erasmus*, I, 261, also Legrand, *Bibliographie hellénique*, I, 89ff.

At the end of October or beginning of November Erasmus departed for Padua,[89] in order to accept a position as preceptor to the son of the king of Scotland.[90] But, as Nolhac has justly affirmed, "Padoue, c'est encore Venise." Hence Erasmus probably maintained close contact with the Aldine group while the press was issuing its impressive edition of the *Rhetores Graeci*.[91]

Padua at this time, in the fields of pure Aristotelian philosophy, medicine, and Hellenic studies, had no peer among the universities of western Europe. There Erasmus spent many profitable hours with the most remarkable of the Greek émigré-scholars, Marcus Musurus, then professor of Greek at the university and a "commuting" member of the Aldine Academy. For Musurus' scholarship Erasmus expressed only the highest praise, terming him "marvelously skilled in the Latin language, an accomplishment attained by scarcely any [other] Greek except Theodore Gaza and Janus Lascaris." [92] Erasmus was also favorably impressed by Musurus' character, a judgment all too rarely expressed by Westerners on the Greek refugees, who, despite the warm reception at first accorded them, found that as the Westerners began to acquire greater mastery of Greek they tended to have less and less use for their teachers.[93] Through association with Musurus, it would seem very plausible that Erasmus increased his knowledge of Greek during his Paduan stay, even by attendance at Musurus' lectures, which, as we have seen, were attracting students from all parts of Europe. As Erasmus was much later to write, as from his vantage point in the North he looked back fondly on his days at Padua: "Padua was the richest and most famous center of exchange for the best disciplines." [94]

Erasmus had come to enjoy Padua thoroughly. He was deeply vexed when it became apparent that the danger threatening Venetia as a result of the formation of the League of Cambrai would force his departure. As he wrote to his "amicissimus" Aldus, "A curse on

[89] See Allen, *Epistolae Erasmi*, I, 447; and Renaudet, *Erasme*, 87 (cf. Mangan, I, 245).
[90] On Erasmus' pupil see Mangan, I, 258.
[91] See Renouard, I, 128.
[92] See Erasmus' letter to Gaverus in Nichols, *Epistles*, I, 449.
[93] Cf. D. Geanakoplos, "A Byzantine Looks at the Renaissance: The Attitude of Michael Apostolis toward the Rise of Italy to Cultural Eminence," *Greek and Byzantine Studies* (1958) 158. Also Nichols, *Epistles*, I, 31, Erasmus on Musurus.
[94] Quoted in Nolhac, *Erasme en Italie*, 57, n. 3.

these wars which prevent our enjoying a part of Italy which pleases me more and more every day." [95]

Erasmus left Padua in December. Although he was never to return to Venice, he forgot neither Aldus' family nor the Aldine circle. Evidence of a continuing friendship between Erasmus and members of the group is provided both by the letters subsequently exchanged [96] and by the warm welcome later extended by old members of the Academy to the German humanist Ulrich von Hutten,[97] on the occasion of his visit to Venice, bearing letters of recommendation from Erasmus.

In later years, when Erasmus became involved in disputes with the Ciceronian purists such as Scaliger and Dolet, and especially Aldus' old Maecenas Alberto Pio,[98] he responded to their attacks with certain exaggerated statements minimizing the extent of his scholarly acquisitions in Venice and particularly his indebtedness to Aldus. Thus in one polemic he wrote that Aldus would be quite amused to hear that Erasmus had learned Greek and Latin from him — to which he added the categorical statement, "For myself, I am not indebted to Italy for any letters that I may have." [99] Elsewhere Erasmus expressly denied acquisition of any languages in Italy, his specious explanation for which was that in Italy he lacked the leisure to learn.[100] But it would be remarkable indeed if the beneficent influences which then made the Queen City of the Adriatic the intellectual center of all Europe did not contribute

[95] See Allen, *Epistolae Erasmi*, no. 213, 449. The War of the League of Cambrai began in April 1509 and ended in 1511.
[96] See, in Nolhac, four letters of Erasmus written in 1523 to Aldus' family. Also see Legrand, p. cxxiii.
[97] On the relations of Erasmus and Hutten, see W. Kaegi, "Hutten und Erasmus," *Historische Vierteljahrschrift*, XXII (1924-25) 200-78 and 461-504, and Nolhac, 43.
[98] On Erasmus' conflict with Scaliger, Dolet, and Pio, see the bibliography in notes 28-29 above. Also add M. Chassaigne, *Etienne Dolet* (Paris, 1930) 93ff., and O. Galtier, *Etienne Dolet* (Paris, n.d.) 137-146, and the older work of Christie, *Etienne Dolet*, 203-11, 224.
[99] See *Apologia* (in Nichols, *Epistles*, I, 446-447). Rhenanus says that Erasmus brought to Italy more dignified erudition than most take from it (Mangan, I, 259), but of course Rhenanus was a partisan and pupil of Erasmus.
[100] Nichols, *Epistles*, I, 448; and see Mangan, I, 259, for Erasmus' argument to Pio: "Where was the leisure for learning Greek and Latin? We were so busy that we had hardly time, as they say, to scratch our ears." But we may here recall Aldus' answer to Erasmus' query as to why he took such pains: "studeo." See above, text and note 52.

considerably to the formation of Erasmus' intellectual constitution. In the light of our evidence, his remarks may be dismissed as the exaggerated protests of a hypersensitive person who felt that his ability as a self-made scholar must, at all costs, be defended.

In summary, to substantiate the view that Erasmus' classical education was broadened during his nine months in Venice and Padua, one need only point to the milieu in which he then moved. Here for the first time he had the opportunity to enjoy the intimacy of a large group of accomplished Greeks who, despite the increasingly able scholarship of the Italians, were by many still considered the final authority for Greek in the West; he could participate in the learned discussions of the exclusive Aldine Academy; he had access to the valuable libraries of Aldus and his associates, containing a wealth of Greek manuscripts, many yet unprinted and hence unknown to large sections of the West; and he had undoubtedly heard Aldus, and perhaps Aleandro, energetically though amicably criticizing the Greek pronunciation of their Byzantine confrères. More concretely, through his exploitation of the contribution of his Hellenist friends in the Aldine publication of his *Adages*, and the wide circulation of this work throughout Europe, Erasmus was enabled to achieve recognition as the foremost scholar of the western world.[101]

When one considers that Erasmus on his return to the North took with him the knowledge he had acquired in Venice (it was not long afterwards that he assumed the chair of Greek at Cambridge University in England), the implications for the diffusion of Greek learning become immediately apparent. Erasmus is quite properly regarded as a major link between southern and northern phases of the Renaissance. One avenue at least of transmission becomes clearer after re-examination of his activities in Venice, for it was his associations with the Aldine community of scholars that enabled Erasmus to perfect his knowledge of Greek. And it was this Venetian episode involving the man who was soon to become the most influential humanist of the age that brought to a climax the process of conveying Greek letters to the West.

[101] See Renaudet, 83 and Tilley, *Dawn of the French Renaissance*, 287.

CONCLUSION
The Contribution of the Greek Scholars

> There are special reasons and the most cogent of motives
> which impel the Venetians to undertake and constantly
> to strive to bring to a happy conclusion the revival of
> Greek letters. You have been provided most liberally with
> the means of bringing to fruition this very noble under-
> taking: you have living among you Greeks as your
> neighbors, you have under your hegemony not a few of
> the Greek cities and islands, and you suffer from no
> lack of as many teachers and books as are needed for this
> task . . .
>
>   — Pietro Bembo, from a speech delivered
>   to the Venetian Senate probably in 1531.

> How deeply it grieves me to see our (Greek) people
> suffering everywhere publicly and privately, esteemed
> lightly, hated, persecuted, abused . . . Learn to bear the
> jealously flourishing everywhere . . . especially against
> foreigners, the more so if they are learned men.
>
>   — Cardinal Bessarion, letter to
>   Michael Apostolis, ca. 1455.[1]

From 1397, when the Byzantine Manuel Chrysoloras delivered
his opening lecture at the *studium* of Florence, to 1534 and the
death in Rome of the last major Greek scholar-exile, Janus Lascaris,[2] western Europe advanced in its knowledge of Greek from
virtual ignorance of the language to the recovery and mastery of
almost the entire corpus of Greek literature in the original. In the

---

[1] Quoted in Ferrai, *L'Ellenismo di Padova*, 9; also see J. Morelli, "Intorno ad
un orazione greca inedita del Cardinale Pietro Bembo alla Signoria di Venezia,"
Memorie dell' R. Istituto del regno Lombardo-Veneto, II (Milan, 1821) 251–62.
Also L. Mohler, *Aus Bessarions Gelehrtenkreis* (Paderborn, 1952) 481.

[2] The traditional date of Lascaris' death is 1535 (Knös, *Janus Lascaris*, 214), but
Mercati, in *Opere minori*, III (1910) 185, on the basis of Ms. Vat. gr. 2240, fol.
49r, has now placed it as December 7, 1534.

fourteenth century Greek had been known only to a few individuals or in isolated areas, southern Italy in particular; by 1534
it had been communicated to every important cultural area of the
West.

But before this process of diffusion could be accomplished, the
many Greek works unknown to medieval western Europe (apart,
that is, from the culturally separate area of southern Italy) — a
large part of the extant ancient literature, including poetry,
history, oratory, and some of Plato, not a few of the patristic
works, and most of the Byzantine writings and commentaries —
had to be introduced from that repository of Hellenic learning, the
Greek East. These writings were brought to the attention of the
West both by Western scholars who traveled to the East, as did
certain of Chrysoloras' pupils and others like Barbaro, Filelfo, and
Aurispa,[3] and, more importantly — as this book has emphasized
— through the mediation of men of letters from the East, who,
before or for some years after 1453, emigrated westward in increasing numbers in order to escape the Turkish domination of their
homelands. These Greek fugitives brought with them not only
whatever manuscripts they were able to carry on their persons but,
much more significantly, as is not fully appreciated by many
Western-oriented historians of the Renaissance, the intellectual
tradition of Byzantium by which their education and general outlook had been to a considerable extent molded. And it was through
their work in the West as teachers, scribes, and editors for the press
that the diffusion of the Greek language and literature was able to
proceed so rapidly in so brief a period.

Opportunistic as perforce they had to be, these Eastern exiles
were naturally attracted to the leading Italian humanist centers of
the time. First they gravitated to Florence, whose period of leadership in Greek studies extended over the greater part of a century,
from Manuel Chrysoloras' appearance in 1396–97 to the collapse
of the Medici regime following upon the French invasion of 1494.
Other Greeks appeared for a time in Rome during the mid-fifteenth

---

[3] Guarino, Filelfo, Aurispa, and Giovanni Tortelli, the first librarian of the
Vatican (who was at Constantinople from 1435 to 1437), actually studied in the
East. Fuchs, *Die höheren Schulen*, 68–69, gives a long list, but several of the names
he cites are certainly wrong. R. Sabbadini, *Le scoperte*, is a much better authority.
See above Chapter 1. South Italian monasteries had a good deal of Greek literature.

century, under the patronage of Pope Nicholas V and his humanist cardinal, the Byzantine Bessarion. Forced by political conditions at the close of the fifteenth century to leave Florence, many of the learned exiles moved northward to Venice, safely isolated for a time at least from the wars and dislocations of the Italian peninsula. There they remained until the decline of Venetian literary primacy following the Venetian defeat at Cambrai (1509) and the death in 1515 of the famous Venetian printer Aldus Manutius. The promise of another Medici golden age under the patronage of Popes Leo X and Clement VII attracted the exiles finally to Rome, the ascendancy of which was in turn brought to a close by the sack of the papal capital in 1527. This pattern of movement from one center to another is clearly apparent in the careers of most of the Greek scholar-exiles discussed in this book — Marcus Musurus, Arsenios Apostolis, Demetrius Ducas, and Zacharias Calliergis. Of this group Musurus and Arsenios, as we have seen, resided for a time in Florence, mainly during the period of their youth and when Florence was already experiencing a loss of prestige. With the subsequent decline of Florence they, along with Calliergis and Ducas (after his return from Spain), moved on to Rome, now rapidly displacing Venice in humanist endeavors. But the careers of the exiles we have treated were most closely associated with the Venetian period of pre-eminence. And it is their activities in Venice and in the areas affected by the influences emanating from that city or its colonies that have constituted the principal focus of this work.

Though the activities of these Greek exiles in the Republic of St. Mark seem almost exactly to coincide with the Venetian period of intellectual supremacy, to say that they alone were responsible for the Venetian advances in Greek scholarship would be to discount other important factors — the contribution of the Latin Hellenists of Venice and, more fundamental, the historical background of the city itself, which seemed to lend itself naturally to the development of an interest in Greek. Actually the Venetian flowering of Greek studies in the early sixteenth century marks the culmination of a tradition of close Venetian involvement with the Greek East that reaches back even earlier than the ninth century. We have shown in an early chapter why for a long period the relations of the two peoples led to little genuine Venetian appreciation of the classical Greek works as literature. But once Venice had become imbued with the rising humanist ideals emanating from Padua and to a lesser extent Florence, she could take advantage of her traditional orientation to the East and make remarkable progress in the cultivation of Greek letters.

With the fall of Constantinople in 1453, the colonial possessions of Venice in the East, acquired as a result of the fourth crusade of 1204, assumed a greater importance in the cultural sphere. For they became a refuge for fugitives coming from all areas of the old Byzantine world. The island of Crete in particular now became what it was never to be again, a prime European center of intellectual activity, especially for the copying and distribution of manuscripts. Prominent in this occupation were two men whose careers have been dealt with in considerable detail, the Byzantine refugee Michael Apostolis and his Cretan-born son Arsenios. Both established schools for scribes on the island in which a surprisingly large number of future copyists, editors, and correctors for the Venetian press were trained, including Laonikos the Cretan, Musurus, John Gregoropoulos, Emmanuel Adramyttenos, and John Rhosos. Indeed, in some respects this Cretan milieu offers a direct anticipation of certain aspects of the work of the Aldine circle. But despite the importance of this Cretan activity, which permitted the island to act as a kind of halfway point for the transmission of Greek letters from Byzantium to Italy, little attention has hitherto been directed by historians to this phase of Cretan history.

The conditions obtaining on the overcrowded island soon began to breed frustration among all groups, not least among the scholars, and a desire spread to emigrate elsewhere. From Crete and the other Venetian colonies a stream of refugees, or in some cases voluntary exiles, now flowed into Venice, the principal port of entry to the West. And by the turn of the century the largest concentration of Greeks in western Europe was to be found in that city. It would be a mistake to think that this Greek community of Venice consisted only of intellectuals; actually it embraced a wide stratum of society, from merchants and intellectuals to soldiers (*estradioti*), shipowners, and laborers. In order to provide a background for this book we have traced the growth of this colony from its early beginnings to its recognition as a corporate body

CONCLUSION

within the Venetian state, and, ultimately, to its assertion in the
sixteenth century of complete independence of the ecclesiastical
authorities of Venice. In the cultural sphere the Venetians were
able to draw considerable profit from the interaction of their
Greek community and colonies with the home city: through increasingly close contact with the Greek language and manner of
life the Venetians gradually developed a predisposition for Greek
studies. And the wealth of manuscripts brought by the exiles or
otherwise procured from the East through their agency — some
such codices being then still unknown to the West — contributed
to make the city one of the principal custodians of Greek manuscripts in this period of the Renaissance. Moreover, as the wealthy
Venetian aristocracy developed its taste for Greek studies, it drew
on the Greeks as teachers, and we find schools established in the
city not only for the practical purpose of training Venetian colonial
officials but to instruct students in the Greek literature and Aristotelian philosophy. Indeed, the Greek chair at the nearby university
of Venetian-controlled Padua, during its occupancy by the Cretan
scholar Marcus Musurus, became the most famous in all Europe,
with students from Italy, France, Germany, the Lowlands, Spain,
and Hungary flocking to hear his lectures.

But it was the economic prosperity of Venice in conjunction
with the advantages provided by her Greek connections that led to
the development of Venice's famous Greek press. Already the
leading international entrepôt for the commerce between East and
West, Venice by the end of the fifteenth century had become the
chief European center for the manuscript and book trade. With
easy access to her Eastern colonies, with the papermaking facilities
of Padua at her disposal,[4] and with a citizenry not only wealthy
but increasingly eager to support humanistic endeavors, Venice
was now in a position to vie with her predecessors in the field of
Greek publication, Milan and Florence.

The invention of printing in movable type had taken place at
almost the moment of Constantinople's fall, thus providing a convenient means of preserving and even multiplying the manuscripts
of the ancient Greek masterpieces, many of which were threatened

[4] Brown, *Venetian Printing Press*, 24. Aldus secured the paper for his book
manufacture from the small town of Fabriano, in the province of Ancona.

by destruction as a result of the Turkish conquest. Of the many scores of presses established in Venice in the late fifteenth and early sixteenth centuries, the most celebrated is certainly that of Aldus Manutius, and it is in his widely distributed productions that we find the instrument for the broadest transmission of Greek.

There can, of course, be no question of Aldus' extraordinary inspiration in inaugurating and directing the activities of his famous publishing house. He was not only a competent printer [5] but an outstanding editor and humanist scholar as well. But it is not generally realized that in the publication of Greek works in Venice Aldus was anticipated by certain little-known Greek émigrés, the Cretans Láonikos and Alexander, and possibly by Zacharias Calliergis and Nicholas Vlastos (themselves preceded by the Italian Peregrino of Bologna). Moreover, a major portion of the vital and difficult work of typesetting and editing at Aldus' press was done by the Greek exiles. His principal editor was the Cretan Marcus Musurus, while his compositors were likewise in large part Cretans (chief among whom was John Gregoropoulos), because of the difficulty of finding persons competent to read the Greek script from which the printing was done. Of some thirty Greek first editions produced by Aldus,[6] Musurus alone was responsible, presumably, for editing no less than eleven or twelve of the more difficult and important authors. Other Greeks such as Arsenios Apostolis supervised at least one volume, and several were edited by Ducas, whose *Rhetores Graeci*, in the view of the authoritative Renouard, may be considered the most valuable of all Aldine editions.

We certainly cannot overlook the fact that Aldus took a keen interest in all the productions of his press, himself editing or collaborating with others, including Italian scholars, in the editing of a number of Greek authors. Nor should we forget that Aldus offered a means of employment — an outlet as it were — for the talents of the Greek émigrés. Had it not been for the prestige of

[5] Some authorities have criticized from a technical point of view his talent or lack of talent as a craftsman of printing. For instance, his adoption of the new cursive hand for his Greek type has been much criticized in favor of the handsome type used in the Alcalá New Testament. See above, especially Chapter 5, note 87; also Chapter 8, note 76; and Chapter 7, note 13.

[6] Out of a total of 127 authenticated editions of all kinds (E. Robertson, "Aldus Manutius, the Scholar-Printer," 72; also C. Bühler, "Aldus Manutius," 211).

the Aldine press, even the valuable editions of Musurus would unquestionably have been less widely known. On the other hand, to take nothing from Aldus, it is doubtful whether without the reservoir of talent provided by his Byzantine associates and workmen, with their mastery of the language and technical skill, he could have offered to the public, in the relatively short period of less than two decades, as much as he did of the corpus of classical Greek authors. To quote Aldus' own words: "Musurus' constant aid in the correction of texts is so precious to me that, had Greece produced two more of his merit as councillors of mine, I would not despair of giving before long to people of taste, in very correct editions, the best works of both literatures [Greek and Latin]." [7] By the time of Aldus' death in 1515 his press had given to the world practically all the major Greek authors of classical antiquity. [8]

But the press of Aldus was not a mere publishing house in the narrow sense. With the Greek exiles as a kind of nucleus, Aldus was able to gather around him a group of Western and Greek Hellenists and to establish an Academy (*Neakademia*) where, as we have seen, it was prescribed that the Greek language alone could be spoken. There the problems involved in the projected publications of his press were discussed and analyzed, there Hellenists of both East and West in friendly camaraderie could exchange manuscripts and ideas, while not infrequently visitors could benefit from the association, to return later to their homelands enriched by their experience. The contribution of Aldus' Academy is more difficult to assess precisely than is that of his press. But there can be little doubt that this select intellectual circle, composed of eminent Western as well as Greek Hellenists, was during the period of its existence the chief focus for the development of Greek studies not only in Venice but in the entire western world.

Let us look more closely at this period of Venetian primacy in order to distinguish the specific advances made by Venetian scholarship and in particular the nature of the contribution of the Greek exiles. Toward the close of the fifteenth century, Western Europe, despite or perhaps because of the significant advances previously made in Greek studies in Florence and other Renaissance centers,

[7] Cf. above, Chapter 5, note 135.
[8] One important omission was Polybius.

began acutely to feel the lack of Greco-Latin grammars, lexica, and especially readable editions of the Greek classics. It was no accident that the first wholly Greek book to appear in the West was a grammar, the *Erotemata* ("Questions") [9] of Constantine Lascaris, published in Milan in 1476 and followed in 1493 by a grammar of the same title written by the fourteenth century Byzantine Manuel Moschopoulos. But, printed as these were entirely in Greek and without Latin translation, their usefulness was somewhat limited. It was in Venice, with her capabilities for Greek printing and scholarship, that the greatest advances were made in providing the tools for instruction in Greek.

There Aldus, following the appearance in 1484 of the first Venetian Greek book, the grammar of Chrysoloras, produced in rapid succession a series of technical manuals: in 1495 Lascaris' *Erotemata*, with Latin translation, and Gaza's grammar, followed the next year by the collaborative *Thesaurus Cornucopiae et Horti Adonidis*, an important collection in Greek of Greek and Byzantine grammatical treatises, some then unknown. Continuing along these lines, Aldus in 1497 published Urbano Bolzanio's grammar, the first to be written in Latin, and, following this, in the same year, the *Lexicon* of Crastoni (probably edited by Musurus), which when published earlier was the first Greco-Latin dictionary printed in the West. Aldus' enthusiasm for the printing of grammars and lexica, so important in his mind for the diffusion of Greek letters, culminated in the publication of a grammar of his own, which was edited after his death by his friend Musurus.[10] It is a fact worthy of repetition that the grammars most often published in the first half century after the beginnings of Greek printing were not those of the ancients but of Byzantines of the Palaeologan or post-Palaeologan era — of the fourteenth century Moschopoulos and of the Greek émigrés themselves: Chrysoloras, Constantine Lascaris, Chalcondyles, and Gaza. The composition and publication of these grammars on the part of the exiles adds credence to the view that

[9] This was a favorite title for a whole series of Byzantine grammars; works of this name were cast in the form of questions and answers (a kind of grammatical catechism).

[10] See Kukenheim, *Contributions à l'histoire de la grammaire*, 7ff. Also Chapter 5, note 153.

in many ways they were but carrying on in another environment the intellectual tradition of their homeland.[11]

Aldus' interest in the publication of aids for Greek instruction is further indicated by his issuing of a number of texts with corresponding Latin translation, the Musaeus, for instance, edited by Musurus, and Aesop's *Fables*. But it was of course, in his famous series of first editions of the classical authors that Aldus made his chief contribution to scholarship. We have already noted how much he was indebted to his Greek collaborators, especially Musurus, about whose work a word is here in order.

Of the many editions for which Musurus was primarily responsible (it is only in the nineteenth and twentieth centuries that philological methods have permitted more conclusive identification of Musurus' editorial contributions), five are works of poetry (Musaeus, Aristophanes, Sophocles, Euripides, and perhaps Pindar); two are philosophic, the writings of Plato and of Alexander of Aphrodisias on Aristotle; two, the Hesychius and Athenaeus, belong to the category of lexica or literary prose. Still another work comprises the orations of the Byzantine church father Gregory of Nazianzus. There is also an epistolographic collection of ancient and early medieval authors and the edition done later in Rome of Oppian's *Halieutica*. Gifted as he was in the various fields of Greek literature, Musurus' true genius, however, lay in his grasp of the art of Greek poetry. More even than his teacher the eminent Janus Lascaris, he had a keen sensitivity for the style and meters of the ancient poets; and he understood the difficult art of versification with its problems of meter and quantity as did no other person of the age. The editions he produced of the ancient tragedies, comedies, and lyric poets, despite the failings that can be noted by modern philologists with respect to some of his textual changes, are

[11] Cf. Krumbacher, *Byzantinischen Litteratur*, 501, who had realized the continuity of the Byzantine tradition in Italy on the part of the Greek exiles. As he writes: "Wer künftig eine Geschichte des Humanismus schreiben will, muss auf Moschopulos, Planudes, ja bis auf Eustathios, Psellos, Arethas, und Photius zurückgehen. Dass sich die Sache geschichtlich so verhält, geht schon aus der einfachen Beobachtung hervor, dass gerade die Werke, durch welche ein Theodoros Gazes, ein Konstantin Laskaris, ein Manuel Chrysoloras das Studium der griechischen Sprache am meisten beförderten aus älteren byzantinischen Vorlagen, aus Arbeiten des Theodosios, Moschopulos u.a. abgeleitet sind."

probably the best examples of Renaissance Greek textual criticism, surpassing in insight and technical skill the similar work of any of his contemporaries. A main contribution, in fact, of later Greek Renaissance scholarship (not of the *quattrocento* as a whole but of the late fifteenth and the early sixteenth century) is the editing of Greek poetry, which had hitherto not been attempted, certainly not by Western scholars. And here, of course, Musurus' name is in the foreground.

Despite Musurus' undeniable talent, it must be noted, however, that he too, like all of the exiles, was in many respects but following in the footsteps of his Byzantine predecessors of the Palaeologan era, who, as we have seen, had, as early as the later thirteenth century, instituted a revival of classical criticism and of the editing of the old texts. Thus the greatest philologist of the nineteenth and early twentieth centuries, the German classicist U. von Wilamowitz-Moellendorff, could refer justifiably to Musurus as a continuator of Moschopoulos.[12] Nonetheless, despite his debt to his Byzantine forebears, Musurus possessed considerable originality and insight of his own, as may clearly be observed from some of his textual corrections which seem to be based on no known manuscript evidence, the felicitousness of which readings must therefore be attributed to his own remarkable powers of critical divination.

But Musurus' work as editor, as we have noted, was only part of his contribution to Venetian intellectual life. For in his instruction at Padua and later at Venice he attracted pupils from practically every country of the West — ambassadors, men of state, aspiring or established scholars, other refugees. Though it would be difficult to assess the precise influence of his teaching unless one could examine the intellectual development of each of his many students, the vast popularity of his courses and the high regard in which he was held by the Venetian government, the papacy, and many contemporary Hellenists, including the discerning Erasmus, attest to an influence paralleled only by that of Chrysoloras in Florence and Guarino at Ferrara. Neither Chrysoloras nor Guarino, of course,

---

[12] See U. von Wilamowitz-Moellendorff, *Einleitung in die attische Tragödie* (= *Euripides Herakles erklärt*, von U. von W.-M., Band I, Berlin, 1889) 194, and cf. 220f. for another extremely complimentary passage on Musurus' talent in textual criticism. These passages also refer to other fourteenth and sixteenth century Greeks.

had any connection with the press, and therefore, when one considers Musurus' double editorial and pedagogical career, one is tempted to term him the greatest Hellenist of the entire Renaissance period.

Though none of the other Greek exiles could match Musurus in the number of editions they produced, their work was often of first importance. Ducas' edition of the *Rhetores Graeci*, referred to above, contained many valuable treatises, among them Aristotle's *Rhetoric* and the first edition of Hermogenes, both of which played a major part in the development of Renaissance rhetoric. And Ducas' *editio princeps* of Plutarch's *Moralia* rendered that work easily accessible in the original to those humanists becoming increasingly concerned with the theory and practice of education, so important for the development of the Renaissance intellect.

It has more than once been emphasized here that the Aldine was not the only press to issue Greek books in Venice. Of an even higher quality of printing and sometimes of textual criticism were the productions of the Cretan Zacharias Calliergis. Independently of Aldus and possibly even before him, Calliergis had conceived the plan of founding in Venice a press to publish all the Greek works of antiquity. In view of the often expressed desire of the exiles of the diaspora to preserve the treasures of the Greek legacy not only for the western world but especially for the benefit of future generations of their countrymen [13] (this deep ethnic pride as a basic dynamic in the activities of so many of the Greek exiles is a point that bears repetition), the intention of Calliergis to print Greek works alone seems only natural. Calliergis' press, which was owned and operated exclusively by Greeks, produced as its first work the most important of the medieval Greek dictionaries, the *Etymologicum Magnum* (pages of which resemble the rich leaves of a Byzantine manuscript) and subsequently the *editiones principes* of the commentary of Simplicius on the *Categories* of Aristotle and of Ammonius Hermeiae on the *Five Voices* of Porphyry.[14] Both editions were to prove of significance for the humanistic in-

[13] This wish of the Greek exiles to preserve their national legacy for their downtrodden people is frequently overlooked by historians in discussing their activities in the West in connection with the development of Greek learning. See above, Chapter 4, text to note 33, for the eloquent speech of Bessarion on salvaging the Greek works for future generations of Greeks.

[14] Calliergis also printed the *Therapeutics* of Galen. See above, Chapter 7, note 29.

terpretation of Aristotle which in this period — and in large part under the influence of the Greeks — had begun to develop independently of the medieval scholastic tradition.

Another Cretan, Arsenios Apostolis, early in his career edited one of the very first Aldine works, the *Galeomyomachia*. After his return, however, from his see of Monemvasia, in Greece, his principal contribution to the cultural life of Venice consisted of important editions for the Giuntine and da Sabio presses — various works of Psellus, an edition of Byzantine poetry, Alcinous' precious philosophic summary of and introduction to Plato, and Arsenios' celebrated scholia on Euripides.

Arsenios' father, Michael Apostolis, never resided for any length of time in Venice but spent most of his life on Crete. From that vantage point in the decades following the fall of Constantinople he scoured the East for manuscripts, which he transcribed and sent on to his patron Bessarion in Rome. Many of these were later to be incorporated into the great collection of manuscripts Bessarion bequeathed to the Venetian government. Codices from this library served as the basis for not a few editions produced by Aldus and other Venetian printers. Michael, as we have mentioned, established some kind of school in Crete, and among his pupils was one of the teachers of Pico della Mirandola and of Aldus himself, Emmanuel Adramyttenus, who, along with Apostolis, seems to have had some as yet undefined connections with the pioneer Cretan printers of Venice. It is to be noted, however, that Michael's method of transcribing manuscripts, however useful for their ultimate preservation, was from the standpoint of modern philology inferior. For his aim, like that of his fellow Cretan scribes, was primarily to provide a complete text of a given author for the amateur patron of the moment, scholarly faithfulness in the process of copying being of only secondary importance. Nor can it be said in general that the Greeks of Venice followed strict standards of philological scholarship in their work of editing for the press. Such canons were not to be formulated until the nineteenth century. Yet it cannot be denied that the editions produced by Musurus and his Greek colleagues at Venice were correct within the limits of Renaissance scholarship, and remained, in many cases, for almost three centuries the vulgate versions accepted in Europe. Even today many of the texts they established are still considered very significant factors in the history of the modern transmission of these texts.

But was this role of the Greek exiles in Venice limited only to the technical one of teacher, grammarian, or editor — in other words to that of purveyor of knowledge? In the case of Musurus the question must be answered in the negative, when we consider the merits of his long poem to Plato prefixed to his edition of that author. Within the difficult metrical and prosodical pattern of the ancients, Musurus expresses true poetic feeling — a moving appeal to the spirit of Plato so to inspire the Pope that he will launch a crusade in behalf of his enslaved Greek compatriots. But Musurus' ability to compose with effect in the larger Greek poetic forms was exceptional among the Greeks. Apart perhaps from some of the well-turned epigrams that all the humanists were in the habit of writing, the exiles seem as a whole rarely to have attempted original composition. This was probably in part because what poetic feeling they possessed they sought to express in the artificial classic language, not in the living demotic Greek. And this attempt to imitate the antique style did not permit the full exercise of imagination. In this respect they were typical of the later phase of Byzantine literature (and not unlike the Western Ciceronians of the Renaissance), which, aside from the Platonic revival at Mistra, was essentially a rhetorical movement, very learned but hampered in the expression of originality by overly strict adherence to the imitation of the antique forms.

And yet one may ask how many of the later Italian humanists reveal genuinely creative literary imagination. Very few, probably, except for the poets Poliziano, Pontano, and Sannazaro.[14a] Even the vaunted Erasmus' main talents lay in the direction of critical scholarship — in the editing and translating of classical authors, the amassing of proverbs from recondite sources, and the utilization of these in the editions he prepared for popular consumption — rather than in true artistic or poetic expression.[15] Moreover, one must not

[14a] This is not, of course, to say that others in other fields, for example, Ficino in philosophy and Poggio and Bruni in history, did not exhibit a certain imagination.

[15] Weiss, "Learning and Education in Western Europe," I, 114, thinks that the works of the Greek poets Homer, Sophocles, and Aeschylus were too difficult for Erasmus: hence his partiality (as he said) for Euripides or Lucian!

forget that the Greek exiles, unlike not a few of their Latin contemporaries, rarely had the leisure to indulge whatever creative impulses they might have possessed. As displaced persons they were preoccupied with eking out a living as best they could. Constantly busy at the press, teaching, or copying manuscripts, they had to carry out whatever demands were made upon their time by their patrons of the moment.[16]

It would appear, however, that in one important respect at least the Greeks did, if almost inadvertently, contribute something more than merely the mechanical to Western humanism. In accordance with the Byzantine rhetorical tradition (the orations of the fourteenth century Thomas Magister are a good example), they emphasized the reading, memorization, and imitation of the style of the original texts,[17] and through this procedure something of the content of these works could not but have been absorbed by their Western students. This would be especially true of the philosophic and educational writings of such authors as Aristotle, Plato, and to a lesser degree Plutarch, a translation of which, however careful, would almost invariably lose some of the nuances of thought or expression of the original. As a result of this method, then, which produced a growing familiarity with the original texts of Greek works containing some of the noblest concepts of classical antiquity, the intellectual horizon of the western world during the *quattrocento* and *cinquecento* could not help being expanded. And this, in fact, to a degree that it had not been since the reception of Aristotle's scientific works from the Arabs several centuries before.[18]

Having examined the contribution of the Greek exiles, in par-

[16] The Greek exile Marullus wrote some very good Latin poetry in Florence, as did Rhalles. Janus Lascaris wrote some Latin epigrams. Cf. above, Chapter 5, note 12, and Knös, *Janus Lascaris*, 168–69. The verses by Ducas translated above are of course not important.

[17] Cf. W. Woodward, *Studies in Education during the Age of the Renaissance* (Cambridge, Eng., 1924) 18, who says that at the schools of Guarino and Vittorino the study of Greek was mainly for its content. Among the Byzantines, the fourteenth century Thomas Magister wrote orations deliberately imitating the form and style of the ancients: see F. Lenz, "On the Authorship of the Leptinean Declamations Attributed to Aristides," *American Jl. of Philology*, LXIII (1942) 154ff., esp. 167.

[18] Of course the contribution of the Greek exiles of Venice was only part of the broad movement for the restoration of Greek letters, which began at least as early as the fourteenth century. This point bears repetition.

ticular with regard to Venice, let us attempt to evaluate the role of that center in transmitting Greek letters to the West. Chronologically the Venetian period of leadership in Greek studies lasted approximately twenty-five years, that of Florence an entire century. Yet within her relatively brief span of time, Venice, in this particular respect, the diffusion of Greek, seems proportionally to have made the greater strides. We have, it is true, not attempted in a rigidly systematic manner to delineate the role of Venice in spreading Greek letters. But on the basis of the variegated experiences of the six representative figures treated in this book, we may derive a reasonably adequate impression of the Venetian part in this process. For in the careers of these figures may be clearly observed the various methods or channels of diffusion of Greek as well as the distant areas to which a knowledge of the language was carried. In their very movement from Venice to other areas the exiles were themselves responsible for a good deal of dissemination of Greek. Ducas, for example, after being summoned by Cardinal Ximenes to Spain and appointed the first professor of Greek at the newly founded University of Alcalá, spent much of his time surpervising the editing of the Greek New Testament of Cardinal Ximenes' celebrated Polyglot Bible. And through his teaching as well as his other publications (it was at his own expense that the first Greek books were printed in Spain), he provided no little impetus to the development of Greek studies in that country. Calliergis, after many years of residence in Venice, introduced the art of Greek printing to Rome, where under the patronage of members of Leo X's court he edited as well as printed some significant first editions, notably the scholia on Pindar and several Byzantine religious works. Arsenios Apostolis too, the exigencies of whose ecclasiastical career made him a frequent commuter between East and West, worked in the later portion of his career in Rome and in Florence, tirelessly copying, printing, or editing texts of both ancient and Byzantine writers. And the great Musurus, whose career, as we have seen, was passed almost entirely in Venice, spent the last year of his life at Rome, teaching and editing while moving in the circle of Pope Leo X as one of its chief ornaments.

The influence of the Venetian-based émigrés is also apparent in the activities of their many students, who came from various far-flung areas of Europe. Such persons as Girolamo Aleandro, after a period of tutelage under Musurus at Padua and the closest of associations with the Aldine group (it will be recalled that he lived in Aldus' own house), left Venice to go directly to Paris, where he instituted the first public lectures in Greek. And John Conon, after pursuing the course of study at Padua under Musurus, returned to Germany to become what one scholar has called the "true founder" of Greek studies in that country.[19] We might briefly mention also, among others who studied in Venice, Germain de Brie of France, Janus Vertessy of Hungary, the young Gelenius of Prague (who later settled in Basle, where he produced some Greek editions), and again the cosmopolite Erasmus of Rotterdam, who, soon after leaving Venice, accepted an appointment as professor of Greek at Cambridge University.

In the Venetian sojourn of this most influential of all Western humanists we see what is probably the prime example of a Latin Hellenist who was able not only to assimilate but in his unique manner to exploit the Greek learning of the Aldine circle and to transmit it to the West on a wider and more popular level. Erasmus, as we have noted, acquired from the Eastern exiles not only manuscripts — we have tried to give some idea of which of these were as yet unknown to the West — but, hardly less important, advice in the interpretation of difficult Greek passages as well as ideas that would later assist him in the formulation of his program for the reform of Greek pronunciation. In the career of Erasmus, who is generally regarded as the chief link between the northern and southern phases of the Renaissance, we may see the culmination of the process of disseminating Greek learning from Venice to northern Europe.

But there were still other methods of transmitting Greek learning. Venice, as the center of the book trade, attracted many foreign book agents and buyers, eager to purchase not only Aldine and other publications but, no less important for the development of Greek studies in their homelands, Greek manuscripts. Thus it was in Venice that Vittorino da Feltre procured numerous old codices for his library, while Venetian nobles like Barbaro and Lipo-

---

[19] The honor of founding Greek studies in Germany is often awarded to John Reuchlin and Rudolph Agricola.

manno were able to secure theirs in Venetian-dominated Crete.
Giorgio Valla, who taught Greek in Venice in the last years of the
fifteenth century, amassed a remarkable collection of manuscripts
there,[20] no few of which were used by Aldus in producing his
famous Greek editions. Aldus himself had a rich library, which we
know was accumulated in considerable part in Venice. Musurus,
too, as we have seen, owned a number of valuable manuscripts, and
Pietro Bembo formed his library while he was in retirement in
Padua. Even after Venetian intellectual primacy had declined,
Venice continued to be an important mart for the purchase and
exchange of Greek codices. From there in the mid-sixteenth century the wealthy Spanish diplomat Don Diego Hurtado de Mendoza
sent the Corfiote Nicholas Sophianos to Greece and Mount Athos,
and he returned with no less than 300 Greek manuscripts.[21] Guilel-
mus Pélicier, then the French ambassador to the Serenissima (1539–
1542), bought many valuable manuscripts in that city,[22] and Jean
de Pins, another French envoy, also gathered works there. Moreover, Cardinals Domenico and Marino Grimani (pupils of Musurus) in the early sixteenth century left a library in Venice containing hundreds of volumes of Greek and Latin authors.[23] All of
these activities helped in one way or another to further the diffusion
of Greek learning.

Since during the Renaissance a knowledge of Greek was not so
widespread as one might expect — after all, not even all the humanists could read the language — the diffusion of Greek literature
depended no less on Latin translations than on editions of the
original Greek texts.[24] The Greek exiles, of course, for obvious
reasons (including in most cases an insufficient knowledge of

[20] These are the manuscripts that were later purchased by Alberto Pio and are
today housed in Modena.
[21] See above, Chapter 8, note 120. Of course the value of all these manuscripts
must have been very uneven.
[22] On Pélicier see the preface to L. Cohn, *Verzeichniss der von der königlichen
Bibliothek zu Berlin erworbenen Meermanhandschriften des Sir Thomas Phillipps* (Berlin, 1892) p. i, which lists the many manuscripts he collected ("quorum
codicum maior pars iussu Pelecerii ipsius vel ab hominibus Graecis vel ab Italis
doctis, quos per tempus illud quo Venetiis morabatur mercede conductos habebat,
Venetiis exarata est").
[23] See Mercati, *Pio*, 14ff. Also P. Paschini, *Domenico Grimani* (Rome, 1943) 141.
[24] See Bolgar, *Classical Heritage*, 277f., and especially Kristeller, *Classics*, 16.
Also Lockwood, "Aristophanes in the 15th Century," *Transactions and Proceedings of the American Philological Association*, XL (1909) p. lvi.

Latin) preferred to edit Greek texts for the press. The medieval world, to be sure, had produced a surprisingly large number of translations from the Greek, especially of the Aristotelian philosophic and scientific works. But these were done in a crabbed, overly literal style that did not make for readability and hence for any degree of popularity except within select groups. The humanists, on the other hand, as a result of training from the Greek exiles, had acquired a superior knowledge of Greek syntax and idiom and some awareness of textual variants, together with a greater freedom in word order, style, and terminology. And as a consequence they were now able to produce works that were attractive to a much wider audience.[25] The first substantial humanist translations from the Greek had been made in Florence in the early fifteenth century by Chrysoloras' student Leonardo Bruni and very soon thereafter in Rome by the circle of Bessarion and Pope Nicholas V, where George of Trebizond, Theodore Gaza, and Bessarion himself joined Western humanists in converting Greek texts into Latin.

The Greeks of Venice, however, had little to do with translation into Latin, one of the very few exceptions being Musurus, who did a version of *Musaeus* for Aldus and translated the commentary of the Byzantine John Philoponos on Aristotle's books on generation and corruption. The reason for these exiles' lack of interest in translation (besides an insufficient command of Latin) lay probably in the fact that adequate Latin versions of most of the Greek works by then already existed: the primary task now was rather to prepare the original texts for the press, an undertaking for which the Greeks were well qualified. So thoroughly was this task accomplished — and by the Greeks centered in Venice particularly — that by the time the last important Greek exiles had disappeared from the scene the body of Greek material that the Latin humanists were able to translate included almost all of Greek poetry, historiography, oratory, much of Greek patristic theology and of non-Aristotelian philosophy, and some writings on mathematics and medicine.[26]

[25] See Kristeller, *Classics*, chap. i.
[26] Cf. Kristeller, *Classics*, 16. By 1600 virtually all of Greek literature was available in Latin.

But the chief vehicle for the transmission of Greek in the early sixteenth century was undoubtedly the printed book, especially the Aldine productions. It was Aldus' aim to issue each month from his press an edition of one thousand copies.[27] The great demand for his books throughout Europe is evident from the catalogues he frequently printed (on occasion he even listed the publications of his rivals such as Calliergis), and from the orders for Greek books he received from almost every region of the West, including distant Poland, England, Spain, even Crete. His voluminous correspondence with scholars — with Erasmus, Reuchlin, Bonamico, Vertessy, William Latimer, Celtis, Aleandro, to cite only a few important names — reveals requests for newly printed Greek grammars and lexica and manuals of style and syntax as well as for his eagerly awaited editions of the classic masterpieces.[28] His invention of the small octavo volume, designed to reduce the price of his books and the cost of production (a volume could now be carried in a reader's pocket) helped to increase the circulation of his books far beyond the confines of the Italian peninsula.[29] As we have seen, though Erasmus was not without some reputation on his arrival in Venice, it was the Aldine publication of his *Adages* that established his reputation on a pan-European scale. Aldus' efforts in behalf of Greek learning did not go unappreciated. The great German humanist John Reuchlin (with whom Aldus enjoyed close relations) could declare that without the work of Aldus in providing Greek texts his own endeavors at teaching Greek in Germany would have been fruitless.[30] But perhaps the most striking testimony to Aldus' efforts is the remark of Beatus Rhenanus, the pupil of Erasmus, who informs us that so successful was Aldus in spreading abroad a knowledge of Greek that he was accused by a fellow-Venetian of a lack of patriotism, as students

[27] Preface to Aldine Euripides (1503), in Botfield, *Praefationes*, 226. Also see Putnam, *Books and Their Makers*, I, 423.

[28] A rapid perusal of E. Pastorello, *L'epistolario Manuziano* (Florence, 1957), gives an idea of Aldus' vast, far-flung correspondence; for instance, Aleandro from Paris requests a Greek grammar (210); Celtis makes a request (27); Reuchlin (26); Vertessy, 35; and Latimer, from Padua (21).

[29] See Putnam, I, 424ff. (who notes that the sales in Paris were interfered with by Lyons piracy editions); Brown, *Venetian Printing Press*, 48, and Robertson, "Aldus Manutius, the Scholar-Printer," 64.

[30] See Putnam, I, 430.

would no longer find it necessary to come to Italy to learn Greek.[31]

A complete picture of the role of Venice in transmitting Greek letters to the West would of course have to include an equally intensive treatment of the careers of all the other Greeks connected with the period of Venetian primacy [31a] — and notably of Janus Lascaris (of whom several biographies are available), who for a time was closely associated with the Aldine press. And it would have to delineate in equivalent detail the role of the Latin Hellenists of Venice, who were at least as numerous as their Greek associates and were able (or thought they were), several of them, to vie with the Greek exiles in their mastery of the Hellenic language. Nevertheless, recognition has been given in these pages to the work of the more important of these Western Hellenists of Venice, including, besides Aldus, Scipio Carteromachus, cofounder with Aldus and Gregoropoulos of the Aldine Academy; Urbano Bolzanio, who acquired much of his Greek in the East and was responsible for the first Greek grammar written in Latin; [32] Varinus Favorinus of Camerino, whose career is more intimately associated with Leonine Rome; and the Venetian nobleman and later Cardinal Pietro Bembo, whose cogently expressed sentiments on the significance of Greek learning and the role of the Greek colonies of Venice therein have been prefixed to this chapter.

Impressive as was the Venetian achievement in the dissemination of Greek, there were in the early sixteenth century certain obstacles which impeded an even more rapid diffusion of the language. In the first place (and in contradiction to the sage advice

---

[31] See Beatus' introduction to the works of Erasmus: "Quidam Venetiis olim Aldo Manutio commentarios Graecos in Euripidem et Sophoclem edere paranti dixit: Cave, cave hoc facias, ne barbari istis adjuti domi maneant et pauciores in Italiam ventitent."

[31a] As has frequently been stressed, this book focuses primarily on the Greek exiles in or connected with Venice during the period when she attained the primacy in Greek studies. But of course the Venetian role in the transmission of Greek did not cease in 1535 (with the disappearance of the scholars whose biographies have been given here). Venice remained for some years an important center for the manuscript trade, and in fact Greek scholars of lesser importance from Crete, Corfu, and other areas continued to come to Venice until long past the end of the sixteenth century. Some of these, nearly all of whom were copyists, were Anthony Eparchos, Nicholas Sophianos, Angelo Vergikios, Andreas Darmarios, Constantine Palaeokappas, and John and Thodosius Zygomalas. On all these see esp. Legrand, *Bibliographie hellénique*, vols. I and II.

[32] According to Rhenanus, Erasmus had a high regard for Bolzanio's Greek knowledge.

contained in the 'discourse of Michael Apostolis to the Italians'),
Greek was always taught through the instrumentality of Latin.
And among the exiles — whose role, as we have seen, was so central for the Venetian period of primacy — very few, except for
Musurus, Lascaris, and George of Trebizond, were competent in
Latin,[33] a fact which was a certain handicap in their instruction.
Moreover, in the later stage of the development of Greek learning
in the West, the exiles, Musurus and Lascaris again excepted, were
no longer looked upon with the respect, even adulation, that had
greeted the earlier arrivals such as Chrysoloras and Bessarion. As
the Westerners drew their knowledge of Greek from the émigrés
and began in turn to consolidate their own skills, some, like Poliziano, began to believe that their command of the language even
surpassed that of their Greek masters. And as more and more
émigrés arrived from the East, many from among the lower classes
and many pseudo-intellectuals, the Latin feeling of disdain, even
mistrust, for the Greeks became more pronounced. But for this
attitude, it must be admitted, the exiles were themselves far from
blameless. For the most part they would not, or perhaps could not,
recognize the exigencies of life in the new world they entered.
Bearded, as they often remained, viewing themselves in the traditional Byzantine manner as superior to the Westerners whom they
considered it their mission to Hellenize, expressing lip service to
Catholicism but at heart retaining their Orthodox loyalties, they
aroused a good deal of resentment. This was especially true when,
as not infrequently happened, a Greek proved more successful
than his Latin opponent in capturing a coveted professorial post.
Musurus, to be sure, despite his great learning and success in the
West, remained modest in word and act. But his was an exceptional
case, and even he was slandered after death. On the other hand,
Michael Apostolis, possibly Ducas in Spain, and certainly the
devious Arsenios aroused deep feelings of antagonism and professional jealousy and were therefore never able to secure permanent professorial positions. Even so, more important obstacles
to the diffusion of Greek than the prejudice and presumptuous
ignorance of the Western humanists were certain practical considerations: for all the Hellenists, Latin as well as Greek, there

[33] Gaza and Bessarion had also been good Latinists.

were too few stable university chairs; Greek books, despite the rapid development of the press, remained relatively costly; and it was not always easy to find expert transcribers of Greek texts.[34]

A few years before Janus Lascaris' death in 1534, Greek studies in Italy began noticeably to decline from the pitch of contagious enthusiasm fostered by the propaganda of the Greek exiles[35] — in the last analysis perhaps the émigrés' chief contribution to Renaissance Greek learning — to the narrower, more specialized interests of the native Italian professional scholars. It would be difficult to affirm categorically that it was the gradual disappearance of the Greek exiles that brought about this situation, although, as Burckhardt points out, more than mere coincidence seems to be involved.[36] It should be noted, however, that almost all of the ancient Greek works had now been printed, and that, with the excitement diminished for the production of new ones, a certain satiety with Greek learning had begun to set in. Part of this lessening of interest in Greek may also have stemmed from the developing interest in the Italian vernacular as a literary medium.[37] Important, finally, was the severe blow dealt to Italian humanism by the sack of Rome in 1527, with the consequent ending of the lavish patronage of the papal court — a factor of vital significance in view of the leading role patronage had played in the furtherance of Greek studies in Florence and Venice, as well as in the mid-fifteenth century Rome of Bessarion's circle. After all, like the exiles themselves, the Greek language, for all the admiration of the Westerners, was never really a part of the native Western culture.

The emphasis placed by historians on Venice's economic, political, and artistic life has served to obscure her purely intellec-

[34] Cf. V. Rossi, *Il Quattrocento*, 93.

[35] Of course certain exceptions can be cited in the late sixteenth century, such as the excellent Hellenists Pier Vittorio and Francesco Patrizi, and we know that additional translations were made. On the decline of enthusiasm for Greek see Sandys, *Classical Scholarship*, II, 100 and 133 ("Before 1525 the study of Greek had begun to decline in Italy"). Also Burckhardt, *Civilization of the Renaissance* (Oxford and London, 1945) 118. Meanwhile, under the influence of Italy, Greek studies had begun to flourish north of the Alps, especially with Budé, Erasmus, and the Stephani.

[36] Burckhardt, *Civilization of the Renaissance* (Oxford and London, 1945) 119.

[37] On the development of the vernacular see Kristeller, *Studies*, 492, who affirms that study of the vernacular was influenced by the techniques (on vocabulary, syntax, forms) perfected for the study of Latin. Greek study also, if indirectly, probably played a part here.

tual achievements. Of even greater importance, however, with respect to her role in the development of Greek learning, has been the lack of understanding of the interaction of Venice's intellectual life with that of the Byzantine and post-Byzantine East, in particular the Venetian colony of Crete. It has been the aim of this book to provide such a composite picture of East and West by means of a detailed examination of the careers of five little-studied and in many ways representative Greek émigré scholars who (except for the preparatory figure of Michael Apostolis) came to reside in Venice during the years of her intellectual primacy but did not cut the ties with their Greek homeland. In the background of the émigrés was the Greek community of Venice, which was constantly being reinforced by new arrivals from the East and from which, whether the émigrés chose to live in the colony or not, they were able to derive a sense of security which caused them to look upon Venice as almost a second Byzantium. It was chiefly this magnetlike attraction of Venice for the Greek exiles, based on a centuries-old tradition of close relations with Byzantium — not to overlook, of course, the city's economic prosperity and the opportunity for employment afforded by the Aldine press — that enabled Venice not only to appropriate but, with remarkable success, to diffuse Greek letters throughout the Western world.

BIBLIOGRAPHY

BIBLIOGRAPHY[1]

PRIMARY SOURCES

(Documentary, Literary, Bibliographical)

Alberi, Eugenio, *Relazioni degli ambasciatori veneti al senato*, 15 vols. (Florence, 1839–1863).

Aleandro, Girolamo, *Journal Autobiographique du Cardinal Jérôme Aléandre (1480–1530)*, ed. H. Omont, in *Notices et extraits des manuscrits de la Bibliothèque Nationale et autres Bibliothèques*, XXXV (Paris, 1895).

——— *Lettres familières de J. Aléandre (1510–1540)*, ed. J. Paquier (Paris, 1909).

Allen, P. S. and H. M., *Opus epistolarum Des. Erasmi Roterodami* (Oxford, 1906–1958) 12 vols.

Allen, T. W., *Notes on Greek Manuscripts in Italian Libraries* (London, 1890).

Antoniadis, Sophia, "Πορίσματα ἀπὸ τὴν μελέτην προχείρων διαχειριστικῶν βιβλίων τῶν ἐτῶν 1544–1547 καὶ 1549–1554 τῆς παλαιᾶς κοινότητος Βενετίας," Πρακτικὰ Ἀκαδημίας Ἀθηνῶν, XXXIII (1958) 466–487.

Antonius, Nicolaus, *Bibliotheca hispana nova* (Madrid, 1783).

Apostolis, Arsenios, *Violetum [Ionia]*, ed. C. Walz (Stuttgart, 1832).

Apostolios, Michael, *Paroemiae: nunc demum, post epitomem basiliensem . . . cum Petri Pantini versione . . . editae* (Leyden, 1619).

Bandini, A. M., *De Florentina Juntarum Typografia et Juntarum Typog. Annales*, 2 vols. (Lucca, 1791).

Baschet, Armand, *Aldo Manuzio, lettres et documents 1495–1515* (Venice, 1867).

Bembo, Giovanni, "In obitum Cyurcω incoris suae Corcyriensis ad Andream Anesinum, an. 1536," Marc. Lat. MS. XIV, 235 (= 4714), no. v, fols. 13v ff.

Bembo, Pietro, *Della istoria viniziana*, 2 vols. (Venice, 1790).

[1] Works cited only once in the book are generally not included in the Bibliography, nor of course is the primary focus here on the early period of the Renaissance.

Bertanza, Enrico, *Documenti per la storia della cultura in Venezia* (Venice, 1907), vol. I, *Maestri, scuole, e scolari in Venezia fino al 1500.*

Biedl, A., "Beiträge zur Geschichte der Codices Palatini," *Byz. Zeit.,* XXXVII (1937) 36–38.

Boissonade, J. F., *Anecdota graeca,* 5 vols. (Paris, 1829–1833).

Botfield, Beriah, *Praefationes et Epistolae Editionibus Principibus Auctorum Veterum Praepositae* (Canterbury, 1861).

Branca, Vittore, "Un trattato inedito di Ermolao Barbaro," *Bibliothèque d'humanisme et Renaissance,* XIV (1952).

Browning, R., "Recentiores non deteriores," *University of London Institute of Classical Studies Bulletin* no. 7 (1960) 11–21.

Calogerà, Don A., *Raccolta d'opuscoli,* 51 vols. (Venice, 1728–1757).

Cantacuzene, John, *Historia,* ed. L. Schopen, 3 vols. (Bonn, 1828).

Cantarella, Raffaele, *Aristofane, Le Commedie* (Milan, 1953).

Cessi, Roberto, *Deliberazioni del Maggior Consiglio di Venezia,* 2 vols. (Bologna, 1931).

Cicogna, E. A., *Saggio di bibliografia veneziana* (Venice, 1847).

——— *Delle inscrizioni veneziane,* 6 vols. (Venice, 1824–1853).

Cohn, Leopold, "Griechische Lexicographie," appendix in I. Müller, *Handbuch der Kl. Altertums-Wissenschaft,* II 1, *Griechische Grammatik* of K. Brugmann (Munich, 1913).

——— *Verzeichniss der von der königlichen Bibliothek zu Berlin erworbenen Meermanhandschriften des Sir Thomas Phillipps* (Berlin, 1892).

Cornelius, Flaminio, *Creta Sacra,* 2 vols. (Venice, 1755).

——— *Ecclesiae venetae antiquis monumentis,* 12 vols. (Venice, 1749).

Cramer, J. A., *Anecdota graeca e codicibus Bibliothecarum Oxoniensium,* III (Oxford, 1836).

Cranz, F. E., "Alexander Aphrodisiensis," in P. O. Kristeller, *Catalogus Translationum et Commentariorum: Mediaeval and Renaissance Latin Translations and Commentaries,* I (Washington, 1960).

Crusius, Martin, *Turcograeciae libri octo* (Basle, 1584).

Dain, A., "Un manuscrit de Thucydide, le Mon. gr. 126," *L'Antiquité Classique,* VI (1937) 119f.

Dallari, U., *I rotuli dei lettori legisti, e artisti dello studio bolognese dal 1384 al 1799,* 4 vols. (Bologna, 1888–1924).

Delisle, L. V., *Le Cabinet des manuscrits de la Bibliothèque Nationale* (Paris, 1868) vols. 2–3.

Demetracopoulos, Andronikos, Ἐθνικὸν Ἡμερολόγιον Βρεττοῦ (1870), 359–367.

Devreese, Robert, *Introduction à l'étude des manuscrits grecs* (Paris, 1954).

——— *Les manuscrits grecs de l'Italie méridionale* (Vatican, 1955).

Dindorf, G., *Scholia graeca in Euripidis tragoedias* (Oxford, 1863).

Donati, L., "Bibliografia Aldina," *La Bibliofilia*, LII (1950) 188–204.

Drachmann, A., *Die Ueberlieferung des Cyrillglossars* (Copenhagen, 1936).

Ducas, M., *Historia byzantina* (Bonn, 1834).

Ebert, F., *Allgemeines bibliographisches Lexikon* (Leipzig, 1821) I.

Erasmus, Desiderius, *Adagiorum Collectanea* (Paris, 1500).

——— *Adagiorum Chiliades tres, ac centuriae fere totidem* (Aldine ed.; Venice, 1508).

——— *Adagiorum Opus* (Froben ed.; Basle, 1526).

——— *Desiderii Erasmi Roterodami Opera omnia*, ed. Jean Le Clerc, 10 vols. in 11 (Leyden, 1703–1706).

——— *De recta, latini graecique pronuntiatione* (Basle, 1528).

Fabricius, I. A., *Bibliotheca Graeca sive notitia scriptorum veterum Graecorum*, 12 vols. (Hamburg, 1790–1809).

Facciolatus, Jacopo, *Fasti Gymnasii patavini*, 2 vols. (Padua, 1757).

Fantuzzi, Giovanni, *Notizie degli scrittori bolognesi*, 9 vols. (Bologna, 1781–1794).

Favaro, A., *Saggio di bibliografia dello studio di Padova*, 2 vols. (Venice, 1922).

Festa, Nicola, "Indici dei codici greci Bolognesi," *Studi italiani di filologia classica*, III (1895) 371ff.

Frati, Carlo, *Dizionario bio-bibliografico dei bibliotecari e bibliofili italiani dal sec. XIV al XIX* (Florence, 1933).

Fulin, Rinaldo, "Documenti per servire alla storia della tipografia veneziana," *Archivio veneto*, XXIII (1882) 84–212, 390–405.

Fumagalli, Giuseppe, *Lexicon Typographicum Italiae* (Florence, 1905).

Gaisford, Thomas, *Etymologicon Magnum* (Oxford, 1848).

Gallavotti, Carlo, *Theocritus* (Rome, 1946).

Gamba, Bartolomeo, *Serie degli scritti impressi in dialetto veneziano* (Venice, 1832).

Geisler, E., *Beiträge zur Geschichte des griechischen Sprichwortes*, in *Anschluss an Planudes und Michael Apostoles* (Breslau, 1908).

Gerland, Ernst, *Das Archiv des Herzogs von Kandia im Königl. Staatsarchiv zu Venedig* (Strassburg, 1899).

Gerola, Giuseppe, *Monumenti veneti dell' isola di Creta*, 4 vols. (Venice, 1905–1932).

Gherardi, Alessandro, *Statuti della università e studio fiorentino dall'
anno MCCC LXXXVII* (Florence, 1881).

Gill, Joseph, *Quae supersunt Actorum graecorum Concilii Florentini*
(Rome, 1953).

Golubovich, Girolamo, *Biblioteca bio-bibliografica della Terra Santa
e dell' Oriente francescano* (Quaracchi, 1906–1927).

Gómez de Castro, A., *De rebus gestis a Francisco Ximenio Cisnerio*
(Alcalá, 1569), and in *Hispaniae illustratae scriptores* (Frankfort,
1623–1628).

Graesse, J. G., *Trésor de livres rares et précieux ou Nouveau Dictionnaire*, 7 vols. (Dresden, 1859–1900).

Graux, Charles, *Essai sur la formation du fonds grec de l'Escurial* (Paris,
1880).

——— *Notices sommaires des manuscrits grecs d'Espagne et de Portugal* (Paris, 1892).

Gregoras, Nikephorus, *Bizantina historia*, ed. L. Schopen, I. Bekker, 3
vols. (Bonn, 1830–1845).

Gregory, C. R., *Textkritik des Neuen Testamentes*, II (Leipzig, 1902).

Gyraldi, L. G., *Dialogi duo de poëtis nostrorum temporum* (Florence,
1551).

Haeghen, Van der, F. Vanden Berghe and T. Arnold, *Bibliotheca
Erasmiana (Bibliographie des oeuvres d'Erasme), Adagia* (Gand,
1897).

Hain, Ludwig, *Repertorium bibliographicum*, 2 vols. (Stuttgart, 1826–
1838).

Halm, C. and G. Meyer, *Catalogus codicum latinorum Bibliothecae
regiae Monacensis . . .* , II (Munich, 1874) pt. 1.

Heiberg, J. L., "Beiträge zur Geschichte Georg Vallas und seiner Bibliothek," *Centralblatt für Bibliothekswesen*, XVI (Leipzig, 1896)
106ff.

Hofmann, Georg, "Nuove fonti per la storia profana ed ecclesiastica
di Creta nella prima metà del secolo XV," *Actes du IX ͤ Congrès
Intern. des études byz.*, II (Athens, 1956) 462–69.

Hunger, H., "Joannes Tzetses Allegorien zur Odyssee, Buch 1–2," *Byz.
Zeit.* XLIX (1956) 250f.

Hyperides, G. M., Μιχαήλου Ἀποστόλη πονήματα τρία (Smyrna, 1876).

"Inventario delle scritture, documenti, e libri appartenenti alla Scuola di
S. Nicoló e Chiesa di San Giorgio" (ms. at San Giorgio, Venice).

Iovius (Giovio), Paulus, *Elogia doctorum virorum ab avorum memoria
publicatis ingenii monumentis illustrium* (Antwerp, 1557).

——— *Elogia virorum literis illustrium* (Basle, 1577).

——— Le iscrittioni poste sotto le vere imagini degli huomini famosi, trans. H. Orio (Florence, 1552).

Irigoin, Jean, Histoire du texte de Pindare (Paris, 1952).

Kristeller, P. O., Catalogus Translationum et Commentariorum: Mediaeval and Renaissance Latin Translations and Commentaries, I (Washington, 1960).

Krumbacher, Karl, Geschichte der byzantinischen Litteratur (Munich, 1897).

Lamius, Iohannes, Deliciae eruditorum seu veterum ἀνεκδότων opusculorum collectanea, 16 vols. (Florence, 1736–1754).

Lampros, S. P., " Ἀνέκδοτος Ἐπιστολὴ τοῦ Βησσαρίωνος," Νέος Ἑλληνομνήμων, VI (1909) 393ff.

——— " Ἀθηναῖοι βιβλιογράφοι καὶ κτήτορες κωδίκων κατὰ τοὺς μέσους αἰῶνας," Ἐπετηρὶς Παρνασσοῦ, VI (1902) 159–218.

——— " Ὁ κατ᾽ Ἀρσενίου τοῦ Ἀποστόλη ἀφορισμὸς τοῦ Πατριάρχου Παχωμίου Α᾽," Νέος Ἑλληνομνήμων, III (1906) 56ff.

——— Παλαιολόγεια καὶ Πελοποννησιακά, 4 vols. (Athens, 1912–1930).

Laourdas, Basil, " Ἐπικήδειος εἰς Καλοτάρην καὶ Γαλατηνόν," Κρητικὰ Χρονικά, IV (1950) 251–56.

——— "Κρητικὰ Παλαιογραφικά," Κρητικὰ Χρονικά, V (1951) 231–62.

——— "Κρητικὰ Παλαιογραφικά . . . Ἰωάννης Συμεωνάκης καὶ Πέτρος Λαμπάρδος," Κρητικὰ Χρονικά, II (1948) 540–45.

——— "Μενέξενος," Κρητικὰ Χρονικά, VI (1952) 51–58.

——— "Μιχαὴλ Ἀποστόλη ἀνέκδοτα ἐπιγράμματα," Ἐπ. Ἑτ. Βυζ. Σπουδῶν, XX (1950) 172–208.

——— "Μιχαὴλ Ἀποστόλη, Ἐπικήδειος εἰς Ἀνδρέαν Καλέργην," Κρητικὰ Χρονικά, XI (1958) 381–86.

——— "Μιχαὴλ Ἀποστόλη, λόγος περὶ Ἑλλάδος καὶ Εὐρώπης," Ἐπ. Ἑτ. Βυζ. Σπουδῶν, XIX (1949) 235–44.

——— " Ἡ πρὸς τὸν Φρειδερῖκον Γ᾽ ἔκκλησις τοῦ Μιχαὴλ Ἀποστόλη," Γέρας Α. Κεραμοπούλλου (1953) 516–27.

——— "Προσευχὴ πρὸ τῆς μεταλήψεως," Tome commémoratif du millénaire de la Bibliothèque Patriarcale d'Alexandrie (Alexandria, 1953) 47–52.

Latte, Kurt, Hesychii Alexandrini Lexicon (Copenhagen, 1953) I.

Lazzarini, V., Lettere ducali veneziane del secolo XIII, in Paleografia diplomatica in onore di V. Federici (Florence, 1945).

Legrand, Emile, Bibliographie hellénique ou description raisonnée des ouvrages publiés en grec par des grecs au XVᵉ et XVIᵉ siècles, 4 vols. (Paris, 1885–1906).

—— *Bibliographie hispano-grecque*, pt. 1 (New York, 1915).

Leutsch, E. L., and F. G. Schneider, *Paroemiographi graeci*, 2 vols. (Göttingen, 1839–1851).

Levi, L., "Un carme greco medievale in lode di Venezia," *Ateneo Veneto*, XXV (1902) 188ff.

Lobel, Edgar, *The Greek Manuscripts of Aristotle's 'Poetics'* (Oxford, 1933).

Malaxos, Manuel, *Historia Patriarchica*, in Bonn ed. (1849) and in M. Crusius, *Turcograecia* (Basle, 1584).

—— *Manoscritti e stampe venete dell' Aristotelismo e Averroismo (Secolo X–XVI)* (Venice, 1958).

Manousakas, M. I., " Ἡ ἀλληλογραφία τῶν Γρηγοροπούλων χρονολογουμένη (1493–1501)," Ἐπετηρὶς τοῦ Μεσαιωνικοῦ Ἀρχείου, VII (1957) 156–209.

—— " Ἀρσενίου Μονεμβασίας τοῦ Ἀποστόλη Ἐπιστολαὶ Ἀνέκδοτοι (1521–34)," Ἐπ. τοῦ Μεσαιωνικοῦ Ἀρχείου, VIII–IX (1961) 5–56.

—— "Βενετικὰ ἔγγραφα ἀναφερόμενα εἰς τὴν ἐκκλησιαστικὴν ἱστορίαν τῆς Κρήτης τοῦ 14 ου καὶ 16 ου αἰώνος," Δελτίον Ἱστ. Ἐθν. Ἑτ. Ἑλλάδος, XV (1960) 149–233.

Martini, A., and D. Bassi, *Catalogus codicum graecorum Bibliothecae Ambrosianae* (Milan, 1906).

Mazzuchelli, G. M., *Gli scrittori d'Italia*, 6 vols. (Brescia, 1753–1763).

Mehus, L., *Ambrosii Traversarii epistolae* (Florence, 1759).

Mercati, Giovanni, *Codici Latini Pico Grimani Pio . . . e i Codici greci Pio di Modena* (Vatican, 1938).

—— "Indici di manoscritti greci del Cardinal N. Ridolfi," *Mélanges d'arch. et d'hist.*, XXX (1910) 51–55.

—— *Notizie di Procoro e Demetrio Cidone Manuele Caleca e Teodoro Meliteniota*, in *Studi e Testi*, LVI (Vatican, 1931).

—— *Se la versione dall'ebraico del codice veneto greco VII sia di Simone Atumano, Arcivescovo di Tebe*, in *Studi e Testi*, XXX (Rome, 1916).

Meyer, P., *Die theologische Litteratur der griechischen Kirche im sechzehnten Jahrhundert* (Leipzig, 1899).

Meyier, K. De, "Two Scribes Identified as One," *Scriptorium*, XI (1957) 99ff.

—— "More Mss. Copied by George Trivizius," *Scriptorium*, XIII (1959) 86–88.

Miklosich, F., and J. Müller, *Acta et diplomata res graecas italasque illustrantia* (Vienna, 1860–1890).

Mioni, Elpidio, *Aristotelis Codices Graeci qui in Bibliothecis Venetis Adservantur* (Padua, 1958).

Mittaire, D., *Annales typografici*, 3 vols. (Nurnberg, 1795).

Mohler, Ludwig, "Aus Bessarions Gelehrtenkreis Abhandlungen, Reden, Briefe von Bessarions, Theodoros Gazes, Michael Apostolios, Andronikos Kallistos, Georgios Trapezuntios, Nicollò Perotti, Nicollò Capranica," *Quellen und Forschungen aus dem Gebiete der Geschichte*, XXIV (Paderborn, 1942).

Mommsen, T., "Autobiographie des Venezianers Giovanni Bembo," *Sitzungsb. der bayerischen Akad. der Wissensch.*, I (1861) 584ff.

Montfaucon, Bernard de, *Palaeographia Graeca* (Paris, 1708).

Morelli, J., "Intorno ad un' orazione greca inedita del Cardinale Pietro Bembo alla Signoria di Venezia colla quale la esorta a promuovere e conservare lo studio delle lettere greche," *Memorie dell'imperiale regio istituto del regno Lombardo-Veneto*, II (Milan, 1821) 251–62.

―― *Operette di Iacopo Morelli*, II (Venice, 1820).

Müller, K. K., "Neue Mittheilungen über Janos Laskaris und die Mediceische Bibliothek," *Centralblatt für Bibliothekswesen*, I (1884) 333–412.

Müntz, E. and P. Favre, *La bibliothèque du Vatican du XV e siècle d'après des documents inédits* (Paris, 1887).

Mystakides, B., "Μαρτῖνος ὁ Κρούσιος καὶ 'Ανδρέας Δαρμάριος ὁ 'Επιδαύριος ἐν Τυβίγγῃ 1584," *Forschungen und Versuche für Geschichte des Mittelalters und Neuzeit* (Jena, 1915) 501–26.

Nelson, E., "Recent Literature Concerning Erasmus," *Journal of Modern History*, I (1929) 88–102.

Nichols, F., *Epistles of Erasmus*, 3 vols. (London, 1901–1918).

Noiret, Hippolyte, *Documents inédits pour servir à l'histoire de la domination vénitienne en Crète de 1380 à 1485* (Paris, 1892).

―― *Lettres inédites de Michel Apostolis* (Paris, 1889).

Nolhac, Pierre de, "Les correspondants d'Alde Manuce: Matériaux nouveaux d'histoire littéraire (1483–1514)," in *Studi e documenti di storia e diritto*, VIII (Rome, 1887) 247–99, and IX (1888) 203–48.

―― *La bibliothèque de Fulvio Orsini*, in *Bibliothèque de l'école des hautes études* (Paris, 1887).

―― "Inventaire des manuscrits grecs de Jean Lascaris," *Mélanges d'archéologie et d'histoire*, VI (1886) 251–74.

Novati, F., *Epistolario di C. Salutati*, 4 vols. (Rome, 1891–1911).

Omont, H. A., *Catalogue des manuscrits grecs de la Bibliothèque Royale de Bruxelles* (Gand, 1885).

―― *Catalogue des manuscrits grecs d'Antoine Eparche (1538)* (Paris, 1892).

—— *Catalogue des manuscrits grecs de G. Pélicier* (Paris, 1886).

—— *Catalogues des manuscrits grecs de Fontainebleau sous François I et Henri II* (Paris, 1889).

—— *Fac-similés de manuscrits grecs des XV*ᵉ *et XVI*ᵉ *siècles* (Paris, 1887).

—— "Inventaire de manuscrits grecs et latins donnés à Saint-Marc de Venise par le Cardinal Bessarion en 1468," *Revue des bibliothèques*, IV (1894) 129–87.

—— *Inventaire sommaire des manuscrits grecs dans les bibliothèques autre que la Bibliothèque Nationale*, I (Paris, 1886).

—— *Notes sur les manuscrits grecs du British Museum* (Paris, 1882).

—— "Un premier catalogue des manuscrits grecs du Cardinal Ridolfi," *Bibliothèque de l'école des chartes*, XLIX (1888) 313–24.

Pachymeres, George, *De Michaele et Andronico Palaeologis*, ed. I. Bekker, 2 vols. (Bonn, 1835).

Papadopoli, N. C., *Historia gymnasii patavini*, 2 vols. (Venice, 1762).

Pasquali, G., *Bibliotheca Smithiana* (Venice, 1785).

Pastorello, Esther, *L'epistolario Manuziano. Inventario cronologico-analitico (1483–1597)* (Florence, 1957).

—— *Inedita Manutiana 1502–97* (Florence, 1960).

Paton, W. R., *The Greek Anthology*, Eng. transl., 5 vols. (Cambridge, Mass., 1928–1948).

Paton, W. R., and I. Wegehaupt, *Plutarchi Moralia*, I (Leipzig, 1925).

Patrinelis, Christ, " Ἕλληνες Κωδικογράφοι τῶν χρόνων τῆς Ἀναγεννήσεως," Ἐπετ. τοῦ Μεσ. Ἀρχείου, VIII–IX (1958–59) 63–121.

—— "Νόθα, ἀνύπαρκτα καὶ συγχεόμενα πρὸς ἄλληλα ἔργα τοῦ Μιχαὴλ Ἀποστόλη," Ἐπ. Ἑτ. Βυζ. Σπ., XXX (1960) 203–13.

Powell, J. E. "Michael Apostolios gegen Theodoros Gaza," *Byz. Zeit.*, XXVIII (1938) 71–86.

Puntoni, Vittorio, "Indice dei codici greci della Bibliotheca Estense di Modena," *Studi italiani di filologia classica*, IV (1896) 379–536.

Puscolo, Ubertino, "Constantinopolis," in A. Ellissen, *Analekten der mittel- und neugriechischen Literatur*, III (Leipzig, 1857) Appendix.

Quintanilla y Mendoza, Pedro de, *Archetypo de virtudes, espejo de prelados: el Venerable Padre y Siervo de Dios Fray Francisco Ximénez de Cisneros* (Palermo, 1653).

Reitzenstein, R., *Zur Geschichte der griechischen Etymologika* (Leipzig, 1897).

Renouard, A. A., *Annales de l'imprimerie des Alde*, 2nd ed., 3 vols. (Paris, 1825); 3rd ed. (Paris, 1834).

Richard, Marcel, *Répertoire des bibliothèques et des catalogues de manuscrits grecs*, 2nd ed. (Paris, 1958).

Sabbadini, Remigio, *Centotrenta lettere inedite di F. Barbaro* (Salerno, 1884).

Sánchez, Alonso B., *Fuentes de la historia española e hispano-americana*, 3 vols. (Madrid, 1952).

Sanudo, Marino (Torsello), *Istoria del regno di Romania*, ed. C. Hopf, in *Chroniques gréco-romanes* (Berlin, 1873) 99–170.

Sanuto, Marino, *I diarii di Marino Sanuto (1496–1533)*, ed. R. Fulin, F. Stefani, N. Barozzi, G. Berchet, M. Allegri, 58 vols. (Venice, 1879–1903).

—— *Vite dei Dogi*, in Muratori, *RISS*, XXII, pt. 4 (Città di Castello, 1906).

Sathas, Konstantine, *Documents inédits relatifs à l'histoire de la Grèce au Moyen Age*, 9 vols. (Paris, 1888–1890) VII.

—— Νεοελληνικὴ φιλολογία (Athens, 1868).

Schmidt, M., *Hesychii Alexandrini Lexicon*, 5 vols. (Jena, 1858–1868).

Scholderer, Victor, *Catalogue of Books Printed in the XV Century Now in the British Museum*, pt. 5 (London, 1924).

Spandugnino, Theodore, *De la origine degli imperatori ottomani*, in K. Sathas, *Documents inédits relatifs à l'histoire de la Grèce*, IX (Paris, 1890).

Sphrantzes (Phrantzes), George, *Chronicon*, ed. J. B. Papadopoulos (Leipzig, 1935).

Stefano Magno, *Estratti degli Annali Veneti di Stefano Magno*, ed. C. Hopf, in *Chron. gréco-romanes* (Berlin, 1873) 179ff.

Stevenson, Henricus, *Codices manuscripti Palatini Graeci Bibliothecae Vaticanae* (Rome, 1885).

Syropoulos, Sylvester, *Historia vera unionis non verae . . . Concilii Florentini*, ed. M. Creyghton (The Hague, 1660).

Tafel, G., and G. Thomas, *Urkunden zur älteren Handels- und Staatsgeschichte der Republik Venedig*, pts. 1–3, in *Fontes rerum austriacarum*, II, *Diplomataria et acta*, XII–XIV (Vienna, 1856–1857).

Thaunus, Jacques Auguste, *Historiarum sui temporis libri CXX* (Paris, 1606–1609).

Theotokes, Spyridon, Εἰσαγωγὴ εἰς τὴν ἔρευναν τῶν μνημείων τῆς ἱστορίας τοῦ Ἑλληνισμοῦ καὶ . . . Κρήτης ἐν τῷ Κρατικῷ Ἀρχείῳ τοῦ Βενετικοῦ Κράτους (Corfu, 1926).

Thomas, G., and R. Predelli, *Diplomatarium Veneto-levantinum*, I, II (Venice, 1880–1899).

Tomasini, J. F., *Bibliothecae Venetae* (Udine, 1650).

Torre del Cerro, A. de la, "La Universidad de Alcalá; datos para su historia, Catedras y Catedraticos desde la inauguración del colegio de San Ildefonso hasta san Lucas de 1519," *Revista de Archivos, Bibliotecas y Museos*, ser. 3, XXI (1909) 48–71, 261–85, 403–33.

Treu, Max, *Zur Geschichte der Überlieferung von Plutarchs Moralia*, 3 vols. (Waldenburg in Schlesien, 1877–1884).

Turyn, Alexander, *The Byzantine Manuscript Tradition of the Tragedies of Euripides* (Urbana, 1957).

—— *De codicibus pindaricis* (Cracow, 1932).

—— *The Manuscript Tradition of the Tragedies of Aeschylus* (New York, 1943).

—— "The Sophocles Recension of Manuel Moschopulos," *Transactions of the American Philological Association*, LXXX (1949) 94–173.

—— *Studies in the Manuscript Tradition of the Tragedies of Sophocles* (Urbana, 1952).

Valeriano, Giovanni Pierio, *De litteratorum infelicitate* (Venice, 1620; new ed., Geneva, 1821).

Vogel, M., and V. Gardthausen, *Die griechischen Schreiber des Mittelalters und der Renaissance* (Leipzig, 1909).

Wilamowitz-Moellendorff, U. von, *Einleitung in die attische Tragödie*, I (Berlin, 1889).

Wittek, Martin, "Manuscrits et Codicologie," *Scriptorium*, VII (1953) 274–96.

—— "Pour une étude du *scriptorium* de Michel Apostolès et consorts," *Scriptorium*, VII (1953) 290–97.

Young, D. C., "A Codicological Inventory of Theognis Manuscripts," *Scriptorium*, VII (1953) 3–36.

Zanetti, A. M., and A. Bongiovanni, *Graeca D. Marci Bibliotheca Codicum Manu Scriptorum* (Venice, 1740).

Zavira, G., Νέα Ἑλλὰς ἢ Ἑλληνικὸν Θέατρον (Athens, 1872).

SECONDARY WORKS

Agostini, Giovanni degli, *Notizie istorico-critiche intorno la vita, e le opere degli scrittori viniziani*, 2 vols. (Venice, 1752–1754).

Alazard, Jean, *La Venise de la Renaissance* (Paris, 1956).

Alexiou, S., " Ὁ Χαρακτὴρ τοῦ Ἐρωτοκρίτου," Κρητικὰ Χρονικά, VI (1952) 351–422.

Allen, P. S., *The Age of Erasmus: Lectures Delivered in Oxford and London* (Oxford, 1914).

Allen, T. W., *Miscellanea Francesco Ehrle, IV*, in *Studi e Testi*, XL (Rome, 1924).

Anastos, Milton, "Pletho's Calendar and Liturgy," *Dumbarton Oaks Papers, No. 4* (Cambridge, Mass., 1948) 183–303.

Antoniadis, Sophia, " Ἡ βιβλιοθήκη τοῦ Ἑλληνικοῦ Ἰνστιτούτου Βενετίας," Νέα Ἑστία (1960) 1134–41.

———"Museo di Dipinti Sacri" [in Italian and Greek] (Venice, 1959).

———"Νέα Στοιχεῖα ἀπὸ κατάστιχα τῆς Ἑλληνικῆς Ἀδελφότητος Βενετίας (16 ου αι.)," Ἀφιέρωμα Μ. Τριανταφυλλίδη (Athens, 1960) 63–67.

Antonius, Nicolaus, *Bibliotheca hispana nova* (Madrid, 1783).

Appelt, T., "Studies in the Contents and Sources of Erasmus 'Adagia' with Particular Reference to the First Edition, 1500, and the Edition of 1526" (dissertation, University of Chicago, 1942).

Armingaud, J., *Venise et le Bas-Empire* (Paris, 1868).

Atiya, A. S., *The Crusade in the Later Middle Ages* (London, 1938).

Aubreton, Robert, *Démétrius Triclinius et les recensions médiévales de Sophocle* (Paris, 1949).

Babinger, Franz, *Mehmed der Eroberer und seine Zeit* (Munich, 1953); also Italian trans. by E. Polacco (Turin, 1957).

Barbarich, E., "Gli stradioti nell'arte militare italiana," *Rivista di cavalleria*, XIII (1904) 52–72.

Baron, Hans, "Fifteenth-Century Civilization and the Renaissance," *The New Cambridge Modern History*, I, (Cambridge, Eng., 1957) 50–75.

Bataillon, Marcel, *Erasme et l'Espagne* (Paris, 1937).

Battagia, Michele, *Delle Accademie Veneziane* (Venice, 1826).

Beck, H. G., *Theodoros Metochites: Die Krise des byzantinischen Weltbildes im 14. Jahrhundert* (Munich, 1952).

———*Kirche und theologische Literatur im Byzantinischen Reich* (Munich, 1959).

Beloch, G., "La popolazione d'Italia nei secoli XVI–XVIII," *Bulletin de l'Institut international de statistique*, III (1888).

———"La popolazione di Venezia nei secoli XVI e XVII," *Nuovo archivio veneto*, n.s., III (Venice, 1902) 1–49.

Beltrami, Daniele, *Storia della popolazione di Venezia dalla fine del secolo XVI* (Padua, 1954).

Bertoni, Giulio, *Il Duecento*, 3rd ed. (Milan, 1939).

Bires, Kosta H., Ἀρβανίτες: Οἱ Δωριεῖς τοῦ Νεωτέρου Ἑλληνισμοῦ (Athens, 1960).

Bolgar, R. R., *The Classical Heritage and its Beneficiaries* (Cambridge, Eng., 1958).

Börner, C. F., *De doctis hominibus graecis litterarum graecarum in Italia* (Leipzig, 1750).

Boutierides, E., Ἱστορία τῆς Νεοελληνικῆς λογοτεχνίας (Athens, 1924).

Bréhier, Louis, *La civilization byzantine* (Paris, 1950).

Brightman, F. E., *Liturgies Eastern and Western*, I (Oxford, 1896).

Brown, Horatio R., *Studies in the History of Venice*, 2 vols. (London, 1907).

———— *The Venetian Printing Press* (London, 1891).

———— "The Venetians and the Venetian Quarter in Constantinople to the Close of the 12th Century," *Journal of Hellenic Studies*, XL (1920) 62–88.

Brugi, Biagio, *Gli scolari dello studio di Padova nel Cinquecento* (Padua, 1905).

Brunetti, Mario, "L'Accademia Aldina," *Rivista di Venezia*, VIII (1929) 417–31.

Bühler, Curt, "Aldus Manutius and his First Edition of the Greek Musaeus," *Scritti sopra Aldo Manuzio* (1955) 3–7, 106–107.

———— "Aldus Manutius and the Printing of Athenaeus," *Gutenberg-Jahrbuch* (1955) 104–106.

———— "Aldus Manutius: The First Five Hundred Years," *Papers of the Bibliographical Society of America*, XLIV, 205ff.

Burckhardt, Jacob, *The Civilization of the Renaissance in Italy*, new ed. (Oxford-London, 1945).

Bury, J. B., "The Lombards and Venetians in Euboia," *Journal of Hellenic Studies*, VII (1886) 309–52.

Butler, C., *The Life of Erasmus with Historical Remarks on the State of Literature between the Tenth and Sixteenth Centuries* (London, 1825).

Bywater, Ingram, *The Erasmian Pronunciation of Greek and its Precursors: Jerome Aleander, Aldus Manutius, Antonio of Lebrixa* (London, 1908).

Calonaros, P., *Venezia nelle canzoni e leggende del popolo greco* (Athens, 1942).

Cammelli, Giuseppe, "Andronico Callisto," *Rinascita*, XXIII–XXIV (1942) 3–64.

———— *Demetrio Calcondila* (Florence, 1954).

———— *Giovanni Argiropulo* (Florence, 1941).

———— *Manuele Crisolora* (Florence, 1941).

Cappelletti, Giuseppe, *Storia di Padova dalla sua origine alla presente*, 2 vols. (Padua, 1874–1875).

Castellani, Carlo, *La stampa in Venezia* (Venice, 1889).

Castellani, G., "Giorgio da Trebisonda maestro di eloquenza a Vicenza e a Venezia," *Nuovo Archivio Veneto*, XI (1896) 123ff.

Cecchetti, Bartolomeo, *Venezia e la corte di Roma*, 2 vols. (Venice, 1874).

Cecchini, Giovanni, "Anna Notara Paleologa: Una principessa greca in Italia e la politica senese di ripopolamento della Maremma," *Bulletino Senese di storia patria*, XVI (1938) 1–41.

Cessi, Roberto, *Storia della Repubblica di Venezia*, 2 vols. (Milan, 1944–1946).

Chacon, A., *Tiara et purpura veneta ab anno 1379 ad 1759* (Brescia, 1761).

Chassaigne, M., *Etienne Dolet* (Paris, 1930).

Chiti, Alfredo, *Scipione Forteguerri (Il Carteromaco)* (Florence, 1902).

Christie, R. *Etienne Dolet, The Martyr of the Renaissance 1508–1546*, new ed. (London, 1899).

Cermenati, M., "Un diplomato Naturalista del Rinascimento Andrea Navagero," *Nuovo Archivio Veneto*, XXIV (1912) 164–205.

Ciampi, Sebastiano, *Memorie di Scipione Carteromaco* (Pisa, 1811).

Cian, Vittorio, *La cultura e l'italianità di Venezia nel Rinascimento* (Bologna, 1905).

Cicogna, E. E., *Della vita e delle opere di Andrea Navagero* (Venice, 1855).

Cogo, C., "La guerra di Venezia contro i Turchi (1499–1501)," *Nuovo Archivio Veneto*, XVIII (1899) 5–76 and 348–421, and XIX (1900) 97–138.

Courcelle, P. P., *Les lettres grecques en Occident* (Paris, 1943).

Croce, Benedetto, *Michele Marullo Tarcaniota* (Bari, 1938).

Cugnoni, Giuseppe, *Agostino Chigi il Magnifico* (Rome, 1878).

Dain, Alphonse, "Le Moyen-Age Occidental et la tradition manuscrite de la littérature grecque," *Association G. Budé, Congrès de Nice* (Paris, 1935) 358–78.

Darko, E., "Michael Apostolios levelei Laonikoshoz," *Csengers Emlék-könyv* (Szeged, 1926) 108–12.

Darlow, T. H. and H. F. Moule, *Historical Catalogue of the Printed Editions of Holy Scripture in the Library of the British and Foreign Bible Society*, 2 vols. (London, 1911).

Davies, T. *The Golden Century of Spain* (London, 1937).

Delaruelle, Louis "La carrière de Janus Lascaris depuis 1494," in *Revue du 16ᵉ siècle*, XIII (1926) 95–111.

———"Un vie d'humaniste au XVᵉ siècle, Gregorio Tifernas," *Mélanges de l'Ecole Française de Rome*, XIX (1899) 9–33.

Delitzsch, Friedrich, *Studien zur Entstehungsgeschichte der Polyglottenbibel des Cardinal Ximenes* (Leipzig, 1871).

Demaras, K. T., " Ἡ φωτισμένη Εὐρώπη," Νέα Ἑστία, LI (1952) 228ff.

Denifle, H., *Die Universitäten des Mittelalters bis 1400* (Berlin, 1885).

Denisoff, Elie, *Maxime le Grec et l'Occident* (Paris-Louvain, 1943).

Dibdin, T. F., *Introduction . . . to the Greek and Latin Classics*, 2 vols. (London, 1827).

Diehl, Charles, "Byzantine Civilization," *Cambridge Medieval History*, IV (New York, 1927) 745–77.

———*Byzantium: Greatness and Decline* (New Brunswick, 1957).

———"La colonie vénitienne à Constantinople," *Etudes byzantines* (Paris, 1905) 204ff.

———"Le monastère de S. Nicolas di Casole, près d'Otrante d'après un manuscrit inédit," *Mélanges d'archéologie et d'histoire*, VI 1886) 173–88.

Dölger, Franz, "Der Titel des sogenannten Suidas Lexikons," *Sitzungsberichte der bayerischen Akademie der Wissenschaften, Philosophisch — historische Klasse* (Munich, 1936) VI.

Donati, Lamberto, "La seconda Accademia Aldina ed una lettera ad Aldo Manuzio trascurata dai bibliografi," *Bibliofilia*, LIII (1951) 54–59.

Dorez, Léon, "Antoine Eparque," *Mélanges d'archéologie et d'histoire*, XIII (1893) 281–364.

———"Joannes Lascaris, frère de Janus Lascaris," *Revue des bibliothèques*, V (1895) 325–29.

———"Recherches sur la bibliothèque du Cardinal Girolamo Aleandro," in *Revue des bibliothèques*, II (1892) 49–68. Also "Nouvelles recherches sur la bibliothèque du Cardinal Girolamo Aleandro," *ibid.*, VII (1897) 293–304.

Douglas, R. M., *Jacopo Sadoleto 1477–1547: Humanist and Reformer* (Cambridge, Mass., 1959).

Drerup, Engelbert, *Die Schulaussprache des Griechischen von der Renaissance bis zur Gegenwart*, 2 vols. (Paderborn, 1930–1932).

Drummond, R., *Erasmus: His Life and Character as Shown in his Correspondence and Works* (London, 1873).

Ducas, T., *Travels in Various Countries in Europe* (London, 1822) I, 12–14.

Dudan, Bruno, *Il dominio Veneziano di Levante* (Bologna, 1938).

Egger, Emile, *L'hellénisme en France* (Paris, 1869).

Elwert, W. T., "Pietro Bembo e la vita letteraria del suo tempo," in *La Civiltà Veneziana del Rinascimento* (n.d.).

——"Venedigs literarische Bedeutung," *Archiv. für Kulturgeschichte*, XXXVI (1954) 261–300, and amplified version, "L'importanza letteraria di Venezia," *Studi di letteratura veneziana* (Venice-Rome, 1958) 1ff.

Embiricos, Alexander, *La Renaissance Crétoise: XVI e et XVII e siècles* (Paris, 1960).

Emerton, Ephraim, *Desiderius Erasmus of Rotterdam* (New York-London, 1899).

Esperabé y Arteaga, E., *Historia pragmatica e interna de la Universidad de Salamanca* (Salamanca, 1914–1917).

Essling, V., *Les livres à figures vénitiens de la fin du XV e siècle et du commencement du XVI e*, 4 vols. (Florence-Paris, 1907–1914).

Fabris, G., "Professori e scolari greci all' università di Padova," *Archivio Veneto*, XXX (1942) 120–65.

Ferguson, W. K., *The Renaissance in Historical Thought* (Boston, 1948).

Ferrai, Eugenio, *L'Ellenismo nello studio di Padova* (Padua, 1876).

Ferrajoli, A., "Il ruolo della corte di Leone X: Prelati domestici," *Arch. della Soc. Rom. di St. Patria*, LI (1928) 462ff.

Ferrigni, Mario, *Aldo Manuzio* (Milan, 1925).

Feugère, Gaston, *Erasme: Etude sur sa vie et ses ouvrages* (Paris, 1874).

Fiorentino, Francesco, *Pietro Pomponazzi: Studi storici sulla scuola bolognese-padovana del sec. XVI* (Florence, 1868).

Fioretto, G., *Gli umanisti, o lo studio del Latino e del Greco nel secolo XV in Italia* (Verona, 1881).

Firmin-Didot, A., *Alde Manuce et l'hellénisme à Venise* (Paris, 1875).

——"La Renaissance de l'hellénisme et Alde Manuce," *Revue de France* (Paris, 1875) 1–31.

Fletcher, J., *Literature of the Italian Renaissance*, 2 vols. (New York, 1934).

Foffano, Francesco, "Marco Musuro professore di greco a Padova e a Venezia," *Nuovo Archivio Veneto*, III (1892).

Fortescue, Adrian, *The Uniate Eastern Churches* (London, 1923).

Foscarini, M. (Doge), *Della letteratura veneziana* (Venice, 1854).

Foulché-Delbosc, R., "Le 'commandeur Grec,' y-a-t'il commenté le Laberinto?," *Revue hispanique*, X (1903) 105–16.

Franchini, V., "Note sull' attività finanziaria di Agostino Chigi nel Cinquecento," *Studi in onore di G. Luzzatto*, II (Milan, 1950) 156–75.

Freudenthal, Jacob, *Der Platoniker Albinos und der falsche Alkinoos* (Berlin, 1879).

Frothingham, A., Jr., "Byzantine Art and Culture in Rome and Italy," *American Journal of Archaeology*, X (1895) 160ff.

Fuchs, Friedrich, *Die höheren Schulen von Konstantinopel im Mittelalter* (Leipzig-Berlin, 1926).

Fumagalli, Giuseppe, "Saggio bibliografico sulla Galeomiomachia di Teodoro Prodromo," *Rivista delle biblioteche*, II (Florence, 1889) 49–56.

Gabotto, F., *Il trionfo di Venezia nell 'umanesimo* (Venice, 1890).

Gabrielli, G., "Gl'italo-greci e le loro colonie," *Studi bizantini*, I (1925) 97–121.

Gallavotti, Carlo, "Da Planude e Moscopulo alla prima edizione a stampa di Teocrito," *Studi italiani di filologia classica*, XIII (1936) 45–59.

———— "Per l'edizione di Teocrito," *Atti della reale accademia d'Italia, Rendiconti, Cl. Scienze Morali e Storici*, ser. VII (Rome, 1943) 1–19.

García López, J. Catalina, *Ensayo de una tipografía complutense* (Madrid, 1889).

García López, Santiago and Paulino Ortega Lamadrid, *Fiesta del libro, XIV Exposición: Obras de filósofos griegos romanos y comentaristas. Manuscritos, incunables e impresos (siglos XV–XVIII) Catálogo* (Valladolid, 1958) 1–58.

Garin, Eugenio, *L'educazione in Europa (1400–1600)* (Bari, 1957)

———— *Medioevo e Rinascimento* (Bari, 1954).

———— "Le traduzioni umanistiche di Aristotele nel secolo XV," *Atti dell' Accademia Fiorentina di Scienze Morali 'La Columbaria,'* VIII (1950) 1–50.

Gay, Jules, "Etude sur la décadence du rite grec dans l'Italie méridionale à la fin du XV e siècle," *Revue d'histoire et de littérature religieuses*, II (1897) 481–95.

———— *L'Italie méridionale et l'empire byzantin* (Paris, 1904).

———— "Notes sur le conservation du rite grec dans la Calabre et dans la terre d'Otrante au XIV e siècle," *Byz. Zeit.*, IV (1895) 59–66.

Geanakoplos, Deno J., "A Byzantine Looks at the Renaissance: The

Attitude of Michael Apostolis toward the Rise of Italy to Cultural Eminence," *Greek and Byzantine Studies*, I (1958) 157–62.

—— "The Council of Florence (1438–39) and the Problem of Union between the Greek and Latin Churches," *Church History*, XXIV (1955) 324–36.

—— *Emperor Michael Palaeologus and the West, 1258–82: A Study in Byzantine-Latin Relations* (Cambridge, Mass., 1959).

—— "Erasmus and the Aldine Academy of Venice: A Neglected Chapter in the Transmission of Graeco-Byzantine Learning to the West," *Greek, Roman, and Byzantine Studies*, III (1960) 107–34.

Geiger, L., "Beziehungen zwischen Deutschland und Italien zur Zeit des Humanismus," *Zeitschrift für deutsche Kulturgeschichte* (1875) n.s., 104–24.

Gercke, Alfred, *Theodoros Gazes. Festschrift der Universität Greifswald* (Greifswald, 1903).

Gerini, G. B., *Gli scrittori pedagogici italiani del secolo XV* (Turin, 1896).

Gerland, Ernst, "Histoire de la noblesse crétoise au Moyen Age," *Revue de l'Orient Latin*, X (1903–1904) 172–247; XI (1905–1908).

—— "Kreta als Venetianische Kolonie, 1204–1669," *Historisches Jahrbuch*, XX (1899) 1–24.

Gerola, Giuseppe, "Gli stemmi cretesi dell' Università di Padova," *Istituto Veneto di Scienze Lettere ed Arti*, 239–278, in *Atti del Reale Istituto Veneto di Scienze Lettere ed Arti* (1928–29).

—— *Monumenti Veneti dell'isola di Creta*, 4 vols. (Venice, 1905–1932).

—— *I francescani in Creta al tempo del dominio veneziano* (Assisi, 1932).

—— "Οἱ Ἕλληνες ἐπίσκοποι ἐν Κρήτῃ ἐπὶ Ἐνετοκρατίας," Χριστιανικὴ Κρήτη, II (1915) 313.

—— *Per la cronotassi dei vescovi Cretesi all' epoca Veneta* (Venice, 1914).

—— *Una descrizione di Candia del principio del 600* (Rovereto, 1908).

Gidel, C. A., *Nouvelles études sur la littérature grecque moderne* (Paris, 1878).

Gilmore, Myron, *The World of Humanism* (New York, 1952).

Gill, Joseph, *The Council of Florence* (Cambridge, Eng., 1959).

Goldsmid, E., *A Biographical Sketch of the Aldine Press at Venice* (Edinburgh, 1887).

Goldsmith, E., *The Printed Book of the Renaissance* (Cambridge, Mass., 1950).

González Palencia, A. and E. Mele, *Vida y obras de Don Diego Hurtado de Mendoza*, 3 vols. (Madrid, 1941–1943).

Gothein, Percy, *Francesco Barbaro. Frühhumanismus und Staatskunst in Venedig* (Berlin, 1932).

——— "Zaccaria Trevisan il Vecchio: la vita e l'ambiente," *Dep. St. Patria, Miscell., Studi e Mem.* (1942).

Gradenigo, Giangirolamo, *Lettera all' Emin. e Rev. Cardinale Angelo Quirini bibliotecario . . . di Brescia* (Venice, 1744).

Graux, Charles, *Essai sur les origines du fonds grec de l'Escurial* (Paris, 1880).

Gravino, Donato, *Saggio d'una storia dei volgarizzamenti d'opere greche nel secolo XV* (Naples, 1896).

Gray, H., "Greek Visitors to England 1455–56," in *Haskins Anniversary Essays* (Boston, 1929) 81–116.

Groussac, Paul, "Le commentateur du 'Laberinto,'" *Rev. Hisp.*, XI (1904) 164–224.

Grunzweig, Armand, "Philippe le Bon et Constantinople," *Byzantion*, XXIV (1954) 47–61.

Guilland, Rodolphe, "Les appels de Constantin XI Paléologue à Rome et à Venise pour sauver Constantinople," *Byzantinoslavica*, XIV (1953) 226–44.

——— *Essai sur Nicéphore Grégoras: L'homme et l'oeuvre* (Paris, 1926).

Halecki, Oskar, *From Florence to Brest (1439–1596)* (Rome, 1958).

Hall, F., *A Companion to Classical Texts* (Oxford, 1913).

Hall, Vernon, "Life of Julius Caesar Scaliger (1484–1558)," *Transactions of American Phil. Society*, XL (1950) 83–170.

Hartmann, G., "Die Bedeutung des Griechentums für die Entwicklung des italienischen Humanismus," in J. Irmscher, *Probleme der neugriechischen Literatur*, II (Berlin, 1960), 3–36.

Haskins, C. H., "The Greek Element in the Renaissance of the 12th Century," *American Historical Review*, XXV (1920) 603ff.

——— *Renaissance of the Twelfth Century* (Cambridge, Mass., 1927).

——— *Studies in the History of Medieval Science*, 2nd ed. (Cambridge, Mass., 1927).

Hatzes, A., Οἱ Ῥαούλ, Ῥάλ, Ῥάλαι *(1080–1800)* (Kirchhain, 1909).

Hatzidakes, M., " Ἡ συλλογὴ εἰκόνων τῆς Ἑλληνικῆς Κοινότητος τῆς Βενετίας," Κρητικὰ Χρονικά, III (1949) 574–82.

Hazlitt, W., *The Venetian Republic: Its Rise, Growth, and Fall*, 2 vols. (London, 1900).

Hefele, K. J., *The Life and Times of Cardinal Ximenes*, trans. J. Dalton, 2nd ed. (London, 1885).

Heisenberg, Auguste, "Das Problem der Renaissance in Byzanz," *Hist. Zeit.* 133 (1926) 393–412.

Hernand y Espinosa, Benito, "Cisneros y la fundación de la Universidad de Alcalá," *Boletín de la Institución libre de Enseñanza*, XXII (December 1898).

Hesseling, L. and H. Pernot, "Erasme et les origines da la prononciation érasmienne," *Revue des études grecques*, XXXII (1919) 278–301.

Heyd, Wilhelm, *Histoire du commerce du Levant au Moyen-Age*, 2 vols. (Leipzig, 1885–1886; reprinted 1936).

Hodius, H., *De doctis hominibus* (London, 1742).

Hofmann, Georg, "Wie stand es mit der Frage der Kircheneinheit auf Kreta?" *Orientalia Christiana Periodica*, X (1944) 91–115.

Hraban, Gerézdi, "Amis hongrois d'Aldus Manutius," *Magyar Könyvszemle*, LXIX (Budapest, 1945) 38–98.

Huizinga, J., *Erasmus of Rotterdam* (London, 1952).

Hunger, Herbert, "Theodoros Metochites als Vorläufer des Humanismus in Byzanz," *Byz. Zeit.*, XLV (1952) 4–19.

———"Von Wissenschaft und Kunst der frühen Palaiologenzeit," *Jahrbuch der Osterreichischen byz. Gesellschaft*, VIII (1959) 123–55.

———"Zeitgeschichte in der Rhetorik des sterbenden Byzanz," *Studien zur älteren Gesch..te Osteuropas*, II (1959) 152–61.

Hutton, James, *The Greek Anthology in Italy to the Year 1800* (Ithaca, 1935).

Irmscher, Johannes, *Probleme der neugriechischen Literatur*, II (Berlin, 1960).

Jorga, Nicolas, *Byzance après Byzance* (Bucharest, 1935).

Jugie, Martin, "Barlaam," *Dict. d'hist. géog. ecclés.*, VI, cols. 817–34.

———"Démétrius Cydonès et la théologie latine à Byzance au XIVe et XVe siècles," *Echos d'Orient*, XXXI (1928) 358–402.

Kaegi, W., "Hutten und Erasmus," *Historische Vierteljahrschrift*, XXII (1924–25) 200–278 and 461–504.

Kalitsounakes, J., Article on Marcus Musurus (in Greek) in *Encyclopedia Helios*, XIII (1953) 848–49.

———"Ματθαῖος Δεβαρῆς καὶ τὸ ἐν 'Ρώμη 'Ελληνικὸν Γυμνάσιον," 'Αθηνᾶ, XXVI (Athens, 1914) 81–101.

BIBLIOGRAPHY

Kalogeras, E., Μονεμβασία ἡ Βενετία τῆς Πελοποννήσου (Athens, 1956).

Kalokyres, K., Ἡ ἀρχαία Ῥίθυμνα (Athens, 1950).

Kalonaros, P., Ἡ Βενετία εἰς τοὺς θρύλους καὶ τὰ τραγούδια τοῦ Ἑλληνικοῦ λαοῦ (Athens, 1942).

Kampanes, A., Ἱστορία τῆς Νέας Ἑλληνικῆς Λογοτεχνίας (Alexandria, 1925).

Kampouroglou, D., Οἱ Χαλκοκονδύλαι (Athens, 1926).

Karapiperis, M., Nicephorus Blemmydes as teacher and master (in Greek) (Jerusalem, 1921).

Keller, A., "Two Byzantine Scholars and their Reception in Italy," Journal of the Warburg and Courtauld Institutes, XX (1957) 363–70.

Kerofilas, Costas, Une famille patricienne crétoise: les Vlasto (New York, 1932) 79–112.

Kibre, Pearl, The Library of Pico della Mirandola (New York, 1936).

Kleehoven, H. von, "Aldus Manuzio und der Plan einer deutschen Ritterakademie," Bibliofilia, LII (1950) 169–77.

Klibansky, Raymond, The Continuity of the Platonic Tradition during the Middle Ages (London, 1939).

Knös, Börje, Un ambassadeur de l'hellénisme: Janus Lascaris et la tradition greco-byzantine dans l'humanisme français (Upsala-Paris, 1945).

Kontosopoulos, N., "Τὰ ἐν Βενετίᾳ τυπογραφεῖα Ἑλληνικῶν βιβλίων κατὰ τὴν Τουρκοκρατίαν," Ἀθηνᾶ, LVIII (1954) 286–342.

Koukoules, Phaidon, Βυζαντινῶν βίος καὶ πολιτισμός, I (Athens, 1948).

—— "Συμβολὴ εἰς τὴν Κρητικὴν Λαογραφίαν ἐπὶ Βενετοκρατίας," Ἐπ. Ἑτ. Κρητικῶν Σπουδῶν, III (1940) 1–101.

Kournoutos, G. Λόγιοι τῆς Τουρκοκρατίας, I (Athens, 1956).

Kotta, B., "Ὁ Ἅγιος Γεώργιος τῶν Ἑλλήνων στὴ Βενετία," Νέα Ἑστία, XX (1936) 1612–15.

Kretschmayr, H., Geschichte von Venedig, 3 vols. (Gotha, 1905–1934).

Kristeller, Paul O., The Classics and Renaissance Thought (Cambridge, Mass., 1955).

—— "Humanism and Scholasticism in the Italian Renaissance," Byzantion, XVII (1944–1945).

—— "Die italienischen Universitäten der Renaissance," Schriften und Vorträge des Petrarca—Instituts Köln, I (n.d.).

—— The Philosophy of Marsilio Ficino (New York, 1943).

—— "The Place of Classical Humanism in Renaissance Thought," Journal of the History of Ideas, IV (1943).

—— *Studies in Renaissance Thought and Letters* (Rome, 1956).

—— "The University of Bologna in the Renaissance," *Studi e Memorie per la Storia dell' Università di Bologna*, n.s., I (1956) 313–23.

Kukenheim, Louis, *Contributions à l'histoire de la grammaire grecque, latine, et hébraïque à l'époque de la Renaissance* (Leiden, 1951).

Kyriakos, D., Ἐκκλησιαστικὴ Ἱστορία (Athens, 1898).

Kyrou, Achilles, "Les Byzantins à Venise" (in Greek), *Ekloge*, III (1947) 70–77.

—— " Ἡ πνευματικὴ ἀκμὴ τῆς Κρήτης κατὰ τὸν 15 ᵒʸ καὶ 16 ᵒʸ αἰῶνα," Ἐπ. Ἑτ. Κρητικῶν Σπουδῶν (1938) 302–15.

Lamansky, V., *Secrets d'état de Venise* (St. Petersburg, 1884).

Lampros, Spyridon, "Τὸ Βενετικὸν προξενεῖον ἐν Θεσσαλονίκῃ," Νέος Ἑλληνομνήμων, VIII (1911) 206–28.

—— "Λακεδαιμόνιοι βιβλιογράφοι," Νέος Ἑλληνομνήμων, IV (1907) 303–57.

Laourdas, Basil, " Ἡ Γόρτυνα καὶ ὁ Μιχαὴλ Ἀποστόλης," Κρητικὰ Χρονικά, IV (1950) 240–42.

Lazzari, V., "Nota sulle truppe marittime e terrestri della Republica di Venezia," in *Venezia e le sue lagune*, I (Venice, 1847).

Lazzarini, Lino, *Paolo de Bernardo e i primordi dell'umanesimo in Venezia* (Geneva, 1930).

Legrand, Emile, *Bibliographie hellénique ou description raisonnée des ouvrages publiés en grec par des grecs au XV ᵉ et XVI ᵉ siècles*, 4 vols. (Paris, 1885–1906).

—— *Bibliographie hispano-grecque*, pt. 1 (New York, 1915).

—— *Dossier Rhodocanakis* (Paris, 1895).

—— *Notice biographique sur Jean et Théodose Zygomalas* (Paris, 1889).

Leicht, P., *Ideali di vita dei veneziani nel cinquecento* (Venice, 1933).

Lemke, A., *Aldus Manutius and his Thesaurus Cornucopiae of 1496* (Syracuse, 1958).

Leva, G. de, *Della vita e delle opere del Card. Gasparo Contarini* (Padua, 1863).

Lockwood, D. P., "De Rinucio Aretino Graecarum Litterarum Interprete," *Harvard Studies in Classical Philology*, XXIV (1913) 51–109.

—— "Aristophanes in the 15th Century," *Transactions and Proceedings of American Philological Association*, XL (1909).

Lockwood, D. P. and R. Bainton, "Classical and Biblical Scholarship in the Age of the Renaissance and Reformation," *Church History*, X (1941) 3–21.

Loenertz, Raymond, "Démétrius Cydonès, citôyen de Venise," *Echos d'Orient*, XXXVII (1938).

——— "Pour la biographie du Cardinal Bessarion," *Orientalia Christiana Periodica*, X (1944) 116ff.

Lo Parco, Francesco, *Petrarca et Barlaam* (Reggio di Calabria, 1905).

Losada, A., *Juan Gines de Sepúlveda* (Madrid, 1949).

Loomis, Louise, *Medieval Hellenism* (Lancaster, Pa., 1906).

Lyell, J. P., *Cardinal Ximenes, Statesman, Ecclesiastic, Soldier and Man of Letters* (London, 1917).

Mandalari, Mario, *Fra Barlaamo Calabrese, maestro del Petrarca* (Rome, 1888).

Major, E., *Erasmus von Rotterdam* (Basle, 1926).

Manfroni, Camillo, *Storia della marina italiana dalle invasioni barbariche al trattato di Ninfeo* (Livorno, 1899).

Mancini, Augusto, "Spirito e caratteri dello studio del greco in Italia," *Italia e Grecia* (Florence, 1939) 411–33.

Mangan, J. J., *Life, Character, and Influence of Desiderius Erasmus of Rotterdam*, 2 vols. (New York, 1927).

Mann, M., *Erasme et les débuts de la réforme française (1517–36)* (Paris, 1934).

Manousakas, M. I., " Ἀρχιερεῖς Μεθώνης, Κορώνης καὶ Μονεμβασίας γύρω στὰ 1500," Πελοποννησιακά, III (1959) 95–147.

——— Ἡ ἐν Κρήτῃ συνωμοσία τοῦ Σήφη Βλαστοῦ *(1453–54)* καὶ ἡ νέα συνωμοτικὴ κίνησις τοῦ *1460–62* (Athens, 1960).

——— "Μέτρα τῆς Βενετίας ἔναντι τῆς ἐν Κρήτῃ ἐπιρροῆς τοῦ Πατριαρχείου Κωνσταντινουπόλεως," Ἐπετηρὶς Ἑταιρείας Βυζαντινῶν Σπουδῶν, XXX (1960) 85–144.

——— "Προσθῆκαι καὶ συμπληρώσεις εἰς τὴν Ἑλληνικὴν Βιβλιογραφίαν τοῦ E. Legrand (Συμβολὴ πρώτη)," Ἐπετηρὶς Μεσαιωνικοῦ Ἀρχείου Ἀκαδημίας Ἀθηνῶν, VII (1958) 34–83.

——— "Recherches sur la vie de Jean Plousiadénos (Joseph de Méthone) (1429?–1500)," *Revue des études byzantines*, XVII (1959) 28–51.

Marangoni, G., "Lazaro Bonamico e lo studio padovano nella prima metà del Cinquecento," *Nuovo Archivio Veneto*, I (1901) 118–51 and II (1901) 131–96.

Marconi, S., "La Raccolta di Icone Veneto-Cretesi della Communità Greco-Ortodossa di Venezia," *Atti dell' Istituto Veneto di scienze lettere ed arti (1947)* (Venice, 1948) 104–47.

Marinesco, Constantine, "L'Enseignement du grec dans l'Italie méridionale avant 1453, d'après un document inédit," *Académie des inscriptions et belles-lettres, Comptes rendus* (1948) 304–12.

———— "Notes sur quelques ambassadeurs byzantins en Occident à la veille de la chute de Constantinople sous les Turcs," *Mélanges Henri Grégoire*, II (Brussels, 1950).

Marzi, D., *Una Questione librarie fra i Giunti ed Aldo Manuzio* (per nozze) (Florence, 1895).

Masai, François, "Περὶ τῆς οὐσίας faussement attribué à Michel Apostolis," *Scriptorium*, I (1946–7) 162ff.

————*Pléthon et le Platonisme de Mistra* (Paris, 1956).

Mazzoni, G., "Le piu importanti traduzioni italiane di classici greci," *Italia e grecia* (Florence, 1939) 425–33.

Mazzuchelli, G. M., *Gli scrittori d'Italia*, 6 vols. (Brescia, 1753–1763).

Menéndez y Pelayo, M., "Humanistas esp. del siglo XVI," *Revista de Madrid*, V (1883) 89–111.

Menge, Rudolf, *De Marci Musuri Cretensis vita, studiis, ingenio narratio*, in M. Schmidt, ed., *Hesychii Alexandrini Lexicon*, V (Jena, 1868) 1–57.

Mercati, Angelo, "Le spese private di Leone X nel maggio-agosto 1513," *Atti della Pontif. Accademia Romana di Archeologia*, ser. 3, *Memorie*, II (1928) 99–112.

Mercati, Giovanni, *Se la versione dall' Ebraico del Codice veneto-greco VII sia di Simone Atumano* (Vatican, 1916).

Mercati, Silvio G., "Di Giovanni Simeonachis Protopapa di Candia," *Miscellanea Giovanni Mercati*, III, in *Studi e Testi*, CXXIII (Vatican, 1946) 1–30.

———— "Venezia nella poesia Neo-greca," *Italia e Grecia* (Florence, 1939) 307–39.

Merores, M., "Der Venezianische Adel," *Vierteljahrschrift für Sozial- und Wirtschaftsgeschichte*, XIX (1936) 137–237.

Mertzios, Constantine, Θωμᾶς Φλαγγίνης καὶ ὁ Μικρὸς Ἑλληνομνήμων, in Πραγματεῖαι τῆς Ἀκαδημίας Ἀθηνῶν, IX (1939).

———— " Ἡ διαθήκη τῆς Ἄννας Παλαιολογίνας Νοταρᾶ," Ἀθηνᾶ, LIII (1949) 17–21.

————"Περὶ Παλαιολόγων καὶ ἄλλων εὐγενῶν Κωνσταντινουπολιτῶν," Γέρας Α. Κεραμοπούλλου (Athens, 1953), 355–72.

Mestica, E., *Varino Favorino Camerte* (Ancona, 1888).

Meyer, M., "Ein Kollegheft des Humanisten Conon," *Zentralblatt für Bibliothekswesen*, LIII (1936) 281–84.

Michalopoulos, A., " Ἐνετία καὶ Βυζάντιον," Ἔρευνα (Alexandria, 1934) 47ff.

Michaud, J. F., ed., "Marcus Musurus," *Biographie Universelle*, XXIX, 655–56.

Miller, William, *Essays on the Latin Orient* (Cambridge, 1921), esp. "Crete under the Venetians (1204–1669)," 177–98.

———— *Latins in the Levant* (London, 1908).

———— "Monemvasia," *Journal of Hellenic Studies*, XXVII (1907) 238ff.

Minio-Paluello, L., "Jacobus Veneticus Grecus," *Traditio*, VIII (1952) 265–304.

Mohler, Ludwig, *Kardinal Bessarion als Theologe, Humanist und Staatsmann*, 3 vols. (Paderborn, 1923–1942).

Molmenti, Pompeo, *Venice: Its Individual Growth from the Earliest Beginnings to the Fall of the Republic*, trans. H. F. Brown, 6 vols. (Chicago, 1907).

Monnier, P., *Le Quattrocento*, 2 vols. (Paris, 1912).

Morel-Fatio, A., *L'historiographie de Charles-Quint*, I (Paris, 1913).

Morelli, J., *Della pubblica libreria di San Marco in Venezia* (Venice, 1774).

Motta, E., "Demetrio Calcondila editore," *Archivio storico lombardo*, X (Milan, 1893) 143–66.

Moustoxydes, Andreas, "Arsenios" (in Greek), Πανδώρα, VI (1855–56) 493–94; also "Zacharias Calliergis," *Hellenomnemon*, I, 328–336.

———— "Τὸ ἐν Ῥώμῃ Ἑλληνικὸν Γυμνάσιον," Ἑλληνομνήμων, I (1843) 234.

Muckle, J., "Greek Works Translated Directly into Latin before 1350," *Medieval Studies*, IV (1942) 33–42, V (1943) 102–14.

Nardi, B., "Letteratura e cultura veneziana del Quattrocento," in *La Civiltà Veneziana del Quattrocento* (Florence, 1957) 99–147.

———— *Saggi sull' Aristotelismo padovano dal secolo XIV al XVI* (Florence, 1958).

Netzhammer, Raymund, *Das griechische Kolleg in Rom* (Salzburg, 1905).

Neumann, Carl, "Byzantinische Kultur und Renaissance Kultur," *Historische Zeitschrift*, XCI (1903) 215–32.

Nolhac, Pierre de, *Erasme en Italie* (Paris, 1898).

———— *Erasme et l'Italie* (Paris, 1925).

———— "Le grec à Paris sous Louis XII," *Revue des études grecques*, I (1888) 61–67.

———— *Pétrarque et l'humanisme*, 2nd ed. (Paris, 1907).

Nordström, J., *Moyen Age et Renaissance* (Paris, 1933).

Norton, F. J., *Italian Printers 1501-1520* (London, 1958).

Nulli, S., *Erasmo e il Rinascimento* (Milan, 1955).

Oleroff, A., "L'humaniste Dominicain Jean Conon et le Crétois Jean Grégoropoulos," *Scriptorium*, IV (1950) 104-107.

Olmedo, F., *Nebrija en Salamanca* (Madrid, 1944).

Omont, Henri, "Hermonyme de Sparte, maître de grec à Paris et copiste de manuscrits (1476)," *Mémoires de la Société de l'histoire de Paris et de l'Ile-de-France*, XII (1885) 65-78.

Ostrogorsky, George, *History of the Byzantine State*, trans. J. Hussey (New Brunswick, 1957).

Palau y Dulcet, A., *De los origines de la imprenta y su introducción en España* (Barcelona, 1952).

———— *Los origenes de la imprenta en España* (Barcelona, 1948).

Pantelakes, E., "Τὸ Σινᾶ καὶ ἡ Κρήτη," Ἐπ. Ἑτ. Κρητικῶν Σπουδῶν, I (1938) 165-85.

Papadopoli, N. C., *Historia gymnasii patavini*, 2 vols. (Venice, 1762).

Papadopoulos, C., "Σχέσεις ὀρθοδόξων καὶ λατίνων κατὰ τὸν 16ον αἰῶνα, Θεολογία, III (1925) 103-107.

Papadopoulos-Kerameus, A., "Μάρκος ὁ Ξυλοκαράβης, Πατριάρχης Οἰκουμενικὸς καὶ εἶτα πρόεδρος τῶν Ἀχριδῶν," Βυζαντινὰ Χρονικά, X (1903) 402-15.

Papadopoulos-Vretos, A., Νεοελληνικὴ Φιλολογία (1854-1857).

Papamichael, G., Μάξιμος ὁ Γραικός (Athens, 1951).

Paquier, J. A., "Erasme et Aléandre," in *Mélanges de l'Ecole Française de Rome*, XV (1895) 351-374.

———— *L'humanisme et la réforme: Jérôme Aléandre de sa naissance à la fin de son séjour à Brindes* (Paris, 1900).

Paschang, J. L., "The Popes and the Revival of Learning" (dissertation, Catholic University, Washington, D.C., 1927).

Paschini, Pio, *Domenico Grimani Cardinale di S. Maria* (Rome, 1943).

Paspates, A. G., Βυζαντιναὶ Μελέται (Constantinople, 1877).

Pastor, Ludwig von, *History of the Popes, from the Close of the Middle Ages* (London, 1891-1940) vols. 2-12.

Pastorello, Esther, *Bibliografia storico-analitica dell' arte della stampa in Venezia* (Venice, 1933).

———— *Tipografi, editori, librai a Venezia nel secolo XVI* (Florence, 1924).

Paulsen, F., *Geschichte des gelehrten Unterrichts*, 2 vols. (Leipzig, 1919-1921).

Pears, Edwin, *The Destruction of the Greek Empire and the Story of the Capture of Constantinople by the Turks* (London, 1903).

Pernot, H. O., "Les Crétois hors de Crète," *Etudes de Littérature grecque moderne* (Paris, 1916) 129–94.

Pernot, H. O., and L. Hesseling, "Erasme et les origines de la prononciation érasmienne," *Revue des études grecques*, XXXII (1919) 278–301.

Pertusi, A., "Leonzio Pilato, Petrarca e Boccaccio: Omero e la cultura greca nel primo umanesimo" (not yet published).

——— "La scoperta di Euripide nel primo Umanesimo," *Italia medioevale e umanistica*, III (1960) 101–52.

Pertusi, A., and E. Franceschini, "Un' ignota Odissea latina dell' ultimo Trecento," *Aevum*, XXXIII (1959) 323–55.

Phillips, M., *Erasmus and the Northern Renaissance* (New York, 1950).

Pierling, Paul, *La Russie et le Saint-Siège*, I (Paris, 1896).

Pisani, P., "Les Chrétiens de rite oriental à Venise et dans les possessions vénitiennes (1439–1791)," *Revue d'histoire et de littérature religieuses*, I (1896) 201–24.

Pizzi, C., *Un amico di Erasmo: L'umanista Andrea Ammonio* (Florence, 1956).

——— "La grammatica greca di T. di Gaza ed Erasmo," *Atti dello VIII Congresso Intern. di Studi Bizantini*, I (Rome, 1953) 183–88.

Politis, L., "Eine Schreibschule im Kloster τῶν 'Οδηγῶν," *Byz. Zeit.*, LI (1958) 278ff.

Powell, J. Enoch, "Cretan Manuscripts of Thucydides," *Classical Quarterly*, XXXII (1938) 102–108.

Prescott, H., *Friar Felix at Large* (New Haven, 1950).

Prezziner, Giovanni, *Storia del pubblico studio e delle società scientifiche e letterarie di Firenze*, 2 vols. (Florence, 1810).

Proctor, Robert, *The Printing of Greek in the Fifteenth Century* (Oxford, 1900).

Psilakes, B., Ἱστορία τῆς Κρήτης, 3 vols. (Canea, 1909–1910).

Pusino, I., "Der Einfluss Picos auf Erasmus," *Zeitschrift für Kirchengeschichte*, XLVI (1927) 75–96.

Putnam, G., *Books and their Makers during the Middle Ages*, I, 2nd ed. (New York, 1898).

Quaranta, E., "Osservazioni intorno ai caratteri greci di Aldo Manuzio," *La Bibliofilia*, LV (1953) 123–30.

Rackl, Michael, *Miscellanea F. Ehrle*, I, in *Studi e testi*, XXXVII (Rome, 1924).

Ranke, L. von, *History of the Popes during the Last Four Centuries*, trans. E. Foster, 3 vols. (London, 1912).

—— *The History of the Popes, their Church and State in 16–17th Centuries*, trans. W. Kelly (Philadelphia, 1844).

—— *Zur Kritik neuerer Geschichtsschreiber* (Leipzig, 1874).

Rashdall, Hastings, *The Universities of Europe in the Middle Ages*, 3 vols. (Oxford, 1936).

Renaudet, Augustin, "Erasme et l'Italie," in *Travaux d'humanisme et Renaissance*, XV (Geneva, 1954).

—— "Erasme et . . . langues antiques," *Bib. hum. Ren.*, 18 (1956) 190–96.

—— *Préréforme et humanisme à Paris pendant les premières guerres d'Italie (1494–1517)* (Paris, 1916).

Renazzi, F. M., *Storia dell' Università degli studi di Roma*, 3 vols. (Rome, 1803–1806).

Renieris, M., Ὁ Ἕλλην Πάπας Ἀλέξανδρος Εʹ (Athens, 1881).

Reusner, Nicolaus, *Icones sive Imagines virorum literis illustrium* (Frankfurt-am-Main, 1719).

Reynier, G., *La vie universitaire dans l'ancienne Espagne* (Paris, 1902).

Riccoboni, Antonio, *De Gymnasio Patavino* (Padua, 1598).

Ridolfi, Roberto, *La biblioteca del Cardinale N. Ridolfi (1501–50)*, *Bibliofilia*, XXXI (1929) 173–93.

—— *Scritti sopra Aldo Manuzio* (Florence, n.d.).

—— *La Stampa in Firenze nel Secolo XV* (Florence, 1958).

Robb, N., *Neoplatonism of the Italian Renaissance* (London, 1935).

Robertson, E., "Aldus Manutius, the Scholar-Printer," *Bulletin of J. Rylands Library*, XXXIII (1950).

Rocholl, R., *Bessarion, Studien zur Geschichte der Renaissance* (Leipzig, 1904) 79–85.

Rodocanachi, Emmanuel P., *La première Renaissance: Rome au temps de Jules II et de Léon X* (Paris, 1912).

Rodotà, P., *Dell' origine, progresso, e stato presente del rito greco in Italia*, III (Rome, 1763).

Romanin, Samuele, *Storia documentata di Venezia*, 2nd ed. (Venice, 1912–1925) vols. I–VI.

Rosalia, A. de, "La vita di Costantino Lascaris," *Archivio storico siciliano*, III (1957–58) no. 9, pp. 21–70.

Roscoe, William, *The Life and Pontificate of Leo X*, 4 vols. (Liverpool, 1805–1806).

Rosmini, C. de', *Vita di Francesco Filelfo*, 3 vols. (Milan, 1808).

Rossi, V., *Il Quattrocento*, 3rd ed. (Milan, 1933).

Rubio, P. Lemus, "El Maestro Elio Antonio de Lebrixa," *Revue hispanique*, XXII (1910) 478ff.

Rupprecht, Karl, *Apostolis, Eudem und Suidas, Studien zur Geschichte der griechischen Lexica* (Leipzig, 1922).

Sabbadini, Remigio, *Centotrenta lettere inedite di Francesco Barbaro* (Salerno, 1884).

—— *Giovanni da Ravenna, insigne figura d'umanista* (Como, 1924).

—— *Il metodo degli umanisti* (Florence, 1922).

—— *Le scoperte dei codici latini e greci nei secoli XIV e XV*, 2 vols. (Florence, 1905–1914).

—— *La scuola e gli studi di Guarino Veronese* (Catania, 1896).

—— "L'ultimo ventennio della vita di M. Crisolora," *Giornale ligustico*, XVII (1890) 321ff.

Salaville, Sévérien, "Arsenios Apostolios," "Michael Apostolios," *Dict. d'hist. géog. eccl.*, III, cols. 1027–35.

Saitta, Giuseppe, *La filosofia di Marsilio Ficino* (Messina, 1923).

Sandys, John E., *Harvard Lectures on the Revival of Learning* (Cambridge, Eng., 1905).

—— *A History of Classical Scholarship*, 3 vols. (Cambridge, 1903–1908) (reprinted 1958).

Sathas, Konstantine, " Ἕλληνες στρατιῶται ἐν τῇ Δύσει," Ἑστία, XIX (1885) 370–76, and later issues.

—— Νεοελληνικὴ φιλολογία (Athens, 1868).

Scaffini, G., *Notizie intorno ai primi cento anni della dominazione Veneta in Creta* (Alexandria, 1907).

Schmidt, A., "Ingratitude des Humanistes envers Byzance," *Permanence de la Grèce* (Paris, 1948) 135–41.

Scholderer, Victor, *Greek Printing Types 1465–1927* (London, 1927).

—— "Printers and Readers in Italy in the Fifteenth Century," in *Proceedings of the British Academy*, XXXV (1949) 1–23.

—— *Printing at Venice to the End of 1481* (London, 1925).

Schück, J., *Aldus Manutius und seine Zeitgenossen in Italien und Deutschland* (Berlin, 1862).

Seebohm, F., *The Oxford Reformers* (London, 1914).

Segarizzi, Arnaldo, "Cenni sulle scuole pubbliche a Venezia nel secolo XV e sul primo maestro d'esse," *Atti del R. Ist. Veneto*, LXXV (1915–16) 638ff.

—— "Lauro Quirini Umanista Veneziano del Secolo XV," *Memorie della Reale Accademia delle Scienze di Torino*, LIV (1904) 1–28.

Semper, H., F. Schulze, and W. Barth, *Carpi: Ein Fürstensitz der Renaissance* (Dresden, 1882).

Sephakes, G., "Μάρκου Μουσούρου τοῦ Κρητὸς ποίημα εἰς τὸν Πλάτωνα," Κρητικὰ Χρονικά, VIII (1954) 366–88.

Setton, Kenneth M., "The Byzantine Background to the Italian Renaissance," *Proceedings of the American Philosophical Society*, C, no. 1 (1956) 1–76.

——— *Catalan Domination of Athens, 1311–88* (Cambridge, 1948).

Sicilianos, D., Ἕλληνες ἁγιογράφοι μετὰ τὴν Ἅλωσιν (Athens, 1935).

Siegmund, A., *Die Ueberlieferung der griechischen cristlichen Literatur in der lateinischen Kirche bis zum zwoelften Jahrhundert* (Munich, 1949).

Sigala, A., Ἱστορία τῆς Ἑλληνικῆς Γραφῆς (Salonika, 1934).

Signorelli, Giuseppe, *Il Card. Egidio da Viterbo, Agostiniano, umanista e riformatore* (Florence, 1929).

Simar, T., *Cristophe de Longueil, humaniste* (Louvain, 1911).

Simeoni, L., *Storia della Università di Bologna*, 2 vols. (Bologna, 1940).

Simons, H. de, "Erasmo y sus impresores," *Humanidádes*, XI (1925) 313–19.

Skasses, E., " Ἡ Κρήτη καὶ οἱ Λατῖνοι συγγραφεῖς," Κρητικὰ Χρονικά, VII (1953) 119–26.

Smith, Preserved, *Erasmus* (New York, 1923).

——— "A Key to the Colloquies of Erasmus," *Harvard Theological Studies*, XIII (1927).

Soteriou, George, " Ἡ Ἑλληνικὴ Ἐκκλησία τοῦ Ἁγίου Γεωργίου ἐν Βενετίᾳ," Ἡμερολόγιον τῆς Μεγάλης Ἑλλάδος (1930) 79–90.

Spingarn, J., *History of Criticism in the Renaissance*, 2nd ed. (New York, 1908).

Stephanides, Basil, Ἐκκλησιαστικὴ Ἱστορία (Athens, 1948).

Symonds, J. A., *The Renaissance in Italy*, 7 vols. (New York, 1914–1915).

Tannery, P., *Mémoires scientifiques*, V, *Sciences exactes chez les Byzantins* (Paris, 1920).

Tassini, Giuseppe, *Curiosità veneziane*, ed. E. Zorzi (Venice, 1933).

Tatakis, Basil, *Histoire de la philosophie byzantine* (Paris, 1949).

Tatham, E., "Erasmus in Italy," *English Historical Review*, X (1895) 649ff.

Taylor, J. W., "Bessarion the Mediator," *Transactions and Proceedings of American Philological Association*, LX (1924) 120–27.

——— *Georgius Gemistus Pletho's Criticism of Plato and Aristotle* (Menasha, 1921).

Thiriet, Freddy, *Régestes des délibérations de Venise concernant la Romanie* (Paris, 1959).

——— *Histoire de Venise* (Paris, 1952).

—— *La Romanie vénitienne au moyen âge* (*XIIᵉ–XVᵉ siècles*) (Paris, 1959).

Thomas, H., *Periods of Typography: Spanish 16th Century Printing* (London, 1926).

Thompson, J. W., *The Medieval Library* (New York, 1957).

Tilley, Arthur, *Dawn of the French Renaissance* (Cambridge, Eng., 1918).

Tiraboschi, Girolamo, *Storia della Letteratura Italiana*, 9 vols. (Modena, 1787–1794) (new ed., Milan, 1833).

Tischendorf, Constantin von, *Novum Testamentum graece*, vol. III (Leipzig, 1894).

Toffanin, Giuseppe, "La lettera del Papa Pio II a Maometto II," *Ultimi Saggi* (Bologna, 1960) 81–124.

—— *Storia dell'umanesimo* (Naples, 1933).

Tomadakes, Nicholas, " Ἀμιρούτζης καὶ Μιχ. Ἀποστόλης," Ἐπ. Ἑτ. Βυζ. Σπουδῶν, XVIII (1948) 130ff.

—— "Αἱ Ἑλληνικαὶ Κοινότητες τοῦ ἐξωτερικοῦ," Ἀθηνᾶ, LVII (1953) 3–34.

—— Ὁ Ἰωσὴφ Βρυέννιος καὶ ἡ Κρήτη κατὰ τὸ *1400* (Athens, 1947).

—— "Μιχαὴλ Καλοφρενᾶς Κρής, Μητροφάνης Β' καὶ ἡ πρὸς τὴν ἕνωσιν τῆς Φλωρεντίας ἀντίθεσις τῶν Κρητῶν," Ἐπ. Ἑτ. Βυζ. Σπουδῶν, XXI (1949–51) 110–44.

—— "Οἱ Ὀρθόδοξοι παπάδες ἐπὶ Ἑνετοκρατίας καὶ ἡ χειροτονία αὐτῶν," Κρητικὰ χρονικά, XIII (1959) 39–72.

—— "Répercussion immédiate de la prise de Constantinople," *L'Hellénisme Contemporain*, VII (1953) 55–68.

Torre, A. de la, "La Casa Nebrija en Alcalá de Henares y la Casa de la Imprenta de la 'Biblia Poliglota Complutense,'" *Miscelanea Nebrija*, I (Madrid, 1946) 175–82.

Torre, A. della, *Storia dell' Accademia Platonica di Firenze* (Florence, 1902).

Tuilier, André, "Recherches sur les origines de la Renaissance byzantine au XIIIᵉ siècle," *Bulletin de l'association Guillaume Budé*, III (1955) 71–76.

Udalcova, Z. V., "The Struggle of Parties in 15th Century Byzantium and the Role of Bessarion of Nicaea" (in Russian), *Vizantiysky Vremennik*, II (1949) 249–307, and III (1950) 106–32.

Ughelli, Ferdinando, *Italia Sacra*, 2nd ed., 10 vols. (Venice, 1717–1722).

Ullmann, B. L., *The Origin and Development of Humanistic Script* (Rome, 1960).

———— "Some Aspects of the Origin of Italian Humanism," *Philological Quarterly*, XX (1941) 20–31.

Vailhé, Siméon, "Constantinople (Eglise de)," in *Dict. Théol. Cath.* (1908), section entitled "L'Italie byzantine, VIIIᵉ–XVIᵉ siècles."

Valery, A. C., *Voyages historiques et littéraires en Italie, a. 1826–28*, 3rd ed. (Brussels, 1842).

Vannutelli, Vincenzo, *Le colonie Italo-greche* (Rome, 1890).

Vasiliev, Alexander, *History of the Byzantine Empire* (Madison, 1952).

Vast, Henri, *Le Cardinal Bessarion* (Paris, 1878).

———— *De vita et operibus Jani Lascaris* (Paris, 1878).

Vaughan, Dorothy, *Europe and the Turk: A Pattern of Alliances, 1350–1700* (Liverpool, 1954).

Veludo, Giovanni, Ἑλλήνων Ὀρθοδόξων ἀποικία ἐν Βενετίᾳ, 2nd ed. (Venice, 1893); earlier Italian ed. "Cenni sulla colonia greca orientale," *Venezia e le sue lagune* (Venice, 1847) I, pt. 2, 78ff.

Verpeaux, J., "Byzance et l'humanisme: Position du problème," *Bulletin de l'association G. Budé*, 3rd ser. (October 1952).

———— *Nicéphore Choummos homme d'état et humaniste byzantin (ca. 1250/1255–1327)* (Paris, 1959).

Verveniotes, G., " Ἑλληνισταὶ τῆς Ἀναγεννήσεως. Μᾶρκος Μουσοῦρος," Νέα Ἑστία, II (1927) 792–97.

Villemain, A., *Lascaris ou les Grecs du XVᵉ siècle* (Cambridge, Eng., 1875).

Viller, Marcel, "La question de l'union des églises entre Grecs et Latins," *Revue d'histoire écclésiastique*, XVII (1921) 260–305, 515–32; XVIII (1922) 20–60.

Vindel, Francisco, *Origen de la imprenta en España* (Madrid, 1935).

Visconti, Alessandro, *La storia dell' Università di Ferrara* (Bologna, 1950).

Vitaliani, Domenico, *Della vita e delle opere di Nicolò Leoniceno Vicentino* (Verona, 1892).

Vogel, E., "Litterarische Ausbeute von Janus Lascaris' Reisen im Peloponnes um's Jahr 1490," *Serapeum*, XV (1854) 154–60.

Voigt, Georg, *Die Wiederbelebung des classischen Alterthums*, 3rd ed. (Berlin, 1893). *Pétrarche, Boccace et les débuts de l'humanisme en Italie*, trans. P. Le Monnier (Paris, 1894).

Voltz, L., "Zur Uberlieferung der griech. Gramm. in byzant. Zeit," in Fleckeisen's *Neue Jahrbücher für Philologie und Paedagogik* XXXIX (1889), 579.

Weiss, Roberto, *The Dawn of Humanism in Italy* (London, 1947).

———— "England and the Decree of Vienne on the Teaching of Greek,

Arabic, Hebrew and Syriac," *Bibliothèque d'Humanisme et Renaissance*, XIV (1952) 1ff.

—— "The Greek Culture of South Italy in the Later Middle Ages," *Proceedings of the British Academy*, XXXVII (1951) 23–50.

—— *Humanism in England during the Fifteenth Century* (Oxford, 1941).

—— "Italian Humanism in Western Europe," in *Italian Renaissance Studies*, ed. E. Jacob (London, 1960) 69–93.

—— "Learning and Education in Western Europe from 1470 to 1520," *The New Cambridge Modern History*, I (Cambridge, Eng., 1957) 95–126.

—— "Lo studio del greco all' Università di Parigi alla fine del Medioevo," *Convivium*, XXIII (1955) 146–49.

—— *Un umanista veneziano papa Paolo II* (Venice-Rome, 1958).

—— "The Translators from the Greek at the Angevin Court of Naples," *Rinascimento* (1950) 195–226.

Wendel, C. T. "Planudes, Maximos," *Real Encycl. Klass. Altert.*, XL (Stuttgart, 1950) cols. 2202–53.

Wilkins, E. H., *Petrarch at Vaucluse* (Chicago, 1958).

Witt, R. E., *Albinus and the History of Middle Platonism* (Cambridge, Eng., 1937).

Wittek, Martin, "Pour une étude du *scriptorium* de Michel Apostolès et consorts," *Scriptorium*, VII (1953) 289–97.

Woodward, W. H., *Studies in Education during the Age of the Renaissance, 1400–1600* (Cambridge, Eng., 1924).

—— *Vittorino da Feltre and Other Humanist Educators* (Cambridge, Eng., 1905).

Xanthoudides, Stephanos, Ἡ Ἐνετοκρατία ἐν Κρήτῃ (Athens, 1939).

Xerouhakes, Agathaggelos, Ἡ Βενετοκρατουμένη Ἀνατολή: Κρήτη καὶ Ἑπτάνησος (Athens, 1934).

Young, D. C., "A Codicological Inventory of Theognis Manuscripts," *Scriptorium*, VII (1953) 3–36.

Ypselantes, A., Τὰ μετὰ τὴν ἅλωσιν 1453–1789 (Constantinople, 1870).

Zakythinos, Dionisios, Ἡ Ἅλωσις τῆς Κωνσταντινουπόλεως καὶ ἡ Τουρκοκρατία (Athens, 1954).

—— *Le Despotat grec de Morée 1262–1460*, II (Athens, 1953).

—— *La Grèce et les Balkans* (Athens, 1947).

—— "Μιχαὴλ Μάρουλλος Ταρχανιώτης," Ἐπ. Ἑτ. Βυζ. Σπ., V (1928) 200–42.

—— "Τὸ πρόβλημα τῆς ἑλληνικῆς συμβολῆς εἰς τὴν Ἀναγέννησιν," Ἐπιστημ. Ἐπετ. Φιλοσοφ. Σχολῆς, Παν. Ἀθηνῶν (1954–55) 126–38.

Zanelli, Domenico, *Il pontefice Niccolò V ed il risorgimento delle lettere, delle arti e delle scienze in Italia* (Rome, 1855).

Zanotto, Francesco, "Pittura, Architettura, Scultura, e Calcografia," *Venezia e le sue lagune* (Venice, 1847) I, pt. 2, 290ff.

Zoras, George, Γεώργιος ὁ Τραπεζούντιος καὶ αἱ πρὸς Ἑλληνοτουρκικὴν Συνεννόησιν προσπάθειαι αὐτοῦ (Athens, 1954).

———"Κάρολος ὁ Ε′ τῆς Γερμανίας καὶ αἱ πρὸς ἀπελευθέρωσιν προσπάθειαι," Περὶ τὴν ἅλωσιν τῆς Κωνσταντινουπόλεως (Athens, 1959) 193–211.

Zoudianos, Nicholas, Ἱστορία τῆς Κρήτης ἐπὶ Ἐνετοκρατίας, I (Athens, 1960).

INDEX

Accolti, Benedetto, 187n
Acropolites, George, 23
Adages, 119, 257n, 260, 263–273
Adramyttenos, Emmanuel, 85, 108, 116, 282, 290
Adrian VI, Pope, 65, 187, 221, 249
Aelian Dionysius, 172n
Aesop, 287
Agapetus, 213
Agricola, Rudolph, 5, 294n
Albanians, 56n
Alberto Pio. *See* Pio, Alberto
Alcalá Bible. *See* Polyglot Bible
Alcalá, University of: Greek studies, 223, 232–237; paucity of Greek materials, 235–236; teaching of Greek by Demetrius Ducas, 238, 250, 254, 293
Alcionio, Pietro, 145, 166n
Alcinous, 290
Aldine Academy, 132, 150, 211, 213, 223, 256–257, 277, 285, 294, 298; founding, 128; influence on Erasmus, 257, 263–266, 270–278; membership, 128–130; relations with Musurus, 131, 139; and transmission of Greek to western Europe, 128–129
Aldine Press, 128, 132, 157, 193, 204, 220, 284–286, 289–290; closing, 142, 213; establishment, 117–120; reopening in Venice, 146; relations with Musurus, 120–121, 139, 146, 156, 284–285, 287–289; and transmission of Greek to western Europe, 284–285, 297
Aldus Manutius, 58, 60, 85, 108, 116, 121, 130–131, 139–140, 143, 145, 154–155, 157, 172–175, 177, 193, 204, 207, 209, 211–212, 215, 221, 284–285, 295–297; death, 156, 248, 281; early years, 116; plans for Polyglot Bible, 245; preface to Erasmus' *Adages*, 268–270; publication of Greek grammars, 285–287; relations with Alberto Pio, 125; with Arsenios Apostolis, 171–176, 182,

186; with Demetrius Ducas, 223, 226–227, 229–230, 232, 262, 284; with Erasmus, 246, 257, 259–261, 263, 266, 268–272, 274–278; with his employees, 261–262; with Leo X, 150, 153–154; with Musurus, 120, 131, 146, 262; with Zacharias Calliergis, 207; role in dissemination of Greek to western Europe, 284–285, 297; studies in Greek pronunciation, 274, 278. *See also* Aldine Academy; Aldine Press
Aleandro, Girolamo, 4, 129, 131, 135, 220n, 226n, 229–230, 261, 267n, 270, 274–275, 278, 294, 297
Alexander V, Pope, 41, 163
Alexander VI, Pope, 58, 160
Alexander of Aphrodisias, 140, 154, 174, 249–259, 287
Alexander, son of John the Priest, 58, 284
Alopa, 219n
Amaseo, Gregorio, 144
Amiterno, Antonio, 162
Anesinus, Andreas, 130–131
Anselm, 51
Antenoreus, Carolus, 172
Anthology, 23n, 115, 137n, 145
Anthony of St. Bergen, 258
Antonio, Luca, 123
Aphthonius, 141, 264
Apollonius of Rhodes, 169
Apostolis, Aristovoulos. *See* Apostolis, Arsenios
Apostolis, Arsenios, 8, 45, 49, 51, 67, 100, 107, 112, 125n, 130–131, 161, 249, 265, 270, 282, 284, 299; ambitions for see of Monemvasia, 177–179, 183–184, 187–188, 191–192; archbishop of Monemvasia, 179–181, 187, 189–191, 200; birth, 168; copying manuscripts, 177, 182, 185; death, 199–200; director of Greek school in Florence, 187; education, 168–169; exile from Monemvasia, 181–182; in Crete, 167–169, 172–173, 176, 182–183, 187–188; in Flor-

38–39, 211; Paris, 230; pronunciation,
273–275, 278; Rome, 4, 6, 91, 147, 159,
161, 167, 184, 201, 214, 216–218, 248–
249, 279–281, 300; Spain, 5–6, 229–236,
238–239, 253–255, 293; Venice, 2–4,
6–8, 25–30, 32–35, 37–40, 50, 57–59,
68n, 69n, 116–119, 122, 128, 132, 139,
142–145, 166–167, 201, 264–265, 277,
279–290, 294–298, 300–301; western
Europe, 3–6, 101–106, 279–280
Gregoropoulos, George, 54, 115n, 172,
176–177
Gregoropoulos, John, 54–55, 60n, 112–
113, 115n, 120, 128–129, 130n, 136,
169, 172–174, 176–177, 205, 207n, 232n,
261n, 282, 284, 298; relations with
Arsenios Apostolis, 174–175; with
Musurus, 123–124, 126; with Zacharias
Calliergis, 135n, 209–211
Gregory of Nazianzus, 50, 138, 157,
264n, 287
Grimani, Domenico, 295
Grimani, Marino, 145, 295
Grolier, Jean, 157
Guarino, Battista, 106, 107n, 116
Guarino of Verona, 4–5, 26, 28–30, 32,
101, 106, 107n, 116, 135, 280n, 288,
292n
Gyraldi, Lilio, 163

Haskins, C. H., 17
Helladios, Gregory, 175–176
Hermeiae, Ammonius, 208, 289
Hermogenes, 138, 140, 227–228, 264, 289
Hermonymus, George, of Sparta, 4, 258
Herodian, 172n
Herodotus, 51
Hesiod, 264
Hesychius, 154–155, 287
Hierapetra, Bishopric of, 160
Hodius, 240
Holobolos, Manuel, 23
Homer, 21, 22n, 25n, 57–58, 94n, 99, 104,
137, 185, 194, 196, 213, 216, 249n, 264,
268
Humanism, 18–19, 39n
Hungary, Greek studies, 145
Hurtado de Mendoza, Don Diego, 296
Hutten, Ulrich von, 277

Innocent III, Pope, 16
Ipsilla, Peter, 259n
Isaias, 87

Isidore, Constantinople Patriarch and
Roman Cardinal, 77n, 78–79, 100, 163
Isocrates, 146
Italy, Greek studies, 6, 21–22, 300. See
also Ferrara; Florence; Mantua; Mi-
lan; Padua; Rome; Venice

James of Venice, 17
Jenson, Nicholas, 57, 156
John I, of Aragon, 6n
John the Grammarian, 172n
John of Speyer, 57
Joseph of Modon, 45, 95
Julius II, Pope, 147, 201
Justinian, Emperor, 212

Kalosenas, Anthony, 255
Kartanos, Joannikios, 199
Kounades, Andrew, 240n
Kyrou, A., 42

Lampridio, Benedetto, 161, 215
Landi, Jerome, 101, 182
Laonikos the Cretan, 58–59, 85, 107–108,
282, 284
Lascaris, Constantine, 1, 6n, 57, 138, 201,
224, 231, 273n, 286
Lascaris, Janus, 1, 4, 49, 51, 73, 91, 112,
114–115, 116n, 130–131, 136–137, 139,
147–148, 150–151, 158–159, 161–162,
163n, 170–171, 177, 184–188, 191, 193,
194n, 202, 213, 216–217, 219–220, 225,
230n, 248–249, 252, 257n, 263, 264n,
265n, 266n, 274n, 276, 279, 286, 292n,
298–300; teaching of Greek in Rome,
147, 161, 217, 252; views on crusade
against the Turks, 158
Lascaris, Theodore, 49
Lascaris, Theodore II, Emperor, 23
Latimer, William, 297
Laurentius Martinus Bradyglossus de
Lillo. See Balbo, Lorenzo
Lebrija. See de Lebrija, Antonio
Legrand, Emile, 73, 139, 150, 195, 199,
209, 212, 240; absence of biography of
Demetrius Ducas in Bibliographie hél-
lenique, 223; on Arsenios Apostolis,
167, 172, 180n, 181, 182n, 185n; on
Marcus Musurus, 111n, 120n, 131; on
Zacharias Calliergis, 204n, 210, 219; on
Michael Apostolis, 74, 79, 105n, 107n
Leo X, Pope, 35, 45n, 64–65, 129, 147,
149–151, 153–154, 156, 158–161, 165,
170–171, 182–186, 191–193, 201, 213–